U.S. Colored
Troops Defeat
Confederate Cavalry

U.S. Colored Troops Defeat Confederate Cavalry

Action at Wilson's Wharf, Virginia, 24 May 1864

EDWIN W. BESCH

Edwin W. Besch

McFarland & Company, Inc., Publishers

Jefferson, North Carolina

LIBRARY OF CONGRESS CATALOGUING-IN-PUBLICATION DATA

Names: Besch, Edwin W., 1936– author.
Title: U.S. colored troops defeat Confederate cavalry :
action at Wilson's Wharf, Virginia, 24 May 1864 / Edwin W. Besch.
Description: Jefferson, North Carolina : McFarland & Company, 2017. |
Includes bibliographical references and index.
Identifiers: LCCN 2017005802 | ISBN 9781476666631
(softcover : acid free paper) ∞
Subjects: LCSH: United States—History—Civil War, 1861–1865—
Participation, African American. | Virginia—History—Civil War,
1861–1865—Participation, African American. | Wilson's Wharf,
Battle of, Va., 1864. | United States. Army—African American troops—
History—19th century. | United States—History—Revolution, 1775–1783—
Participation, African American. | United States—History—
War of 1812—Participation, African American. | African American soldiers—
History—19th century. | African American soldiers—History—18th century.
Classification: LCC E540.N3 B47 2017 | DDC 973.7/415—dc23
LC record available at https://lccn.loc.gov/2017005802

BRITISH LIBRARY CATALOGUING DATA ARE AVAILABLE

ISBN (print) 978-1-4766-6663-1
ISBN (ebook) 978-1-4766-2737-3

Front cover: 1st U.S. colored infantry (Library of Congress)

Printed in the United States of America

*McFarland & Company, Inc., Publishers
Box 611, Jefferson, North Carolina 28640
www.mcfarlandpub.com*

To the men of every race, from North and South, who fought to restore the Union and end slavery.

And from me personally, this book is dedicated to the Marines of Echo Company, 2nd Battalion, 4th Marines who were killed, wounded, or traumatized while serving under my command during August 1966 while fighting for the freedom and independence of the people of South Vietnam.

"We hold these truths to be self-evident, that all men are created equal, that they are endowed by their Creator with certain unalienable Rights, that among these are Life, Liberty, and the pursuit of Happiness."

—The Declaration of Independence, 1776

Table of Contents

Preface

The Action at Wilson's Wharf on 24 May 1864 was a land-naval action that pitted defending 1st and 10th Regiments of United States Colored Troops (USCT)—black soldiers under their white officers—supported by New York artillerymen manning two cannons, a small Signal Corps detachment, and two U.S. Navy gunboats, against detachments from eleven regiments of veteran Confederate cavalrymen from Virginia, North Carolina, and South Carolina. The Union commander, a one-armed Abolitionist and temperance-minded physician–brigadier general from Massachusetts, faced a flamboyant, West Point–educated Confederate major general from Virginia. It was the first major clash between U.S. Colored Troops and Robert E. Lee's Army of Northern Virginia, resulting in a victory won by a Union force "of nearly all U.S. colored troops."

In Chapters I and II are biographies of three very different men who were present during the Action at Wilson's Wharf: Union Brig. Gen. Edward A. Wild and Confederate Maj. Gen. Fitzhugh Lee, the respective commanders; and the chaplain of the 1st Regiment, U.S. Colored Troops, the Rev. Henry McNeil Turner, who was born free in South Carolina and educated there against the law by white lawyers. Turner was the first of only 14 black chaplains in the 185,000-strong U.S. Colored Troops (including 7,000 white officers). He later became a prominent bishop in the African Methodist Episcopal Church.

There are accounts of General Wild having three female slaves whip their "notoriously cruel slave-owner," and his defiant replies to Fitzhugh Lee's surrender demands, including when he told Lee to "go to hell!" Corporal Charles T. Price, 2nd Virginia Cavalry, later wrote a chilling statement: "We were ordered to take our sabres along (when fighting dismounted), because we were ordered to kill every man in the fort if we had taken them."

1

Chapter IX, "Fort Pocahontas," describes the history of a site dating from the 17th century. Known as "Kennon's Landing" and later "Wilson's Wharf or Landing" until fortifications there were completed, and then was named "Fort Pocahontas" on 6 August 1864. It was occupied from 5 May 1864 by U.S. Colored Troops who were replaced in mid–June 1864 by "100 Days" Ohio National Guard soldiers (who suffered high losses to disease); and then by New Hampshire, New York and New Jersey soldiers. Their stories, those and of the units they commanded, are briefly told in Chapter IX.

There is a 21st-century "Hero of Fort Pocahontas": Harrison Ruffin Tyler, descendant of famed Pocahontas, namesake of the fort; grandson of U.S. President John Tyler, and great-grandson of Edmund Ruffin, a famed Virginia agriculturalist and pro-secession "Fire-eater"; and a very accomplished industrialist in his own right. He purchased the Fort Pocahontas site, cleared it (doing much of the work himself), had signs denoting its significance put up on the main southern route between Williamsburg and Richmond, paid for archeological studies by the College of William & Mary (his alma mater), and sponsored annual reenactments nearest to May 24, the date of the Action in 1864. Stories of the rediscovery, purchase, preservation, and interpretation of the Kennon's Landing/Wilson's Wharf/ Fort Pocahontas site, its early and later history, and the Tyler Family history, are told in Chapter X.

There are two appendices. Appendix A lists units, names, types of wounds, etc., of Federal and Confederate casualties suffered during the Action on 24 May 1864. Appendix B is a graph that shows numbers and types of known losses suffered by all units that occupied Wilson's Wharf/Fort Pocahontas during May 1864–June 1865. There, or nearby, at least 369 Americans: 143 Federal and 226 Confederate officers; soldiers and civilians of white, black, and mixed-races, were killed, wounded, or captured; or else died of disease, were accidentally shot or drowned, or deserted their units. "Wilson's Wharf/Fort Pocahontas" symbolizes the intermingled bitterness, brutality, humanity, and valor of America's Civil War.

My research about the Action at Wilson's Wharf on 24 May 1864, the fortifications that were later named Fort Pocahontas, and the men on both sides who fought or served there, continued from 1993 through 2016 and was conducted at the National Archives and Records Administration (NARA), the Naval Historical Center in the Navy Yard, and Library of Congress Archives in Washington, D.C.; the Library of Virginia, Museum of the Confederacy, and Virginia Historical Society in Richmond; the Library and Museum at the Virginia Military Institute at Lexington, and the Charles City County Local History Center, in Virginia; the U.S. Army

Military History Institute at Carlisle, Pennsylvania; the North Carolina State Archives and Department of Cultural Resources at Raleigh, Duke University Library, and University of North Carolina Library at Chapel Hill, in North Carolina; the South Carolina Department of Archives and History and State Library at Columbia, and the Chester County Library at Chester, South Carolina; the Swan Library at the College of William & Mary at Williamsburg, and History and Genealogical Sections at libraries in Fairfax and Loudoun Counties, Virginia; at libraries at Birmingham and Mobile in Alabama; and in my own extensive library. I visited Civil War collections to find related artifacts at the Atlanta History Center, Milwaukee Public Museum, Wisconsin State Archives at Madison; the National Civil War Museum at Harrisburg, Pennsylvania; and at Pamplin Historical Park and National Museum of the Civil War Soldier near Petersburg, Virginia. My subscriptions to Civil War magazines often provided new information or fresh insights. Attendance with my wife Donna at annual Civil War reenactments sponsored by Harrison R. Tyler 1997–2013 provided opportunities for on-site research at Fort Pocahontas itself and obtaining insights and new information from local and visiting historians.

I am indebted to very many persons for their assistance during my archival research during 1993–2005. I borrowed very heavily from works of three outstanding biographers: Frances H. Casstevens (*Edward A. Wild and the African Brigade in the Civil War*), James L. Nichols (*General Fitzhugh Lee: A Biography*), and C.R. Gibbs (*Black, Copper & Bright*, a history of the 1st Regiment, USCT, and biography of Chaplain Henry M. Turner). Diaries, letters, and postwar reminiscences of officers and soldiers who fought at Wilson's Wharf or were posted there, were provided by their descendants, augment contemporary official reports by senior officers on both sides.

I was privileged to have served with many African American civilians, Marines, navymen, and soldiers, and became interested in studying their military forbears, but I would never have selected the subject of the Action at Wilson's Wharf to study and write about if my friend Ken Bako had not initiated contacts with the American Battlefield Protection Program. We were assigned Wilson's Wharf, where "Black Union soldiers fought," as one of twelve Civil War battlefields to survey. It was a challenge, because the military history of blacks, including the "U.S. Colored Troops," was largely neglected except by a very few historians.

I especially wish to thank my beloved wife Donna Steadham Besch, whose assistance, encouragement, historical interests, and patience were blessings in themselves. I made no mistake when I proposed to her on our first date. She was my assistant and driver while researching this book as well.

Prelude

The Significance
of the Emancipation Proclamation

The U.S. Constitution Defers
the "Slavery Question"

The early antislavery movement wanted the Nation's founders to embody the sacred text "all men are created equal" from the Declaration of Independence in the U.S. Constitution of 1789. Instead, that document clearly recognized slavery as an existing institution in the new country, but didn't refer to it by name.[1] The vexing "Slavery Question" soon generated political conflicts and regionalism that resulted in secession of eleven slave states, and ended in bloodshed.

The National Election of 1860:
Abraham Lincoln Is Elected
President of the United States

In the election on 6 November 1860, Abraham Lincoln carried all Northern States except New Jersey, which split its vote between him and Stephen A. Douglas; Missouri, a border slave state, went for Douglas. *Constitutional Union Party* candidates John Bell and John C. Breckinridge divided the remaining slave states. Lincoln won 180 electoral votes and just over 40 percent of the popular vote. Lincoln's election over three candidates with only 40 per cent of the popular vote, was unacceptable to Southern politicians.[2]

Six weeks later the General Assembly of South Carolina held a

4

convention to draw up an Ordinance of Secession. Six other Southern states soon followed South Carolina's lead.[3]

Two attempts after Lincoln's Election to achieve compromises: the Crittenden "compromise" and The Washington Peace Conference in February 1861, failed to avoid dis–Union.[4]

On 13 December 1860, before any compromises were debated, and before any states had seceded, senators and representatives from seven states signed an address to their constituents: "The argument is exhausted. All hope of relief in the Union, through the agency of committees, Congressional legislation, or constitutional amendments, is extinguished.... The honor, safety, and independence of the Southern people are to be found in a Southern Confederacy."[5]

Secession of Eleven Southern Slave States from the Union

Seven States seceded before Abraham Lincoln was inaugurated as President on 4 March 1861: South Carolina on 20 December 1860, Mississippi on 9 January 1861, Florida on 10 January, Alabama on 11 January, Georgia on 19 January, Louisiana on 26 January, and Texas on 23 February; four more States seceded after the fall of Fort Sumter: Virginia on 17 April, Arkansas on 6 May, North Carolina on 20 May, and Tennessee on 8 June 1861.[6]

In February 1861, at the Confederate convention at Montgomery, delegates drafted a temporary constitution, turned themselves into a provisional Congress, and elected Jefferson Davis as provisional president and Alexander Stephens as provisional vice-president. As the provisional president Jefferson Davis was directed to call for volunteers for not more than 12 months. On 6 March, 100,000 men were called for, and by mid-April 35,000 were in the field[7]

By 1861 one-third of the 12,000,000 population of the South were Negro slaves who were owned by only 384,000 whites, and only about 1,800 of them owned 100 or more. Three-fourths of Southern families owned no slaves at all. But Slavery, which its defenders called "the peculiar institution," dominated Southern life after most of the civilized world had abandoned it. "Slavery itself did not cause the Civil War, but it was intertwined in every sectional dispute."[8]

Writing for "Fellow Southerners!" Gordon Rhea describes "*Why*" the Southern States seceded to form the Confederate States of America:

The short answer to why our ancestors decided to leave the United States, of course, was Abraham Lincoln's election and his opposition to expansion of slavery in the territories. If new states could not be slave states, then the South's political clout would fade, abolitionists would be ascendant, and the South's "peculiar institution"—the right to own human beings as property—would be in peril....

The Confederacy's founders were unabashedly frank about their motives. [After stating that the "Old" Union "rested upon the assumption of the Equality of races,"] Alexander Stephens, the Confederacy's vice president, proclaimed [in a speech at Savannah, Georgia on 4 March 1861] that the new nation's "foundations are laid, its cornerstone rests, upon the great truth that the negro is not equal to the white man; that slavery, subordination to the white man; is his natural and normal condition. This, our new government, is the first in the history of the world, based on this great physical, philosophical and moral truth."[9]

Confederate Vice-President Alexander H. Stephens (courtesy Cary Delery, Metairie, Louisiana).

The constitution of the new Confederacy was modeled after the U.S. Constitution with two important additions:

- Article I, Section 9, Paragraph 4, provided: "No bill of attainder, ex post facto law denying or impairing the right of property in negro slaves shall be passed."
- Article IV, Section 3, stated: "The Confederate States may acquire new territory ... In all such territory, the institution of negro slavery, as it now exists in the Confederate States, shall be recognized and protected by Congress and the territorial government."[10]

The "Bloodiest Day of the War" at Antietam on 17 September 1862 Gives Lincoln the Opportunity to Issue His Emancipation Proclamation.

Tactically a draw, history records Antietam as a Union strategic success. At Whitehall in London and the White House in Washington, the battle went down as a Union victory. It frustrated Confederate hopes for British recognition, and it precipitated the *Emancipation Proclamation.* Antietam thereby was one of the war's great turning points.[11] Five days after a "down payment" was paid in blood at Antietam, President Abraham Lincoln issued his Emancipation Proclamation.

President Abraham Lincoln (Library of Congress, Washington, D.C.).

The Emancipation Proclamation's Meanings and Its Aftermath

President Lincoln's executive order that took effect on 1 January 1863 proclaimed the freedom of slaves in the ten states that were then in rebellion, applying to 3.1 million of the approximately 4 million slaves living in the United States according to the 1860 Census. The Proclamation did not compensate owners, did not by itself outlaw all slavery, and it did not make ex-slaves, who were called freedmen, citizens. The *Emancipation Proclamation* was never challenged in court. Lincoln did not have authority over four slave-holding border-states that had not seceded: Missouri, Kentucky, Maryland, and Delaware; separate state and Federal actions freed the slaves in those states. To ensure abolition of slavery everywhere in the United States, Lincoln pushed for passage of the Thirteenth Amendment to the U.S. Constitution, which was passed by Congress by the necessary two-thirds vote in February 1865; it was ratified by the states and took effect on 18 December 1865.[12]

The *Proclamation* would turn Union armies and naval forces into an army of liberation after January 1, 1863—if they could win battles and conquer the South. And it invited slaves to help them win it. Ex-slave Frederick Douglass wrote in his October *Douglass's Monthly*: "We [black and white abolitionists] shout for joy that we live to record this righteous decree"; William Lloyd Garrison wrote in his *Liberator* that it was "an act of immense historical importance." A British abolitionist said that September 22nd was "a memorable day in the annals of the great struggle for the freedom of an oppressed and despised race."[13]

General Robert E. Lee, who later as Confederate General-in-Chief would advocate enlistment and arming of slaves as Confederate soldiers himself, saw Lincoln's *Proclamation* only as a way for the North to increase the number of soldiers it could field and thus it was an imperative to increase the number of Confederate soldiers as well. Lee wrote in December 1862:

> In view of the savage and brutal policy he has proclaimed, which leaves us no alternative but success or degradation worse than death, if we would save the honor of our families from pollution, *our social system from destruction,* let every effort be made, every means be employed, to fill and maintain the ranks of our armies, until God, in his mercy, shall bless us with the establishment of our independence.

Lee's request for a dramatic increase in recruits for the Confederate army went unfulfilled,[14] and the Confederacy did not enlist slaves as soldiers until March 1865, when it was far too late.

The *Emancipation Proclamation* authorized eventual recruitment of nearly 200,000 black and mixed-race soldiers (most of them ex-slaves) into the U.S. Colored Troops (USCT); a few State colored artillery, cavalry, and infantry units; and some 17,000 sailors in the U.S. Navy. The USCT provided the North with additional manpower during the latter part of the War. Among them were the 1st and 10th Infantry Regiments, USCT which fought at Wilson's Wharf on 24 May 1864.

I

The Commanders
at Wilson's Wharf

A Massachusetts Physician-Soldier
vs. a Virginia Professional Soldier

Edward Augustus Wild

Edward Augustus Wild was born 25 November 1825 at Brookline, Massachusetts, the third of nine children born to Dr. Charles Wild and Mary Joanna Rhodes Wild, who was a descendant of Roger Williams (1602–1683), an early advocate of religious freedom who preached separation of church and state, and founded Providence, Rhode Island. His family attended, and Edward ("Ned") played the bass viola and trombone "in the choir of Dr. [John H.] Pierce's [Unitarian] church" in Brookline. Rise of the Abolitionist movement began during the 1830s in New England, and Brookline became part of the "underground railroad" that helped slaves escape to the North. "Edward Wild learned to hate the institution of slavery and those who protected and prolonged it." Wild graduated from Harvard in 1844 and from Jefferson Medical College at Philadelphia in 1846, "upon a brilliant examination and a full year in advance of the regular course." He became a doctor in Brookline, and he joined the Independent Corps of Cadets of Boston. In 1848 he traveled to Europe; in Italy he was arrested twice as a "spy" but was released once by famed Giuseppi Garibaldi.[1]

In 1850, Dr. Edward A. Wild joined the Massachusetts Medical Society, and the Massachusetts Society of Homeopathy in 1853. ("'Homeopathy' is a method of treating diseases by minute doses of drugs that in a healthy person would produce symptoms similar to those of the disease.") In June

1855, Edward married Frances Ellen Sullivan, who was from a prominent Boston family. On their honeymoon, the couple cruised to Turkey, where Dr. Wild offered his services to the Turkish Sultan and was commissioned Surgeon of Artillery with rank of lieutenant colonel. He spent 15 months in Turkey, nine of them serving Sultan Abdul Mejid. He was initiated into the order of Freemasonry at Malta before returning to Brookline to resume his medical practice in late 1857.[2]

Captain Edward A. Wild (Mass. Commandery, Military Order of the Loyal Legion of the United States (MOLLUS), United States Army Heritage and Education Center, Carlisle, PA).

When the Civil War began with the attack on Fort Sumter, South Carolina, during 12–14 April 1861, Edward A. Wild already was an ardent abolitionist who sympathized with fugitive slaves he had seen at Brookline, and his travels abroad had shown him that the United States was a wonderful country that "must be kept intact to grow and become a great nation which could never be divided." He recruited and became captain of Company A, 1st Massachusetts Infantry Regiment. By 19 June 1861 the regiment was camped on the Upper Potomac near the "Chain Bridge," and on 21 June it marched in review for President Lincoln. The regiment saw its first action at Blackburn's Ford over Bull Run on 18 July 1861, when the Federals suffered 83 casualties, including 1 officer and 9 enlisted men killed, and 22 wounded in the 1st Massachusetts; the Confederates suffered 68 casualties. During the First Battle of Bull Run (or First Manassas) on 21 July 1861, Brig. Gen. Irvin McDowell's Union army was routed after an initial success. Captain Wild later wrote about his first battle:

> I was sent in command of two companies to hold a small wood in advance of our Front … and protect the artillery that opened the fight. But the chief battle took place on our right. The enemy also attacked to the left of us smartly. Stampede [of Union forces] in the afternoon from 4–5. But we could see nothing of it, only judge by hearing, that our men were driven back…. Finding ourselves abandoned, and apparently surrounded, I started, after six o'clock, and marched back in good order … to Centreville heights and found our Brigade drawn up in hollow squares…. We brought up the rear for several miles. Were afterwards relieved by the German Regiments.[3]

After serving on courts-martial duty, Captain Wild was arrested on 14 April 1862 for appearing on parade in his gray overcoat he had worn on guard duty, because his dress uniform was unavailable. On 26 April he participated in capture of a "Lunette by storm" [assault]. During the Battle of Williamsburg on 4–5 May 1862, Wild's sword was hit by a bullet and his head was injured by a tree splinter. During the Battle of Fair Oaks (Oak Grove), the first of the "Seven Days' Battles" during McClellan's Peninsular Campaign (March–July 1862), Wild was wounded on the knee by a Minié ball and through his right hand by a "small rifle ball," causing loss of use of two fingers. While recuperating, Wild was promoted major in the 32nd Massachusetts Volunteers, which became the 35th Massachusetts, with Wild as its colonel.[4]

As the regiment passed through Philadelphia, Col. Wild, "a firm believer in total abstinence of alcoholic beverages," ordered "the stock of drinking shops to be cleaned out at two places, a hotel and a saloon." City authorities followed him with two "writs of arrest," but he refused to accept them. His biographer Frances H. Casstevens writes: "Wild dared defy authority on any level, and he bluffed his way out of being arrested in Philadelphia…. He would not be so fortunate as to escape consequences in the future when he attempted to act both as judge and jury of those he believed were wrongdoers. Over the next few years … he used his rank and power of the military to right wrongs, according to his personal beliefs and puritanical upbringing."[5]

About the Battle of South Mountain, Maryland, on 14 September 1862, Wild wrote: "My regiment [35th Massachusetts Volunteer Infantry] entered the fight about 4 p.m. Drove the enemy through the forest, over rough, rocky, and mountainous ground—and then rejoined the brigade. [We] were forming line to pass the night, just about dusk, when the enemy attacked us suddenly from a dark wood; they were repulsed. *I was wounded, my left arm being shattered by an explosive bullet.*" Wild found his way down the mountain to a crude building that sheltered wounded men. As a surgeon in the Crimean War, Wild had seen many similar wounds; he demanded that his arm be amputated: "Take it off at the shoulder and don't let me wake and find it here."[6]

Colonel Wild recuperated at Middletown, Maryland, where his wife joined him, and then at his sister's house in Philadelphia. In December 1862 at Boston, almost helpless, it was the low point in Edward Wild's life. While in fighting "for less than six days," they included six battles during 18 July 1861 through 14 September 1862, besides skirmishes and siege operations. Now, with permanent injuries to his right hand and loss of his left arm, and in constant pain, his future appeared dim. On New Year's Eve 1863, however, his Harvard classmates sent him "an elegant sword of regulation pattern, very elaborately chased, heavily gilded, with gold and tassels and a shark-skin scabbard."[7]

Organizing Units and Recruiting Black Soldiers and Their White Officers Begins; It Meets Serious Opposition in the North and South

After the Emancipation Proclamation was proclaimed on 1 January 1863, measures were taken to enlist black soldiers. Besides efforts in the East, the Army Adjutant General began recruiting and organizing blacks in the Mississippi Valley, and Maj. Gen. Nathaniel P. Banks organized a "Corps d'Afrique" of colored troops in Louisiana. General Order No. 143, dated 22 May 1863, established a Bureau of United States Colored Troops. Major Charles W. Foster was appointed chief of the central bureau in Washington, D.C., as Assistant Adjutant General.[8] Per Dana B. Shoaf: "Union General Orders No. 143, issued on May 22, 1863, is one of the war's most important but little-known documents. The order laid out nine points establishing a bureau for 'the organization of Colored Troops' and began the process of recruiting and forming black regiments commanded by white officers. Former slaves were transformed into paid agents of the Federal government, armed and given sanction to kill those who had enslaved them. The order jump-started the process of black equality in the nation."[9]

The term "Freedmen" was applied to slaves who became free men after Congress had passed the Confiscation Act of 1862, which punished Confederates who did not surrender within 60 days of its passage by having their slaves freed as Union armies advanced. The Confiscation Act solved the dilemma facing Union commanders about the status of refugee slaves within their jurisdiction. Many were herded into camps of "contrabands" (a term coined by Maj. Gen. Benjamin F. Butler at Fort Monroe in 1861 to identify runaway slaves who had been used to aid Confederate military efforts); others were hired out to loyal Unionist planters for low wages; and still others were recruited into the Union Army or Navy. In mid–1863 the War Department established the American Freedmen's Inquiry Commission, which reported: "Docility, earnestness, and instinct of obedience" were qualities that made a good soldier, and that these were qualities, "as a general rule, of the colored refugees who enter our lines." The commissioner surmised, however, that efficiency of black troops would depend upon their having white officers who were "in sympathy with them, having gained their confidence, and can arouse their devotion."[10]

At first there was an almost "impenetrable wall of prejudice" against colored men in military service. It was widely believed "they could not be made into soldiers; that they could not fight; that to employ them would prolong the war; that white soldiers would not serve in the same army with them; and that they would prove a source of demoralization to our [Union] armies in the field." It was also feared that black soldiers would cause "civil discord" in states loyal to the Union, and that they would prove "ruinous to the Union cause."[11]

Meanwhile, as battle casualties mounted, and terms of many Union soldiers who had volunteered in 1861 were soon to expire, more men would be needed to replace them. The Enrollment Act of 3 March 1863 resulted in bloody riots. When Northern state governments were ordered to impose a draft, anti-draft riots broke out in Wisconsin and Indiana, and later in Vermont, New Hampshire, and Ohio. In July 1863, hatred of blacks erupted in violence during anti-draft riots in New York City; a Negro church and an orphanage for 250 Negro children were burned there. Troops were called in to reinforce the police, but over 1,000 people were killed. The mob targeted military officers and beat and killed an Army colonel. In Boston, a mob stoned Federal troops and dispersed only after some rioters were killed. The draft was wisely postponed until 19 August 1863, and to ease the need for the draft, it was imperative that black volunteers refill Union army ranks.[12]

The 54th Regiment of Massachusetts Volunteer Infantry (often incorrectly identified as the Massachusetts Volunteers (*Colored*)—Massachusetts never used "Colored" or "African Descent" as part of its unit designations),[13] a regiment of free blacks from many states recruited in Massachusetts, was largely the idea of Governor John A. Andrew, but it was supported by Frederick Douglass, Harriet Beecher Stowe, and other abolitionists. The governor envisioned the 54th as "a model for all future Colored Regiments." Robert Gould Shaw, a veteran captain from the 2nd Massachusetts Infantry, became colonel of the 54th. He died along with two other white officers and 31 black enlisted soldiers; 11 officers and 135 enlisted soldiers were wounded; and 92 became "missing" (some possibly executed by the Rebels); a total of 272 casualties out of 650 men of the 54th Regiment who participated in the attack on Confederate Battery Wagner on Morris Island in Charleston Harbor on 18 July 1863.[14] Although the attack was unsuccessful, the 54th Regiment of Massachusetts Volunteer Infantry proved that black soldiers could and would fight ... bravely.

While Colonel Edward A. Wild recuperated, he worked during early 1863 assisting Governor Andrew to organize colored troops, including the 54th Regiment of Massachusetts Infantry. The governor initially wanted Wild to command the new 55th Regiment of Massachusetts Volunteer Infantry, but he decided to form an entire brigade of colored regiments, and he recommended Wild be promoted to "facilitate work of forming a brigade."[15]

"Wild's African Brigade"

On 1 April 1863, Governor Andrew urged Secretary of War Edwin M. Stanton to find some "able, tried, and *believing man*" who could organize 2,500 to 5,000 colored troops in North Carolina into a brigade. However, Maj. Gen. John Gray Foster, who headed the Department of North Carolina, believed "not more than one Regiment could be raised in this Department." Foster was concerned that troops raised from among contrabands or freedmen would be "antagonistic … to the feelings of white troops."[16]

General Foster's attitude was typical of many officers in his department and in Union armies in general.

On 13 April 1863, Secretary of War Edwin M. Stanton authorized Wild to "raise a brigade (of four regiments) of North Carolina volunteer infantry to serve for three years or the duration of the war." On 24 April, Wild was appointed "Brigadier General of Volunteers," and officers of his first regiment were appointed. He understood the psyche of his men. They "are not veterans … they must be led, you cannot order them forward and expect them to go alone, you cannot station them in a heavy fire and expect them to stay without flinching … though they may be the bravest men on earth; *example*

Brigadier General Edward A. Wild, USA (Mass. Commandery, MOLLUS, United States Army Heritage and Education Center, Carlisle, PA).

is everything." Wild knew that *he* must set the example. "They are not afraid to do what they think you are not afraid to lead them in yourself, but let them suspect you of flinching, they think something is impossible or going wrong, [then] they are like sheep without a shepherd; [but] one firm man can support a whole corps." Governor Andrew wrote to General Foster on 14 May 1863: "[Wild] is one of the bravest men and one of the most accomplished and experienced officers in the Massachusetts Volunteer Service."[17] The governor and Secretary Stanton had found their "able, brave, tried, and *believing man.*"

Wild screened officer applicants at New York, staffing his regiments with officers who were "committed to abolition and temperance." There were some black officers, but most were white. Wild had problems finding enough white noncommissioned officers with military experience to promote as officers because he could not take them from the Army of the Potomac, so he chose them from units elsewhere, *or from among disabled soldiers.* Within three days of accepting his appointment as brigadier general, Wild had most of the officers for his 1st North Carolina Colored Volunteer (NCCV) Regiment. He got his brother Walter H. Wild transferred from the 54th Massachusetts to serve as his aide-de-camp. With only some officers commissioned, Wild sailed with them from New York to General Foster's headquarters at New Bern, North Carolina, in mid–May; there they began enlisting black men. Wild gave "much time and labor to care and provision of Negro families." Proud colored women of New Bern ordered a flag made in Boston of "blue silk, with a yellow fringe," on which the Goddess of Liberty rested her foot on a copperhead snake. Governor Andrew consecrated the flag.[18]

On 25 July 1863, the 55th Massachusetts Volunteer Infantry Regiment joined Wild in North Carolina. His two regiments of colored troops became part of Maj. Gen. Foster's Department of North Carolina. As recruiting began, Wild wrote that he had "much more on my hands now than I can do well, between the military general business, the military recruiting business, the colonization scheme [for the Roanoke Island Freedmen's Colony], and endless appeals for protection…. All seem to look to me…. At times when I see the weak, or the false and rotten course pursued by different provost marshals, it exasperates me so."[19]

Wild was ordered to move with his incomplete African Brigade from New Bern, North Carolina, to Charleston, the "Cradle of Secession," where Foster now believed colored troops would "do well and fight well under their fighting general." Wild left on 30 July with 2,154 men in the 1st NCCV Regiment, the 55th Massachusetts Volunteer Infantry Regiment, a detachment of the 2nd NCCV Regiment, and a company of the 3rd NCCV. The 1st NCCV Regiment, organized at New Bern and Portsmouth, Virginia, and later redesignated the 35th Infantry Regiment, U.S. Colored Troops (USCT), was made up entirely of men of African descent who were former slaves who had deserted their plantation homes and sought refuge with the Union army only a few months earlier. The 55th Massachusetts, in contrast, was made up of free black enlisted men from many Northern states. The 2nd NCCV Regiment was organized at Portsmouth, Virginia, and became the 36th Regiment, USCT in February 1864. The 3rd NCCV regiment was partially completed in January 1864 and redesignated the 37th Regiment, USCT in February.[20]

From 3 August to 20 October 1863, Wild's African Brigade was assigned to the north end of Folly Island, closest to Morris Island. Wild soon clashed with his superior, Brig. Gen. Israel Vogdas, who threatened to charge Wild with being absent without leave for not reporting to him as soon as Wild arrived, and who harassed Wild's brigade adjutant with trivial matters. Wild was not intimidated, and he forcefully stated his case in matters relating to his troops and to himself. Wild's men, however, had hurriedly sailed from New Bern and arrived with only their arms needed for field service, having left behind their knapsacks, camp equipage, and baggage. By the time a transport steamer could be procured to bring those items, most had been destroyed or stolen, and the men had to do without them for a while. Diseases, illnesses, and deaths took their toll on Wild's men, and Captain Walter Wild noted that the General's arm "troubles him often, and his head swims constantly." General Wild treated himself "with homo [homeopathic medicines] and refused to be waited on, and [his brother Walter hoped] he will weather it through, but it is a hard test for the best constitution." Typhoid and dysentery took its toll on the men, as well as exhaustion due to General Vogdas's having ordered 400 to 500 men to do duty 4 or 5 nights in succession. The 55th Regiment of Massachusetts Infantry, over several months, lost 54 men to combat, 4 to accidents, and 112 to disease. There was "brackish water"; pesky mosquitoes and sand fleas, ticks, and flies; and sand everywhere. Few drugs or medicines were available to treat the sick; the only pain relievers were opium and alcohol.[21]

From 10 August until the opening of fire on Fort Sumter on 5 September, large details of Wild's men were required for day and night fatigue duties, even after the Confederates abandoned Battery Wagner during the night of 6 September. The men cut timber, made gabions,[22] built wharves, loaded and unloaded ammunition and stores, hauled heavy cannon to the front, and worked in the trenches on Morris Island, much of the time under Confederate fire. Fatigue duties consisted of cleaning camps, repairing roads, etc., every day. Colonel James C. Beecher, 1st NCCV Regiment, voiced his anger about his men being treated like servants when they were ordered to "clean up the camps" occupied by white troops: "I have never before known such duty imposed upon any Regiment.... They have been slaves and are just learning to be men. It is a drawback that they are regarded as, and called, 'd——d niggers' by so-called 'gentlemen' in the uniform of U.S. Officers, but when they are set to menial work doing for white regiments what those Regiments are entitled to do for themselves, it simply throws them back where they were before and reduces them to the position of slaves again." When General Wild learned about this situation, he asked Col. N.P. Hallowell of the 55th Massachusetts to tell the officers in charge of the details "to disregard such orders in the future," on Wild's authority. Wild issued an order that forbade Negro troops from digging wells and doing other menial tasks for white troops,[23] but it was rather late.

The black soldiers of the 55th Massachusetts, 1st NCCV Regiment,

"Colored Troops under General Wild Liberating Slaves in North Carolina," *Harper's Weekly*, January 23, 1864 (a 1978 print by the North Carolina Museum of History, Raleigh).

and in other colored units worked hard to become good soldiers, but they constantly met prejudice, resulting in their being given the "worst equipment, the worst supplies, and the worst guns[24] in the army because many high ranking Union officers thought so little of these soldiers." Officers in black units also were looked down upon. There was discrimination in pay. Black soldiers were paid $10 per month, but $3 was deducted for clothing, leaving only $7 per month, while white soldiers received $13 per month plus an additional $3.50 for clothing. Governor Andrew offered to make up the difference, but the 55th Massachusetts black soldiers refused his offer as a matter of principle. Some men wrote to President Lincoln, complaining that they had been in the field for 13 months but had received no pay and been offered only $7 per month. Congress later authorized equal pay for black and white soldiers to date from 1 January 1864; retroactive pay was finally distributed in October 1864.[25]

Six officers answered a circular questionnaire about how black Union troops had performed during the summer and fall of 1863. They concluded that black soldiers:

1. were "more docile and obedient, hence more completely under the control of his [sic] commanders," and were influenced by examples;
2. were less skillful than white troops, but were skillful enough for most work in a siege;
3. could do more work than whites, because they worked more constantly;
4. could not be hurried in their work, no matter what the emergency; and
5. those recruited from free states were superior to those recruited from slave states.

A favorable report by Major C.W. Foster, Assistant Adjutant General of Volunteers, stated that Wild's 2,000 "colored troops have already established for themselves a commendable reputation. Their conduct in camp, on the march, in siege, and in battle attests [to] their discipline, their endurance, and their valor." A commission set up to review the condition of black troops praised them for being neat "in care of their persons, uniforms, arms, and equipments [sic], and in police [cleanliness] of their encampments." The report concluded: "These qualities will be apparent to any one who inspects the Negro regiments under Brigadier-General Wild in North Carolina."[26]

Wild's Raid into Northeastern North Carolina During 5–21 December 1863: Results and Repercussions

At the end of October 1863, there were 58 regiments of colored troops, with a total strength of 37,480 officers and men, in the Union armies.[27] Of those units, Wild commanded the 1st Infantry Regiment, USCT; 2nd NCCV Regiment; 10th Infantry Regiment, USCT (which later fought at Wilson's Wharf on 24 May 1864); and detachments from the 1st NCCV Regiment, 3rd NCCV Regiment (later redesignated the 37th Regiment, USCT and served at Wilson's Wharf/Fort Pocahontas), and 55th Massachusetts Infantry Regiment. The 5th Regiment, USCT was added to his brigade in November. Major General J.G. Foster was replaced by Maj. Gen. Benjamin F. Butler as commander of the Department of Virginia and North Carolina on 10 November. Wild's raids into nearby counties brought in "contrabands" and their families. Some escaped slaves served Union forces as cooks, teamsters, or body servants to officers,[28] *as did thousands of slaves and some free blacks in Confederate armies.*

Wild began his largest raid into North Carolina with a threefold mission: (1) to free slaves and send them north or settle them in the Freedmen's Colony on Roanoke Island; (2) to enlist freedmen as soldiers in his brigade; and (3) *to clear the area of Confederate guerrilla forces and partisan rangers.*[29] He also was to administer the Oath of Allegiance to the United States to white citizens who wanted protection that the oath offered. Wild told slave-owners: "All slaves are now at liberty to go where they please, or stay. By assisting them on their way with food and transportation, you can save yourselves visitations from the colored troops."[30]

A major objective of Wild's raid was to find and destroy camps of Confederate guerrillas that were hidden in swamps and to capture or kill Confederates who operated as guerrillas. Wild hated irregular troops who conducted short but deadly attacks, raids on Union communications and supplies, and other harassing activities. Wild told people in the coastal counties: "All guerrillas are on a par with pirates, and are to be treated as such." The people were also told by Wild that it would be in their best interest not to harbor guerrillas or partisan rangers, and to refuse them food or shelter, and to report their locations to Federal authorities.[31] But it's hard for citizens to refuse hungry men with guns.

On 28 December 1863, after having gained intelligence information about guerrillas and their activities during his raid, Wild reported:

The organization of the guerrillas is loose and improper, and ought not to be recognized. Governor [Zebulon] Vance gave commissions to the officers to raise their companies, ostensibly for State defense. They are entitled "North Carolina Defenders." Each captain is his own mustering officer; [he] musters men into the service of North Carolina, and the men are paid, or expect pay, from the State only. Governor Vance supplied them with excellent arms (new Enfields) and ammunition. There appears to be some person acting as commissary near each company, to keep a small stock of provisions in camp; but the bands do not scruple to live on the inhabitants, individually and collectively. The captain is allowed to encamp where he pleases, and to operate when and where he sees fit, his proceedings being as independent, arbitrary, and irresponsible as those of any chief of bandits....

They are virtually bandits, armed and hired by Governor Vance. They have not defended and cannot defend their State, nor any portion of it. They can only harass us by stealing, murdering, and burning; by stopping negroes from reaching us ... and harass their own State by plundering, terrifying, and even murdering Union citizens. There are jealous disaffections among them—not only between individuals of a company, but between one company and another—amounting to rancor.[32]

In late November 1863, Wild had sent Col. Alonzo G. Draper with the 5th Regiment, USCT on a raid through Princess Anne County, Virginia. Wild ordered Draper to capture bands of guerrillas; but "if fired upon, you will at once hang the man who fired," and if the shots came from a house, "burn the house immediately. In case of a hanging, you will label the body ... as 'Assassin's' 'Guerrilla's' &c." Wild decreed that guerrillas were "not to be taken alive," and if firearms were found "in any house ... bring the owner in as a prisoner." Draper freed hundreds of slaves and enlisted many recruits, and he even captured a guerrilla chief. The results encouraged Wild "with the approbation of Maj. Gen. Butler, to plan a raid of similar character, but on a much more extensive scale, beyond our lines into North Carolina."[33]

For "Wild's Raid," his 2,000-man force consisted of 700 men in Col. John H. Holman's 1st Regiment, USCT (which would bear the brunt of the fighting at Wilson's Wharf on 24 May 1864); 400 men from the 2nd NCCV Regiment, commanded by Col. Draper; 530 men from the 5th Regiment, USCT, commanded by Col. James W. Conines; 100 men from "detached" units of the 1st NCCV Regiment; and Captain Jones's detachment from the 55th Massachusetts Infantry Regiment. They were joined by two companies of cavalry from the 5th and 11th Pennsylvania Regiments and a section (two guns) of the 7th New York Light Battery. Wild's objective was Elizabeth City in North Carolina, 50 miles from his headquarters at Norfolk. Wild and his black soldiers and their white officers began their march at daylight on 5 December, so secretly that only one member of the press, reporter "Tewksbury" of the *New York Times*, came with them. They moved in two columns. Wild took the 1st Regiment, USCT and 400 men from the 2nd NCCV Regiment, 1,100 men in all. They left Portsmouth and marched 27 miles in two days on a towpath along the Dismal Swamp Canal. Supply boats took a wrong turn, so troops began "living off the country."

The second column from the 5th Regiment, USCT; the 1st NCCV Regiment; and the detachment from the 55th Massachusetts Regiment left their camps northeast of Norfolk and marched via Great Bridge to South Mills. Union cavalrymen of Col. John Ward's 8th Connecticut Cavalry Regiment, who were sent in advance, warned the population that "nigger-stealers were coming to plunder them of everything." Wild complained about Col. Ward's interference to Brig. Gen. George W. Getty, who "considered the tone" of Wild's letter "very improper."[34]

On the day Wild began his raid into North Carolina, General Butler issued General Order No. 46, which specified how colored soldiers were to be treated. It declared: "The recruitment of colored troops has become the settled purpose of the Government.... [It is the] duty of every officer and soldier to aid in carrying out that purpose ... irrespective of personal predilection." Assistance was necessary because of new rights acquired by the colored soldiers, and the "new obligations imposed upon them, the duty of the Government to them, the great stake they have in the war, and the claims their ignorance and helplessness of their women and children make upon each of us who hold a higher grade in social and political life." Butler reminded his white

Major General Benjamin F. Butler, USA (Library of Congress, Washington, D.C.).

soldiers that colored soldiers did not have access to "'State aid' for support of their families while fighting our battles … nor the generous bounties given by the States and National Government in the loyal States," but an even greater reward awaited each of them—"freedom for himself and his race forever."[35]

Wild Occupies Elizabeth City; Residents Believe "Beelzebub had taken up residence"

General Wild later reported on tactics of both sides as his raiders headed southward:

> The guerrillas pestered us. They crept upon our pickets at night, waylaid our expeditions and cavalry scouts, firing upon us whenever they could. But in marching, our flankers breaking up the woods, generally drove them. We ambuscaded them twice without success; pursuit was useless. Colonel Holman burned two of their camps between Elizabeth and Hertford, taking some of their property, such as guns, horses, provisions, and clothing; catching some of their abettors, but only one of their number, Daniel Bright, of Pasquotank County, *whom I later hanged….*
>
> Finding ordinary measures of little avail, I adopted a more vigorous style of warfare; burned their houses and barns, ate up their livestock, and took hostages from their families. This course we followed throughout the trip, and we learned that they were disgusted with such unexpected treatment; it bred disaffection, some wishing to quit the [guerrilla] business, others going over the lines to join the Confederate Army.[36]

Approaching Elizabeth City, Wild found that guerrillas had burned the bridge over the Pasquotank River, "leaving nothing of it remaining visible but the charred tops of the piles…. I then built a substantial bridge over the Pasquotank, below South Mills, constructed by Colonel Holman and Major Wright [both 1st Regiment, USCT], of materials taken from the house and barn of a rebel captain nearby. In six hours the whole force had moved across the bridge and on to Elizabeth City," which he captured with loss of only two men wounded, but one was captured by guerrillas. A gunboat transporting their forage had engine trouble, but supplies arrived on another steamer; his promised naval support, the gunboat *North State*, burst a steam pipe and was disabled, but another gunboat, the *Miami*, joined Wild.[37]

Wild established his headquarters in Elizabeth City, where townsfolk believed "Beelzebub himself had taken up residence." Wild: "While there I sent out expeditions in all directions, some for recruits and contrabands' families, some for guerrillas, some for forage, some for firewood, which was scarce and badly needed by us. Every man was constantly employed." The sight of armed black soldiers frightened citizens more than anything they had ever seen, but historians believe the town of Elizabeth City and Pasquotank County suffered "more spoliation from roving bands of 'Buffaloes' [who were Union sympathizers] and [Confederate] guerrillas than from [black] Yankees." The 66th Regiment of North Carolina State Troops, 300–450 men with a field piece, camped near Hertford. Wild sent Col. Holman and his 1st Regiment, USCT to Hertford, but Confederate guerrillas had burned the river bridges on their route. Holman sent his men into a swamp where they burned a Confederate camp, buildings containing forage and provisions, and nearby houses and barns. They returned with one "guerrilla as prisoner."[38]

On 12 December, Wild's men took Phoebe Munden, the 35-year-old wife of Lt. William J. Munden of Company I, 68th North Carolina Regiment, as hostage from her home and placed her in a room at Elizabeth City "without fire, bed, or bedding, with several male prisoners, tied by the feet and hands ... [and even worse in Southern minds] a Negro guard was placed in charge" of her. On 13 December, Col. Holman took another female hostage, Mrs. Elizabeth Weeks, wife of Private Pender Weeks, who was confined with Mrs. Munden at Norfolk. The women were held to assure the safety and good treatment of Private Samuel Jordan, Company D, 5th Regiment, USCT, who had been captured. Wild vowed he would treat the female hostages the same as his Negro soldier held captive by the Confederates was treated, "even to hanging." A special committee of the Confederate Congress obtained depositions regarding the inhumane treatment of Wild's female hostages.[39] Taking of hostages was rare, but not without precedent. Six months before Wild's raid into North Carolina, two Confederate officers, Brig. Gen. William Henry Fitzhugh ("Rooney") Lee and Captain John H. Winder, son of the commandant of Confederate prisons, had been selected as hostages for two Union captains who had been "chosen by lot for execution." Both pairs of officers were exchanged in February 1864.[40]

General Wild's soldiers captured 18 men suspected of being guerrillas. On 17 December, Wild held a "drum-head court" to try the captives, of whom nine were found innocent, and eight were convicted and sent to Norfolk. One, Daniel Bright, whom Col. Holman's men had captured at a guerrilla camp and Wild believed was a guerrilla, was sentenced to death by hanging. Wild then sent a note to Captain John T. Elliott of Company A, 68th North Carolina Volunteers, who held Private Samuel Jordan, 5th Regiment, USCT as a prisoner, to ensure Jordan's safety and good treatment, and (facetiously?) urging Elliott to "renounce" being a guerrilla. On the cold, rainy morning of 18 December 1863, Wild and his 1,300 men marched north toward South Mills but stopped at "Hinton's Crossroads" to hang the condemned prisoner, Daniel Bright. The two lady hostages, Mrs. Munden and Mrs. Weeks, and other prisoners were forced to watch the execution, which also was attended by the colored soldiers. Reporter "Tewksbury" wrote:

> About noon, the sun coming out, a halt was ordered. The General and his staff rode to a small unfinished building designed for a post office, standing upon a knoll at a crossroads.... One of the officers, producing a cord, tied a hangman's knot at one end of it and, standing upon the head of an empty cider-barrel, made the other fast to one of the joists overhead ... the barrel was made to serve for both the scaffold and the drop, being ingeniously balanced upon one of the floor timbers, and held in place by a wedge which could be instantly removed....
>
> Lieut.-Col. [Giles W.] Shurtleff, of the Fifth United States [Regiment, USCT, and a graduate of the seminary at Oberlin College], was appointed spiritual advisor to the criminal, and went back with a guard to bring him to the place of execution. When informed that he had but a few minutes to die, and was counseled to improve this time in making his peace with God, he dropped to his knees in the road and prayed: "O, merciful Father, look down upon me! O, merciful Father, look down upon me!" These words alone he repeated a hundred times, until the acting Chaplain stopped him. He then rose to his feet, walked up the inclined board with a firm step, at the point of the bayonets [of] the colored guard[s], advanced quickly to the head of the cider barrel, and stood under the noose. This being placed around his neck, Col. Shurtleff invoked the throne of grace in behalf of the guilty wretch. As the word "Amen" dropped from his lips, *the General, who had taken charge of the drop, pulled the wedge—the barrel tipped, the guerrilla dropped.* He was a man of about thirty, a rough stout fellow, was dressed in butternut homespun, and looked the very ideal of a guerrilla. He died of strangulation, his heart not ceasing to beat for twenty minutes. Then a slip of paper was pinned to his back, on which the General had previously written, "This guerrilla hanged by order of Brig.-Gen. Wild, Daniel Bright, of Pasquotank County," and the body was left hanging there, a warning to all passing bushwhackers.[41]

General Wild reported that, as they returned:

> [At] South Mills [North Carolina] I dismissed the cavalry and artillery and sent home Colonel Holman's [1st USCT] regiment with our [wagon] trains; marched with the remainder to Indiantown, [there] met Colonel Draper, who had gone southward with his party to Shiloh, thence northward again.
>
> [Draper] had three encounters with guerrillas. At Shiloh they made a strong night attack, driving in his pickets and pouring in volley after volley upon his campfires. But Colonel Draper had previously withdrawn all his men to sleep inside the church, leaving the camp fires burning. The picket reserve having been secretly posted, returned the fire and drove away the enemy before the colonel could form his men and reach them. He pursued them in vain. The next day he [Captain George B. Cock's 200-man detachment of the 5th USCT Regiment] was waylaid at Sandy Hook by a force estimated at 200, who had taken position at the edge of a swamp 400 yards distant, which they held with some determination long enough for the colonel to bring 300 guns to bear upon it, and to send two flanking parties round their right and left. One of these, charging with the bayonet, they did not wait to receive, but vanished in the

swamp. The guerrillas, as we afterward learned, lost 13 killed and wounded, although [they were] sheltered, thus faring worse than our men, who lost 11, though exposed.

After crossing Indiantown Bridge, his rear guard holding the bridge was attacked, but drove back the enemy. The next day, with our combined force, I went back to meet them, drove them a long chase into their swamp, and after much trouble struck their trail, viz., a succession of single felled [tree] trunks leading to their citadel. We filed in single, burned their camp, took many guns, chiefly new Enfields (Tower mark, 1863), considerable fine [imported English?] ammunition, drum, clothes, provisions, &c.[42]

On 23 December, Wild sent Col. Alonzo Draper and a detachment to Knott's Island; that foray resulted in taking a third female hostage, 23-year-old Miss Nancy White.[43]

Perhaps Wild's most tragic victim was a Major Gregory, about whom Wild wrote to "Willis Sunderlin, Captain of Guerrillas," on 22 December: "Sir: I hold Major Gregory as a hostage for the colored soldier captured near Shiloh. I shall treat him exactly as your people treat that soldier. If they hang him I shall hang Major Gregory. And you know by this time I keep my word." In his deposition to the Confederate special committee, 1st Lt. William J. Munden wrote: "Among others arrested was Major Gregory, about seventy years old, who, while gone [as Wild's hostage], became paralyzed and died soon after his release and return home. All his property was destroyed by fire."[44]

Wild's force marched back to Norfolk in three columns, but two vessels were loaded with the "sick, lame, and wounded, a few prisoners, and a good pile of contrabands, with their baggage" for the return. As Wild's men reached the Virginia line, Confederates tried to trap them near Suffolk, and "several stragglers were surrounded in a house on the far side of town." They killed one man from Brig. Gen. Matt Ransom's North Carolina brigade as they attacked the house, which was set on fire with the black soldiers still inside. After 20 days of "hard scouting, without overcoats or blankets," the rest of Wild's African Brigade returned safely to their camps at Fortress Monroe in Virginia.[45]

"Wild's Raid" in northeastern North Carolina was significant because it was the first undertaken on a large scale with Negro troops and settled questions about their efficiency as soldiers. They scouted, skirmished, did picket and guard duty, and fought well while being "thoroughly obedient to their officers, [and] during a march of three hundred miles their conduct on every occasion, was truly admirable." Union cavalrymen said "no soldiers have ever done as hard marching through swamps and marshes as cheerfully" as Wild's black troops.

The results of Wild's Raid were impressive: 2,500 slaves freed, of whom only 70 to 100 were recruited as soldiers because most able-bodied men had previously fled to freedom or been "run over into Dixie"; four guerrilla camps were burned; more than 50 rifles, a drum, some ammunition, and four large boats engaged in contraband trade were captured. Ten prisoners, including 6 Confederate soldiers on furloughs to obtain horses, were taken, besides three female hostages and one old man. They "burned over a dozen homesteads, 2 distilleries, &c." Wild's men lost 7 soldiers killed, and one who died of poison and three from illness, a total of 11. Another 9 were wounded, and 2 captured (1 escaped). Many became ill from fatigue or exposure. Nine soldiers contracted smallpox, and many caught mumps. Three horses were shot and killed; 7 guns were lost and one captured.[46] "Tewksbury" added: "100 Enfield rifles captured; 350 ox, horse, and mule teams and 50–75 horses seized." His article summarized it as "the first raid of any magnitude undertaken by negro troops since their enlistment was authorized by Congress. And any question of their efficiency in any branch of service has been practically set at rest."[47]

Citizens of northeastern North Carolina were terrified by Wild and his men. People were "panic-stricken" due to rumors, and many families fled to the swamps. It was believed Wild's men had seized $100,000 worth of personal property. Confederate authorities described conditions in northeastern North Carolina as "deplorable." Horses and mules had been "objects of plunder," and Wild's men not only foraged for food, but they (probably white officers) also had seized valuable household furniture and sent it North.[48]

"Tewksbury" also described Wild's style as a commander and administrator: "The General imposes very little office work on members of his staff, *doing nearly all the writing himself.* Having but one arm, this is especially laborious, but it is his way. *Nothing, however trivial, escapes his notice, and he personally supervises everything.*"[49] In short, Edward A. Wild lived up (or down) to his surname on occasion, and he was a "one-man show."

But it wasn't over. Retaliation for Daniel Bright's hanging by Wild was not long in coming. A special committee of the Confederate Congress inquired into the matter of Daniel Bright. It reported he was a member of the 62nd Georgia Regiment (or 2nd Georgia Cavalry, a unit of partisan rangers organized from seven Georgia companies and three North Carolina companies), commanded by Col. Joel R. Griffin, and Bright had authority from Governor Vance of North Carolina "to raise a company for local defense." Daniel Bright, however, failed in this effort, and "retired to his farm, and was there seized, carried, off, and executed."[50] Colonel Griffin wrote to Wild, chastising him for his treatment of hostages and prisoners, and to describe what Confederates had done in retaliation:

Your Negro troops fired on Confederates after they had surrendered and were only saved by the exertions of the more humane of your white officers. Last, but not least, you hanged Daniel Bright, a private of Company L, Sixty-second Georgia regiment[,] forcing the ladies and gentlemen whom you held in arrest to witness the execution. Therefore, I have obtained an order from the General commanding for the execution of Samuel Jones [*sic*, Jordan], a private from Company B, Fifth Ohio [*sic*, USCT], whom I hang in retaliation. I hold two more of your men—in irons—as hostage for Mrs. Weeks and Mrs. Munden. When these ladies are released, then these men will be … treated as prisoners of war.[51]

By mid–January 1864, Private Jordan's body was found, and eleven citizens of Pasquotank County, fearing retaliation against themselves, had "made a suitable box and buried him near the place he was found hung." A placard stated: "Here hangs Private Samuel Jones [*sic*] of Company B, Fifth Ohio [*sic*] Regiment, by order of Major-General [George] Pickett, in retaliation for Daniel Bright … hanged December 18, 1863, by order of Brigadier-General Wild."[52]

Confederates saw Wild's actions as criminal, uncivilized, and unjustified, and even Wild's fellow officers were unhappy with him. Colonel J.W. Shaffer urged Butler to "get rid of him," and tell the Secretary of War to "give us one good common sense man…. I wish Wild was elsewhere. He has no common sense and does harm!" Frances H. Casstevens:

Perhaps only his "sable soldiers" believed Wild was "the right man in the right place." One of them wrote that, although Wild had lost an arm, "*with his revolver in hand, he was at the head of our regiment cheering us on to victory*" [as he probably was on 24 May 1864 at Wilson's Wharf]. What greater praise could a commander wish for than the approval of his men? But it is not the opinion of the common foot soldier that matters, for they have no power to make or break brigadier generals…. Because of the actions of Wild and his men in North Carolina, Brig. Gen. Wild suffered to his reputation and his military career.[53]

The hangings of both Daniel Bright as a "Guerrilla" by General Wild, and of Private Samuel Jordan, 5th Regiment, USCT by order of Maj. Gen. Pickett in retaliation, as horrible and unjustified as they were, pale in comparison to Confederate atrocities committed earlier in Louisiana. Just before Wild began his raid, a letter to Secretary of War Stanton published in the *New York Times* on 28 November 1863 pointed out that death awaited Union officers of colored troops who were captured by Confederates. None had been captured alive and held as prisoners of war in the South, nor had any Union colored soldier who was captured been "accounted for as a prisoner of war." A letter dated 3 November 1863 from a captain in the "7th Regiment" reported that "First Lieut. George B. Coleman, Jr., of New York City, who was captured about two months ago while on a raid, was hanged within twenty-four hours afterward, together with some twenty privates (colored) who were taken with him." The letter also stated that those men serving with the "Corps d'Afrique" when captured were "murdered, cast into prison, or sold into slavery. They are not regarded in the South as soldiers."[54]

Although Miss Nancy White had been released, in mid–January Wild's other two female hostages were still being held. After President Lincoln contacted General Butler about the hostages, Butler replied to him: "All executions have been stayed until further orders from you." Butler assured their Confederate husbands, Lt. W.J. Munden and Private Pender Weeks, that their wives would not be hanged, and he overrode Wild's threats and declared that Wild's order to execute the women in retaliation would be revoked. Butler tried to calm the situation with a "judicial" proposal that the two women be exchanged for their husbands. Butler believed he needed hostages because Confederates were "still talking about reprisals." Butler had the women released; however, he required the two husbands to take their wives' places indefinitely. Despite protests about Wild's actions, Butler neither demoted nor reprimanded Wild. Instead, he gave Wild command of all black and white troops in the Norfolk-Portsmouth area. Wild's command consisted of the African Brigade, the 27th Massachusetts Infantry and 20th New York Cavalry Regiments, six companies of the 2nd Massachusetts Heavy Artillery Regiment, and the 7th New York Independent Light Artillery Battery.[55]

During April 1864, prior to the beginning of Butler's James River Campaign, Wild was replaced by another general, Charles C. Graham. Wild remained under Butler, but during build-up and organization of the Army of the James, he became part of Maj. Gen. William F. Smith's XVIII Corps, in its 3rd Division under Brig. Gen. Edward W. Hinks. Wild commanded the 1st Brigade, consisting of Col. John H. Holman's 1st Regiment, USCT; 10th Regiment, USCT under Lt. Col. E. Henry Powell; and 22nd Regiment, USCT, commanded by Col. Joseph B. Kiddoo.[56]

Recruitment of black soldiers was occurring elsewhere as well. In the upper Mississippi Valley, Brig. Gen. Lorenzo Thomas raised 20,830 black troops from Alabama, Arkansas, Louisiana, Mississippi, Missouri, Kentucky, and Iowa, who were organized under white officers into 29 regiments of cavalry, artillery, and infantry. They had suffered some 5,000 losses—men were killed, died of wounds or diseases, and had deserted or were missing in action. Some 15,000 colored troops had been organized by Generals Benjamin F. Butler, Nathaniel P. Banks, and Daniel Ullmann in the lower Mississippi Valley; and others were raised in Middle Tennessee.[57]

General Thomas cited an engagement involving both black and white Union cavalrymen:

> On the 17th instant, thirty men of Company A, First Mississippi Cavalry (African), in connection with fifty men of the First Battalion, Fourth Illinois Cavalry, while on a scout up the Yazoo Valley, met 150 picked men of the First and Third Texas Cavalry. The First Mississippi behaved nobly, neither lacking courage nor steadiness, firing with coolness and precision. The engagement lasted half an hour, the Texans being routed and demoralized, we capturing 28 stands of arms and 7 prisoners.[58]

Fitzhugh Lee

Fitzhugh Lee was Union Brig. Gen. Edward A. Wild's Confederate antagonist on 24 May 1864. He was born on 19 November 1835 at Clermont in Fairfax County, Virginia. He was the son of Sydney Smith Lee, a distinguished U.S. Navy officer who had served as a fleet captain under Commodore Matthew Perry in Japanese waters and rose to commodore; and Ann Maria Mason Lee, granddaughter of George Mason of Gunston Hall, the "Plato of the American Revolution." Fitzhugh's paternal grandfather was Henry Lee III, or "Light Horse Harry" Lee, a renowned cavalry leader during the American War for Independence and later governor of Virginia and a U.S. congressman. Fitzhugh ("Fitz") was the nephew of Confederate Generals Robert E. Lee and Samuel Cooper, and a cousin of George Washington Custis Lee, W.H.F. "Rooney" Lee, and Robert E. Lee, Jr. Fitzhugh had five younger brothers and a sister who died in infancy. The boys had their early schooling in Alexandria in Northern Virginia. One author suggested that Fitz's lifetime disposition for fun and frolic came from his Mason blood, while Lees were "quiet folk." Biographer James L. Nichols states: "Fun or no, the Lees respected education," and they sent Fitz to secondary school at Timothy's Hall in Catonsville, Maryland, in April 1850. "Fitz's delight with drama and poetry was consistent with his lifelong attention to romance, opera, theater, and style in the flow of words. He later applied for an appointment to West Point, where reading of fiction would prove less rewarding academically."[59]

Fitzhugh Lee's U.S. Military Education and Early Service

Fitzhugh Lee was appointed by President Millard Fillmore from the District of Columbia to the U.S. Military Academy at West Point, New

York, on 1 July 1852. He was 16 years, seven months old when he entered a class of seventy-seven. Mathematics gave him the most trouble; he did best in French and English. Academy Library circulation records reflect his lack of interest in works on military science or mathematics; he seemed to confine himself in his four years to recreational reading of novels. Fitz was often cited in daily journals of student demerits for failing to control his hearty laugh while in ranks, "tobacco in his possession, dancing across the parade ground, dancing in front of guard tent, absent from quarters 11:40 a.m. until 5:20 a.m., failure to make proper recitation in Mathematics Academy, allowing boisterous noise in his tent at one a.m., etc., etc."[60]

Where was Fitz when off the post during forbidden hours? James L. Nichols: "The answer is most likely Benny Havens Tavern down the road from the Academy." The song "Benny Havens, Oh," became the cadets' theme song during that era. Benny Havens excursions got him in serious trouble during his second year, when Superintendent "Uncle Robert" turned him in for court-martial. Robert E. Lee was especially dismayed when he found Fitz among five young cadets who were absent from their barracks on the night of 16 December 1853. All five admitted their guilt, and nephew or not, Col. Lee recommended Fitz and the other cadets for dismissal or court-martial. Then the entire third class "pledged themselves for the remainder of the session not to commit the offense of which their comrades were accused." Lee endorsed the proposal, but Secretary of War Jefferson Davis turned it down and insisted on a court-martial. Stiff penalties were imposed on Fitz and his classmates; the two first-year cadets were allowed to resign. Fitzhugh Lee finished 45th of 49 cadets in the West Point Class of 1856.[61]

As Fitz Lee graduated, the War Department was organizing a new regiment, the United States 2nd Cavalry, with Albert Sydney Johnston as its colonel and Robert E. Lee as its lieutenant colonel. Fitz Lee drilled cavalry recruits at Carlisle Barracks in Pennsylvania for a year while awaiting orders to join the regiment, which was spread along the Comanche frontier of Texas. In 1857 in Washington, Elizabeth Lindsay Lomax recorded in her diary, "It is always a pleasure to have dear Fitz with us. He is so light-hearted and gay—will never grow up." Writing to his godmother, Fitz Lee described the life of a soldier on the western frontier and the "rough service of the horse: I put on a blue flannel shirt, top boots & soldier pants & I am equipped. Carry along a pack mule for provision and wander over the prairies, having no fixed direction, except to try and get on a trail & then follow it, until we come up with the Indians."[62]

In spring of 1859, Fitz Lee was at Camp Radziminski, the base for launching expeditions against the Comanche located at the edge of the Washita Mountains. Major Earl Van Dorn led six companies of cavalry and a company of infantry toward the headwaters of the Canadian and Arkansas Rivers. Kirby Smith was second-in-command and Fitz Lee the adjutant. Without tents and on scanty rations, the troops and 46 friendly Indians left in early May. At the Washita, they captured an Indian boy who told them about a great encampment of Kiowas and Comanche five days' travel to the north. Based on the report, officers thought they might be up against ten thousand Indians. Van Dorn made the boy guide the troops, threatening to shoot him if he made a wrong move. After days and nights marching, they crossed the Cimarron and skirmished with a party of Comanches, killing one Indian. Further on, they found where two thousand Indians had encamped, but they had fled northward. Van Dorn pressed on. On 13 May, a small force pushed some Indians into a wooded ravine and captured their horses. Kirby Smith ordered his company to dismount and go into the thicket. Smith was wounded by a ball in the thigh, but he stayed in the fight during which the Indians were killed at a cost of 13 soldiers killed and wounded.[63]

In the fight, Fitz Lee had the fight knocked out of him when an arrow passed under his arm and through both lungs. He survived despite being dragged across the plains on a litter. He wrote home on 3 June 1859:

> I have been as near to death's door, as it falls to the lot of a mortal to be, & still not enter…. I was leading the charge through a dense thicket, had just shot & killed an Indian, & was within a dozen yards of them, dispatching another, he shooting and I shooting, a sort of duel, I had shot him twice … & was about firing a third time, having my pistol raised when an Indian about 10 yds. on my right shot me as I have described…. I have just been brought 200 miles in a mule litter & of course feel a little tired, but hope after being still a few days to rally fast.

He was given salt water to stop the flow of blood, but blood only came from Fitz's mouth. Surgeons regarded the wound as fatal. Fitz expressed a special obligation to sixteen-year-old bugler boy Edward "Jack" Mortimer Hayes for having nursed him all the way across the prairie during the "Wichita Expedition." Three months later, Fitz wrote he was "entirely recovered, minus a little, very little strength."[64]

On 17 January 1860, Fitz and twenty men of Company B, 2nd U.S. Cavalry, caught up with a party of Comanche driving a herd of animals, and charged them. Fitz pursued one Indian: "I dismounted and finally after a search of between two and three hours came suddenly upon him hidden behind a ledge of rocks, and after a short struggle *killed* him … with pleasure I report that none of my command received the slightest injury…. I recovered *all their animals*, 24 in number." Jack Hayes remembered that the Indian leaped on Fitz, and the two wrestled on the ground before the Indian got off a shot through Fitz's sleeve. Lee finally maneuvered his enemy into a position where he could blow out his brains. Kirby Smith wrote that Lee paraded into camp bearing the Indian's "shield, head dress and arms with great pride."[65]

In the summer of 1860, Fitz was ordered to West Point to instruct cavalry tactics to cadets, among whom were George A. Custer and Judson Kilpatrick, both of whom he later faced in battle. National political tensions building up during the winter of 1860–1861 must have been distracting for a Virginian of his age and disposition. He had previously expressed being unhappy with abolitionists in general. Two months after the Confederate government was formed at Montgomery, Alabama, and one month after President Lincoln's inauguration, Fitz wrote to his mother, charging the politicians with creating the crisis and threat of civil war:

> You need be under no apprehension about my injuring myself talking secession—T''is only occasionally, when I hear something exceedingly hard and unjust about the South that I am unable to hold in—I wrote Papa a letter not long ago, telling him I wanted to resign—That I was tired of serving a Black Republican administration.
>
> ... T''is a short-sighted policy to think the reinforcement of these Southern forts will restore the condition of things in this country—The Army, while it rather likes occasionally a little brush with a foreign foe, equally loathes the idea of civil war—and our only wish is to be allowed to stand aside and let the politicians who have got us into all this trouble, fight it out—were that the case—viz: those who gave the orders had the execution of them, the speck of war now visible upon the horizon would soon disappear.... I see by the papers that 7 co's of my Regt. will soon arrive in New York— my own is one of them—I wonder where they will be sent—I am now a First Lieutenant in my Regt., only 8 above me for a Captaincy—There have been 8 resignations and one officer drummed [out] recently—Did you see an account of my resignation in the N.Y. Herald and other papers.... I have T''is true been offered a position in the Southern Army....
>
> Fitz
> I WANT TO RESIGN

Many other Virginians and other Southerners felt the same way in March and April 1861, but like Robert E. Lee, they waited for the decision in the Old Dominion, which only came after the Fort Sumter "incident" in mid–April. After Virginia seceded on 17 April, Robert E. Lee resigned on 20 April. In late April Fitz left West Point, shaking hands with each cadet, his parting words delivered "with tears in his eyes and [in] a voice tremulous with emotion." On 16 May he tendered his resignation, which was accepted by the War Department on 21 May 1861.[66]

Fitzhugh Lee's Confederate Military Service, Beginning in July 1861

Fitzhugh Lee's first Confederate appointment was as a first lieutenant of artillery. But in late July 1861, Governor John Letcher commissioned Fitzhugh Lee as lieutenant colonel in the Virginia Volunteers, and on 27 September 1861 he was assigned to the 1st Virginia Cavalry Regiment. Meanwhile, he served as acting assistant adjutant general to Brig. Gen. Richard S. Ewell, who commanded the Second Brigade, First Corps, of General P.G.T. Beauregard's army at the First Battle of Manassas on 21 July 1861, but he saw little action.[67] Fitz Lee also formed a close friendship with Colonel J.E.B. ("Jeb") Stuart.[68]

On 18 November 1861, the 1st Virginia Cavalry was in the vicinity of Falls Church, where his men encountered a Federal picket post. Fitz reported: "[G]etting as near as possible, I charged them, they retiring rapidly toward the woods and pines, while we quickly lessened the distance, driving one picket upon another.... Followed by a portion of my command, I got in between them and ... completely surrounded them." Lee then ordered his men to dismount and fight. The Federals fought with determination, but they lost 2 killed, one mortally wounded, and 10 prisoners. Fitz withdrew with his prisoners and captured wagons as Union troops from Falls Church began arriving. Lee lost 2 men—a private and a civilian guide—killed, and had three horses killed, including his own. Frank Bond described the action in the 1898 *Confederate Veteran*: "Col. Lee with heavy black ostrich plume in a broad-brimmed slouch hat, and mounted on his horse Dixie was well to the front." Bond heard a command from "a small man, on foot, and covered with mud.... To my horror I saw it was Col. Lee," whose horse Dixie had been killed under him while going at speed, and "had taken a header into the mud."[69]

John Singleton Mosby, later a famed partisan scout and ranger, was with Fitz Lee. Mosby was adjutant of the 1st Virginia Cavalry; he and Fitz clashed from the start. Frank Bond explained:

> There could not have been greater contrast between the two men.... Lee was the precise and punctilious soldier, with great regard for all the etiquette of the profession. Mosby was absolutely careless of all this, and seemed to take pride in violating every rule that it was safe to do.... [Once, when Col. William E. "Grumble"] Jones was absent, and Col. Lee was in command and waiting in front of his tent for his horse, Mosby sauntered up, and with a drawl more pronounced than usual, said, "Colonel, the horn has blowed for dress parade." Lee [replied:] "Sir, if I ever again hear you call that bugle a horn, I will put you under arrest."

For his part, James L. Nichols states: "Mosby consistently reflected his dislike of Fitz throughout his *Memoirs*."[70]

A full-strength Confederate cavalry regiment consisted of 5 squadrons, each squadron having 2 companies or troops. A troop had an authorized strength of 3 officers: a captain and 2 lieutenants, and 60 to 80 enlisted men, including 5 sergeants, 4 corporals, a farrier, and a blacksmith. A squadron was led by the senior company commander. Each regiment was commanded by a colonel, a lieutenant-colonel, and a major. The staff included an officer adjutant, a sergeant-major, and a quartermaster-sergeant. On paper, a regiment numbered about 800 men in 1861. Seldom during the war did gray regiments average above 500 men due to casualties, sickness, and men on leave to obtain new horses, etc. Studying strength returns, John W. Thomason discovered that Confederate cavalry regiments in 1862 averaged about 500 men; in 1863, from 350 to 500 men; and after that, never above 350 men. Four or more regiments composed a brigade. A cavalry division contained two or more brigades. Horse artillery batteries of 3 to 6 guns were directed by the brigade commander.[71] Captain Charles Blackford, 2nd Virginia Cavalry, wrote in late 1862: "My company is becom-

"The 1st Virginia Cavalry at a halt," Sketch by Alfred W. Waud, Sept. 1862, during the Antietam Campaign (LC-62–157, Library of Congress, Washington, D.C.).

ing smaller and smaller through sickness, wounds, and lack of horses, chiefly the latter.... I believe this is the only army in history where the men have to furnish their own horses [in contrast to the Federal cavalry where the government provided the initial horse and remounts] and it is the main weakness of our cavalry. To me to lose a horse is to lose a man, as they cannot afford a remount, and new recruits with horses of their own are almost nil."[72]

Confederate cavalry tactics in the East followed the *Trooper's Manual*, adapted by Col. J. Lucius Davis of Stuart's brigade from the *Poinsett Tactics* used by United States mounted units during 1841–1861. Squadrons formed on line in double or single ranks—single for combat and double for ceremonial reviews that Stuart favored. In combat, a regiment normally deployed on a two-squadron front, some two hundred men abreast, supported by two more squadrons in lines of companies, each company in a column of fours or twos, depending on the terrain. *Dismounted tactics* [as used mostly at Wilson's Wharf on 24 May 1864] *called for deployment as skirmishers, while one man in each "set" of four remained to the rear as a horseholder for the other three men.* These were outlines for drill and maneuver; it's questionable whether the manual was exactly followed as time progressed and men and horses were lost to attrition.[73]

In May 1862, a giant Prussian officer, Heros von Borcke, spent a rainy night in now–Colonel Fitz's "spacious" tent and enjoyed a supper of turtle eggs, while "one of the younger officers played many tunes on a banjo accompanied by jolly old soldier songs [despite] incessant thunder and rain." Von Borcke saw in Fitz "an unusually cheerful disposition and indestructible humor." Well-known in the whole army, Fitz was the "greatest favorite with his men."[74]

The "Chickahominy Raid," 12–15 June 1862

After McClellan's great offensive against Richmond had been halted, General Robert E. Lee decided to bring Maj. Gen. "Stonewall" Jackson from the Shenandoah Valley to flank Fitz-John Porter's 25,000-man Union corps on McClellan's extreme right. Lee wanted Stuart to find that unanchored flank and discover if it was "in the air." Stuart received orders to reconnoiter the Federal right, but Stuart wanted to do more—"to ride entirely around McClellan's army." He selected Col. Fitz Lee's 1st Virginia, "Rooney" Lee's 9th Virginia, and William C. Wickham's 4th Virginia split between them because Col. Wickham had received a bad saber wound, and

Lt. Col. William Martin's Mississippi "Jeff Davis Legion," making 1,200 horsemen in all. Captain James Breathed's Horse Artillery, 2 guns, came along. Mosby and von Borcke came as volunteers. At 2:30 a.m. on 12 June the column moved out in column of fours on the Brooke Turnpike, before heading westward toward Louisa Court House and crossing the South Anna and heading east. Near Hanover Court House, Fitz's 1st Virginia pursued a patrol from Fitz's old U.S. 2nd Cavalry, now the U.S. 5th Cavalry. He captured a sergeant who had fallen out, and together they laughed and joked about the "old days."[75]

By late 13 June 1862, Stuart knew Brig. Gen. Fitz-John Porter's dispositions, and that the Federals probably were trying to cut off his return westward. He was well in the rear of McClellan's infantry, so going entirely around McClellan would be unexpected, and in Stuart's mind, "the quintessence of prudence." At Christian Ford on the Chickahominy, they built a pedestrian crossing on ruins of an old bridge while their horses swam across. Last across was Fitz Lee. Five men fired the crude bridge just as the 6th Pennsylvania Lancers rode up and opened fire. At 11 p.m., Fitz put the column on the road for Richmond, returning with 165 prisoners and 260 captured animals. The only fatality was Captain William Latane of the 9th Virginia, who also killed a Federal captain in a "duel," and only 4 men were missing.[76]

The value of Stuart's raid was obvious: Robert E. Lee had his information, and its morale-building for civilians and military alike was invaluable. James L. Nichols: "Yet, at the same time, it well may be that Stuart should have somehow slipped away to the north and around to the west with his valued report. He had jeopardized his entire command and had caused McClellan to consider establishing a base on the James, since the York line's power had been precarious. This he did and, in a sense, was braced for the Jackson-Lee blows of late June." General Lee's superb plan to roll up McClellan's flank "like a carpet" from his right to his left, or from north to south, went awry early. Thomas J. "Stonewall" Jackson was late and failed to tell anyone where he was on 25 June, and R.E. Lee made no effort to find him. There was no contact between Jackson and A.P. Hill, staff work was almost nil, and maps and overlays were faulty and scarce. Fitzhugh Lee and his 1st Virginia rode out again with Stuart on 25 June to find Jackson, who arrived at Ashland, north of Richmond. On 27 June, at Gaines's Mill, the Confederates achieved a great victory, but suffered over 5,000 casualties.[77]

Stuart's cavalry was sent along the old York River line "to cut the enemy's [now abandoned] line of communications with the York" and to intercept McClellan's retreat along the Chickahominy. But the ponderous quarry had escaped to Harrison's Landing on the James. McClellan then marched back to Malvern Hill, where he repulsed Robert E. Lee's bloody and uncoordinated attacks. Stuart came up with another "ride around McClellan." The victory over McClellan's attempt to capture Richmond had been so complete, "so dramatically done in one short week, that few people questioned the competence of Confederate command. Even so, the drama had been frightfully expensive, as Lee's losses exceeded 20,000" (3,478 killed, 12,261 wounded, and 875 missing, a total of 16,614 reported losses). James L. Nichols states:

Lieutenant General Thomas Jonathan "Stonewall" Jackson, CSA. Fitzhugh Lee reconnoitered with Jackson shortly before Jackson launched his great flank attack and was mortally wounded by his own men (courtesy Cary Delery, Metairie, Louisiana).

> Actually, [R.E.] Lee had only carried [won] one attack, Gaines's Mill. He had been thrown back every other time, but McClellan had decided on [his own] defeat. Perhaps not the least of his weakness was his feeble cavalry arm which told him nothing. Operating in an even denser "fog of war" than Lee, it is indeed remarkable and a compliment to his credit and to the Federal army, that they were able to extricate themselves so adroitly, sustaining a gross loss of 15,849 men (1,734 killed, 8,062 wounded, and 6,053 missing)—"prisoners mostly."[78]

In July 1862, Stuart was promoted to Major General, and Wade Hampton, Beverly Robertson, and Fitz Lee, the junior in precedence, were promoted to brigadier generals. In forwarding his commission to Fitz Lee, Stuart wrote: "My dear General, Please accept Gen R.E. Lee's and my own congratulations on the within, but I am free to say I reserve the 'main body' of my congratulations for myself and the Country in having such a Brigadier. I hope you will report

Major General James Ewell Brown (J.E.B.) Stuart, CSA (Library of Congress).

soon." Wade Hampton was given the First Brigade, and Fitz Lee the Second Brigade, consisting of the 1st, 3rd, 4th, 5th, and 9th Virginia Cavalry Regiments. In early August 1862, Fitz Lee's force struck the rear of two Union infantry brigades and some cavalry that were raiding the Virginia Central Railroad and had captured Mosby at Beaver Dam Station. The Rebels were forced to retreat, but they held on to 85 prisoners, 11 wagons and teams, and 15 cavalry horses they had captured. Two of Fitz's men died of their wounds; other casualties were not reported.[79]

During mid–August at Orange Court House, Robert E. Lee explained his plan for an assault on Maj. Gen. John Pope's left near Manassas, so as to place Lee between Pope's army and Washington. Stuart sent orders for Fitz to come to Raccoon Ford on the Rapidan; Jackson and Longstreet were already on the move. Then, Stuart and his staff rode down the road. Fitz received Stuart's order, but it had no prescribed time for his arrival at Raccoon Ford. His men were low on rations, so Fitz rode 30 miles to Louisa Court House to get them supplied. Thus, his brigade had to ride 60 miles to get to Raccoon Ford. Fitz sent his route decision via courier to Stuart, who left Orange before the courier arrived. Stuart rode on, annoyed he did not run into Fitz's brigade.[80]

James L. Nichols: "The 'imponderables,' the 'incalculable elements of luck and chance' were working against the Confederates." After Stuart and his staff stopped near Verdiersville to stay the night, Stuart then foolishly sent his aide, Major Norman R. Fitzhugh, alone to find Fitz Lee. Major Fitzhugh had the written copy of Robert E. Lee's plan of attack against Union General John Pope, which Stuart had given him for temporary "coat-pocket filing." Federal cavalry captured Major Fitzhugh with the attack plan, and they nearly captured Stuart, von Borcke, and others. In wild haste, Stuart and his staff scrambled to get away, leaving Stuart's plumed hat and his scarlet-lined cloak behind.[81]

Late on the night of 18 August, Fitz Lee reached Raccoon Ford with tired horses and men. General R.E. Lee ordered a day of rest and set 20 August for the river crossing to begin the new campaign. But *the great opportunity was now lost, because Pope now knew Lee's attack plan.* In his report, Stuart blamed Fitz for the delay, but Stuart's biographers defend Fitz, feeling that his orders must have been vague about the time factor. Unaware of Stuart's urgency, Fitz had notified R.E. Lee that his horses were not fit for hard service. Douglas Southall Freeman wrote: "Fitz Lee ... was not solely responsible for delaying the offensive. Even had he arrived on schedule on the 17th, the Army would not have been able to carry out its original plan of advancing on the 18th. The commissary was not ready; Anderson's Division was not at hand."[82]

Early on 20 August, Fitz Lee crossed the Rapidan at Raccoon's Ford. At Kelly's Ford on the Rappahannock, Fitz captured a flag and prisoners and drove other Federals across the river. Robertson, and "Grumble" Jones with his 7th Virginia, drove Kilpatrick's force behind the Rappahannock, taking 64 prisoners while losing 3 men killed and 13 wounded. Stuart asked R.E. Lee to let him move around Pope's communications, and another great adventure began.

Riding past Warrenton, the troopers reached Auburn near Catlett's Station that night. They fell on the picket guard and captured everything in sight, despite heavy rain. A negro who knew Stuart showed him Pope's wagon park. Then, "Rooney" Lee's 9th Virginia struck the Federal camp and captured some of Pope's staff along with much money, headquarters papers, and Pope's baggage, including his hat, military cloak, and frock coat. Later, Fitz halted General Charles Field to show off his captures. Fitz "slipped behind a big oak-tree, and emerged dressed in a long blue coat [and] a general's hat with its big plume. The masquerade was accompanied by a jolly laughter from him that might have been heard for a hundred years."[83]

Besides 8 cannon and 300 prisoners, Jackson had seized enormous stores of food and clothing at Manassas, which he evacuated on 27 August. The Rebel cavalry was widely scattered by 28 August, the day Jackson's corps fought the Union "Iron Brigade" to a bloody draw at Brawner's Farm, a mile west of the First Manassas Battlefield fought a year earlier. During 29–30 August, the Second Battle of Manassas was fought mostly by infantry and ended in another great Confederate victory. On 31 August, Fitz captured a company of regular U.S. cavalry from the old U.S. 2nd Dragoons. Fitz occupied Fairfax Court House on 2 September.[84]

The Antietam Campaign into Maryland

On 4 September from Leesburg, Robert E. Lee wrote President Davis that he was "more persuaded of the benefit that [would] result from an expedition into Maryland," and he would make the move unless Davis disapproved. Lee's cavalry crossed the Potomac on 5 September 1862 and established a long picket line. Fitz Lee was at an advanced position on the left at New Market. At Poolesville, Maryland, on the 5th, Fitz Lee "encountered a body of the enemy's cavalry, which he attacked, capturing the greater portion." Fitz later wrote:

> On the morning of the 15th, when the Federal army debouched from the mountains, the cavalry brigade was alone between the Federals [cavalry and infantry] and [R.E.]

Lee at Sharpsburg to dispute every foot of ground between the base of the mountains and Boonsboro. This was done with artillery, dismounted cavalry, and charges of mounted squadrons. The object having been accomplished, the brigade was slowly withdrawn and placed on the left of the line of battle of Sharpsburg [or Antietam].

The Battle of Antietam [the "bloodiest single day of the war," with an estimated 4,808 killed, not counting other casualties] on 16 September 1862 was an infantry fight, while the cavalry formed a provost screen at the rear of Lee's army to halt the many stragglers, except for those severely wounded. Anyone who could still handle a musket was pressed back to fight; Robert E. Lee had no unused reserves. Fitz's conduct in the campaign merited praise from both R.E. Lee and "Jeb" Stuart. But a mule kicked Fitz soon after he returned to Virginia, and his cousin Rooney Lee took his place. Fitz missed Stuart's famous Chambersburg Raid into Maryland and Pennsylvania in October because of his "muleitis." By mid–November, Fitz was back with his brigade.[85]

The Battle of Fredericksburg and the Winter of 1862–1863

The Battle of Fredericksburg on 13 December 1862 was again primarily an infantry action in which Union Maj. Gen. Ambrose P. Burnside lost 12,000 men in futile charges, compared to R.E. Lee's 5,000 casualties. During the battle, Stuart ordered Fitz Lee to make a cavalry charge against oncoming Federals. The effort would have been another Crimean War–style "Balaklava" suicidal charge, but Fitz said he would obey orders. "Stonewall" Jackson recognized the hopelessness of the mounted attack and stopped it before it could begin.[86]

During the winter of 1862–1863, shortages of forage and corn aggravated disease in Stuart's horses, which already suffered from mange, sore-mouth, and foot-evil. As miserable weather continued, Fitz's brigade covered the upper Rappahannock. North of the river were 130,000 Federal soldiers under "Fighting Joe" Hooker; Maj. Gen. George Stoneman commanded Hooker's newly formed Cavalry Corps, estimated at 12,000 men. Lee's army was reduced to about 50,000 men, including Stuart's two brigades (Fitz Lee's and "Rooney" Lee's), since Wade Hampton's brigade went to the Carolinas to recruit men and find mounts. General R.E. Lee wanted to penetrate Hooker's lines to get information, so Stuart sent Fitz Lee with 400 selected men to cross Kelly's Ford on 24 February. The next day, Fitz "drove the enemy's pickets near Hartwood Church, and attacked his reserve and main body. Routed them, and pursued them within 5 miles of Falmouth to their infantry lines." He captured 5 officers and 145 enlisted men; his cavalry lost 14 men.

In late February, he showed another side to Constance Cary, who went with an aunt to "Belpre" near Fitz's headquarters at Culpeper. He gave her a Smith & Wesson revolver and taught her how to shoot it. She also was daily feted with the "jollity and good fellowship" of Fitz Lee. During one outing, the young general entertained her with his riding abilities, as he "rode standing in the saddle, picking dried wayside flowers at a gallop, backward, forward, in every attitude that one can assume upon a steed."[87]

West Pointers William Averell vs. Fitzhugh Lee at Kelly's Ford, Virginia, 17 March 1863

The 1863 campaign began on 14 March when William Averell's 2nd Division of the Union Cavalry Corps, 3,000 men, set out to crush Fitz Lee's brigade at Culpeper. Averell and Fitz had been classmates at West Point, and Fitz had taunted Averell to cross the Rappahannock, and asked him to bring coffee. Hooker's orders were "to attack and rout or destroy Fitz Lee's brigade of cavalry." Reports from R.E. Lee at 11 a.m. on the 16th alerted Fitz, who then alerted his pickets on the Rappahannock but kept his main force of 800 troopers close to Culpeper. Fitz had 1,900 men on muster rolls, but the number was severely reduced by failed horses and sickness. He also had James Breathed's horse artillery battery with three English Blakely cannon.[88]

Averell came on cautiously, keeping 900 men to his right rear to cover the advance. Early on 17 March, the 1st Rhode Island Cavalry forced a crossing of Kelly's Ford, where it overran and captured 25 troopers of the 2nd Virginia Cavalry under Captain James Breckinridge. Word came to Fitz at 7:30 a.m. at Culpeper; he led his men forward at a rapid trot to challenge Averell. Stuart and young Artilleryman John Pelham rode along to see the action that followed.[89]

When conferring with Stuart, Fitz reportedly said, "General, I think there are only a few platoons in the woods yonder. Hadn't we better 'take the bulge' on them at once?" By mid-morning, Lee attacked Averell, who had advanced only a half-mile from the ford along the Kelly's Ford-Brandy Station Road. Sharpshooters from the 1st Virginia Cavalry led the way, followed by the 3rd Virginia Cavalry. Fitz reported the Federal position as "a very strong one, sheltered by woods and a long, high stone fence" which served as a breastwork for Averell's skirmishers. Preceded by a squadron deployed as skirmishers, Fitz's troopers charged the fence, "wheeled about," and delivered "their fire almost in the faces of the enemy." They hoped to find a gate or low spot that would enable them to scatter the sharpshooters and strike the Federal rear. Finding no passage, they rode down the fence toward the Federal right while firing at the defenders. Captain Harry Gilmor of the 12th Virginia Cavalry led an unsuccessful rush at the fence by the dismounted 3rd Virginia. The 3rd Virginia then turned and ran away despite Gilmore's shouts to stand and fight. Stuart rallied the demoralized 3rd Virginia and placed them beyond a fence facing the Federals. There was too much "Blue," and Fitz pulled back to wait for his artillery. During the charge, the "Gallant Pelham" was mortally wounded by a Federal shell fragment; his death was mourned by the whole Confederacy.[90]

The 5th Virginia Cavalry now joined the 3rd Virginia, and, with Breathed's guns up, Fitz ordered a general advance by his entire force. Fitz Lee reported: "[I]t was a succession of gallant charges by the various regiments and once by the whole brigade in line, whenever the enemy would show mounted men ... sabers were frequently crossed and fences charged up to, the leading men dismounting and pulling them down, under a heavy fire of canister, grape[shot] and carbine balls." The 3rd and 5th Virginia regiments fought the 4th and 16th Pennsylvania Cavalry Regiments, while on the opposite flank, the 1st Rhode Island, 4th Pennsylvania, and 6th Ohio Cavalry Regiments attacked the 1st, 2nd, and 4th Virginia Cavalry Regiments. Federal accounts speak of the Confederate line being driven back in confusion, while Southern accounts point out that only nine of their men were captured here, and their final and successful stand was only a mile behind their initial position.

At 5:30 p.m., the Federals stubbornly withdrew under close fighting. The Rebels were relieved when Averell pulled back toward Kelly's Ford, and he was back across the river by nightfall. Averell lost 78 men (including 29 whom Lee reported as prisoners) to Fitz Lee's 133 (11 killed, 88 wounded, and 34 captured). With 2,100 men, Averell should have been able to drive Fitz Lee into Culpeper; thus Averell gained no stature at Kelly's Ford. But Fitz was unhappy. At best he had driven a much larger force back across the Rappahannock, but Averell had gotten away. Fitz must have grimaced when he read Averell's note left behind with a sack of coffee: "Dear Fitz, Here's your coffee. Here's your visit. How do you like it." But on 21 March, Fitz congratulated his men for their stand at Kelly's Ford:

Rebel cavalry have been taught that Yankee (would be) horsemen, notwithstanding their numbers, can be confronted and hurled back.

… Rebel cavalry have been taught that a determined rush upon the foe is the part of sound policy as it is the part of true courage. Rebel cavalry have taught an insolent enemy that, notwithstanding they may possess advantages of chosen positions, superiority in numbers and weapons [breechloading carbines], they cannot overwhelm soldiers fighting for the holiest cause that ever nerved the arm of a freeman or fired the breast of a patriot. You have taught certain sneerers in our army that placing a Southern soldier on horseback does not convert him into a coward; and, last but not least, you have confirmed Abolition cavalry in their notions of running.[91]

Brigadier General Fitzhugh Lee, CSA, c. 1863 (Library of Congress, Washington, D.C.).

Stuart lavishly praised Fitz as the "noble chief" of the brigade, and whose report was so "very graphic." Stuart noted that Fitz Lee "exhibited … the sagacity of a successful general" and the victory at Kelly's Ford "was one of the most brilliant achievements of the war." Thus, by their rhetoric, Fitz and Stuart turned a minor action that repulsed a very tentative attack resulting in few casualties on either side, into a "most brilliant achievement." Although the Federals had fallen far short of fulfilling their orders to rout or destroy Fitz's small brigade, their cavalry had given a good fighting account of themselves.[92]

Battle of Chancellorsville, 1–4 May 1863: Fitzhugh Lee Plays a Key Part in the Victory

After Maj. Gen. Joseph Hooker began a new offensive in late April, Fitz probed Hooker's lines to find his extreme right and determined it to be just west of Wilderness Church on the Plank Road. The Union right flank was "in the air," exposed to an attack from the northwest. Generals R.E. Lee and Thomas J. Jackson used Fitz's information to plan the famous flank movement that evening. Jackson, with 25,000 men, began moving westward through the Wilderness at 4 a.m. on 2 May. Fitz's troopers rode at the head of Jackson's column to scout, screen, and picket road crossings. After marching 12 miles over roads and forest paths, Jackson came to the Orange Plank Road, 2.5 miles southwest of Melzi Chancellor's or Dowdall's Tavern, from where Jackson planned to attack. After riding beyond the Plank Road, Fitz recounted: "Seeing a wooded hill in the distance, I determined, if possible, to get upon its top … reaching the open space upon its summit without molestation. What a sight presented itself before me! I was in rear of [Union General] Howard's right.… The soldiers were in groups in the rear, laughing, chatting, smoking … feeling safe and comfortable."[93]

Fitz Lee "rode rapidly back" and urged Jackson to ride a little way with him to a point on the Plank Road. On the crest, Jackson could see the right of Hooker's line, the XI Corps under Maj. Gen. Oliver Otis Howard. Fitz closely watched Jackson's face as he studied Howard's troops. Fitz recalled that Jackson's "eyes burned with a brilliant glow, lighting up a sad face," and "his face was colored slightly with the paint of approaching battle and radiant at the success of his flank movement." Jackson soon made his dispositions to roll up Howard. Fitz was to maneuver his squadrons on the road as if to charge, while Jackson's infantry crossed the road unobserved.

Meanwhile, Stuart found Averell and intended to attack him, when he learned that both Jackson and A.P. Hill had been wounded (Jackson mortally, as it turned out; he later died of pneumonia), and that Hill had directed Stuart to take command of Jackson's Corps. Throughout the night of 2–3 May, Stuart readied the corps to resume the furious attack begun by Jackson the night before. Hooker yielded the Wilderness until early 6 May, when all of his army, minus its dead and seriously wounded left behind, was again north of the Rappahannock. Hooker's Army of the Potomac suffered 17,278 casualties, or 13 percent of his original 133,000 men, while Lee's Army of Northern Virginia lost 12,821 men, or 21 percent of its 61,000 men.[94]

The Cavalry Battle of Brandy Station, 9 June 1863; Fitz Lee Misses the Battle Because of Illness

After Chancellorsville, Fitz's regiments got some veterans returning with mounts, and some new men, helping to swell Stuart's total force to 10,000 men, supported by horse artillery with 20 guns. As General Robert E. Lee decided to invade the North again, via the valley into Maryland

and Pennsylvania, Stuart based himself at Culpeper and proudly held troop reviews of his command, attended by gentlemen and ladies. On 5 June, Stuart had his own review, complete with artillery salutes. A parade for R.E. Lee was set for 8 June. Stuart then moved northward to Fleetwood Hill near Brandy Station on the Orange & Alexandria Railroad. Fitz Lee's brigade moved to Oak Shade Church north of Hazel River, where Fitz became ill with severe rheumatism or arthritis, and he temporarily turned over command to Col. Thomas T. Munford of the 2nd Virginia Cavalry.[95]

On 8 June, Maj. Gen. Alfred Pleasanton came across the Rappahannock in two columns of cavalry, with six light artillery batteries, about 11,000 men, and supported by two infantry brigades. The Battle of Brandy Station, the largest cavalry battle fought in the Western Hemisphere, involved a series of charges at the gallop, with clashes of sabre to sabre. Fitz was out of action, but his brigade fought under command of Col. Munford. In one action, the 4th Virginia was routed and half the regiment was captured; Stuart wrote it was "unaccountable," as that regiment usually fought well. Munford blamed an "uncertainty" in his orders for his slowness in getting his other regiments off to the scene of battle. Confederate losses were 523 men; the Federal loss was 936, including 486 captured. But Pleasanton had accomplished his mission, since Hooker now knew that Lee was leaving Fredericksburg and heading north. Stuart had been surprised; the *Richmond Sentinel* chided: "'Vigilance, vigilance, more vigilance,' is the lesson taught us by the Brandy surprise…. Let all learn from it, from the Major General down to the picket." Stuart's image was tarnished, and his subsequent Gettysburg raid was prompted largely by a desire to re-establish his reputation. Major Henry B. McClellan also wrote later: "[Another] result of incalculable importance certainly did follow this battle … it *made* the Federal cavalry. Up to that time confessedly inferior to the Southern horsemen, they gained on this day that confidence in themselves and in their commanders which enabled them to contest so fiercely the subsequent battlefields."[96]

Gettysburg

Two weeks after Brandy Station, Robert E. Lee's army was on its second invasion, which would culminate in the Battle of Gettysburg (1–3 July 1863) in Pennsylvania. Sharp cavalry screening actions at Aldie, Middleburg, and Upperville in Virginia again demonstrated Federal cavalry confidence and fighting abilities. Stuart suggested to R.E. Lee that a move across the Potomac to strike at Hooker's supply lines would pull Federal cavalry after Stuart and remove the threat to Lee's own extended communications. On the night of 23 June, Stuart received a key order from R.E. Lee, a dispatch that led to considerable controversy later. R.E. Lee wrote:

> If you find that [Hooker] is moving northward, and that two brigades can guard the Blue Ridge and take care of your rear, you can move with the other three into Maryland, and *take position on General Ewell's right, place yourself in communication with him, guard his flank, and keep him informed of the enemy's movements. You will, however, be able to judge whether you can pass around their army without hindrance, doing them all the damage you can,* and cross the [Potomac] river east of the mountains. *In either case, feel the right of Ewell's troops, collecting information, provisions, etc.*[97]

The next day, Stuart directed "Grumble" Jones and Beverly Robertson with their brigades to watch the south and east, covering R.E. Lee's rear.[98]

Stuart took with him the three brigades of Fitz Lee, who had recovered from his rheumatism; Wade Hampton; and John R. Chambliss, who commanded in place of "Rooney" Lee, who had been wounded at Brandy Station. Marching east toward Hooker, Stuart encountered Winfield Scott Hancock's northbound Union II Corps, and he detoured around the Federals to Buckland without conferring with his officers. Robert E. Lee was then notified of the Federal movement, but Stuart didn't ask for further orders regarding his own movements. James L. Nichols writes:

> Although Lee had authorized the earlier stages of Stuart's movements, he certainly would not have approved the isolation from his cavalry that followed after June 24. Lee wrote that after the Army of the Potomac had crossed the Potomac, "Stuart would give no notice of its movements." Since Lee had not heard from Stuart, "it was inferred that the enemy had not yet left Virginia." Instead, Stuart now headed north to the Potomac via Fairfax Court House to Rowser's Ford on June 28. Stuart was isolated; out of contact, and Ewell, with whom he was supposed to join hands, was already at Carlisle, Pennsylvania, over seventy miles away. Stuart's diversion to move in isolation around the Federal army has been a topic of criticism and controversy ever since.[99]

Henry B. McClellan, on Stuart's staff, described the Potomac crossing at Rowser's Ford: "No more difficult achievement was accomplished by the cavalry during the war." Then Stuart's men rode north through Rockville, Maryland, capturing and encumbering Stuart with a 125-wagon commissary and forage train and 400 prisoners. Stuart decided to keep the wagons with him, slowing him even more. On 29 June, Fitz Lee's Virginians destroyed a bridge and tore up tracks of the Baltimore & Ohio Railroad, but they failed to capture an alerted train that backed away in time. At Westminster, Fitz's men fought two Delaware cavalry companies. On 30 June at Hanover, Kilpatrick's cavalry clashed with Stuart's small force; Stuart barely escaped by jumping a fifteen-foot ditch. The tardy cavalrymen then rode eastward to Dover, 15 miles from Gettysburg. Fitz went to York, Pennsylvania, looking for Confederate infantry; he learned that Maj. Gen. Jubal Early had been there but was heading west. Stuart sent Major A.R. Venable after Early for information, and Fitz sent his brother and aide, Captain Henry Lee, toward Gettysburg. The main body rode on to Carlisle, where they expected to find Ewell, who had long since left there. They did find Maj. Gen. William F. "Baldy" Smith and a Union volunteer infantry brigade who garrisoned the town. Stuart had Fitz Lee send a flag of truce demanding surrender or suffer a bombardment. Smith refused, and the Rebels shelled as promised. Fitz later wrote his mother about destruction of his former barracks and noted that the "citizens were furious," and "I feel highly flattered at the Yankee notice of me."

On 2 July, the second day of the battle, Stuart finally reported to R.E. Lee, who asked angrily: "General Stuart, where have you been?" A chastened Stuart explained his movements and mentioned the captured wagons, which Lee derided as an "impediment." Then Lee reverted to character and asked for Stuart's help dealing with the Federals at hand.[100] Earl B. McElfresh later summarized:

> Typically, cavalry provided guidance, protection and screening—to mask the intentions and movements of the army—on a campaign of this nature [invasion of a hostile and unfamiliar territory]. They also gathered ground-to-saddle topographical intelligence. This last function, adequately performed, could have provided [R.E.] Lee with sufficient updated topographical data to annotate his small-scale maps. But Stuart, embarrassed by criticism about Brandy Station, had planned a grand gesture to avenge his honor and humiliate the Union army. He attempted to ride a circle around the Union forces, expecting to bring himself back on the right front of Lee's forces as they moved into Pennsylvania. Instead Stuart rode himself and his best troopers completely out of the campaign. They spent days searching for the army they were supposed to be scouting for [while Meade's Union cavalry had fought a delaying action on the first day that determined Gettysburg as Lee's unplanned battlefield, and] roving Union cavalry under Ulrich Dahlgren had captured a lone Confederate messenger who was carrying an uncoded note from Jefferson Davis advising Lee that General P.G.T. Beauregard could not reinforce him—intelligence that may have influenced Meade to stay in place and finish the battle. When Stuart's command finally plodded into Gettysburg on the 2nd [of July, and the second day of the battle], some of his troops were led to the battlefield by their horses as the men slept in the saddle.[101]

East Cavalry Field: The Cavalry Action in Meade's Rear Area on 3 July 1863

By noon on the 3rd, Stuart was on the Federal north flank on what is now called "East Cavalry Field." While the artillery concentration and infantry charge by ten brigades ("Pickett's Charge") was to be mounted against General George G. Meade's center, Stuart was supposed to cut Meade's communications along the Baltimore Pike. Stuart ordered the firing of four guns to signal R.E. Lee that he was in position, a foolish error that also alerted Union Brig. Gen. David McM. Gregg, who positioned the brigades of McIntosh and Custer to block Stuart. As Stuart's Confederate horsemen approached, they were opposed by Gregg's cavalry brigades of J.I. Gregg, John B. McIntosh, and George Armstrong Custer. Stuart was repulsed after a heavy encounter in which both sides fought mounted and dismounted. Although Stuart's four cavalry brigades should have numbered about 5,000 men, they probably had only 3,430 men, with 13 guns, who opposed McM. Gregg's 3,250 Union troopers.[102] The action is described in more detail below.

Stuart, with two brigades, went eastward on the York Turnpike behind Ewell; Fitz Lee and Wade Hampton were to follow. Before Pickett's, Pettigrew's, and Trimble's divisions, some 12,000 infantry, made their magnificent yet costly and futile infantry charge against Meade's center, Maj. Gen. George E. Pickett saw Fitz Lee riding by and confidently called out, "Come on, Fitz, and go with us; we shall have lots of fun there [on Meade's lines] presently."

But the cavalry mission was "to protect Ewell's left and observe the enemy's rear, looking for an opportunity to strike anything vulnerable." James L. Nichols: "From Cress Ridge, Stuart could see the road leading to Meade's position. Most surely, he meant to strike [somewhere] behind Meade." Major McClellan wondered why Stuart ordered an artillery salvo at no target in particular (it was the signal to R.E. Lee). No Federals were seen on the York Road or in front of Cress Ridge, but if Stuart wanted to stir up Federal cavalry, he got results. He urged Hampton and Fitz Lee forward to assault Meade's rear, but Gregg engaged Stuart in an artillery duel. Superior skills of the Union horse artillerymen bested James Breathed's gunners, and it seemed many Confederate shells were defective. Stuart's plan was to pin down McIntosh's and Custer's skirmishers around the Rummel farm and swing over Cress Ridge, around the left flank of the defenders, but the Federals pushed back tenaciously. Troopers of the 5th Michigan Cavalry were armed with Spencer 7-shot repeating rifles, multiplying their firepower. Stuart ordered the 1st Virginia Cavalry to charge mounted at about 1 p.m., the same time Col. Edward Porter Alexander's artillery barrage opened up against Union-held Cemetery Ridge. Fitz Lee's troopers came through the Rummel farm, scattering the Union skirmish line. Gregg ordered Custer to counterattack, and Custer personally led the 7th Michigan, shouting, "Come on, you Wolverines!" Seven hundred men fought furiously with carbines, pistols, and sabers at point-blank range along the farm fence line. Custer's horse was shot out from under him, but he got on a bugler's horse. Custer's men broke down the Rummel fence and caused the Virginians to retreat. Stuart sent in reinforcements from all three brigades: Chambliss's 9th and 13th Virginia, Hampton's 1st North Carolina and the Jeff Davis Legion, and Fitz Lee's 2nd Virginia. Custer's pursuit was broken up, and the 7th Michigan fell back in a disorderly retreat.[103]

When Hampton and Fitz Lee came up, Stuart had enough men and tried for a breakthrough, sending in most of Wade Hampton's brigade, which moved from a walk to the gallop, with sabers flashing. Union horse artillery attempted to block the advance with shell and canister, but the Confederates moved too quickly and filled in their vacant ranks. Custer and Col. Charles H. Town led the 1st Michigan into the fray, also at a gallop; a Pennsylvania trooper observed: "As the two columns [of squadrons] approached each other the pace of each increased…. So sudden and violent was the collision that many horses were turned end over end and crushed their riders beneath them." As horsemen fought desperately in the center, McIntosh led his brigade against Hampton's right flank, and the 3rd Pennsylvania and 1st New Jersey hit his left flank. Hampton received a serious sabre wound to the head; Custer lost his second horse of the day. At Rummel's Barn, "the battle was renewed back and forth across the plain … all of Fitz's brigade except the 4th Virginia Cavalry, were engaged in the fierce hand to hand that followed." The Federal canister was almost too much for faltering gray ranks, but Confederates held their ground before withdrawing. After 40 minutes of intense fighting, losses were relatively minor (or underreported): the Federals reported 254 casualties, 219 of them from Custer's Michigan brigade; Stuart reported 181. The fight was a draw, "but Gregg had stopped Stuart's move on Meade's rear, [*if*] indeed Stuart had intended to go so far."[104]

During Lee's retreat from Gettysburg, which began on the 4th of July, the same day Vicksburg surrendered to Ulysses S. Grant, Fitz Lee's troopers, along with most of Stuart's force, fought in heavy rain to cover the rear of Lee's army in the passes through the Catoctin Mountains. On 16 July, Fitz attacked Gregg at Kearneyville and drove him to Shepherdstown. From Culpeper on 26 July, Fitz wrote to his mother about the campaign: "My dr Mama…. I am once more at my starting point. Have had many fights, and as customary some narrow escapes but with exception of my four horses being shot, escaped without harm."[105]

Major General Fitzhugh Lee

During the Battle of Gettysburg, Fitz Lee's brigade fought unsuccessfully in the action on East Cavalry Field. But in Stuart's after-action report he singled out no officer for praise except Fitz Lee, who he said was "one of the finest cavalry leaders on the continent, and richly [entitled] to promotion." *Fitzhugh Lee was promoted to major general on 3 August 1863.*[106] On 9 September, Fitz wrote in good humor to Stuart that he was pleasantly headquartered on Marye's Heights overlooking Fredericksburg. He noted "ladies & pretty ones still exist" in the city and that his "staff fly around, ride horseback & serenade them." The reason for his good humor was that Fitz Lee and Wade Hampton had been promoted to major generals after Richmond approved two divisions of cavalry in the army. Stuart wrote Fitz on 10 September: "Accept my hearty congratulations on your long earned promotion, you will command the 2nd Div. Cav. Corps, Hampton having the 1st. Your com[mission] dates Aug. 3. Same day with [J.M.] Wilcox and S.D. Lee & Hampton. You will have the Brigadier I mentioned—I command the two divisions as Major Genl— can't say whether it is contemplation to promote me or not…. Gen. Wickham can for the time being take your place. Present my congratulations to Wickham."[107]

Major General Fitzhugh Lee, CSA, in the middle of the war (Mass. Commandery, MOL-LUS, United States Army Heritage and Education Center, Carlisle, PA).

On 10 October 1863, a division of Federal cavalry under John Buford crossed the Rapidan at Germanna Ford. The next day, Fitz launched a frontal assault against the Federals with Lunsford L. Lomax's and Rooney Lee's brigades, while Fitz attacked them on their flank and rear with Wickham's and Johnston's brigades. Fitz reported the Federals were "driven to Stevensburg ... to the Rappahannock River, being dislodged from every position in which they made a stand by simultaneous attacks in front, rear, and flank, with considerable loss to them." On 19 October, Stuart and Fitz planned to lure Kilpatrick's 2,000 men into a trap at Buckland, southwest of Manassas. Fitz would spring the trap by getting on Kilpatrick's rear when he passed through Buckland. The plan worked well, but not as intended, since Fitz ran into Custer along Broad Run. Surprised and eventually routed, Custer delayed Fitz's flank effort. Brig. Gen. James B. Gordon's North Carolinians hit the hard-pressed Federals, but Kilpatrick's two brigades charged Fitz's ranks, breaking through and getting away, losing 300 men. All the wagons of Kirkpatrick's division, and Custer's papers and personal baggage, were taken. Fitz reported "considerable" loss of horses—Wickham's brigade reported "107 [horses] killed in action."[108]

At the end of February 1864, the failed Kilpatrick-Dahlgren Raid with 5,000 troops against Richmond occurred while Stuart was spread along the Rapidan, with Fitz Lee on the left northwest of Charlottesville. To occupy Stuart, Union General John Sedgwick's VI Corps pressed Fitz's division, seizing Madison Court House by 28 February. From there, Custer headed west via Stanardsville and sent a squadron to surprise Breathed's horse artillery encamped on Rio Hill northwest of Charlottesville. Fighting desperately, the artillerymen saved their guns, but lost a limber and their personal baggage. Stuart ordered Wickham's brigade to ambush Custer's men on their return, but Custer's men cut through them, ending the 1863–1864 winter campaign. Rebel cavalrymen were as gay-hearted as ever; Fitz Lee sponsored a black-faced minstrel troupe that toured army camps to entertain the men, and review followed review.[109]

The 1864 Campaign: Todd's Tavern and Spotsylvania Court House

By spring of 1864, Hampton's and Fitz Lee's divisions had 8,000 men, but many new recruits were mere boys. Major General Philip H. Sheridan, the new Union Cavalry Corps commander, had 12,000 men, some of whom were armed with Spencer 7-shot repeating carbines or rifles, while most were armed with Sharps, Burnside, Smith, and other breech-loading, but single-shot carbines.[110] At Culpeper, Ulysses S. Grant, the commander-in-chief of all Federal armies, placed himself with Meade's Army of the Potomac. Grant was determined to keep all Union armies on the offensive to prevent inter-theater transfer of forces by Robert E. Lee, et al., and to drive south across the Rappahannock at whatever the cost to annihilate if possible, or to wear down, R.E. Lee's 60,000 men by attrition. On 1 May, Fitz Lee reported that he had about 3,000 men in his cavalry division in front of Orange Court House as the campaign opened.[111]

About this time, in late June 1864, Sergeant John Wise "beheld Fitz Lee with his staff, making a jolly night of it" at a party in Richmond. He described Fitz, 28 years old, as being "short, thick-set, already inclined to stoutness, [having] a merry eye, and a joyous voice of great power; ruddy, full-bearded, and overflowing with animal spirits as he sang duets with the sister of one of his favorite young staff officers."[112]

On 4 May, Fitz's pickets were driven away at Ely's and Germanna fords, and large Federal columns crossed the Rappahannock. When the Federals reached Chancellorsville, it was evident that this was Grant's general offensive. On the 5th, Fitz moved through Spotsylvania Court House, keeping south and a little to the rear of the Federal cavalry's left. Near Todd's Tavern, Lomax's brigade, Fitz's advance, struck David Gregg coming from the tavern, driving his men back in a sharp skirmish. During 5–6 May, Ewell and A.P. Hill hit Grant and Sheridan, resulting in Grant's losing 18,000 men to Lee's 7,000 or so, but General James Longstreet was wounded. On 7 May, Fitz Lee learned that Grant's wagons were moving east. (Grant always had to move southeast to outflank R.E. Lee because his supplies came via bases on the Potomac River to avoid raids on a vulnerable overland supply line.) Also on 7 May, Fitz was driven back from Todd's Tavern by Grant's cavalry coming from the Brock Road. "Fitz Lee's men fought stubbornly … against relentless dismounted U.S. Regulars in the (Cavalry) Reserve Brigade. But the Southern line had to retreat. Of the casualties, none hurt more than the loss of Col. [Thomas H.] Owen. He was directing fire of [the 3rd Virginia Cavalry] regiment when he was painfully wounded in the left hand … and he lost use of the hand." During dismounted fighting that lasted all day, "Fitz's command fought most gallantly" and "resisted the ferocious onsets of the evening to dislodge them and open the way to Spotsylvania C.H.," but his "loss was heavy in officers and men." Union Maj. Gen. Phil Sheridan reported to Maj. Gen. Humphrey: "Todd's Tavern, 7 May 1864 … I captured prisoners from Lomax's, Wickham's … [and] Gordon's brigades and killed Colonel [Charles Read] Collins, of the Fifteenth Virginia Cavalry."[113]

At daylight on the 8th, Brig. Gen. Alfred T.A. Torbert's Union cavalry hit Fitz's line unsuccessfully, as Fitz Lee reported, although Torbert was supported by V Corps infantry. The Battle of Spotsylvania Court House began on 8 May when Sheridan found Fitz still in his path. However, Maj. Gen. James H. Wilson reported to Lt. Col. Forsyth: "We cleaned out Wickham's brigade in about two minutes, scattered him in all directions, killed quite a number, and wounded 20 or 30. (41) Prisoners from (Wickham's) cavalry brigade and two divisions of Longstreet's corps."[114]

At this time, Sheridan persuaded Grant to turn him loose with three divisions, those of Wilson, Torbert, and Gregg, for a raid against Richmond. If Stuart got in the way, Sheridan planned to fight him. On 9 May, Sheridan's column left from north of Spotsylvania and started south on the Telegraph Toad, leaving Lee's army to his right and rear as he came around Grant's extreme left flank. At 1 p.m., Fitz's horsemen were relieved by infantry; Fitz already had reported to Stuart the movement by Sheridan's cavalry. Quickly mounting his reduced division, Fitz overtook and attacked Sheridan's rear just before dark, the 3rd Virginia Cavalry leading the charge. Just after dark, Stuart rode up alone to join Fitz. Learning that Sheridan had destroyed supplies and released 75 prisoners at Beaver Dam, the Confederate brigades of Lomax and Wickham followed him toward Richmond. Fitz Lee described Stuart's plan: "Discovering Richmond to be the object of the enemy, and knowing the absence of troops on its western side, Genl Stuart determined to move up the chord of the arc the enemy was advancing upon, & by outmarching them interpose our little force in the enemy's front at some point contiguous to the city." Riding through the night, they reached Ashland at 3 a.m., and discovered a detachment of Sheridan's occupying the city. "The 2nd Va of Wickham's Brigade was quickly dismounted, and under its efficient Colonel [Thomas T. Munford], gallantly charged this force and drove them from the village." They prevented the 1st Massachusetts Cavalry from burning the village.[115]

Yellow Tavern, 11 May 1864: Stuart Is Mortally Wounded; Fitzhugh Lee Takes Command

The next encounter occurred at a junction six miles from Richmond known as Yellow Tavern. Stuart ordered Fitz "to make dispositions to resist their further advance." The battle plan placed Lomax's three regiments "directly across the road Sheridan was moving upon, whilst Wickham's four were placed in line at right angles to that occupied by Lomax." The capability to attack the Federals' flanks hopefully would allow the gray cavalry "to retard the overwhelming numbers of the enemy." Breathed's artillery "was placed upon a little eminence in rear of Lomax's right." Meanwhile,

Richmond's defenders had been alerted to Sheridan's proximity. When Sheridan attacked the Confederate cavalry's L-shaped roadblock in the forenoon, Fitz's 3,200 dismounted troopers fought valiantly against elements of Sheridan's 12,000 men. The dismounted Federals hit again and again at Wickham's ranks. Around 2 p.m., firing became sporadic. Major

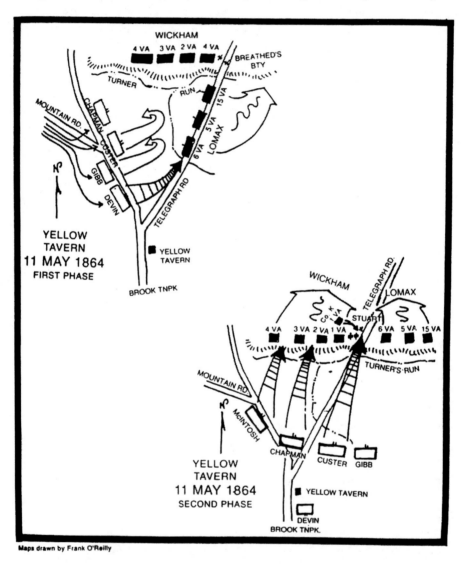

Maps drawn by Frank O'Reilly

Sketch map showing actions at Yellow Tavern on 11 May 1864 that resulted in death of Maj. Gen. J.E.B. Stuart and heavy losses on both sides (*5th Virginia Cavalry*, courtesy of Lt. Col. Robert J. Driver, Jr., U.S. Marine Corps [Ret.]).

McClellan reported that Stuart appeared confident of success, if General Braxton Bragg would come out of Richmond with some infantry support.[116]

Repulsed by Wickham, Sheridan decided to attack Lomax. At 4 p.m., Custer's Michigan regiments captured the artillery battery on Telegraph Road, and Lomax was pushed back several hundred yards. Stuart hastily rode up to rally the left, just as the 1st and 7th Michigan Cavalry Regiments charged at a gallop. Stuart ordered a flanking volley into the blue ranks, softening them for an attack by the 1st Virginia Cavalry that sent the Michigan troopers back, mounted and dismounted. Thom Hatch:

> Stuart rode to the left flank to join the 1st Virginia, just as a combined force of blue-clad cavalrymen assailed that position…. "Steady, men; steady; give it to them!" Stuart calmly advised. He emptied his pistol at the onrushing Union troopers, but his line virtually dissolved…. Nearby, 44-year old Private John A. Huff of Company E, 5th Michigan [Cavalry], a veteran of the 2nd U.S. Sharpshooters, steadied his .44-caliber Colt [Model 1860 Army] pistol upon a fence rail. He peered through the sights to observe an officer wearing a plumed hat who sat astride his horse—only 10 to 15 yards distance—while firing his own pistol in the midst of the confusion. Huff took careful aim and squeezed the trigger. Jeb Stuart was about to shout a command when a sudden, stabbing pain in his right side knocked him off balance. He reeled in the saddle, his head dropping, his hat tumbling to the ground, but remained astride his horse.[117]

Too weak to ride away, Stuart was helped off his horse by Captain G.W. Dorsey. Fitz Lee and Dr. J.B. Fontaine were summoned as combat continued and the Federals appeared ready to charge again. As Fitz rode up on "Nellie Gray" and dismounted, Stuart looked up and seemed to urge Fitz to take command: "Go ahead, old fellow: I know you'll do what is right." Fitz later wrote, "My own time was so much occupied I could not give more of it to his comfort at this time, and did not even know the extent of his wounds." Fitz met Stuart's eyes and then rode quickly toward the troops, while the doctor and his staff officers gathered around their fallen leader. As he left in an ambulance, Stuart cried out to some demoralized men who appeared to be skulking, "Go back! Go back! Go back, and do your duty as I have done mine, and our country will be safe! Go back! Go back! I had rather die than be whipped!" The doctor and two men took Stuart into Richmond, where he died the next day, 12 May, at Dr. Charles Brewer's house on Grace Street at the age of thirty-one.[118]

John Gill, a Confederate Signal Corps sergeant and courier on Fitzhugh Lee's staff from Baltimore, later wrote:

> It was a desperate fight along the entire line. General Stuart was wounded and brought off the field by some gallant members of Company K, First Virginia Cavalry. I am proud to say that this company was commanded by Capt. Gus Dorsey of Howard County, Maryland, and was composed principally of Marylanders. Major

[J.D.] Ferguson, our chief of staff, had his horse shot under him in the fight, and in the confusion the members of our staff were widely scattered....

I was standing on the Richmond road, our cavalry having just been driven back to the right, when Stuart was wounded. That night I saw him placed in an ambulance. He insisted on being taken to his wife. I have always felt that Stuart might have lived if he had been kept quiet that night. In a few days the report came of his death. This was a great loss to the country, an irreparable loss to the cavalry.[119]

Very concerned for his beloved chief, Fitz found himself in command at Yellow Tavern.

Outnumbered, and with Federal pressure now too great as Federal cavalry had ridden around Lomax to seize the Brooke Turnpike, he was in a situation that seemed desperate. But Fitz learned that Confederate infantry had arrived to protect Richmond on the west, and defenses on the north and east were deemed adequate to repel Sheridan's cavalry. With Richmond safe, Fitz withdrew across the upper Chickahominy to Meadow Bridge to block Sheridan that way. Sheridan did come that way after finding Richmond's defenses well-manned. Driven from Meadow Bridge, Fitz moved to Pole Green Church, four miles from Mechanicsville, where he positioned his force across Sheridan's path to prevent him from going north to rejoin Grant or to the base at White House Landing. Some of Sheridan's force attacked Fitz, but the main Federal cavalry force headed down the Chickahominy toward the James River and Union Navy gunboats at Curl's Neck. Nine days' fighting had exhausted his cavalry's ammunition and rations, so Fitz Lee took his men to Mechanicsville on 13 May to resupply.[120] Lee had about 2,400 men left, a loss of about 900 since the campaign began.[121]

Gordon's North Carolina Brigade Joined Fitz at Mechanicsville; Fitz Receives Orders to Attack Black Union Soldiers at Wilson's Wharf

While attacking Sheridan's rear on 12 May, Brig. Gen. James B. Gordon had received a severe arm wound which proved mortal six days later. Colonel Clinton M. Andrews took command of Gordon's North Carolina brigade from 12 May until 26 May (two days after the Action at Wilson's Wharf on 24 May) when Col. John A. Baker took command as senior colonel.[122] Keeping up with Sheridan's movements, *the gray cavalry ended up at Atlee's Station on the Central Railroad.* During the night of 20 May, Federals destroyed the trestle on the rail bridge at Hanover Court House but

General Braxton Bragg, CSA. As military advisor to President Jefferson Davis, and possibly at the latter's direction, he "verbally" ordered Maj. Gen. Fitzhugh Lee to "capture a garrison of Negro Soldiers at Kennon's" (Wilson's Wharf) (Library of Congress).

withdrew before Fitz could attack them. *Fitz Lee also had been reinforced by the 5th South Carolina Cavalry Regiment, which came from its home state.*[123]

"Fitz's cavalrymen returned to *Atlee's Station, where they received orders from General Braxton Bragg* [the military advisor to President Jefferson Davis] *on 23 May to move against a garrison of Black soldiers at Kennon's* [Wilson's Wharf] *in Charles City County on the James.* Fitz's '*object was to break up the nest & stop their uncivilized proceedings in the neighborhood.*'"[124] Corporal Charles T. Price, Company C, 2nd Virginia Cavalry, recalled: "Fitz Lee had ten well mounted and equipped men detailed from each company in [Wickham's] brigade ... to carry carbine, sabre and pistol and 125 cartridges."[125]

After an all-night march, Fitz reached the enemy at Kennon's just before noon on 24 May. His force consisted of detachments from ten regiments in Wickham's, Lomax's, and Gordon's brigades, along with the 5th South Carolina Cavalry and one piece of artillery. "Lomax remained at Atlee's with the remainder of the division."[126]

II

The Federal and Confederate Units That Fought

The 1st Regiment, United States Colored Troops

Hi rally! Ho rally! To the war we'll go
And we'll show those Traitors south the courage of their foe!
Come what may—now's the day
The year of jubilee!
Dawn is nigh with freedom's ray
Mankind must now be free![1]

Author C.R. Gibbs writes:

From the first, black men in the District of Columbia sought to fight for the Union. The news of the rebel attack on Fort Sumter struck the nation's capital with trip hammer force ... thousands of residents, irrespective of color, had to choose allegiances that sharply affected their lives for the next four years.

President Lincoln's Proclamation [on] April 15, 1861, declaring a state of insurrection and calling out 75,000 militia, transformed the initial confusion and distress into grim resolve. And yet, incongruously, because of the city's strong economic, political, and social ties to the South, it was known as a hotbed of secession and was widely believed filled with residents of "doubtful loyalty." Neighbor to two slaveholding states, Maryland and Virginia, the defenseless city daily received reports of activities of groups of southern sympathizers: bridges down, northern troops attacked, and telegraph lines cut.

Many pro-southern white males crossed the Potomac to Alexandria to enlist in units like the Washington Volunteers....

African Americans in the city were well aware of the immediate danger facing the besieged capital in the critical period (April 10–24) before sizable reinforcements from northern states arrived. They were eager to show their martial spirit in helping to subjugate the rebellion and serve in a struggle that most believed would turn into a war for the extirpation of slavery.[2]

On 23 April 1861, Jacob Dodson, a black resident of the city who had accompanied Major John Charles Fremont, the "Pathfinder," on his western expeditions during the 1840s, sent a note to Secretary of War Simon Cameron: "Sir: I desire to inform you that I have some three hundred reliable *colored free citizens* of this City, who desire to enter the service for defense of the City.... I can be found about the Senate Chamber, as I have been employed about the premises for some years." On 27 April 1861, Secretary Cameron responded: "In reply to your letter of the 23rd instant, I have to say that this Department has no intention at present to call into service of the Government any colored soldiers." Black men across the country made similar overtures during the first year of the war and all received similar rebuffs. Because of severe manpower shortages, however, the Union Navy began enlisting blacks during September 1861.[3]

An 1871 special report to Congress stated:

> [T]he colored people who first settled in Washington, constituted a very superior class of their race. Many ... were favorite family servants who came here with congressmen from the South, and with families of other public officers, and who by long and faithful services had secured, by gift, purchase, or otherwise, their freedom.
>
> Others were superior mechanics, house servants, and enterprising in various callings, who obtained their freedom by their own persevering industry. Some, also, received their freedom before coming to this city.

Nevertheless, aspirations and movements of African Americans in 1861 were made difficult by local laws. The severe black code derived from old Maryland statutes was the law of the District, never modified by Congress. The District had an unsavory early history of kidnapping and selling freemen. Slave trading had been abolished there in 1850, but participation of magistrates and constables in fees paid by runaways' masters still degraded the courts and corrupted police. No free Negro, without a certificate of freedom on his person, was safe from arrest. City police and District marshals spent most of their time hunting and seizing colored people, while white unofficial slave catchers also engaged in the business.[4]

District blacks resisted the oppressive laws, and they built strong social institutions and participated in diverse skilled trades, service occupations, and small businesses. The city also drew an imposing class of black leaders, male and female, who often were intellectuals doubling as ministers, businesspersons, and tradesmen. The 1860 Census reported 11,131 free blacks and 3,185 slaves; in both cases women outnumbered men by significant margins.[5]

Northern white attitudes very slowly began to change. In September 1861, Republican Senator Charles Sumner of Massachusetts said: "It is sometimes stated that this war ought to be carried into Africa. There is something better: carry Africa into this war ... in Virginia alone there are

121,564 male slaves of an age for military service. Can we afford to reject this national alliance, inspired by a common interest and consecrated by humanity?" In January 1862, Congressman Thaddeus Stevens of Pennsylvania, another advocate of emancipation and use of black troops, presented a bill urging enlistment of 150,000 black men. The bill died in the Senate. Congressman Robert Mallory of Kentucky raised the prospect of servile insurrection and "indiscriminate slaughter of men, women, and children," adding that "one shot of cannon would disperse thirty thousand." Thaddeus Stevens responded with irony: "Why then object to them as a savage and barbarous race, if one gun will disperse an army? History tells us that they make the best and most docile soldiers in the world. They are not barbarous by nature. They are a people as well calculated to be humanized as any other."[6]

On 16 April 1862, President Lincoln signed into law "An Act of the Release of Certain Persons held to Service or Labor in the District of Columbia." The word "slavery" was omitted, but everyone understood the law's letter and spirit. Not only was emancipation immediate, slave-owners who were loyal Unionists were compensated up to $300, and each newly freed African American who consented to emigration outside the United States would receive up to $100. The U.S. government paid several hundred claimants nearly a million dollars for the "release" of approximately 3,100 "persons held to service or labor within the District of Columbia by reason of African descent." The New York newspaper *Anglo-African* editorialized: "It was a fitting celebration of the anniversary of Fort Sumter, that Congress should pass a bill to emancipate the capital from the thrall of slavery forever. Henceforth, whatever betide the nation, its physical heart is freed from the presence of slavery."[7]

In January 1863, when Governor John A. Andrew began raising funds and recruiting men of African descent for the 54th and 55th Massachusetts Regiments of Infantry, a few men from the District enlisted in these units. Amid pressure for raising more regiments of black troops in the spring of 1863, two ambitious former hospital chaplains, J.D. Turner and W.G. Raymond, wrote to President Lincoln about organizing a regiment of black men in the District of Columbia. Raymond told the president he was "anxious to put down the rebellion," and he wanted "to command a regiment of colored men in the District of Columbia and vicinity." Turner felt he could be of "more good both to my country and my race in command of a colored regiment. My motives are good. My experience is considerable in the Army," since he had served 18 months as an army chaplain, including during the Peninsula Campaign. Both men asked influential friends to provide introductions and recommendations. Despite many endorsements, their actual qualifications for commanding a regiment were slim. Union army chaplains were "ministers in uniform," and whatever their personal valor, both men lacked critical military skills. Neither man provided examples of his contacts with the city's black community.[8] Nevertheless, during the first week in May 1863, a circular appeared throughout the District:

> The President has authorized Col. J.D. Turner, late Chaplain in the Army, and Lieutenant Col. W.G. Raymond, late Chaplain in Trinity Hospital in this city, to raise a Regiment of Colored Troops in the District of Columbia. A meeting will be held in Asbury Chapel, corner of 11th and K Streets, on the Monday evening next, May 4th, 7:30 o'clock, to organize and make arrangements to visit the President and receive his orders.... All who desire to enlist in the 1st Regiment of District of Columbia Volunteers, and thus demonstrate their manhood, are earnestly invited to be present, and hear, consult, and decide.
>
> By order of J.D. Turner, W.G. Raymond

They received assurances from Lincoln that the regiment they raised would be accepted for service when 640 men were listed on the rolls.[9]

The 5 May 1863 *Washington Star* reported on Turner's and Raymond's initial recruitment efforts. The Reverend Mr. Jenkins; A.L. Sanborn, a clerk at Columbia Hospital; and a camp assistant "are expecting to be officers in the new regiment." Sanborn brought 15 potential recruits from two hospitals, and about 30 men were recruited that afternoon. That night, at Asbury United Methodist Church, the new recruits were displayed during a large, animated meeting. Turner and Raymond opened with prayers before giving speeches. Several white dignitaries and observers were present, and a Col. Bingham of New York who hoped to raise "a colored brigade." A squad of armed white soldiers from the 39th Massachusetts Regiment were posted there to prevent trouble, since tension between blacks and whites was growing. Contrabands, singly or in groups, were assaulted by pro–Confederate rowdies and thugs.[10]

The Rev. Henry McNeal Turner from South Carolina: Student, Preacher, Pastor and Union Army Recruiter and Chaplain

Recruiting accelerated with the appearance of the Rev. Henry McNeal Turner, pastor of Israel Bethel African Methodist Episcopal (A.M.E.) Church at South Capitol and B Streets (now Independence Avenue) at the foot of Capitol Hill. His charisma, powerful oratory, organizational skills, and leadership of the second largest black church in the District, with 500 members, added new energy to recruiting efforts. Turner had been one of the first local black religious leaders to favor black enlistment. He wrote in the *Christian Recorder* in 1862 that so long as emancipation was a goal, African Americans would be willing to serve. On 8 May 1863, Turner became part of a recruiting committee that included other prominent black pastors. Turner also turned his church into the main recruiting center for the regiment.[11]

Henry McNeal Turner was born free in 1833 or on 1 February 1834[12] at Newberry Court House, South Carolina. He was the son of Hardy and Sarah Turner, who nurtured his spirituality and racial pride by telling him stories of his mother's noble African blood. Her father, David Greer, was the son of a king who had been kidnaped, enslaved, and brought to the English colony of South Carolina; David Greer obtained his freedom before his death in 1819. Blacks recalled with pride his commanding presence and scrupulous reputation in that part of Newberry County, which had been established during 1785 in the Ninety-Six District in central uplands of the state. Timberlands and farmlands there had been settled by English, Scots-Irish, and Germans who brought their slaves with them from the low country.[13]

State governments' attitudes throughout the South during the 1830s were driven by the 1830 Nat Turner Rebellion in southern Virginia and subsequent rumors of slave plots and revolts within their borders. They passed laws that banned any teaching of slaves; restricted black preachers; outlawed use of whistles, drums, and other musical instruments that might be used as signals; and curtailed manumission of slaves. In South Carolina, it was unlawful to keep a school for teaching blacks; penalties were a fine of up to $100 and six months' imprisonment for whites, or a $50 fine and 50 lashes for free blacks or slaves. The informer was declared a competent witness and given one-half of the fine. Authorities viewed free blacks as potential leaders of revolts, and their very existence vexed those who believed in enslavement of all "inferior" blacks. Free blacks, such as the Turner family, constantly walked a tight-rope of fear and suspicion.[14]

The death of Henry's father was a catastrophic blow to his family's fragile economic circumstances. Henry experienced long, hot, tiring labor as he picked cotton alongside slaves or pounded an anvil as a blacksmith's apprentice. But something in his character gave him strength to resist his fatherless, poverty-stricken circumstances: "He generally whipped all the overseers that tried to whip him, knowing he was free-born and could never be reduced to slavery." There also were stirrings in his spirit; his friend Bishop Benjamin T. Tanner wrote: "It is said that at the tender age of twelve, he had a dream in which he saw a multitude of men coming to him to be taught. That dream made an impression on him that followed him … and no doubt had much influence in shaping the course of his life. He was licensed to preach before his twenty-first year." Before he could answer the Lord's call, much had to happen. He hungered for knowledge and craved to learn the secrets in books, but Turner understood that state law "manacled" him to ignorance, just as it did any slave.[15]

Henry Turner procured a spelling book and was helped by an old white lady and a white playmate to learn the alphabet and spell two-syllable words, then by an illiterate old colored man who was a prodigy in sounds. One Sunday at church, the preacher said that whatever you ask God for in faith will be granted. Turner, age thirteen, began to fast and pray God would grant him a way to learn. A white woman briefly taught him until she was threatened by her neighbors that her teaching would be reported. On his own and with barest knowledge, and after working all day, Turner committed each night to intensive prayer and study:

> I would kneel down and pray, and ask the Lord to teach me what I was not able to understand myself, and as soon as I would fall asleep an angelic personage would appear with open book in hand and teach me how to pronounce every word I failed in pronouncing while awake…. This angelic teacher, or dream teacher, carried me through the old Webster's spelling book and thus enabled me to read the Bible and hymn book….
>
> I may note, however, that this angelic teacher would never come to my assistance unless I would study the lessons with the greatest effort and kneel down and pray for God's assistance before going to sleep….
>
> By the end of my fifteenth year I was providentially employed to wait around an office of white lawyers at Abbeville court-house, where I filled the exalted station of fire making, room sweeping, boot blacking, etc. I soon won the favor of every lawyer in the office, especially the younger portion of them. My tenacious memory being such an object of curiosity, I soon attracted special attention. They thought it marvelous that a common Negro boy could carry any message, however many words it contained or figures it involved, and repeat them as accurately as if written upon paper. In many cases, the messages contained a multiplicity of the highest law terms. The sequel was … *those lawyers taught me, in defiance of state laws forbidding it, to read* accurately, history, theology, and even works of law. [They] Also taught me arithmetic, geography, astronomy and anything I desired to know except English grammar, which I manifested no desire to study….
>
> I shall always regard my contact with those lawyers, and the assistance given me by the young lawyers in the office, as an answer to my prayer.[16]

In 1848, Turner joined the Methodist Episcopal Church South. The Methodist Episcopal Church in the United States had split into southern and northern conferences in 1845 after Georgia Bishop James O. Andrew's refusal to give up his slaves or resign his bishopric. In 1853, Turner felt a need to proclaim God's word and was licensed to preach by the Reverend Boyd at the Abbeville Court House. Turner preached throughout the South for four years; he married Eliza Ann Peacher in 1856. He left the M.E. Church South and joined the African Methodist Episcopal (A.M.E.) Church. Later a bishop himself, he came under the guidance of Bishop Daniel Alexander Payne, a fellow South Carolinian also born free, and who had by the late 1850s emerged as one of the A.M.E. Church's leading intellectuals. Payne guided Turner's education, placing him with professors and theologians who cultivated his mind and prepared him for greater work. Payne sent Turner to Baltimore to run a small mission and to receive a formal education at Trinity College. Turner impressed his professors with his powerful preaching style, but his grammar needed improvement. Turner received lessons in Latin, Greek, German, and theology. He took elocution from Bishop Cummings of the Protestant Episcopal Church, and instructions in Hebrew from Rabbi Ginsburg. Turner had a prodigious memory and an insatiable taste for learning. He went with Bishop Payne to A.M.E. churches and missions in Washington and Georgetown, and was ordained as a deacon in 1860.[17]

When he became the pastor of Israel Bethel A.M.E. Church, Turner was married and father of two sons, David and John. Henry McNeal Turner presented himself as "a good sized, fine looking, brown-skinned man ... with a splendid voice, fluent in speech, pleasing in gestures, and powerful in delivery." Israel Bethel's members in 1862 were slaves and free, laborers and washerwomen, hackmen, servants, cooks and carpenters, waiters and mechanics.[18]

Meanwhile in Washington, news of the "magnificent behavior" of black Union soldiers from Louisiana and Mississippi helped spur enlistment in the First District of Columbia Regiment, Infantry, African Descent.[19] Before new volunteers could be mustered in, they were physically examined at the Israel Bethel lyceum by Major Alexander T. Augusta, a black American physician who had left a lucrative practice in Canada to return for an army surgeon's commission. He was assisted by Dr. Theodore Seeley, a surgeon at the Armory Square hospital. Seeley said he had never seen such fine physical specimens than these recruits, and he noted their "determined" looks. The 15 May 1863 *Washington Star* reported:

FIRST APPEARANCE OF THE NEGRO SOLDIERS

Company I of the colored regiment of this District made their appearance on our streets this forenoon. They numbered some forty or fifty and wore a red, white and blue badge [in lieu of military uniforms].

Some ... wore also a cockade of the same colors. They seemed to bear their honors well, notwithstanding the derisive remarks they met with as they marched along— coming in several instances from those of their own color. Their drillmaster—as we presume—a colored man, seemed to appreciate the dignity of his position to the fullest.[20]

On 18 May, "Colonel" J.D. Turner held a meeting at Israel Bethel. The Rev. David Smith opened with prayers and a hymn, "Am I a Soldier of the Cross." Then "Lieutenant Colonel" W.G. Raymond reported on recruiting progress, saying he expected to have two companies mustered that day and quarters for them. His request, however, was inexplicably held up inside the War Department. A beautiful banner made by a black woman, Julia Henderson, draped the pulpit. She hoped the flag might be the first to enter Richmond, capital of the Confederacy. A British Royal Navy captain testified to personally having seen successes of African and West Indian regiments employed by England. Henry Johnson, a black man from North Carolina, recalled when black folks were spoiling for a fight—when they were ready and anxious to die for their race—but where are they now? They had this, that, and the other to say against going. "What do you want Mr. Lincoln to do," he mocked, "feed you ice cream?" Johnson's appeals to their racial pride, with colorful taunts and humor, were the hit of the evening.[21]

The next day, 19 May 1863, two companies of over 130 men were mustered at Israel Bethel and marched to No. 3 Barracks at Soldier's Rest, a huge transient camp at Delaware and C Streets N.W. (near present Union Station). They drilled there under "Captains" Anson 1. Sanborn and Sylvester Birdsall. On 22 May, the War Department issued General Order No. 143, which established the Bureau of Colored Troops and more directly involved the U.S. Army in recruiting black soldiers and organizing regiments. The mustered companies of the First District of Columbia Regiment, Infantry, African Descent, were moved from Washington to Analostan Island (now Theodore Roosevelt Island), a 75-acre rock in the Potomac River opposite Georgetown, where they were uniformed in Army blue. Their strict isolation and secret move may have been prompted by fear of race riots and bloodshed when they would be armed. The colored volunteers arrived to find cleared land for a parade and drill field; wooden barracks, officers' quarters, a cook's shack, a small infirmary; and a firing range. The Army called it "Camp Greene." However, "Colonel" Rev. J.D. Turner and "Lieutenant Colonel" Rev. W.G. Raymond were banished. In early June, Col. William Birney, son of abolitionist James G. Birney and recently appointed to organize the 2nd Regiment, U.S. Colored Troops, was ordered to the island to complete mustering and begin formal military training.[22]

Colonel Birney set up a strenuous schedule to train the colored volunteers in drill, ceremonies, respect for their officers and noncommissioned officers, obedience to orders, care of their uniform and equipment, and proper deportment and hygiene. All soldiers had to learn them, but there was a special urgency since many men of the First District of Columbia Regiment, Infantry, African Descent, were ex-slaves who had suffered from dehumanization, and some still bore deep, burning scars. The metamorphosis from slave and civilian to soldier and full citizen was aided by an unvarying schedule from reveille at 5 a.m. followed by roll call, breakfast, sick call, cleaning the company area, guard or picket duty, and hours of drill before lunch; then more drill in the afternoon, training for corporals and sergeants, and afternoon or evening dress parade, followed by supper. The men had open time between 6:30 and 9:30 p.m., when the haunting new bugle call "Taps" signaled the day's end.[23]

Recruiting continued. At a meeting at Asbury Methodist Church, during which over 100 men signed the rolls, a speaker enthralled the crowd:

> When we show we are men, we can then demand our liberty, as did the revolutionary fathers—peaceably if we can, forcibly if we must. If we do not fight, we are traitors to our God, traitors to our country, traitors to our race, and traitors to ourselves. (Applause.)
>
> Richmond is the place for us, and we mean to go there. (Applause.)
>
> Our friend, Jeff. Davis, says we shall go there (Laughter), and we will go; but they won't be glad to see us.[24]

Men now flocked to Analostan Island. The men were issued their uniforms: a loose-fitting navy blue wool sack coat with four brass eagle buttons down the front that soon were polished to brilliance, a white or gray flannel shirt, and sky-blue kersey wool trousers worn with suspenders. Uncomfortable flannel drawers, thick woolen socks and heavy leather square-toed "bootees," a blue forage cap, long blue frock coat, and a sky-blue overcoat completed their clothing issue. Individual equipment consisted of: knapsack, haversack, tin canteen, tin drinking cup and plate, waist belt with metal "U.S." buckle, leather cap pouch, cartridge box with sling and its round brass plate with an eagle design, rubber blanket, wool blanket, poncho, and shelter half. Their weapons consisted of a musket and a bayonet with its scabbard worn on the belt. Author C.R. Gibbs eloquently states: "The uniform was the first solid sign of Uncle Sam's commitment and signaled manhood, honor, and freedom. Military service, despite its inequities, was the path to a higher destiny. Backs straightened, chins lifted. More

potent was the issuance of muskets. With these, by the power of
their own hands, black men
could purchase justice, respect,
and deliverance."[25] The muskets
initially issued were Model 1842
.69 caliber smoothbore muskets
that weighed about 9½ pounds.[26]
These were replaced in 1864 by
standard Model 1861 or 1863 .58
caliber rifle-muskets, with which
they fought at Wilson's Wharf
on 24 May 1864 and elsewhere.
The older Model 1842 and the
newer Models 1861/1863 were all
very deadly weapons.

By late June 1863, six companies (A through F) of volunteers had been mustered in, and
their white officers had been
selected by a special board of
examiners who appraised applicants for commissions in black
regiments, and who determined
the rank of each officer candidate. Unlike rather arbitrary
methods, including elections,
used in most white volunteer
regiments to select officers, the
U.S. Army had exacting requirements regarding military knowl-

U.S. Colored Soldier in field uniform, holding a rifle-musket with fixed bayonet, and
wearing accouterments: cap box (front) and
cartridge box on hip, and has eagle breast
plate and "U.S." belt buckle From a recruiting poster c. 1863 (postcard, Leib Image
Archives, York, PA).

edge and experience, moral character and deportment, literacy, and physical
fitness in order to grant commissions. Each company had a captain, a 1st
lieutenant, and a 2nd lieutenant.

The new commanding officer was Colonel John H. Holman, 38 years
old, who was born in North Livermore, Maine, on 27 October 1824. An
architect before the war, Holman had joined the 4th Missouri Corps as a
2nd lieutenant in May 1861, and he saw action in eastern Missouri. When
that three-month regiment mustered out, he became lieutenant colonel of
the 26th Missouri Infantry Regiment, which saw bitter fighting during

Grant's Mississippi Campaign in 1862; he resigned in January 1863. From Chelsea, Massachusetts, he had been assigned to duty with the examining board until the opportunity to command the District's black volunteers presented itself. Holman reported in June. Holman was a Unionist who believed that slavery was a "curse" that "hung like a pall over the southern country," and use of black troops was a practical way to defeat the rebellion. His fairness, courage, and insistence on high standards of discipline, training, and leadership would later endear him to his men. He even penned the rallying song for his new regiment. Other assigned field and staff officers were Major Elias Wright, former captain of Company A, 4th New Jersey Volunteers, and 1st Lieutenant Myron W. Smith, the Adjutant. Colonel Holman's son, C.

Colonel John H. Holman, 1st Infantry Regiment, U.S. Colored Troops (Mass. Commandery, MOLLUS, United States Army Heritage and Education Center, Carlisle, PA).

Hiram Holman, became a 1st lieutenant in Company H. *On 30 June 1863, the First District of Columbia Regiment, Infantry, African Descent, was designated the First Regiment of United States Colored Troops, the first unit of black troops formally mustered into Federal Service.*[27]

The Second Regiment of U.S. Colored Troops was also recruited in the District of Columbia, and the City of Washington organized numerous white units: 1 cavalry regiment, 2 infantry regiments, 4 infantry battalions, and 33 militia companies.[28]

Walt Whitman, poet and self-described "Army Hospital Visitor," mentioned the regiment: "June 1863—There are getting to be *many black* troops. There is one very good regt. here black as tar; they go around, have the regular [Army] uniform—they submit to no nonsense. Others are constantly forming. It is getting to be a common sight." At Camp Greene, Whitman observed: "The tents look clean and good; indeed, altogether, in locality especially, the pleasantest camp I have yet seen."

Trouble, however, continued between the regiment's off-duty soldiers and those who opposed black enlistment. The *Christian Recorder*, an organ of the A.M.E. Church, published a soldier's statement: "We have had several fights this week between colored soldiers and white rowdies, or pretended citizens. But Mr. Colored Soldier has come out triumphant every time…. The soldiers all ride in the street cars or any other cars they want to ride in; and you might just as well declare war against them, as to declare that they can't ride there because they are colored."[29]

Heavy summer rains made Camp Greene a quagmire, however, and ankle-deep mud, wet clothes, soggy salt pork or beef, bland beans, tasteless hardtack, gritty greens, and bad coffee (some of which their white Confederate counterparts in camps elsewhere might have considered luxuries) discouraged all but the most committed men. A handful deserted; some others died of disease, and one drowned in the Potomac.[30]

Abolitionist and journalist Jane Grey Swisshelm sent a dispatch about the regiment to the *St. Cloud Democrat* in Minnesota: "July 21, 1863…. Their officers appear to have been very carefully chosen and are men who are anxious they should succeed. In addition to military tactics [the enlisted men] are learning to read and may be seen between their drills, in little groups with primers and spelling books conning over their lessons. People here are becoming accustomed to see them in United States uniform, and they are more frequently hailed with signs of approbation than with sneers of scorn."

But while on detached recruiting duty in Norfolk, 2nd Lt. Anson Sanborn, who had been with the regiment since its beginning, was murdered on 11 July 1863 by Dr. D.M. Wright, "a prominent secessionist" who said he would kill the first white officer he saw drilling black troops. After an unsuccessful escape, during which he tried to exchange clothing with his daughter, Wright was hanged by Federal forces occupying the city in October. On the gallows, Wright said, "Gentlemen, the act which I committed was done without the slightest malice."[31]

Not all the regiment's white officers were of excellent quality, and the unfit ones had to be weeded out. First Lieutenant John A. David of Company F, appointed in June, turned into a brutal martinet, engaging in a spree of violence in August. David tied several men by their hands, struck men in ranks without provocation, beat several men with his clenched fists, pistol-whipped others, and punished several men by forcing them to carry heavy logs on their backs for hours in violation of regimental orders. In December 1863, Lt. Davis was dismissed from the service for "cruelty to the men of his command" and "disobedience to orders." Acting Assistant

Surgeon J.B. Pettyjohn went AWOL (absent without official leave) on 2 August 1863. Colonel Holman requested a "surgeon be ordered to duty with the regiment without delay," but he was informed that "no medical officer can now be spared." The problem persisted for the regiment during the rest of the war. Black physicians were eager to serve with colored regiments, but the U.S. Army commissioned only eight black physicians, who were assigned to hospitals in Washington.[32]

In September 1863, Walt Whitman wrote: "Sometimes I go up to Georgetown ... just opposite it in the river is an island. Where the niggers have their first Washington regt encamped. They make a good show, and are often seen in Washington in squads. Since they have begun to carry arms, the Secesh here in Georgetown (about three fifths) are not insulting them as formerly."[33] Also in September, the 1st Regiment, USCT was ordered to Portsmouth, Virginia. Secessionists abounded there, too, and the regiment's white officers and colored soldiers alike endured their hateful gestures and sullen faces. In October, Col. Holman reported the regiment at full strength with 990 men. The 1st Regiment, USCT became part of Brig. Gen. Edward A. Wild's "African Brigade."[34] (Its subsequent activities, preceding the Action at Wilson's Wharf on 24 May 1864, were covered earlier in the first part of Chapter I.)

Meanwhile, the Rev. Henry McNeal Turner, who had worked very hard to recruit men at his church for the First District of Columbia Regiment, Infantry, African Descent, which became the 1st Regiment, USCT on 30 June, had wanted to become the chaplain of the regiment. Turner unofficially served the regiment for several months before receiving his commission. He had to be "a regularly ordained minister of some Christian denomination." Turner requested the official chaplaincy in May 1863, submitting a letter of endorsement signed by six of his ordained colleagues. One of them stated: "He was the first in Washington to advocate publicly the utility of colored soldiers. He *can* but be loyal." The *Colored Chaplain* and Turner's compiled service record at the National Archives indicate he was appointed by President Lincoln on 10 September 1863, making Turner the first African American to receive a *Federal* chaplain's commission. However, the Rev. Samuel Harrison earlier received a *state* commission to serve the 54th Massachusetts Regiment.

Turner joined the 1st Regiment, USCT in November. Turner's main duty was to report quarterly to the colonel on "the moral and religious condition of the regiment, and offer such suggestions as may conduce to the social happiness and moral improvement of the troops." Author C.R. Gibbs:

Turner was typical of the better civil war chaplains. He led religious services several times a week, with particular emphasis on Sunday services.... He often conducted services, including revivals, outdoors sometimes at night around a campfire, or in local churches. He prayed during dress parades and conducted weddings, baptisms, and funerals. He often helped write letters or carried them and held money for the men when requested ... he visited the sick and wounded of his regiment. He proved himself faithful, honest, and conscientious. There were two things, however, that endeared him to his regiment: he shared their daily hazards and worked tirelessly in behalf of their educational advancement.[35]

The Rev. Henry McNeill Turner, Chaplain, 1st Infantry Regiment, U.S. Colored Troops. *Harper's Weekly*, December 12, 1863 (courtesy C.R. Gibbs).

The 1st Regiment, USCT acquired a reputation with the commanding general. On 20 April 1864, Maj. Gen. Benjamin F. Butler wrote to Brig. Gen. Innis Newton Palmer, commanding the District of North Carolina:

I send this note with my aide, Captain Shaffer, in order that you may suggest to me what will be the best regiments to form a brigade for the field, consisting of four regiments which can with safety be spared. *I wish you also to send me at once the First U.S. Colored Troops....* Send with this regiment all the men detailed for extra and other duty. Leave not a man that belongs to it who shall not be in their ranks. This is imperative. The fact that they are quartermasters and other clerks must make no difference.[36]

The 10th Infantry Regiment, United States Colored Troops

The 10th Regiment, USCT was recruited on the eastern shore of Virginia and organized by Col. J.A. Nelson at Craney Island near Portsmouth, Virginia, on 18 November 1863. On 12 January 1864, Maj. Gen. Butler sent Brig. Gen. Edward A. Wild an order concerning the 10th Regiment:

General: You will order the Tenth U.S. Colored to break up their camp at or near Craney Island and proceed to the Eastern Shore of Virginia, headquarters at Drummondtown, there to replace the present force....

The officer in command of the Tenth U.S. Colored will caution all his officers that there must be the strictest diligence and vigilance that no outrages of any sort are committed by his troops, for both he and his officers will be held personally responsible by me if any are committed. The inhabitants there fear greatly the quartering of negro troops in their midst. I depend upon him and the good conduct of his troops to correct that misapprehension, for I assure both him and them that the most summary punishment will be visited upon them for any breach of discipline, especially any that shall affect peaceable men. The commanding officer will immediately take measures to recruit his regiment to the fullest extent. He will give receipts to all loyal men who have taken the oath prescribed by the President's proclamation for any slave which may be recruited.

He will report to me immediately any deficiency in his officers, or any vacancy that may exist, that the one may be taken notice of and the other filled. He will call upon the quartermaster for the necessary transportation, and report to these headquarters the execution of this order. I have the honor to be, very respectfully,

BENJ. F. BUTLER,
Major-General, Commanding[37]

On 18 January 1864, under Lt. Col. Edward H. (or E. Henry) Powell, the new regiment moved to Drummondtown on the eastern shore. Lieu-

tenant Colonel Powell: "I took command of the 10th U.S.C.T., then about 300 strong, on Craney Island near Portsmouth, Virginia, the regiment being anchored out at sea beyond reach of harm…. After feeding upon oysters and terrapin in that section for about two months, having recruited the regiment to nearly the maximum, we were suffered to cautiously approach the mainland, upon some portions of which *the enemy at that very moment* were understood to be stationed in force." The regiment soon had 28 officers and 543 enlisted soldiers present for duty out of an aggregate present and absent of 621 total. It moved to Camp Hamilton at Fort Monroe on 26 February. "A detachment at Plymouth, N.C., November 26, 1863, to

Captain Almond J. Pratt, age 28, Co. H, 10th Infantry Regiment, U.S. Colored Troops, and former sergeant in Co. B, 9th New York Heavy Artillery Regiment (Mass. Commandery, MOLLUS, United States Army Heritage and Education Center, Carlisle, PA).

April 20, 1864, participated in the [Confederate] siege of Plymouth April 17–20, 1864, and surrender April 20, 1864."[38]

The Siege and Union Surrender of Plymouth, North Carolina, 17–20 April 1864; and Confederate Atrocities Against Captured Black Union Soldiers and Their Officers

General Braxton Bragg, military advisor to President Jefferson Davis, planned a joint Confederate land-naval operation to capture the port city of Plymouth, located on a bend of the Roanoke River near where it empties into Albemarle Sound. It was garrisoned by 2,834 Federal troops, who included several colored regiments or detachments from the 1st and 2nd Regiments of North Carolina Colored Volunteers; 37th Regiment, USCT; 2nd Colored Cavalry, and *a "detachment" of the 10th Regiment, USCT.* The new Confederate ironclad ram *Albemarle* sank one Union warship and drove off another gunboat which supported the Union garrison, allowing Confederate Brig. Gen. R.F. Hoke, with five infantry brigades and supporting artillery and cavalry, to defeat and force the surrender of the Federal garrison under Col. H.E. Wessels on 20 April. Jefferson Davis promoted Hoke to major general, and some consider the "Battle of Plymouth" to be the last major Confederate victory and most effective use of a Confederate ironclad in the war.[39] A captured Union sergeant, Samuel Johnson, described in an affidavit what happened to black Union soldiers and their white officers after the Confederates captured Plymouth:

All the Negroes found in blue uniform or with any outward marks of a Union soldier upon him were killed. I saw some taken into the woods and hung. Others I saw stripped of all their clothing, and they stood upon the bank of the river with their faces riverwards and then they were shot. Still others were killed by having their brains beaten out by the butt end of the muskets in the hands of the Rebels.

All were not killed the day of the capture. Those that were not, were placed in a room with their officers; they (the Officers) having previously been dragged through the town with ropes around their necks, where they were kept confined until the following morning when the remainder of the black soldiers were killed.[40]

That same April, Bragg wrote to the governor of North Carolina:

The President [Jefferson Davis] directs that the Negroes captured by our force be turned over to you [for execution by state law or enslavement] .... To avoid so far as possible all complications, with the military authorities of the United States in regard to the disposition which will be made of this class of prisoners, *the President respectfully requests Your Excellency to take the necessary steps to have the matter of such disposition kept out of the newspapers of the State, and in every way to shun its obtaining any publicity.*[41]

On 23 April 1864, the rest of the 10th Regiment, now commanded by Col. Spencer H. Stafford, became part of Brig. Gen. Edward A. Wild's 1st Brigade, Brig. Gen. Edward W. Hinks's 3rd Division, XVIIIth Army Corps. On 5 May 1864, during the grand movement of Butler's Army of the James, the 10th Regiment sailed up the James River on the famous side-wheel steamship *Planter*, the former Confederate armed transport. Robert Smalls and 7 (or 12) other enslaved crewmen had sailed the vessel past harbor fortifications at Charleston, South Carolina, to surrender it to Union Navy blockaders during the pre-dawn hours of 13 May 1862, while the ship's three white officers spent the night ashore. On 5 May 1864, the 10th Regiment, USCT landed without opposition at Fort Powhatan on the south side of the James River. On 17 May it moved to Wilson's Landing (or Wharf) on the north side of the James River, where it participated in the Action on 24 May. It then had eight companies (A through H); Companies I and K were formed later in 1864.[42]

In 1893, Lieutenant Colonel E. Henry Powell stated:

> Just five men [in the 10th Regiment, USCT] were killed by the enemy [two were mortally wounded at Wilson's Wharf on 24 May 1864; any men in the "detachment" of the 10th Regiment, who may have been executed at Plymouth in April, may not have been known to Powell] in nearly three years' service, and no officer was ever hit. *Only one in our regiment was ever court-martialed for cowardice, and he was the chaplain.*
>
> That court-martial is worth noting…. *At Wilson's Landing, when the battle was raging, the* [white] *chaplain,* [Alvah R. Jones] *who should have remained with the wounded, managed to get aboard a passing boat, went up the river and was gone three days.* For this and other graver charges, among which was calling the Adjutant a liar, he was tried, convicted, and sentenced to be cashiered. Gen. Butler, while approving the findings,—on account of a technical defect in the proceedings—refused to confirm the sentence, and restored the chaplain to his place.
>
> In General Orders, however, [Butler] held him up to most infinite ridicule before all the regiments in the command…. Among other things, the order says: "Chaplain Jones is gravely admonished that his mission is peace in the midst of war, and not to excite strife in the armies of the Union. It is expressly disgraceful in a chaplain to use words of provocation to a fight, but if he does use such words, he should not hide himself behind the robe he wears, from the personal chastisement which must be expected to follow such provocation, and which Lieut. Glazier was preparing to administer, when the chaplain interposed his robe. Hereafter Chaplain Jones will be closely watched by his commanding officer and the commanding general, and he must walk henceforth in an upright and godly life.
>
> —By command of Major General Butler.

How plainly you can see the playful curl of the lip, and the sly twinkle in the cross-eye of "Old Strabismus" as he penned those words.[43]

Alvah R. Jones, a "regularly ordained Minister of the M.E. (Methodist Episcopal) Church" at Honesdale, Pennsylvania, was appointed "to be Chaplain" by Maj. Gen. B.F. Butler on 26 April 1864, and was elected unanimously as their regimental chaplain by seven officers of the 10th Regiment, USCT the next day. On 16 July 1864, a "General Court Martial [was] appointed ... for the trial of Chaplain A.R. Jones, 10th U.S.C.T." by General Butler, with Lt. Col. A.G. Chamberlain, 37th Regiment, USCT, as President. The Court considered the following:

Chaplain A.R. Jones, 10th United States Colored Troops
CHARGE I. Cowardice.

Specification 1st—In this: *That he ... did, without proper authority, leave the post of the regiment, Wilson's Landing, Va., which place was likely to be attacked, the enemy being near in force, and did leave the landing on board a boat that touched there, bound upward. This at Wilson's Landing, Va., on or about the 24th of May 1864.*

Specification 2d—In this: That he ... did forsake the regiment when it was ordered to relieve a picket line near Petersburg, and remain absent from his post of duty, the regimental headquarters, where wounded men of the regiment were lying, who needed and were entitled to his aid and comfort ... on or about the 22nd day of June 1864.

CHARGE II.
Neglect of Duty.

Specifications 1st and *2d* (Repeat of the two above under *Cowardice*).

Specification 3d—In this: That he ... has kept aloof from the enlisted men, and has not mingled with them, to learn their wants, and to give them the moral and spiritual instruction they require. This generally during the time he has been Chaplain of the regiment aforesaid.

CHARGE III.
Conduct unbecoming an officer and a gentleman (2 specifications)....

Specification 2d—In this: That he ... did, on being urged by some officers of the regiment, to wit: Capt. M. Montgomery and Capt. Anson Withey, to attend to the moral and religious instruction of the men, utter the following language: "I wish it distinctly understood that I did not come here to mingle with niggers, nor to go into their dirty, lousy tents," or words to that effect.

This at Wilson's Landing, Va., on or about the 1st day of June 1864.

CHARGE IV.
Conduct prejudicial to good order and discipline.

The specifications relating to Charge III are repeated.

CHARGE V.
Disobedience of orders.

Specification—In this: That he ... having been ordered by his superior officer, Col. Stafford, 10th [USCT Regiment] and by Capt. Withey, officer of the day in camp of said regiment, to close an uproarious religious meeting, which he was conducting in one of the company streets ... after tatoo, did refuse to do both, and did say to the commander of the regiment, Col. Stafford: "You may stop them, but I sha'nt," or words to that effect ... on or about the 10th of July 1864.

To which charges and specifications the accused pleaded "Not Guilty."

The Court, after mature deliberations upon the evidence adduced, found the accused:

"Guilty" of all Charges and Specifications [except one]: the 3d specification of
Charge II, "keeping aloof from the enlisted men," etc.
     ... And the Court do, therefore, sentence him, Chaplain Alvah R. Jones.... *To be dismissed* [from] *the service of the United States.*

The findings were approved, but the dismissal sentence was set aside, and
General Butler wrote the letter to Chaplain Jones, as quoted by Lt. Col.
E. Henry Powell, preceding the above.[44] Chaplain Jones continued to get
into trouble with military authorities, even in March 1865.

     The 10th Regiment was unique in another way by its being at least
partially uniformed for a time in colorful "Zouave uniform" (baggy red
pants, braid on jackets, etc.) early in its career. From Craney Island on 15
November 1863, Col. John A. Nelson wrote to Major R.L. Davis, AAG
(Acting Adjutant General):

Sir,

     I have the honor to inform you that I am at present engaged in recruiting the 10th
U.S. Col. Troops and have already recruited about 400 men. As a stimulus to enlistments, I would suggest that men of my regiment be dressed in Zouave uniform. Many
would enlist were they to be thus attired who otherwise would remain away. And as
these uniforms are issued by the United States Quartermaster Depart[ment] at Washington and as I have drawn no clothing with the exception of Overcoats, Shirts and
Boaters [*sic*; "bootees," shoes], I see no hindrance to the issuing of these uniforms for
my Regiment....

On 5 December, Lt. Col. H. Briggs, Chief Quartermaster at Fort Monroe,
wrote to Col. Nelson:

In reply to your letter of the 30th Ulto, you are requested to state the authority by
which *Zouave uniforms have been issued to the 10th Colored Regiment*, which it had
already been supplied with the regulation dress....
     It has been the intention of the Department to uniform the Colored Troops precisely
in the *same uniform that is usually issued to the white troops, in order to avoid their being
known to the enemy by a peculiar dress, and thus be made a special object of his attention....*
By order QM Gen'l,
Alex. J. Perry, AQM.

Correspondence available from incomplete records reveals that a sample
Zouave uniform was requested and sent to the Quartermaster Office. A
clothing list dated 31 January 1864 in the Regimental Book of the 10th
Regiment, USCT shows 113 Zouave uniforms having been issued by the
Regimental Quartermaster to the 10th Regiment. On 9 March 1864, Lt.
Col. Briggs wrote to Col. Nelson stating that the sample suit of Zouave
dress had not yet arrived, and as soon as the sample is received, the clothing
will be ordered."

     On 24 March 1864, Alex J. Perry ordered Lt. Col. D.H. Vinton, "Have prepared ... and sent to Lieut C.D. Webster AAQM at Fort Monroe Va. the following articles of Zouave clothing *for intended issue* to the 10th Regiment U.S. Col.d Troops: 739 Zouave scarfs, 744 Zouave jackets Large sizes, 726 Zouave vests Large sizes, 877 Zouave trousers Large sizes, 800 Zouave Felt caps Large sizes, 834 Zouave Linen Leggins [*sic*] Large sizes." It's unknown whether or not the Zouave clothing ordered for the 10th Regiment, USCT actually arrived and was issued to the regiment. Colonel Nelson was the driving force behind the attempt to uniform the regiment in Zouave dress and apparently was removed from command; Lt. Col. E. Henry Powell made no mention of Zouave dress in his paper, "The Colored Soldier in the War of the Rebellion." And no other mention or record of the 10th Regiment, USCT wearing Zouave uniforms is known to exist.[45]

The 10th Regiment, USCT performed picket duty on Federal lines before Petersburg in June 1864. From August 1864 to March 1865 the regiment guarded Grant's headquarters and the large logistical depot at City Point near Hopewell, Virginia. On 3 April 1865, the 10th USCT marched into Richmond. In July 1865, the regiment was posted in Corpus Christi, Texas, where it mustered out in May 1866.[46]

Other Union Army units that served under General Wild's command at Wilson's Wharf and Fort Powhatan included the following:

The 22nd Infantry Regiment U.S. Colored Troops was organized at Camp William Penn near Philadelphia, and sent to Yorktown, Virginia, at the end of January 1864. It landed at Wilson's Wharf on 5 May 1864 and stayed there until transferred to Fort Powhatan and fought a skirmish there on 21 May.[47] It was commanded by Col. Joseph Barr Kiddoo, who had been in many battles with the 137th Pennsylvania Volunteer Infantry; he had commanded the 6th Regiment, USCT and then the 22nd Regiment, USCT. He was severely wounded at Petersburg, but eventually rose to major general of U.S. Volunteers.[48]

The 37th Infantry Regiment, U.S. Colored Troops was organized on 8 February 1864 from the 3rd North Carolina Colored Volunteer Infantry, part of Wild's former "African Brigade." It landed at Fort Powhatan on 5 May and performed duties there or at Wilson's Wharf/Fort Pocahontas until 28 September 1864. It was armed in 1864 with Springfield M1863 rifle-muskets, and some Sharps .52 cal. breech-loading rifles, probably issued to its two flank companies.[49]

Battery "B," 2nd Light Colored Artillery Regiment was organized at Fort Monroe on 8 January 1864. It landed at Wilson's Wharf on 5 May but was transferred prior to the Action on 24 May.[50] It was replaced by:

Battery M, 3rd New York Light Artillery Regiment, which was

"Unidentified 2nd Lieutenant, Company M, 3rd (Artillery) Regiment, New York State." He has crossed cannon insignia on his cap and an Artillery Officers sword (RG98S-CWP 30.53, Robert Borrell Collection, United States Army Heritage and Education Center, Carlisle, PA).

organized from Company I, 75th New York Infantry formed at Auburn, New York, in November 1861. It joined the 3rd New York Light Artillery Regiment on 24 January 1862 and served in the defenses of Washington, in North Carolina, and in the Norfolk area before being reorganized as "Veteran Light Battery M" and becoming part of the Artillery Brigade of the Department of Virginia and North Carolina. Attached to Wild's brigade, it landed at Fort Powhatan on 5 May 1864, serving later during actions at Fort Powhatan on 21 May and *at Wilson's Wharf on 24 May, where a section of two 10-pdr Parrott rifles "did excellent service throughout the fight, and its fire was most effective."* The full equipment of a six-gun battery consisted of limbers to support the cannon trails on the march, six caissons, a traveling forge, a baggage wagon, and a hundred horses, with each gun, caisson, and wagon being drawn by six horses, and extra ones required for officers and to supply the places of those disabled in battle.[51] A "section" consisted of two guns, two limbers, etc.

The Eleven Veteran Confederate Cavalry Regiments That Sent Detachments from Atlee's Station on 23 May to Fight in the Action at Wilson's Wharf on 24 May 1864

(Their prior service is reported in the biographical section about Maj. Gen. Fitzhugh Lee in Chapter I)

Brig. Gen. William C. Wickham's Brigade

William Carter Wickham (1820–1888). Born at Richmond, he graduated from the University of Virginia, practiced law and managed his plantation besides being a legislator, jurist, and militiaman. He initially opposed secession, but he fought at First Bull Run as captain of the Hanover Dragoons. He became lieutenant colonel in late 1861, and colonel of the 4th Virginia Cavalry in August 1862. He was wounded by a saber at Williamsburg, captured while recuperating and then exchanged, and wounded again at Upperville, Virginia, while temporarily commanding Fitzhugh Lee's brigade. Promoted brigadier general on 1 September 1863, he commanded "Wickham's Brigade" during all its battles from then until November 1864, when he took his seat in the Confederate Congress.[52]

The 1st Virginia Cavalry Regiment was organized on 16 July 1861. Its first commander was Col. James Ewell Brown ("Jeb") Stuart, who progressed to brigade, division, and cavalry corps command. Fitzhugh Lee later commanded the regiment until he was promoted to brigadier general in July 1862. *Lt. Col. William Augustine Morgan commanded the regiment in May 1864.*

The 2nd Virginia Cavalry Regiment, originally a Virginia State Regiment, was also composed of companies from western Virginia and was accepted into Confederate service on 1 July 1861. Colonel Thomas T. Munford commanded the regiment from 1862 until 1865. In April 1864, Company A was armed with 50 Enfield rifles, 2 Sharps carbines, 3 Burnside carbines, 35 Colt Army .44 cal. and 24 Colt Navy .36 cal. revolvers, and 59 sabres. A soldier recalled: "Our cavalry, besides their *sabres which were always left on the horses* [when dismounting to fight—*except on 24 May 1864 at Wilson's Wharf*], we had revolvers and musketoons, a very short musket which the cavalry wore

Brigadier General Thomas T. Munford, CSA. As a colonel, he commanded the 2nd Virginia Cavalry Regiment (The Virginia Historical Society/Museum of the Confederacy).

slung across the backs when on horseback. It was a very indifferent weapon."[53]

Early war image of Private David Meade, Co. I, 3rd Virginia Cavalry Regiment, holding fighting knife (from the Collections of the Confederate Memorial Literary Society, under management of the Virginia Historical Society).

The 3rd Virginia Cavalry Regiment, composed of companies from eastern Virginia, was accepted into service on 1 July 1861. Its Company D, the "Charles City Light Dragoons," or "Charles City Troop," was from Charles City County and organized prior to November 1859. On April 16, 1864, two recruits were "Charles Smith and William Cole, free blacks assigned to the regiment as [civilian] blacksmiths by the Secretary of War's Office." "The regiment 'used their carbines and *Belgian rifles* to good effect' at Aenon church on 28 May 1864."[54]

The 4th Virginia Cavalry Regiment was composed of companies from north-central Virginia and organized at Sangster's Crossroads, Prince William County, on 19 September 1861. At Meadow Bridge on 12 May 1864, Lt. Col. Robert Randolph, commanding the regiment, was killed.[55]

Brig. Gen. Lunsford L. Lomax's Brigade

The 5th Virginia Cavalry Regiment was organized in May 1862 with six companies. Its first colonel was Thomas Lafayette Rosser, who was promoted to brigadier general and succeeded by Col. Henry Clay Pate, who was killed at Yellow Tavern on 11 May 1864. The 5th Virginia had gone into battle that day 350 strong, but only 120 men commanded by Captain Reuben B. Boston were present the next day. The 9th New York Cavalry claimed capture of 10 officers and 115 men. On 30 June 1864 the 5th Virginia turned in: "2 Pittsylvania(?) carbines, 2–4 Sharps and Hankins' carbines, 3 Enfield rifles, 52 Austrian [M1854] rifles, 1 Smith carbine, 1 Starr carbine,

1 Sharps carbine, 2 Richmond [Sharps copy] carbines cal. .58, 3 Burnside carbines, 2 Kerr's pistols, and 9 sabers" *that may have seen action on 24 May.* They received 25 Austrian rifles, 72 Sharps rifles, 130 Richmond carbines, and 4 Burnside carbines, indicating the extent and variety of captured and imported arms for which Confederate Ordnance had to supply ammunition. *Captain Reuben Boston commanded the 5th Virginia at Wilson's Wharf on 24 May*; later he was promoted to colonel.

The 6th Virginia Cavalry Regiment was organized during September–November 1861. Lieutenant Colonel Daniel T. Richards commanded the regiment after late 1863, but he was wounded on 11 May 1864, leaving Major Cabell E. Flournoy in command. "From May

Colonel Reuben B. Boston, CSA; as a captain, he commanded the 5th Virginia Cavalry Regiment during the Action at Wilson's Wharf on 24 May 1864 (The Virginia Historical Society).

23 to 26 Fitz Lee led an expedition to Kennon's Wharf [*sic*]…. If it was barren of success, it was also barren of further significant losses in the regiment. Major Flournoy remained in camp during foray." *Captain David A. Grimsley of Company B exercised command of the 6th Virginia Cavalry at Wilson's Wharf on 24 May.*

The 15th Virginia Cavalry Regiment was formed by consolidation of the 14th and 15th Cavalry Battalions, and two independent companies on 11 September 1862. The men came from Richmond and Henrico and Hanover Counties. There are no muster rolls for the regiment after the March–April 1864 roll. It had about 597 men early in May 1864; Col. Charles Read Collins, an 1859 West Point graduate, was killed 7 May at Todd's Tavern. Before 30 June the regiment had lost in battle "118 Enfield rifles, cal. .58 [*sic*; cal. .577], 3 Austrian rifles cal. .54, 3 Sharps carbines cal. .52, 127 sabres, and 179 sabre belts." "In Lomax's brigade, in autumn 1863, each regiment adopted a distinctive cloth patch to be placed on its headgear." *Captain John F. Cooper commanded the 15th Virginia Cavalry during the Action at Wilson's Wharf on 24 May.*[56]

Gordon's North Carolina Brigade
(commanded by Col. Clinton M. Andrews)

Most Tarheel cavalry troopers were recruited from the rural mountain region of North Carolina, but cavalry companies were also recruited throughout the state. Initially, horses were purchased in Kentucky and saddles in New Orleans, but cavalrymen later relied on captured arms and accouterments. After Brig. Gen. James B. Gordon was severely wounded in the arm at Brook Church on 12 May (he died of infection on 18 May), Col. Clinton M. Andrews, 2nd North Carolina Cavalry, took command of the brigade from 12 May until 26 May when the 3rd North Carolina Cavalry joined, and Col. John A. Baker, being senior, took command. In early June, Lt. Col. Rufus Barringer of the 1st Regiment was promoted to brigadier general and took command of the brigade until the end of the war. Colonel Andrews was killed on 23 June 1864 at "Black & Whites." The brigade's 3rd and 4th cavalry regiments were elsewhere, but *the 1st, 2nd, and 5th North Carolina Cavalry Regiments, under Col. Clinton M. Andrews, participated in the Action at Wilson's Wharf on 24 May 1864.* "The brigade was [in camp then] a mere handful, *most of it having gone with Gen. Fitz Lee to attack a negro stronghold on the James River.*"[57]

The 1st North Carolina Cavalry Regiment (9th Regiment, North Carolina State Troops) was organized at Ridgeway, North Carolina, and became one of the finest units in Confederate service; four of its officers became generals. It arrived in Virginia in October 1861. "After Col. [William H.] Cheek was hurt (shot through the shoulder) during the Yellow Tavern Campaign on 12 May, Major William H.H. Cowles and then Lt. Col. Rufus Barringer assumed command of the regiment."

The 2nd North Carolina Cavalry Regiment (19th Regiment, North Carolina State Troops) assembled at New Berne, North Carolina, in March 1862. After a failed attack, it moved to Virginia in September 1862 and fought hard during the Gettysburg Campaign. After 1862, it was "almost entirely armed and accoutered by captures from the enemy, including swords, saddles, and blankets."[58]

The 5th North Carolina Cavalry Regiment (63rd Regiment, North Carolina State Troops) was formed in October 1862 by consolidation of two cavalry battalions and two independent companies. The 5th was organized as a partisan ranger unit, but it operated as regular cavalry. On 2 May 1864, Special Orders issued from the Adjutant and Inspector General's Office at Richmond, stated: "XXV. The Fifth Regiment of North Carolina Cavalry, now stationed near this city, will immediately proceed to headquarters Army of Northern Virginia, and report to General R.E. Lee, commanding, &c., for assignment to duty with Brigadier-General Gordon's brigade."[59]

The following were not in the Action at Wilson's Wharf on 24 May 1864, but fought in other actions:

The 3rd North Carolina Cavalry Regiment (41st Regiment, North Carolina State Troops) was formed in November 1862. In Virginia in May 1864, it participated in the campaign that "bottled up" Butler's army on the Bermuda Hundred Peninsula. Paul B. Means, 5th North Carolina Cavalry, wrote: "About *26* May 1864, the Forty-first North Carolina (Third Cavalry), arrived … in splendid condition [after fighting at Drewry's Bluff and losing 3 men missing on 16 May], joined the brigade."[60] "May 1864: Comp F (Davis Dragoons) [was] armed with a variety of rifles, muskets, and Colt army and navy revolvers."[61]

The 4th North Carolina Cavalry Regiment (59th Regiment, North Carolina State Troops) was organized in August 1862. By 10 June 1864, it was commanded by Col. Dennis D. Ferebee and was part of Brig. Gen. James Dearing's cavalry brigade in General Beauregard's Department of North Carolina and Southern Virginia, operating south of the James River.[62]

The 5th South Carolina Cavalry Regiment (attached)

The 5th South Carolina Cavalry Regiment was formed 18 January 1863 by consolidation of the 14th and 17th Battalions, South Carolina Cavalry, and two independent companies. Some men, armed mostly with shotguns, had fought earlier on the coast. The regiment's most colorful commander was John Goore Dunovant, born at Chester in 1825. A sergeant in the Palmetto Regiment during the Mexican War (1846–1847), he was severely wounded in the attack at Chapultepec. He was captain of Company A, U.S. 10th Infantry Regiment from 1855 until 1860, when as an ardent secessionist, he resigned his commission on 20 December. He became colonel of the 1st South Carolina Regular Infantry Regiment. Disgrace followed, due partly to his drunkenness and partly due to the hostility of his superiors. Ordered to storm Legareville on 9 June 1862, Col. Dunovant allegedly was "lying drunk by the roadside" in view of his officers and men. He was court-martialed and "dismissed from the service." John's brother, General Richard Dunovant, influenced President Jefferson Davis to relent, and Governor Francis Pickens appointed Dunovant as colonel of the 5th

John Dunovant, probably in late 1860 (Library of Congress, Washington, D.C.).

South Carolina Cavalry Regiment on 25 July 1863.[63]

In February 1864, General Robert E. Lee wrote President Davis that "the Fifth, Dunovant's regiment," had a strength of 1,200 men "as represented by General [Wade] Hampton," and requested a trade: his depleted 1st and 2nd South Carolina Cavalry Regiments for the three large South Carolina cavalry regiments (4th, 5th, and 6th) patrolling the coast. A special order directed the three regiments to "proceed in light marching order by highway to the Army of Northern Virginia" and join Brig. Gen. Matthew C. Butler's brigade. Each captain was ordered to reduce his company to 80 men, for a total of 800 men, excluding officers and staffs.[64] The men of the 5th Regiment and their equipment assembled at Columbia and Florence, and were transported to Virginia by railroad. The horses were marched to Virginia by highway in easy stages, escorted by a contingent of about one-third from each company. Captain A.B. Mulligan, who had spent thousands of dollars to equip his Company B of the Fifth, referred to the "whole Regt. ... of 1,000" arriving in Virginia.[65] The "Daily Roster for April, May, and June" [1864] for Company D of the 5th South Carolina Cavalry in John D. Browne's *Orderly Book* lists names of 4 officers, 4 sergeants, 4 corporals, 1 orderly, 2 buglers, a farrier, a blacksmith, and 83 privates; exactly 100 officers and men in all[66] (apparently before being reduced to 80 men).

According to the "Property Account" in Browne's *Orderly Book*, Company D was armed with 22 Enfield [Pattern 1853] rifle-muskets, 31 Enfield [Pattern 1856 or 1858] short rifles, and 33 Enfield [Pattern 1856] cavalry carbines; all 86 of the imported English caliber .577 weapons fired the same ammunition. The men were also armed with 43 pistols and 78 sabers, enabling them to fight mounted as well as dismounted. Captain Zimmerman Davis and 2nd Lt. Deveaux were issued a pistol each. The troopers carried a mix of pistols; 4th Sgt. J.H. Dukes, Co. H, "lost or had stolen his [English] Kers [*sic*; Kerr] Patent pistol" and was charged for it.[67]

Private James Michael Barr, Company I, 5th South Carolina Cavalry, wrote from "Petersburg, May 10th, 1864; My Dear Rebecca…. We have short rifles, *20 inches long* [probably Enfield Pattern 1856 or P1861 Cavalry Carbines, 37 inches long overall, *with 21-inch barrels*], so they are not much in our way. They shoot 300 yards. They were sent to us at the junction of the Danville & R.[Richmond] R.R." Barr apparently had traveled by train to Virginia.[68]

Special Orders No. 118 dated 21 May, issued from the Adjutant and Inspector General's Office in Richmond, directed Brig. Gen. Pierce M.B. Young to "take charge of the bodies of cavalry arriving from the south … prepare [them] as rapidly as possible for active field service and, when prepared, send them forward promptly to Maj. Gen. Fitz Lee."[69] Although the South Carolinians were earlier described as "badly equipped,"[70] Edward C. Wells, a member of the elite "Charleston Light Dragoons," part of the 4th South Carolina Cavalry, described the three regiments of Butler's brigade in April 1864: "[They] had full ranks, and had been accustomed to army life so long, that they might be considered in some sense, as veterans. Moreover, they were well-mounted, each officer and private furnishing his own animal, according to the practice of the Confederate Army."[71]

After the 4th South Carolina Cavalry Regiment arrived in Virginia, it camped on the Brooke Turnpike two miles south of Richmond for two days. On the third day, when the regiment was to march northward to Hanover Junction, "only some 400 men were in [the] saddle, nearly 600 horses being disabled, chiefly by galled backs."[72] The men of the 4th with their equipment road-marched on their horses to Virginia, while two-thirds of the men of the 5th Regiment went by train, which would have greatly reduced the number of that regiment's horses being disabled when they reached Virginia. In fact, the 4th South Carolina Cavalry passed through Richmond on 24 May, when the 5th South Carolina Cavalry was fighting in Virginia for the fourth time at Wilson's Wharf. The 6th South Carolina Cavalry did not arrive until 30 May.[73]

The 4th South Carolina Cavalry Regiment remained in camp; but, as Edward Wells continued:

> The [Charleston Light] Dragoons ate a very slim breakfast, all that their negroes, lords of the frying pan, would allow. These servants proved tyrants of the most merciless kind in Virginia, where only the limited army rations intended for the [enlisted] men could be obtained. On the coast of South Carolina it had been different, for there these could be supplemented by bought supplies. In Virginia the usual daily allowance

to a man was one-third of a pound of bacon and some corn-meal, occasionally varied by wheat-flour, there being no coffee, tea, or other stimulant ... [but] the servants of the messes took good care not to starve themselves, [so this] soon necessitated a reduction of camp followers, but in the meantime much needless suffering was incurred by the men."[74]

The wealthy officers and men of "the Dragoons" had finally come to the "real war" and had to do without their accustomed luxuries and some of their slave cooks and personal servants!

The 5th South Carolina Cavalry Regiment arrived very soon; its last two companies left Cape Fear, South Carolina, on 20 April and arrived on 18 May.[75] One of 15 male prisoners captured by the 1st Regiment, USCT on 9 May was William Kean, Company B, 5th South Carolina Cavalry, who had arrived from South Carolina two weeks previously. Captain A.B. Mulligan, Company B, wrote on June 28, 1864: "I regret to say that Wm. Kean, the brother of Miss. Kean of Graniteville, [South Carolina,] was captured while on picket on the Chickahominy about four weeks ago." Pvt. William L. Kean, Co. B, is listed in *Union records* as a *prisoner of war* at "Wilson's Landing," where he was brought after capture. He was "transferred from Bermuda Hundred to Point Lookout, Maryland on 7/9/64; then to Elmira, NY and exchanged at Point Lookout on 10/29/64."[76] Meanwhile, Col. Dunovant's 5th South Carolina (minus the two companies which arrived on 18 May) was employed as dismounted skirmishers at Chester Station on 10 May, and on the left flank of Maj. Gen. Robert Ransom's division which smashed the Federal right flank at Drewry's Bluff on 16 May, but it contributed little to the Confederate success there, and suffered very few, if any casualties.[77] It also was engaged at Atkinson's Farm on 17 May.[78]

Captain Mulligan wrote home on 18 May: "We live on rare bacon & hard bread except when we eat [captured] yankee crockery ham, coffee, sugar, etc. Myself and men are pretty nearly all supplied with yankee [accouterments] of the finest kind & we keep up & improve in health."[79]

Colonel (later Brigadier General) John Dunovant is significant because he commanded "Dunovant's detachment" which consisted of his 5th South Carolina Cavalry, temporarily commanded by Lt. Col. Jeffords, and also detachments from Lomax's brigade: 5th, 6th, and 15th Virginia Cavalry Regiments, on Fitzhugh Lee's right during the Action on 24 May 1864, in the absence of General Lomax. A Confederate recalled: "General Dunovant owned two beautiful sorrel horses and a negro named Monroe [who may have served Dunovant at Wilson's Wharf], and frequently the couriers would give Monroe a pass to go out foraging, and he being slick of hand and tongue, would always return with something."[80]

Richard J. Sommers provides insights to John Dunovant's subsequent performance as a commanding officer and the 5th South Carolina Cavalry Regiment itself:

> On 28 May, senior colonel Dunovant probably led both the 4th and 5th South Carolina Cavalry Regiments [during the Battle of Aenon Church-Hawe's Shop]. Their full ranks, redoubtable Enfield rifles, and ardent determination made his Carolinians formidable fighters that day—almost too steadfast, for they did not retreat when ordered and were nearly trapped. In this battle *Dunovant was shot* [by a pistol ball] *through the* [left] *hand* [and admitted to Jackson Hospital at Richmond].
>
> Hospitalized until July 8, he missed the 5th's many battles from May 30 to June 29. Even after returning to the front, he was too unhealthy to assume command.... John Dunovant was promoted to brigadier general on 22 August 1864 and assigned to command the brigade consisting of the 4th, 5th, and 6th South Carolina Cavalry Regiments. At McDowell's Farm on September 29 he helped drive the Yankees, but at Armstrong's Hill on September 30 he was surprised and stampeded, and his adjutant (Division commander Butler's cousin) was captured.
>
> That humiliation, on top of his 1862 disgrace, may have made him rash for redemption on the Vaughn Road on October 1. [Butler gave him an order for a flank attack, but Dunovant] saluted and replied, "Oh, General, let me charge 'em, we've got 'em going and let us keep 'em going" [as he kept urging a frontal attack until Butler angrily assented]. Instantly Dunovant wheeled his horse, and his voice rang out.... "Forward, charge!" ... [His courier:] ... "just as he reached the creek, I saw him fall from his horse." Shot through the heart, Dunovant died instantly. Horrified, his brigade was repulsed.[81]

The battle flag of the 5th South Carolina Cavalry, which possibly was carried during the Action at Wilson's Wharf on 24 May, was captured by the 9th New York Cavalry on 11 June 1864 *during, but not in* the Battle of Trevilian Station. Union Colonel Thomas C. Devin reported: "An advance was again ordered ... the connection between the Fourth and Ninth New York [made], and to press on to the [Trevilian railroad] station, which was successfully accomplished, the station occupied, and a number of prisoners cap-

The 5th South Carolina Cavalry Regimental Standard, type used by Department of South Carolina, Georgia, and Florida. It probably was present at Wilson's Wharf on 24 May 1864 before being captured by the 9th New York Cavalry at Trevilian Station on 11 June 1864 (courtesy John M. Bigham, Curator of Education, and South Carolina Confederate Relic Room & Museum, Columbia).

tured from the Fifth South Carolina, together with a hospital wagon, loaded with stores, and *one battle-flag.*" "The battle flag of the 5th SC Cavalry ... was returned to South Carolina in 1990, and is in the collection of the Confederate Relic Room and Museum in Columbia.[82]

Eight companies: A, B, C, E, F, G, H, and K of the 5th South Carolina Cavalry are mentioned as having detachments at "Charles City C.H. (or 'Wilson's Wharf/Kenner's Point') on 24 May 1864."[83] Captain A.B. Mulligan, Company B, 5th South Carolina Cavalry, wrote from "Army of Northern Va. Near Hanover Junction, Thursday May 26th 1864" [to]: "My Very Dear Mother & Sisters.... On Monday last before rejoining the regt *all the effective force of my Regt went out on a raid.* Went after a lot of Negro cavalry [*sic*; infantry] who have been devastating the country in the neighborhood of Charles City. They have not yet returned. I would have been with them had I been in camp when they started."[84]

The author estimates that the 5th South Carolina Cavalry Regiment had about 650 men, of whom one-quarter held horses for dismounted fighters, at Wilson's Wharf on 24 May 1864.

Ten of the eleven Confederate cavalry regiments which sent detachments to fight at Wilson's Wharf on 24 May had suffered heavy casualties in operations during 9–13 May 1864. Major General Fitz Lee reported to General R.E. Lee from "near Pole Green Church" on 13 May 1864:

> *I shall retain Gordon's brigade with me* to watch [Sheridan's cavalry] movements on [the] Peninsula. My division alone was engaged at Yellow Tavern, Gordon's being on their rear some distance behind, delayed by their obstructing the roads. My lines were finally forced back (*a*) three quarters of a mile just before dark by their overwhelming numbers. General Stuart was with me, and I deeply regret that he received a wound which has since proved mortal. *My loss during these engagements has been very heavy, particularly in officers.* In addition to those you already know of, Colonel Pate, of Fifth [Virginia Cavalry], Lieut. Col. Robert Randolph, of Fourth [Virginia Cavalry], were killed, and Major Wooldridge, of Fourth, lost a leg, besides *the loss of many subordinate officers killed and wounded, particularly captains.* Many companies are without a commissioned officer and several squadrons are commanded by second lieutenants. In the fight yesterday, General Gordon was wounded in the arm and will probably lose it [he died of infection on 18 May]. Colonel Cheek, First North Carolina Cavalry, has also been wounded.
>
> Very respectfully, your obedient servant,
> FITZ. LEE,
> *Major-General*
>
> *a* The left of the line was forced back, losing two pieces of artillery [of the Baltimore Light Artillery—one gun had a broken axle] which were posted on extreme left.[85]

The heavy casualties sustained by the seven veteran Virginia Cavalry regiments and three veteran North Carolina Cavalry regiments made the relatively unscathed and untried 5th South Carolina Cavalry Fitzhugh Lee's largest regiment at Wilson's Wharf on 24 May 1864. In comparison, the 1st Regiment, Infantry, USCT had seen hard campaigning in North Carolina but had only fought some guerrillas; the 10th Regiment, USCT had no reported combat experience.

III

The James River Campaign

*Strategy, Preparations and Movement;
Rebel Orders Regarding Captured
U.S. Colored Troops' Officers
and Enlisted Men*

In mid–March 1864, Lieutenant General Ulysses S. Grant, newly appointed general-in-chief of the Armies of the United States, formed his strategy for winning the war. While Major General George G. Meade conducted operations with his Army of the Potomac against General Robert E. Lee's Army of Northern Virginia north of Richmond, Major General Benjamin F. Butler was to operate with his Army of the James to attack the Confederate capital from the east along the south side of the James River.[1]

Detailed Army-Navy planning and extensive preparations took place. Grant ordered Butler to assemble all available troops, including some on garrison duty who could be spared. Major General Quincy A. Gilmore was to bring 10,000 troops from around Charleston, South Carolina, and Col. (promoted brigadier general on 7 May) Augustus V. Kautz was to move his 3,000 cavalry from Suffolk, Virginia, to cover the south side of the James River. Butler assembled his army between Fortress Monroe and Yorktown. On 1 April, Grant inspected Butler's troops at Fortress Monroe, and Brig. Gen. Edward A. Wild's brigade of U.S. Colored Troops at Norfolk.[2]

Butler's joint Army-Navy operation would begin the night of 4 May, with landings the next day at Wilson's Wharf (or "Kennon's Landing" as it was previously known) on the north side of the James; Fort Powhatan, seven miles upriver on the south side of the river; and City Point at the mouth of the Appomattox River.[3] On 25 April, Butler wrote Admiral S.P. Lee: "In order to prevent annoyance by the enemy of [Army] transports and naval vessels, it is prepared to seize and hold Fort Powhatan and Wilson's Wharf ... the only points below City Point from which we can be substantially annoyed by the enemy's light artillery or sharpshooters."[4]

General Butler had 33,000 men in Maj. Gen. William F. Smith's XVIII Corps and Maj. Gen. Quincy A. Gilmore's X Corps for the expedition. Brigadier General Edward W. Hinks issued each soldier in his division of United States Colored Troops (USCT) a half shelter tent, an overcoat, two pairs of drawers, one pair of trousers, two pairs of shoes,

Lieutenant General Ulysses S. Grant, photographed by the Brady studio (Library of Congress, Washington, D.C.).

a rubber blanket, cap, blouse, two shirts, three pairs of stockings, a clothes brush, and a shoe brush. Each soldier carried 60 cartridges in his cartridge box and knapsack, and 40 extra rounds of ammunition per man were carried in boxes aboard the transports. Hinks also ordered each regiment to have one wagon and four horses, and one wall tent, and to bring pioneer tools required by General Smith's order, and only camp kettles and mess pans. His brigade headquarters was to take two wall tents and three fly tents. One wagon and one ambulance were allocated to the two artillery batteries. Five horses were allowed each regiment's field and staff officers. Each brigade was allotted one ambulance, two hospital tents, and one medicine chest. The Medical Director was to instruct what other stores the surgeons will take with them.[5]

General Hinks requested that his division of USCT be armed with repeating arms, "since Colored troops cannot afford to be beaten and will not be taken and ought to have the best arms" [Spencer seven-shot repeating rifles] the country could provide. Bruce Catton: "His request was ignored, but the making of it was significant."[6]

At sunrise on 5 May 1864, the Army-Navy fleet of 120 gunboats, transports, and assorted vessels carrying most of Maj. Gen. Benjamin F. Butler's 33,000 Union soldiers in the X and XVIII Corps, Army of the James, began to ascend the James River to begin the Union attempt to capture Richmond, the Confederate capital and military production and supply base. Lieutenant General Ulysses S. Grant, with Maj. Gen. George G. Meade's Army of the Potomac, simultaneously began operations against Lee's army north of Richmond. Brigadier General Edward A. Wild's 1st Brigade (1st, 10th, 22nd, and 37th Infantry Regiments, USCT), with two artillery batteries, part of Brig. Gen. Edward W. Hinks's 3rd Division, XVIII Corps, led the way aboard Army transports while escorted by U.S. Navy gunboats and ironclads. Wild, who was joined by Signal Officer and 2nd Lieutenant Julius M. Swain and his four signalmen the night before, sailed on the transport *Wilson Small*. Wild's four regiments landed and seized Wilson's Wharf and Fort Powhatan, an abandoned Confederate earthwork seven miles upriver, while Colonel Samuel A. Duncan's 2nd Brigade (4th, 5th, and 6th Infantry Regiments, USCT) landed at City Point, further upriver and 10 miles southeast of Petersburg. The rest of the XVIII Corps and X Corps followed. Lewis Bennett Rice, from Wayne County, New York, an awestruck first lieutenant in Company E (commanded by his brother, Captain Judson E. Rice), 1st Regiment, USCT described events in detail on 5 May in a letter from Chesapeake Hospital on 16 May 1864:

> Dear Friends at Home[:] ... Thursday morning was a beautiful morning as ever dawned upon earth. Before it [was] light the great fleet had commenced to move. It was a grand sight. There were gunboats of all sizes and descriptions, monitors double & single turreted, Ram's, Steam transports of every kind from the ocean Steam Ship, the fast river boats, ferry boats, tug boats & c. These had in tow ships, briggs [*sic*; brigs], larks, schooners, sloops, barges, a great many canal boats from the Erie canal, flat boats, floating docks, pontoon boats &c. all loaded to their fullest capacity with troops and munitions of war....
>
> We landed at Wilson's Wharf opposite Brandon & about 15 miles above the mouth of the Chicahoming [*sic*; Chickahominy River] a little after noon and went at work throwing up breastworks, so that by dark we were prepared for the enemy if he should see fit to come.[7]

Preceding the naval movement, lengthy and detailed instructions were issued on 4 May by Rear-Admiral S.P. Lee from his flagship *Malvern* at Newport News. That evening, a detachment of "army gunboats" (or armed transports), passed up the James at 7 p.m. "to operate against the enemy's signal station and to occupy Fort Powhatan and Wilson's Wharf," possibly landing small bodies of troops to reconnoiter those places for an enemy presence, before the naval column left at 4 a.m. on the 5th. The instructions specified that five slow ironclads, towed by two gunboats each, proceeded in front of the main column of vessels. The fifth ironclad in line, *Atlanta*, captured at Savannah, used a head tow, *Dawn*, and a side tow, *Young America*, another captured Confederate vessel. These three ships would be working together again upriver to support Wild's brigade at Fort Powhatan and Wilson's Wharf. Instructions stated:

> The *Atlanta*, with the *Dawn* and *Young America*, upon arrival at Fort Powhatan, will drop out of line and take up a position to cover our troops, which it is expected will then be in possession of that point, as well as Wilson's Wharf. The *Dawn* will proceed to Wilson's Wharf for the same purpose. The *Young America* will act as guard boat to the *Atlanta*.... The rest of the ironclads will push forward with dispatch to Harrison's Bar, which it is expected they will reach between 1 and 2 o'clock p.m., in time to cross at high water ... they will be taken to designated positions above Bermuda Hundred."[8]

Hinks's Colored Troops Land, Seize and Occupy Wilson's Wharf and Other Key Points Along the James River

General Wild: "May 5. I made the first landing of the Campaign, with half my command, at Wilson's Wharf on the north bank of James River. *Dug rifle pits.* The other half seized and occupied Fort Powhatan, 7 miles farther up, on the South Bank."[9] General Hinks's division of USCT achieved complete surprise on 5 May. Wild landed Col. John H. Holman's 1st, and Col. Joseph B. Kiddoo's 22nd USCT Regiments, with two sections (of two guns each) of Captain Francis C. Choate's Battery B, 2nd U.S. Colored Light Artillery, at Wilson's Wharf without opposition on 5 May and began to fortify it by "digging rifle pits" (above).

Colonel Joseph Barr Kiddoo landed his 22nd Infantry Regiment, U.S. Colored Troops at Wilson's Wharf on 5 May 1864 and later fought an "Action" at Fort Powhatan with it on 21 May 1864 (RG 98S-CWP 21.28, Roger D. Hunt Collection, United States Army Heritage and Education Center, Carlisle, PA).

"The Campaign on the James River—General Butler Landing at Fort Powhatan"
(on top of bank). *Harper's Weekly,* May 28, 1864, p. 148 (courtesy Thomas G. Crump,
Chester, Virginia).

Captain William Davis Parlin had some unique experiences that day:
"My company [E, 1st Regiment, USCT] on a barge pushed ahead to be
thrown ashore as skirmishers at Wilson's Landing, and I have always flattered myself as being *the first soldier ashore of the Army of the James.* [But]
A sailor jumped on land to secure the boat and I followed him. We made
quick time with our skirmisher line, overtaking this family a little way out
& securing a good saddle horse that helped me all day [while] posting &
visiting pickets." Passing by on a steamer, John L. Cunningham, 118th New
York Volunteer Infantry, and other troops cheered the "Stars and Stripes"
floating over "Wilson's Landing." Wild's other troops—Col. Spencer H.
Stafford's 10th and Lt. Col. Abial G. Chamberlain's 37th Infantry Regiments, USCT, with two sections of Captain Robert H. Howell's Battery
M, 3rd New York Artillery—landed unopposed at Fort Powhatan. Colonel
Samuel A. Duncan's brigade of USCT—4th Regiment, Lt. Col. George
Rogers; 5th Regiment, Col. James W. Conine; and 6th Regiment, Col. John
W. Ames, with the remaining sections of Choate's and Howell's six-gun
batteries—landed at City Point. On 8 May, the 37th Regiment was transferred from Fort Powhatan to City Point. General Hinks also stated: "[A]
member of my [brigade] staff [was] left at Wilson's Wharf to lay out and
superintend the construction of proper earth-works.... On Tuesday, 10th
instant, [I] went personally to Fort Powhatan and directed the construction
of earthworks."[10]

A *New York Times* correspondent aboard General Butler's flagboat, the fast steamer *Grayhound*, gave a colorful description of post-landing activities at Wilson's Wharf and Fort Powhatan:

The stalwart Africans gaily run up the bluff (at Wilson's Wharf) and are soon at work swinging axes with a will, and giant trees fall with a mournful crash ... soon a wide space of woods on the high banks are cleared away, and rebels approaching from Richmond must come within sweep of our batteries. Bye-the-bye, nothing better shows the perfect surprise to the rebels than, according to their own admission, they have a strong force at Charles City Court-house, six miles from Wilson's Wharf, engaged in collecting negroes for work on Richmond fortifications.

> If this force was aware of our approach, it is strange they did not come and give us a few shots from a field battery.... The boat is now leaving Powhatan, where a strong sable garrison [is] mounting guns in works so laboriously constructed by the rebels two years ago. The bell rings for the boat to move on to City Point.[11]

From "City Point, May 5, 1864—9 p.m. (Via fortress Monroe 11:30 a.m. 6th)," Maj. Gen. Butler sent a report that summarized results of the day's complex and extensive operations:

> Lieutenant-General Grant:
>
> We have seized Wilson's Wharf, landing a brigade (Wild's colored troops) there; Fort Powhatan, landing two regiments of same brigade. Have landed at City Point Hinks' division of colored troops, remaining brigades, and batteries. Remainder of both Eighteenth and Tenth Army Corps are now landed at Bermuda Hundred, above the Appomattox. No opposition thus far. Apparently a complete surprise. Both army corps left Yorktown during last night. Monitors [ironclads] all over the bar at Harrison's Landing and above City Point. The operations of the fleet have been conducted to-day with energy and success. Generals Smith and Gilmore, with the army gunboats, led the advance during the night, capturing the signal stations of the rebels. Colonel West, with 1,800 cavalry, made demonstrations from Williamsburg yesterday morning. General Kautz left Suffolk this morning with 3,000 cavalry for the service indicated in conference with the lieutenant-general.[12]

Butler later wrote that he entrusted Colored Troops to seize the three key points along his James River line of communications because he knew they would fight more desperately than white soldiers because Confederate policy denied prisoner-of-war status to black Union soldiers and their white officers, if captured.[13] At Fort Pillow, Tennessee, on 12 April 1864, a disproportionate number of black Union soldiers were killed or badly wounded, many while trying to surrender. Captain Solon A. Carter, Hinks's assistant adjutant general, wrote his wife on 1 May: "We must succeed. Failure for us is death or worse."[14]

General Hinks promptly began more offensive division operations. He wrote on 13 May:

> On Sunday evening, 8th instant … Captain Dollard, Company D, Second U.S. Colored Cavalry, reported for duty. On Monday, 9th instant, with 1,800 infantry, one [artillery] battery, and the company of cavalry, I made a reconnaissance toward Petersburg, upon the river road to Spring Hill, and returned to the middleroad, so-called, and pushed up to within 4 miles of Petersburg, drawing the fire of the enemy's batteries; after which I returned to City Point, arriving at 11 o'clock at night.
>
> On Tuesday, 19th instant, went personally to Fort Powhatan and directed construction of earth-works. Learned that [Brig. Gen. Thomas L.] Clingman's Confederate brigade, three regiments of infantry, and a battery of six guns came down from Petersburg to within 2 miles of the works at City Point, and returned by the river road.[15]

Confederate Treatment of Captured U.S. Colored Troops' Officers and Enlisted Men

On 24 December 1862, President Jefferson Davis had issued his General Order No. 111 at Richmond:

> By the President of the Confederate States of America A Proclamation
>
> … 3. That all negro slaves captured in arms be at once delivered over to the executive authorities of the respective States to which they belong to be dealt with according to the laws of said States.
>
> 4. That the like orders be executed in all cases with respect to all commissioned officers of the United States when found serving in company with armed slaves in insurrection against the authorities of the different States of this Confederacy.
>
> In testimony whereof I have signed these presents and caused the seal of The Confederate States of America to be affixed thereto.…
>
> Jeff'n Davis[16]

After Lincoln's Emancipation Proclamation became effective on 1 January 1863, the Confederate government met in secret session on Friday, 1 May 1863, and passed a resolution condemning the "Government of the United States, its authorities, commanders, and forces" who would free slaves in the Confederate States, abduct slaves, incite them to insurrection, or use them in the "war against the Confederate States." Author C.R. Gibbs adds: "No distinction would be made for the black men in any Union regiment who were born free and knew nothing of whips or fetters." The resolution specified that any who attempted to "arm, train, organize, or prepare Negroes or mulattos in any military enterprise … shall, if captured, *be put to death, or otherwise punished, at the discretion of the court.*" The Confederate States thus officially denied prisoner-of-war status to black Union soldiers or their white officers if they were captured. The resolutions were widely published in newspapers. The editor of the *Wilmington* (North Carolina) *Journal* wrote: "The Yankee officers who would put themselves at the head of a Negro brigade ... should fight with a halter around their necks."[17]

This policy was restated by the Confederate Congress later in May 1863: "Officers of black regiments would be treated as criminals and soldiers who had been slaves would be turned over to state authorities." President Abraham Lincoln issued his unequivocal response in General Order No. 252 of 30 July 1863:

> The law of nations, and usages and customs of war as carried on by civilized powers, permit no distinction as to color in the treatment of prisoners.... To sell or enslave any captured person on account of his color is a relapse into barbarism.... The Government of the United States will give the same protection to all its soldiers; and if the enemy shall sell or enslave anyone because of his color, the offence shall be punished by retaliation upon the enemy's prisoners in our possession. It is therefore *ordered, that for every soldier of the United States killed in violation of the laws of war, a Rebel soldier will be executed, and for every one enslaved by the enemy ... a Rebel soldier shall be placed at hard labor on the public works* ... until the other shall receive the treatment due a prisoner of war.

Lincoln's policy of retaliation probably prevented some application of the harsh Confederate policy, but it certainly did not eliminate it in practice.[18]

The Fort Pillow "Massacre" on 12 April 1864 Showed What Treatment Black Union Soldiers and Their White Officers Could Expect from Confederates in Practice

On 12 April 1864, Confederate forces gained a quick and overwhelming victory over 262 black troops and 295 white Unionists at Fort Pillow, Tennessee. Northern accounts, including a Congressional Report (No. 65, 38th Congress, 1864), concluded that the Confederates were guilty of atrocities which included murdering most of the garrison after it surrendered, burying negro soldiers alive, and setting fire to tents containing Federal wounded. Southern accounts claim Federal losses occurred during a fighting retreat to the river and when Federal troops took up arms after surrendering. Of 557 Federal troops, however, 231 were killed, 100 severely wounded, and only 58 black and 168 white soldiers became prisoners.[19]

A 7 May 1864 *Harper's Weekly* article, "Buried Alive," by Daniel Tyler, a Union soldier, must have been read by some officers and men in Hinks's

"Battle of Fort Pillow, Slaughter on the River, April 12, 1864" (Library of Congress).

Colored Division, and perhaps at Wilson's Wharf. In it, he described being shot at Fort Pillow near the river; then while "running for my life, a burly rebel struck me with his carbine, putting out one eye, and then [he] shot me in two places…. With half a dozen others, I was picked up and carried to a ditch, into which we were tossed like so many brutes, white [Tennessee Union cavalrymen] and black together. Then they covered us with loose dirt and left us to die. Oh, how dark and desolate it was! … with only one hand free, I struggled for air and life … yet able to think and pray." He struggled free, passed out, and awoke in a hospital. He concluded: "I hope to recover and get away from here very soon; I want to be in my place again; for I have something to avenge now, and I can not bear to wait…. And may God speed the day when this whole slaveholders' rebellion—what remains of it—shall be 'Buried Alive!'"[20] His account and stirring words must have instilled anger and determination in those Union officers and soldiers—black or white—who read them. Other eyewitness accounts were later published in *Official Records of the War of the Rebellion*. Some allege that Confederates were bent on killing any black soldiers they found. Private George Huston wrote: "A rebel officer rode up to the [river] bank and said General Forrest ordered every damned nigger to be shot down. So the enemy kept on firing on our defenseless men, and killed a great many of them." Other witnesses testified that Union soldiers waving a white flag to surrender were shot down by the Confederates.[21]

On 28 October 1863, Daniel Tyler, age 21 years, a mulatto slave born in South Carolina who had joined a Federal cavalry column while working in a field in Alabama,[22] mustered as a private in Captain Limberg's Memphis Light Battery, African Descent, at Fort Pickering, Tennessee. It became Battery F, 2nd U.S. Colored Light Artillery Regiment, and was posted at Fort Pillow. The Battery Muster Roll for March and April 1864 states that Tyler was "Missing in Action at Fort Pillow, Tenn. April 12th 1864 whether Killed or Missing (Not Known)." At Fort Pillow, he was "paroled" by the Confederates according to Daniel Tyler's "Memorandum From Prisoner of War Records," and sent on the steamer *Platte Valley* to the U.S.A. General Hospital at Mound City, Illinois. He returned to duty with Battery F on 22 June 1864 and was "Present" until 28 December 1864, when he became "Absent without Authority." On 18 March 1865, he was arrested for desertion and confined in Irvington Military Prison. He "Died of Disease" in the prison hospital on 12 July 1865, without enjoying his freedom.[23]

Bruce Catton: "After the surrender [at Fort Pillow] some of Forrest's tough troopers got out of hand and turned the occasion into something like a lynching bee. The colored troops [i.e., most of them] with the Army of the Potomac [and Butler's Army of the James, etc.] could read no newspapers and got their information of far-off events Heaven knows how, but every one of them knew about Fort Pillow."[24]

Confederate atrocities, or the threat of them, continued. A 3 June 1864 article titled "Taking care of Sambo" in the *Montgomery Daily Advertiser* quoted the *Memphis News*: "Before the Battle of Pleasant Hill [in Louisiana on 9 April], General Dick Taylor sent by flag of truce a letter to [Union] General Banks [threatening] that if negro troops were used against the Confederate army, [Taylor] would raise the black flag and show no quarter."[25] At times, Confederates also committed atrocities against white Union soldiers,[26] and vice versa; and black soldiers sometimes shot Confederate prisoners, as during a Union assault on Fort Blakely, Alabama, on 9 April 1865. By early May 1864, news of the Fort Pillow "massacre" would fuel the anger and fears of Hinks's black soldiers and their white officers and influence their attitudes toward both Confederate soldiers and slave masters among the civilian population of Charles City County, Virginia. Frances H. Casstevens: "The effort exerted by Wild's troops in defense of Wilson's

Wharf was perhaps motivated by events at Fort Pillow the previous month."[27]

Andre Noah Trudeau writes: "Tragically the fate of black soldiers captured in [Grant's Overland Campaign] differed little from that suffered by their comrades in the West." Charles Hopkins, a white New Jersey soldier captured during the Wilderness fighting, was marched with other captives to a holding pen in the basement of a building at Orange Court House in central Virginia. On May 9, the captives there heard a cry, "Hey, thar you-uns, if you want to see a nigger hang, look 'round right smart." Hopkins: "[A]nd sure enough they were just pulling up one of Burnside's black heroes in full uniform." Hopkins, who considered himself a "born Abolitionist," muttered aloud that the "soul of that colored patriot had gone to meet the soul of John Brown," and he exclaimed, "God bless that colored Veteran!!!" His outburst was met with leveled muskets and the order to "shut up yer mouth!" On 8 May, Byrd C. Willis, a member of the 9th Virginia Cavalry Regiment, made a matter-of-fact diary entry: "We captured three negro soldiers the first we had seen. They were taken out on the road side and shot, & their bodies left there."[28]

In the Trans-Mississippi Theater General Kirby Smith chided a senior Confederate officer in Louisiana: "I have been unofficially informed that some of your troops have captured negroes in arms. I hope this may not be so, and that your subordinates who may have been in command of capturing parties may not have recognized the propriety of giving no quarter to armed negroes and their officers."[29] Confederate laws and military policies were responses of outrage and intended to discourage black Union enlistments, but they had other unintended effects. Joseph T. Glatthaar states:

> In a peculiar way, Confederates helped to legitimize and enhance the reputation of blacks within the Union Army. Rebels attempted to undermine the effectiveness of black units by singling them out for especially heavy fire, declining to exchange black prisoners of war, or capturing and executing black soldiers and their white officers on the spot. Such practices, however, backfired. They not only bonded black soldiers and their white officers closer, for both faced the same fates, but elevated the standing of the United States Colored Troops in the Union army. White volunteers could not help but notice that officers and men in black units incurred greater risks.[30]

IV

Wild and His
U.S. Colored Troops Create
a Stir in Charles City County

Raid on a Confederate Signal Station at Sandy Point on the James River, 6 May 1864

On 6 May, Union Signal Officer 2nd Lt. Julius M. Swain and two of his men accompanied a detachment from the 1st Infantry Regiment, USCT led by Captain Clifford F. Eagle and Lt. Lewis B. Rice. They left Wilson's Wharf to seize a "Rebel Signal Station" reportedly located in a "huge mahogany tree in front of a house called 'The Rowe'" at Sandy Point on the James River. After coming by gunboat, the Federal detachment landed in small boats two or three miles above the signal station to block any retreating Confederates. After seeing two men watching them from shore, Wild's men arrested James Challiner, an Englishman; his companion escaped and warned the signal station occupants. The Union soldiers found two muskets and old army clothing and equipment, "probably remains of McClellan's Army," on the Challiner premises. At the signal station, Wild's soldiers met some resistance and killed a Confederate sergeant and four others before two privates and a civilian, all slightly wounded, surrendered with their arms, signal equipment, and a cipher code. A Lt. Davis escaped. Wild reported that of the 10 at the signal station, "8 were soldiers and 2 were civilians. One [civilian] was killed and one wounded." The dead were buried on the spot; the wounded Confederates were taken to Fort Monroe. Captain and Chief Signal Officer L.B. Norton reported further details:

[T]he signal officer (2nd Lt. Swain) at Wilson's Wharf accompanied a detachment of the First U.S. Colored Troops, which captured the rebel signal station party and equipments at Sandy Point…. The enemy's signalist made an armed defense, and the sergeant in charge and 3 of his men were killed before the surrender took place.

The record of all the dispatches and reports sent and received through that rebel station was captured and forwarded to the commanding general…. The Sandy Point station [surviving personnel, records, and "equipments"] … would never have been captured had not the sergeant in charge placed a too literal construction upon his orders, which were to remain at his post until "driven off by the Yankees."

Lieutenant Lewis Bennett Rice, Company K, described his participation in the raid:

[O]n friday Genl Wild determined to try and capture one [signal station] 10 miles from our camp, for this purpose 30 men and myself under Capt. Eagle were ordered to do the work. Accordingly we went aboard the gun boat & went down the river about half way when we landed and proceeded along the bushes carefull [sic] to keep out of sight of any parties on the other side who might signal our approach to the Station. As the captain did not [send] out an advance guard I asked him if I should not go ahead so that if there was an enemy on watch I might see him & before he knew of the approach of our forces. After marching 4 or 5 [or "2 or 3"] miles I come to the large open space in front of which the house was standing … from a knoll I took note of the lay of the ground and soon saw its advantages & when the Capt come up I told him that if he would give me a _____ of the men I would keep up under the edge of the woods and get around & surround the house while he would go under the [river] bank with the other men. So he gave me 10 men & around I went.

As we come up acrost the field their [sic] was a man [who] road away from the house on a horse. I fired at him and ordered him to halt but he was to far away … several of the men shot at him but he got away.…

The men mistook the [wrong] house and ran to far and left me alone but I called back three of them and *we then charged on the signal house.* I saw a number of men run from it down into a ravien [sic; ravine] tords [sic; towards] where the Capt. was. We had a great race to see who should get *the flags from the top of the house* [not the tree]. I out ran and was in the house by the time the others got up. Taking the [signal] flags and anything else that I thought would be of interest we followed the [Confederate] men tords the ravien just then the Capt's squad met them and they fired into them. *We had them between two fires & soon used them up.—4 men killed, one a citizen 2 wounded and two taken prisoner.*

The boys with me killed one and wounded one citizen before we got to the house, so we had all of the men belonging to the stations with their books, telescopes &c. The gunboat which had kept along commenced to throw shells as soon as they heard us shoot but they fired at my ___ instead of the Rebels several shots coming quite close to me.

Not being very well so much running in the hot sun used me up could hardly get around. The expedition was a perfect success. The Gen'l gave me one of the flags which we took. I took quite a package of letters. I captured a Richmond newspaper of the 3rd [of May] & a Reb song book. I have written to [Captain] Judson [his brother] to send them to you.

Confederate Cipher Code Captured
on 6 May 1864 at Sandy Point
Signal Station

U.S. Stmr *Dawn*
off Wilsons Wharf V^a
May 6th 1864

Sir

I very respectfully forward to you the original and a copy of rebel code of Signals captured at Sandy Point V^a this day. General Wild has a copy at this point.

I am Sir very Respectfully
Your Obt-Svt-
J.W. Simmons,
A.V. Lieut. U.S.N.

Actg Rear Admiral
S.P. Lee
N.A. B Squadron

(back)
Hand copy to our army Signal Officer & send original to Genl Butler

S.P. Lee
A.R.A.
(Acting Rear Admiral)
(USS) *Malvern*
May 9th p.m.

(Enclosure) Rebel Signal Code captured at Sandy Point Va May 6th 1864
Recd May 9th

A. 22	N. 2211	(?) End? 1211
B. 222	O. 11	
C. 221	P. 1121	No. 1 11112
D. 212	Q. 122	2 11122
E. 2	R. 121	3 11222
F. 2222	S. 111	4 12222
G. 2221	T. 112	5 22222
H. 211	U. 12	6 11111
I. 21	V. 1112	7 21111
J. 2122	W. 1122	8 22111
K. 2121	X. 1221	9 22211
L. 2111	Y. 1111	0 22221
M. 2112	Z. 1222	

Source: Manuscript Division, Library of Congress

Mary Ruffin Copland described the raid from a Southern perspective:

[The Confederate signal station] was detected on May 5th when Butler's army moved up the James, so the next day, a Federal signal officer, accompanied by a detachment of colored troops, was sent by General Wilde [*sic*] to capture it. The six officers at the station refused to surrender to colored troops and tried to make a get-a-way through the swamp. When they would not halt, the order was given to fire upon them and five were mowed down in their tracks. One, a Lieutenant Davis, succeeded in making good his escape. The records and equipment were seized by the enemy and the station burned. The Hammond-Harwood Chapter (of the United Daughters of the Confederacy–UDC) … has wanted to mark the site of the sad event, but the names of the officers at this station cannot be ascertained, although every effort has been made to learn their identity.

Wild complimented the two USCT officers "for skillfully carrying out the plan" at Sandy Point. A second signal station at Mt. Pleasant, south of the James, was destroyed the next day, and a third one near Harrison's Landing on 13 May.[1] However, Private Edward Keelan, Company B, 1st Regiment, USCT was "wounded 6 May during attack on CSA Signal Station."[2]

The 1st Regiment, USCT captured one female and 15 male Confederates on 8 May.[3] That same day, probably after questioning the prisoners, General Wild wrote to General Butler that the Confederates had sent "every spare man, either north to help Lee, or south against yourself" and suggested that it might be the right time "*to destroy the City of Richmond.*" Having learned that the capital was defended only by "home guards," Wild suggested that a "strong cavalry dash" along a southern or western approach might penetrate the defenses.[4]

Wild's suggestion was prompted by the earlier, unsuccessful Kilpatrick-Dahlgren raid by 3,584 Union cavalrymen and six guns to seize Richmond from the north and free Union prisoners. Confederate authorities took emergency measures and Kilpatrick found the fortifications too strong to assault. Colonel Ulrich Dahlgren led a separate column of 500 men toward Richmond that met disaster; Dahlgren was killed in an ambush. Papers found on his body disclosed an intent of the raiders to burn Richmond and kill Jeff Davis and his cabinet, igniting a controversy about their authenticity.[5]

Relations Between Wild's Soldiers and the Citizens of Charles City County Quickly Deteriorate; the Presence of Black Union Soldiers Represents a Long-Dreaded "Slave Revolt"

Relations between Wild's colored troops and the citizens of Charles City County, who had experienced a milder Federal occupation during

McClellan's 1862 Peninsula Campaign, quickly deteriorated to a bitter level. Black Union soldiers, led by white officers, raided the countryside. Virginia State Senator Cyrus A. Branch wrote the Governor of Virginia: "The people [of his district, Charles City County] have been compelled to fly to swamps and marshes with such provisions as they can take off, and leave their homes prey of the voracious and heartless brutes that are prowling in their midst."[6] Mary Ruffin Copland states in *History of Charles City County, Virginia* that "shocking crimes were perpetrated against the defenseless populace, even the old men and boys were taken prisoners."[7] The presence and operations of U.S. Colored Troops represented a long-dreaded "slave revolt" with both real and imagined consequences for a white population whose military-age men-folk were off to war elsewhere.

Mary Ruffin Copland was referring to General Wild's "List of Prisoners" dated 8 May that includes: "Mrs. [Molly] Wilson—wife of Dr. [32-year old John C.] Wilson-runaway (confine 1 month); Mr. Josiah Wilson [the 34-year old son of the late Josiah C. Wilson, who gave his name to "Wilson's Wharf"]—runaway his slaves; [12-year old] Master George W. Wilson- his son," all of whom lived on or near the property of Wilson's Wharf; and eight "prisoners of war" captured on 6 May at the Confederate Signal Station at Sandy Point or elsewhere, including:

> Mr. R.H. Early-scout-head hurt (Prisoner of war), Mr. John H. Freeman-Capt of Rebel Steamer- conscripted & furloughed; Master William P. Bunt- brought in from Major's house (confine 1 month); Mr. George B. Major –brought in by foraging party (confine 1 month); Mr. John Cholliner—Englishman- (detain 1 month); Mr. S.P. Carrington—(Prisoner of war); Mr. J.C. Tyler –citizen [and nephew of the late ex-President John Tyler]- (detain 1 month); Mr. James Vaughn- citizen- (detain 1 month); (Confederate) Signal Corps prisoners of war William G. Smith, and Denison Worthington; wounded prisoners of war W.D. Wise and S.R. Vincen-privates-Signal Corps; Dunbar Gordon, citizen with arms, [all] slightly wounded.

[There were also five "Contrabands" [freed negro slaves]: Richard B. Randall, Samuel Randall, James Hall, Fabornto Randall, Charles White, "& Several others."[8]

Life and Perils of Union Navymen on the James River in May 1864

The U.S. Navy vessels on the James River also conducted their own raids, some to enhance their meager rations and Spartan life aboard ship, and others directed against the enemy. Acting Assistant Paymaster Calvin

Gibbs Hutchinson, from Roxbury, Massachusetts, wrote in his diary aboard the USS *Pequot*, stationed off Fort Powhatan:

[Early] May 1864: ... The country about Powhatan was very fertile and under cultivation when we first went up the [James] river but our presence interfered with it very much. Plenty of cattle were near at hand & we killed all the beef & mutton we required; an old stone filter was found in an abandoned house did us good service, furnishing us excellent water; we appointed a horny handed old sailor as milkmaid, and kept a cow on the riverbank; a plantation ice house supplied us with ice; we improvised a freezer and flavored our ice creams with extract of coffee. The only draw back to our comfort was the venomous water snakes which occasionally crawled up the [anchor] chain cables & came on deck through the hawse holes....

Contrabands brought us information *as usual* and one night a negro came off and said his master, Major Robert Douthat of the rebel service was at home on a visit to his family at Upper Weyanoke on the north side of the [James] river & near by; a boats crew was armed & sent off under charge of Ensign Smalley who captured the Major & he was sent to Point Lookout prison [in Maryland]. I afterwards visited the family which consisted of four daughters aged from 14 to 24 and a second wife of about 30 yrs with an infant in her arms. The ladies were intelligent & well educated but reduced to extremities by the fortunes of war; they wore drapes of coarse homespun negro cloth & mens [*sic*] wool hats instead of bonnets. The house was a fair specimen of a James river mansion and the large hall extending throughout it was hung round with portraits of six or seven generations; some of them in old colonial or British uniforms.[9]

The life of Union Navymen on the James River was not without peril. Lt. Col. Wyatt M. Elliott, 25th Virginia Infantry Battalion, reported the destruction of the U.S. Navy Gunboat *Shawsheen* by artillery fire from the river bank on 7 May:

About 12 n. to-day the command (composed of a detachment of artillery under Major Stark, and a detachment of four companies from my command) encountered the gunboat Shawsheen off Turkey Island, she having either incautiously or defiantly approached the position taken by my command, dropping anchor ... within easy range for effective execution by the artillery and co-operating infantry, which opened upon her with such telling effect as to drive the gunners from their pieces and prevented resistance after the first discharge of same. Very speedily the vessel was completely disabled by the excellent fire of Major Stark's artillery, and though reluctantly, she nevertheless hauled down her colors in token of surrender. A boat was dispatched to enforce the delivery of prisoners on board, the enemy's boats being available to bring them off. The officer was also instructed to fire the vessel, which was effectively done, the fire quickly reaching the magazine, exploding it, and consigning all to the wind and waves. The immediate approach of two ironclads, against which we were not prepared to contend, prevented removal of anything from the vessel except the prisoners.

During the engagement many jumped overboard and attempted to escape to the opposite side of the river, the larger portion of whom were killed by the infantry firing among them, it is thought Ensign Ringot, commanding, being among the number. Not more than 5 made their escape. The number of prisoners taken is 27, one of them being slightly wounded and now in brigade hospital. The crew is reported to have numbered between 40 and 50. She carried three guns—one 30 and one 20 pounder Parrott, and one 12-pounder howitzer (Dahlgren). It may be counted a matter of satisfaction that the vessel was so summarily and effectually destroyed, since we had information deemed satisfactory that it was a party of this vessel who had an hour before fired the barn and corn-houses of Mr. Robert Taylor, adjoining…. There is occasion also for thankfulness that we … sustained no loss whatever.[10]

A "Friendly Fire" Incident at Wilson's Wharf

On the evening of 7 May, 1st Lt. William C. Dutton, adjutant of the 22nd Infantry Regiment, USCT, was killed when he failed to halt and give the countersign as he galloped toward the "farthest east" picket post manned by a corporal and three men of Co. G, 1st Regiment, USCT. Mistaking Lt. Dutton and his party for Confederates in the dark, they shot and killed him.[11] On 12 May, 1st Lt. Marion Patterson, 22nd Regiment USCT, wrote from "Wilson's Landing, Virginia May 12, 1864": "On the night of the 7th while returning from a scout, Adjutant Dutton of our regt. was shot by our own pickets, doubtless through carelessness; and the next day the officers of the regiment accompanied his remains to the boat, and sent them under charge of Lt. Night to Philadelphia to his friends. It was [a] very sad accident and admonishes us to be more mindful of military discipline, now that we are so near the enemy."[12]

A "Court of Inquiry at HQ, 1st Brigade, 3rd Division, 18th Corps at Wilson's Creek [*sic*], Va." was "convened to investigate circumstances attending the death of 1st Lieut. Wm. C. Dutton, Adjutant, 22nd U.S. Colored Troops on the night of 7 instant" (May). Lieutenant-Colonel Elias Wright of the 1st Regiment, USCT, field Officer of the Day, testified: "I visited the farthest [picket] post on the Charles City road at 5 o'clock PM." He questioned Corporal Samuel H. Fletcher, Company G, 1st Regiment, USCT who repeated his orders to "keep one man standing at all times, keeping good lookout, and halt all persons coming in; and to retreat to the reserve in case of attack." Wright: "I told him that was right for that post that was the last post between there and Richmond." Testimony revealed Lieutenant Dutton was on a scout under Major Cook outside the post. Lieutenant Nathan Bishop, 1st Regiment, USCT, testified: "Party came at a gallop, [and was] challenged three times; Corporal Fletcher and three men fired at the same time," thinking they were Rebel cavalry because they heard "clanking" (like from sabers); then "a horse without rider passed me, more followed … [someone shouted] 'You are firing into your [own] men.'"[13]

The Clopton "Whipping Incident"

In 1860, Charles City County was typical of counties in Virginia's "black belt": 52 percent of its 5,609 residents were slaves; only 32 percent were white. Fifteen percent of the people were free blacks, an unusually large proportion and a result of post–Revolution manumissions. John M. Coski described the situation in Charles City County by 1864: "In Charles City County and throughout the South, whites clung to the myth of the faithful bondsman and insisted that Yankees 'stole' their slaves. Not only did Charles City County blacks flee to the Yankees in huge numbers, they often assisted the Union forces against the South." He added: "While most slaves undoubtedly fled to the Yankees on their own accord, the Union army did eventually encourage slaves to run away…. *Because the Confederacy used slave property to aid their rebellion, slaves were legally contraband of war.* The Union army established contraband camps at Fort Monroe and Craney Island."[14]

On 11 May, General Wild sent Hinks's Provost Marshal, Captain John Cassels, a list of seven more prisoners, all farmers except "(Slave trader) M.F. Vaiden –Soldier captured on furlough" and "Geo. M. Vaiden, a farmer who is a particular enemy of Loyal men about Charles City," along with packages of money found on them. The next day, Wild wrote:

Wilson's Wharf, James River May 12, 1864

Sir—

On Tuesday May 10th William H. Clopton [a 53-year old wealthy farmer] was brought in by the Pickets. He had been actively disloyal so that I held him as Prisoner of War, and have sent him as such to Fortress Monroe. He has acquired a notoriety as the most cruel Slave Master in this region. I found half a dozen *women* among our refugees, *whom he had often whipped unmercifully, even baring their whole persons for the purpose in presence of Whites and Blacks. I laid him bare and putting the whip in the hands of the Women, three of whom took turns in settling old scores on their master's back.* A black Man, whom he had abused finished the administration of Poetical justice, and even in this scene the superior humanity of the Blacks over their white master was manifest in their moderation and backwardness. I wish that his back had been as deeply scarred as those of the women, but I abstained and left it to them—I wish it to be distinctly understood by Brig. Genl. Hinks that I shall do the same thing again under similar circumstances. I forgot to state that this Clopton is a high minded Virginia Gentleman, living next door to the late John Tyler ExPresident of the U.S. and then and still intimate with his family.

(Signed) Edwd. A. Wild

In 1860, William Clopton owned 25 slaves, aged 2 to 70. The soldier who tied up Mr. Clopton was Private William Harris, 1st Regiment, USCT, one of Clopton's own former slaves. Harris struck 15 to 20 blows, reportedly each so severe "that blood flew at every stroke."[15] Regardless of the justice of the slave-owner's punishment, Wild had no authority to summarily punish a civilian. Wild also had Clopton and two Confederate soldiers "captured on furlough" treated as prisoners; the others "are only to be detained for one month or less, *to prevent their giving information to the enemy.*"[16]

The *Richmond Examiner* of 13 May 1864 stated briefly: "John Henry Freeman of Richmond, and Lamb Wilcox, son of Col. Wilcox, were captured and murdered in cold blood by the Yankees. We learn that the Yankees are playing sad havoc in this unprotected county."[17] On Tuesday, 19 May, the following article appeared on the front page of *The Sentinel*, a Richmond newspaper:

> *Horrible Outrages Committed By Gen. Wild and His Negro Troops in Charles City*
> We have distressing accounts from the above county. The notorious General Wild landed at the head of about five-hundred negroes at Cannon's [*sic*] wharf, in Charles City county, and protected by a few gunboats, is daily sending out patrols of armed negroes, who are inflicting the most cruel and heartrending outrages upon the defenseless inhabitants…. The negroes are not merely robbing the people of their horses, cattle, provisions, wearing apparel, bed clothing and furniture capable of removal, but for the slightest pretext are laying in ashes every building upon the farms. They visited the premises of Mr. S. Wilcox, a son of Col. James Wilcox … [and] shot him down in his yard, and burned to ashes every building upon his farm. The only cause for this outrage was the refusal of Mr. W. to recognize them as United States soldiers…. The people are compelled to fly to the swamps with such provisions as they can carry, and leave their homes to the fury of the heartless brutes.
> The daughter of a most worthy and respectable citizen has been violated by a band of these villains; and they openly proclaim their purpose to satisfy their vile passions without discrimination.
> A most respectable citizen [William H. Clopton] has been stripped and whipped…. We gather the above facts from the letter of a most respectable citizen of Charles City county, to a gentleman of high official position in the State Government.[18]

The next day, 20 May 1864, *The Sentinel* contained a short paragraph:

> Charles City County
> A gentleman of the above county who has arrived in Richmond, corroborates the account given in the *Sentinel* of yesterday, of the situation of the people in Charles City county. He says the negroes are in larger force than was first supposed. Mesers. W.B. Graves, Franklin Vaiden, and a son of Mr. George Walker, were killed. Mr. Walker was shot through the face, the ball fracturing the jawbone, and he was carried off in that condition. Mesers. Jerome and Robert Vaiden were arrested and taken away by the negroes. A number of little boys, some of them not ten years old[?], have been arrested and held as prisoners.[19]

According to a Confederate deserter, George Walker was "active in carrying out the conscript act … [and] habitually led scouting parties." He often bragged of "killing a Yankee officer during McClellan's retreat from Harrison's Landing" in 1862.[20]

Another version stated that Virginia planter Lamb Wilcox was standing unarmed in his doorway when he was shot dead because he refused to salute Wild's African Brigade. Just who fired the fatal shots is unknown, but as their commanding officer, General Wild was held responsible for his soldiers' actions. Wild described to General Hinks the events that led to the Wilcox shooting. A party was sent out before daylight to surprise a "squad of Rebels, who had been playing as *Guerrillas*," and who had attacked Wild's men three times. Wild knew the Confederates would spend the night at a "certain house," and he sent out his men, who arrived at daylight. They found 11 Rebels commanded by an officer in uniform, reported to be an adjutant. Five mounted Union soldiers advanced on the Confederates, one of whom was killed and another wounded. The other Confederates escaped into a swamp, and then crossed the Chickahominy River in two boats. The citizen killed was believed to be "Wilcox, owner of the house, and the [Confederate] enrolling officer of the District." Wilcox was buried in his yard at the house, which was burned. The Union officers in charge were Major Cook, 22nd Infantry Regiment, USCT and Henry Harris of Battery B, 2nd U.S. Colored Light Artillery. Wild emphatically stated: "I wish it to be distinctly understood by Brig. Gen. Hinks, that I shall continue to kill Guerrillas, and Rebels offering armed resistance, whether they style themselves citizens, or soldiers."[21]

The *Richmond Examiner* editor, John M. Daniel, had made his newspaper a zealous advocate of secession and Southern nationality. In mid–April 1861, Daniel had confidently written: "Slaveholding begets and fosters the war spirit. After a while the *master race* begins to think its whole business is to fight, whilst the *inferior race* does the labor…. Let us all make up our minds for a long and bloody war…. We are prepared for it; and prepared to continue it, if need be, till the North gets sick of it…. War will do us no harm and much good…. The Christian God is a 'God of Battles.'"[22]

On 25 May 1864, Daniel angrily reported—and exaggerated—the Clopton whipping and other incidents:

[A] number of negro troops landed at Kennon's [Wilson's] *wharf* [on 5 May to] *prevent a flank movement by our artillery and keeping open communications by river* [exactly their mission!]…. These black wretches have been scouring the country, committing the most atrocious and devilish excesses. Their [unspecified] deeds exceed in enormity anything we have heard of during the war; we would scarcely believe them if they were not told to us by one of the most honourable men of that section. Robbing, burning, and plundering have not been enough, but these black scoundrels have *literally caught up white men, tied them to trees and whipped them on their bare backs*! It can be proven that *no less than three citizens* have suffered this fiendish enormity.

Perhaps in the re-telling, the William H. Clopton whipping episode involving General Wild himself, and one male and three female ex-slaves, was twisted so that the latter became "black [soldier] scoundrels," and Clopton became "*three* [male] citizens." Editor Daniel continued:

> *It is said* that these black demons, by violence and threats of instant death, have made some ladies, alone and unprotected, the victims of their hellish appetites, and that one after another have polluted their persons.... [After raising these lurid images, Editor Daniel clamored:] Truly the time has come for Mr. Davis's much vaunted retaliation.... [President Jefferson Davis obviously was no favorite of the editor either.] Is our government to submit passively to seeing its citizens hung and shot down like dogs, *its men bayoneted and nailed to trees, its women raped and ravished by negro troops from Boston and New York?*" [Some of their white officers did come from those cities, but Wild's black soldiers were recruited from the District of Columbia (1st Regiment, USCT), Virginia and North Carolina (10th Regiment, USCT), Pennsylvania (22nd Regiment, USCT), and North Carolina (37th Regiment, USCT).][23] If the government submits tamely ... we shall look to our own defenders in the field to avenge the record of negro infamy."[24]

The "defenders in the field"—three Confederate cavalry brigades under Maj. Gen. Fitzhugh Lee—had attempted to "avenge the record of negro infamy" at Wilson's Wharf the previous day.

The lurid accusations of alleged rapes, bayoneting and nailing men to trees, etc., based on one source, "*a gentleman* up from New Kent and Charles City Counties," and "it is said" (rumor) leave some doubt as to their extent and accuracy as well, although foraging and plundering were almost "normal" activities by this stage of the bitter Civil War. Robbing and burning also occurred frequently. The Richmond editor wanted to stimulate action and to criticize the Davis administration; exaggeration wouldn't hurt. An exchange between Generals Hinks and Wild casts doubt on many of the allegations printed in Richmond newspapers.

General Hinks had in fact severely reprimanded General Wild in a letter to him on 11 May after Col. John H. Holman, 1st Regiment, USCT and the provost marshal had informed Hinks about the Clopton whipping incident. Hinks angrily and condescendingly wrote:

> You will at once report to these headquarters all circumstances attending the killing of a citizen by an armed party from your brigade [at the Confederate signal station on 6 May] and whipping of a citizen prisoner within your camp [at Wilson's Wharf], with names of officers concerned. Not withstanding the impossibility of any justification for the first; and extreme improbability of any justification for the other; *I hope for the credit of my command, and honor of our arms* that the extreme acts were not perpetrated without sufficient cause. *I want it strictly understood that I will not countenance, sanction, or permit any conduct not in accordance with principles recognized by belligerents....* [Persons committing such acts] *will be held individually accountable.*

A furious and unrepentant Wild protested in draft notes on Hinks's own letter: "At Sandy Point Signal Station—10 [Rebels]—5 killed, 3 wounded, 2 captured—ran into swamp ... 8 soldiers, 2 citizens, (1 killed, 1 wounded) with 10 guns."[25]

Wild detailed his actions as requested by Hinks, addressing his explanation and a protest of Hinks's accusations to Major Robert S. Davis, Assistant Adjutant General of the Department on 12 May:

Brigadier General Edward W. Hinks, commander, 3rd Division, 18th Corps, Army of the James (courtesy Cary Delery, Metairie, Louisiana).

> Not being in the habit of accepting rebukes for acts not committed, and feeling that I can judge of "the qualities becoming a man or a soldier" quite as well as I can be informed by Brig. Gen. Edw. W. Hinks, in *such a letter....* I protest against the whole tone of the above [Hinks's] letter, as unbecoming and unjustly as being full of harsh rebuke, administered before even making any inquiry; and therefore, as *pre* judging cases against me, and taking for granted that acts perpetrated by me, are necessarily barbarous and cruel, and not admitting the possibility of any justification, nor the probability of any excuse.[26]

General Edward A. Wild was not only a fervid abolitionist, but also a "John Brown in uniform," willing to exceed his authority as an Army officer by exacting retribution on a cruel slave owner as prosecutor, judge, and executioner of justice. General Hinks was certainly correct in questioning the circumstances and insisting that his officers conform to the laws of war. Hinks no doubt recognized that the reputation of his black soldiers (and U.S. Colored Troops in general) depended both on their conduct in battle and their behavior toward white civilians, whichever side the latter were on.

Discipline was enforced in *the U.S. Colored Troops, the largest regular U.S. Army component.* A total of 52 men were hanged or shot for various crimes, including ten for rape and one for rape/murder. The 10th and 37th Regiments of Wild's Brigade had one man each executed for unspecified crimes; the 1st Regiment had none executed.[27] No Virginians seemed to mind, however, that their local authorities had not curbed Mr. Clopton's cruel, even sadistic behavior toward his human male and female "property."

William H. Clopton told his side to Major Robert S. Davis at Bermuda Hundred, stating that "he came into our lines of his own free will to report himself and to obtain such information in relation to his future conduct as would guide him so as not to transgress any of our laws or rules." Clopton told the post commander that upon General Wild's orders, he had been tied up and "flogged by Negroes and that his back and arms bore the marks of the fearful punishment." Clopton said he had been punished because "some one reported he had been a cruel Master," and he asked to be allowed to "contradict" that report from his own servants. After seeing Clopton's body, the post commander sent Clopton to Butler for "personal inspection and investigation," because he knew Butler would not approve such punishment. At Old Point, some officers who had learned of the whipping incident preferred charges against Wild. Butler agreed that Clopton had "been badly treated," and he promised to investigate the matter.[28]

General Hinks said he would not proceed with Wild's arrest, but he hoped that an "order to that effect" would come from Department Headquarters, and that Wild would be tried by a military court and be "relieved of his command and examined by a commission to determine and report on his soundness of mind." Frances H. Casstevens: "For Brigadier General Wild, the animosity generated by ('his rampaging troops' and the planters he had arrested and imprisoned) and other events resulted in scandalous publicity in national and local newspapers, and fed hatred and discrimination toward black troops and their commanders. All these factors combined to culminate [later] in the arrest and court-martial of Brigadier General Wild."[29]

The "Clopton Whipping Incident" even came to the attention of President Abraham Lincoln. Apparently not feeling chastened or humiliated by being whipped by his own former slaves, Mr. Clopton complained in a letter to his neighbor, Julia Gardner Tyler, staunchly pro–Confederate widow of the late President John Tyler, who had left her home at Sherwood Forest and gone to her mother's estate on Staten Island in 1862. She, in turn, wrote letters to President Lincoln and to General Butler, complaining of Clopton's harsh treatment at the hands of General Wild.[30] On 8 June, Clopton wrote to Mrs. Tyler to inform her that Col. John C. Holman, one of Wild's officers, had visited his wife Lucretia and Miss Marie Tyler at Clopton's "Selwood" and showed them "marked courtesy," which he knew was a result of Mrs. Tyler's letter to General Butler. Wild wrote his wife on 22 June, "Mrs. Ex. Pres. Tyler keeps stirring up the Clopton whipping matter." The matter had been referred to the Judge Advocate General, and Wild knew he faced a court-martial.[31]

In another incident, a squad of black soldiers and their white officer cornered a Confederate sharpshooter in a tree, who had been harassing Union shipping on the James River. The Confederate slid down the tree and *spat in the black sergeant's face. The white officer then killed the Confederate with his pistol.*[32] When reported back in camp, the incident must have reinforced the black soldiers' regard for their white officers. (Southerners the author spoke to, considered it "murder" by the white Union officer; the author and others who have military combat experience, including a Mennonite pastor who served as an Army infantryman during combat in Korea, consider it "suicide" by the Confederate.)

New Recruits

Wild's troops freed slaves, and his officers recruited soldiers from among free blacks and freed slaves of Charles City County. Robert P. Brown, a 5 foot 6¼-inch-tall, 20-year-and-one-month-old mulatto, free and a single farmer, was enlisted on 19 May at "Wilson's creek Va" by 1st Lt. Edward Simonton, 29 years old, from Searsport, Maine, commanding Company I, "First Regiment of U.S. Col. Troops," in time to fight five days later. His descendant, Richard Bowman, served in the U.S. Army's 25th Infantry (a Colored Regiment) in 1945, and Mr. Bowman, who also has Native American ancestry, fittingly became Charles City County Historian and served as supervisor of Charles City County during 1971–1978. At least seven other residents, including another Robert Brown, Banks Bradley, Jesse Braxton, Samuel Harrison, Robert Lewis, Robert A. Waters, and Oliver Williams, enlisted in the 1st Infantry Regiment, USCT during 12–23 May.[33]

The Failure of Butler's and Grant's Strategy to Surprise and Capture Richmond

The focus of Butler's operations, meanwhile, moved from City Point toward Richmond. Grant's *Final Report of Operations, March 1864–May 1865* summarizes:

[The 5th of May Butler] occupied, without opposition, both City Point and Bermuda Hundred, his movement being a complete surprise.... On the 6th, he began intrenching. On the 7th he made a reconnaissance. On the 13th and 14th he carried a portion of the enemy's first line of defenses at Drewry's Bluff with small loss. The time thus consumed lost us the benefit of the surprise and capture of Richmond and Petersburg, enabling Beauregard to collect his loose forces in North and South Carolina, and bring them to the defense of those places. On the 16th the enemy attacked General Butler [who] was forced back into his intrenchments between the forks of the James and Appomattox Rivers. His army, therefore, was as completely shut off from further operations directly against Richmond, as if it had been in a bottle, strongly corked.[34]

General Wild confiscated "two canes and a secession flag" from "Sherwood Forest," the former home of President John Tyler, and sent them to Butler. Wild suggested that these items be sent to Philadelphia for the Sanitary Commission Fair, because their sale could raise "a very large sum of money, for the benefit of our soldiers," and "the public good."[35]

Confederate Attacks against Butler's Forts on the James River

By mid–May 1864 it was evident that Wild's camp at Wilson's Wharf on the north bank where fortifications had only begun, and Fort Powhatan, seven miles upriver on the south side, could be attacked. Those posts protected Butler's vital line of communications on the James River, and General Wild and his USCT troops had stirred up a "hornet's nest" in Charles City County. On 13 May, Butler warned General Hinks at City Point: "Look out for Fort Powhatan; the rebel newspapers threaten to attack it." Hinks, in turn, informed Wild the same day that "an attack may be expected at Fort Powhatan." Hinks instructed Wild "in case an attack should be made to send one of your Regiments [1st or 22nd USCT] to the relief of the garrison immediately" [since the 37th Regiment, USCT had been transferred from Fort Powhatan to City Point on 8 May].[36] On 16 May, Hinks ordered Colonel Stafford to proceed to Wilson's Wharf with his 10th Regiment, USCT.[37]

On 18 May, an estimated 600 Confederates, with two 12-pounder howitzers, probed Hinks's [Col. Samuel A. Duncan's] Second Brigade at City Point but were driven off at the cost of two Union wounded. Colonel Duncan:

[T]he enemy made a demonstration against our works yesterday at 11 o'clock. Issuing suddenly and in force from the woods on the Petersburg road, he commenced a vigorous shelling of the reserve of our grand guard; at the same time throwing two squadrons of cavalry into line near his two pieces of artillery, and sending a few skirmishers down along the woods in our front, connecting with a body of 30 or 40 horsemen that appeared upon our left near the house of Mr. Livesay. Our picket-line was immediately disposed as skirmishers. A few well-directed shots from the battery of the enemy caused our right to fall back, which necessitated the retirement of the whole line.

They fell back in excellent order, and firing deliberately with some effect.... As soon as our line of skirmishers was retired, three of our guns replied. The gun-boats also came to our assistance, and a brisk cannonading ensued for half an hour, [after which] the enemy retired. As his force was mainly cavalry, it was impracticable to pursue him.

Captain Dollard went out far enough to get data from the inhabitants by which to estimate the force.... The enemy is believed to have had about 600 mounted men, a small force of infantry, one or two companies, and two 12-pounder howitzers. Most of our fire was well directed. Three or four saddles were emptied by our skirmishers, and some of our shells exploded in the immediate vicinity of the enemy's battery, causing him to move to the rear instantly. A shell from the gun-boats burst directly over the company of rebels near Livesay's, dispersing them at once.... About 6 p.m. a small force was seen by our videttes [mounted pickets] to return along the Petersburg road ... bringing with them three ambulances and one howitzer. The inhabitants stated ... this was for the purpose of removing their wounded, whom they had concealed in the woods.

It is hardly possible that the enemy escaped without considerable damage, subjected as he was to a cross-fire from the gun-boats, in addition to direct fire from our works, at a range of 1,000 yards.

Two of our men only are wounded, one very slightly in the face, the other more seriously in the fore-arm, both by fragments of shells. We fired 44 shots, 13 shells and 3 spherical case. Enemy fired 25 or 30, some exploded over works, most fell short. Much credit due [Navy] gunboats.[38]

General Wild Issues a Military "Code of Conduct" for Each of His Companies

On 20 May, after criticism he received from General Hinks and in the Richmond newspapers, and anticipating imminent combat against regular "armed rebels" and/or "guerrillas," Wild issued instructions "to be read by my company commander [of each company] to his men, with whatever comments may be necessary to make *everyone* understand *fully*:

You should kill all *armed* rebels, whether soldiers or citizens, who are offering resistance.

You should kill all *armed* rebels who are running away.

You should kill all prisoners who are attempting to escape, either by *running* or *fighting*.

You should *not* kill *un*armed rebels, who surrender themselves, nor those who are *not taken in arms*. After they once become prisoners, and do not attempt to escape, they should be regarded as helpless, like women and children.

You should *not* kill guerrillas, *until* it is *proved* that they have been guerrillas. *If found in arms*, it *is* proved at once by *the very arms* themselves, and you should kill them at once. If not found in arms, you should *wait* until it be proved that they *have* carried arms—that is, until they have been *tried* by *court-martial* and condemned—for fear that you may kill some innocent person.

A notation on the side of Wild's order explained that a "recent occurrence has made the issue of these instructions necessary."[39]

The Threats to Wild's Two Posts on the James River Increase

On 30 April, Confederate General Pierre Gustave Toutant Beauregard had sent his chief engineer, Col. David B. Harris, to inspect then-Confederate defenses at City Point and Fort Powhatan. Implementation of Col. Harris's recommendations to strengthen Powhatan and obstruct the James River with "torpedoes" (mines), however, was preempted by Butler's movement on 5 May.[40] On 19 May, after attacking to shorten his lines confronting Butler's force at Bermuda Hundred, General Beauregard wrote to General Braxton Bragg:

I propose to move with all available troops not required here to the south side of the Appomattox, thence down the south side of the James, and assail and carry by storm Fort Powhatan. This position fortified would enable us to cut off altogether water communications with the force operating in my present front.

This done, the enemy would, in my opinion, be forced to abandon this peninsula. Cannot the departure of the troops ordered from here be delayed until the execution of this plan?[41]

After apparently not getting a favorable response from General Bragg, on 21 May, Beauregard, whose 14,530 Confederate troops now confronted Butler, wrote directly to President Davis: [In order to drive Butler from his present position at Bermuda hundred] "send a force of about 4,000 or 5,000 to storm Fort Powhatan and establish there a battery of heavy guns, to command navigation of the James River at that point. This could be accomplished in a very few days ... then putting into the river torpedoes and rope obstructions under guns of the fort."[42]

The estimated "600 mounted men, a small force of infantry, one or two companies, and two 12-pounder howitzers" that "made a demonstration" on 18 May 1864, and "probed the outposts" at Fort Powhatan, probably came from Brig. Gen. James Dearing's recently organized brigade of cavalry, with two cannon. The "small force of infantry, one or two companies," may have been dismounted cavalrymen. James Dearing's cavalry brigade was organized pursuant to "Special Order No. 105 dated 5 May 1864."[43] On 21 May, General Beauregard reported that, besides 13,000 infantry in his Department of North Carolina and Virginia, he had the following "cavalry":

Three companies of [Col. Joel R. Griffin's] Sixty-second Georgia [2nd Georgia Cavalry]-	150
[Another] company of Sixty-second Georgia (2nd Georgia Cavalry)-	40
[Col. John A.] Baker [and his 3rd North Carolina Cavalry Regiment]-	450
	640
Shingler (about)-	40
[Total]-	680[44]

Colonel Joel R. Griffin's "Sixty-second Georgia Regiment (2nd Georgia Cavalry)" had been Brig. Gen. Edward A. Wild's antagonist in northeastern North Carolina. Wild had hanged "Guerrilla" Daniel Bright of Griffin's Company L, and Griffin had hanged Private Samuel Jordon, Company B, 5th Regiment, USCT in retaliation.

On 20 May 1864, General Butler wrote to Brig. Gen. George F. Shepley at Norfolk: "There are not [as many as] 1,000 rebel cavalry south of the James, and *they are Dearing's brigade,* jaded by a 200-mile march from [near New Bern] in North Carolina." On 21 May, Maj. Gen. H.C. Whiting wrote from Petersburg to "General [Beauregard]: ... *General Dearing moved down last night to reconnoiter Fort Powhatan"*[45] [probably with Col. Baker's 3rd North Carolina Cavalry].

At noon on 21 May, a hundred Confederate cavalrymen probed picket outposts at Fort Powhatan. They were checked until Federal infantry formed, and artillerymen drove them off. A larger force appeared in the afternoon. Colonel Joseph B. Kiddoo, 22nd Regiment, USCT, post commander, requested reinforcements from Wild at Wilson's Wharf. But Col. Kiddoo's artillery (from Battery M, 3rd New York Light Artillery) and ten shots from U.S. Navy Gunboat *Dawn* and four from the ironclad *Atlanta* down their flanks, drove off the Confederates. Colonel Kiddoo reported only two men wounded. One of them, on picket, after firing three times, "fenced with a rebel officer till he disabled the officer, and received a saber stroke across the face" himself.

The Confederates disappeared before General Wild arrived with his 1st Regiment. Wild rode the line at Fort Powhatan with Col. Kiddoo and concluded the Confederates had only been a "reconnoitering party." Wild returned to Wilson's Wharf with the 1st Regiment, USCT and a section (two guns) of Howell's Battery [M, 3rd New York Light Artillery Regiment] that Col. Kiddoo had commandeered from a transport passing from City Point to Wilson's Wharf. Colonel Kiddoo added: "I take pleasure in reporting that gunboats Atlanta and Dawn co-operate with me most cordially and faithfully in everything that pertains to safety of the post."[46]

The next day, 22 May, General Wild wrote to Captain Solon Carter: "We need [at Wilson's Wharf] both Heavy and Light Artillery. By special order just received, but one section of artillery and that Light and four companies of infantry is left with us here. If you have none to spare, please forward this to Department Head Quarters."[47]

General Hinks forwarded Wild's request for more artillery on 23 May, endorsed: "I have ordered one section of light artillery [two of Battery M's 10-pdr Parrotts] and four companies of infantry [from the 10th Regiment, USCT, which had only eight companies] *from Wilson's Wharf to Fort Powhatan* and directed that the transport *Wilson Small* be used to communicate and convey troops from one to another in case of attack. I recommend that *no heavy guns* be mounted at Wilson's Wharf.... *It does not appear that Wilson's Wharf is threatened by anything but Guerrillas who are not likely to use artillery.*" Butler referred the matter to his Chief Engineer, Brig. Gen. Godfrey Weitzel, who supported Hinks's view as late as 25 May.[48]

On 22 May, Brig. Gen. Hinks wrote about several matters from City Point:

> Regular daily communication by water is now established between all points occupied by my division.... Colonel Stafford has been relieved of the command at Fort Powhatan, and ordered with his regiment [10th USCT] to Wilson's Wharf.
>
> Colonel Kiddoo, commanding Twenty-second U.S. Colored Troops, has been stationed at Fort Powhatan. A detachment of the Third Pennsylvania Heavy Artillery, commanded by Capt. F. von Schilling, has been stationed at Fort Powhatan. I have now mounted at Fort Powhatan three 20-pounder Parrotts and one 4 1/2-inch siege gun, and one additional gun, [a] 32-pounder Rodman, mounted on my works at City Point. On the 16th instant a foraging party of 20 men, under command of Lieutenant Cunningham of the Thirty-seventh U.S. Colored Troops, sent out without orders from these headquarters, were attacked by a largely superior force with the loss of 1 killed, 4 wounded, and 2 captured. An investigation of the whole matter by a military commission is now in progress. The questionable behavior of Lieutenant Cunningham ... in this affair stands in strange contrast with the soldierly behavior of Sergeant Frazier, Fifth U.S. Colored Troops.[49]

Hinks ordered: "leave 2 sections [2 guns each] of Captain Howell's battery [M] Third New York Arty. at Fort Powhatan—*one section* [2 guns] *at Wilson's Wharf.*"[50]

While Union Generals Argue About Artillery, Confederate "Storm Clouds" Gather

Wild's futile request of 22 May for more artillery was already too late because Confederate cavalry units were gathering on the afternoon of 23 May to attack Wilson's Wharf, where construction of earthworks continued while "a strong detachment of troops" stood picket duty some distance away.[51] Fortunately for Wild, captured Richmond newspapers commenting bitterly on the presence of black troops also forewarned the U.S. Navy, and Acting Rear Admiral S.P. Lee stationed the gunboat USS *Pequot* above Fort Powhatan, the gunboat USS *Dawn* below Wilson's Wharf, and the captured Confederate ironclad USS *Atlanta* between the two.[52]

The subsequent "Action at Wilson's Wharf" would entail an attack by a much larger force of Confederate cavalry than the Union generals anticipated, and would come from an unexpected direction. *On 23 May, General*

The USS *Atlanta*, a captured Confederate ironclad which supported Wild's troops at Fort Powhatan. The former CSS *Atlanta*, a Scottish-built merchant vessel converted into a casemate ironclad at Savannah, Georgia, was captured by the U.S. Navy Monitor *Weehawken* when she ran aground in Wassau Sound and was later commissioned into the U.S. Navy in February 1864 (NARA File "Atlanta" [Confederate Ram] on the James River, NARA 527533jpg; National Archives and Records Administration, Washington, D.C.).

Braxton Bragg, military advisor to President Jefferson Davis, gave "verbal instructions" to Maj. Gen. Fitzhugh Lee to "surprise and capture if possible a garrison of Negro Soldiers at Kennon's [Wilson's] *Wharf on James River, in Charles City County." Lee: "My object was to break up the nest and stop their uncivilized proceedings in the neighborhood."*[53] Reports of General Fitzhugh Lee and his assistant adjutant general, Major J.D. Ferguson, provide Confederate perspectives about events, numbers of troops, etc., during the "Action."[54]

Fitzhugh Lee's Cavalry Division consisted of Brig. Gen. William C. Wickham's Brigade: 1st, 2nd, 3rd, and 4th Virginia Cavalry Regiments; and Brig. Gen. Lunsford L. Lomax's Brigade: 5th, 6th, and 15th Virginia Cavalry Regiments, from which were selected the best mounted men. The 3rd Virginia Regiment included Company D, the "Charles City Cavalry."[55] General Lomax remained behind in camp. In addition, Gordon's Brigade—1st, 2nd, and 5th North Carolina Cavalry Regiments, commanded by Col. Clinton M. Andrews; and the recently arrived 5th South Carolina Cavalry Regiment under Colonel John Dunovant—were attached to Lee's force. According to Major Ferguson, troops from Lomax's Brigade numbered 750; there were 800 from Wickham's Brigade; and 420 from Gordon's Brigade; for a *total of 1,970 well-mounted, mostly veteran cavalry from the three brigades,*[56] excluding the large 5th South Carolina Cavalry Regiment. Corporal Charles T. Price, Company C, 2nd Virginia Cavalry, recalled that "Fitz Lee had ten well-mounted and equipped men from each company in [Wickham's] brigade … to carry carbine, sabre and pistol and 125 cartridges."[57]

Assuming that a much smaller percentage of the thousand horses of the 5th South Carolina Cavalry had been disabled by the road march from South Carolina to Virginia because two-thirds of their riders came by train, compared to the nearly 60 percent of the 4th South Carolina Cavalry Regiment's horses that were disabled after all were ridden from South Carolina, and recovery of many of the 5th regiment's disabled horses after 2–3 weeks' rest, *an estimated 650 horses should have been healthy and available for Fitzhugh Lee's raid that began on the afternoon of 23 May 1864.* Douglas Southall Freeman states that at Hawe's Shop–Enon Church on 28 May (four days after the Action at Wilson's Wharf), "Hampton's Division supplied … from Calbraith Butler's reorganized Brigade, *the Fifth South Carolina and half of the Fourth … 1,100 finely equipped, well-mounted men.*[58] If the two regiments had approximately the same total number of men, the 5th South Carolina Cavalry Regiment could have numbered as many as 734 men on 28 August. *An estimate of about 650 men of the 5th South Carolina Cavalry Regiment leaving on the raid to Wilson's Wharf on 23–24 May seems reasonable, even conservative.*

On 23 May, Fitzhugh Lee left with the best mounted men in his division who remained after engagements with Grant's army and Sheridan's cavalry earlier in May had resulted in heavy losses in officers, men, and horses. The three Confederate cavalry brigades totaled 1,970 men; adding an *estimated 650 men* of the 5th South Carolina Regiment brings *Lee's total strength for the Action on 24 May to some 2,620 men, of whom one-fourth, or about 655 would be horse- holders for some 1,965 troopers who dismounted to fight.* (In some cases, however, it appears that a horse-holder held 5 or 6 horses, including his own, not 4.) *Shoemaker's battery of horse artillery sent along one gun under Lt. Marcellus Moorman, Virginia Military Institute Class of 1856.* Lee also would have brought along a few ambulances, supply wagons, and possibly a few slaves and hired free blacks who served as cooks, personal servants, or teamsters.

However, not everyone who started on the raid participated in the Action. Private James Michael Barr, Company I, 5th South Carolina Cavalry, wrote on 27 May: "I did not get to Charles City. My horse became very lame and *I was left behind with a good many others that were lame,* so *I was not nearer than five or six miles,* but was in the enemy's lines[?] for two days. We get very little corn for our horses and slim rations for ourselves."[59]

On 23 May, Captain and Assistant Adjutant General W.F. Hullehen wrote: "Colonel Critcher, Commanding Lomax's Brigade: I am directed by General Lomax to say that you are now in command of this brigade. You will go into camp on this place (Miss Crenshaw's), unsaddle tonight, and saddle at daylight. General Lomax's headquarters will be at Atlee's Station."[60]

General Lomax and two field officers thus did not accompany their men of the 5th, 6th, and 15th Virginia Regiments on the expedition; all three of his regiments had lost colonels during recent fighting and his detachments were commanded by captains.

Charleston Light Dragoons veteran Edward Wells described the Confederate cavalry at this time:

> *Most of the cavalry (of the Army of Northern Virginia),* with exception of the newly arrived Division [Wade Hampton's, including Butler's Brigade with the detached 5th South Carolina] from the South were well uniformed in gray jackets, and *were armed generally with breech-loading carbines captured from the enemy.* The fresh Division (Hampton's) were chiefly clad in "homespun," a brown cloth unserviceable, and very unsoldierly in style, and they carried muzzleloaders not quite as long as infantry [rifle-muskets]. Butler's Brigade was armed with sabres, and most of the men had revolvers, but the rifles carried by all (enlisted soldiers) were the important weapon.[61]

Not all of the cavalry in the Army of Northern Virginia were "armed generally with breech-loading carbines captured from the enemy," even in the veteran 2nd Virginia Cavalry. Private H. St. George Tucker Brooke of Company B wrote years later:

> On the 7th of May [1864], we fought [Hancock's Union Corps] all day. Our arms were greatly inferior to those of the enemy [he thought *incorrectly* that "most of their [Union] cavalry, which we fought most of the time, had seven-shooting breech-loading Spencer rifles ... that could shoot seven times without reloading while the Confederate cavalryman was loading his musketoon with just one cartridge]. Our cavalry, besides their sabres which were always left on the horses, we had revolvers and *musketoons*.
>
> A musketoon was a very short musket which the cavalry wore slung across their backs when on horseback. *It was a very indifferent weapon.... The musket[oon] was smoothbore....* In this battle of the Wilderness my musketoon became very foul with so much firing and my cartridge [with powder and bullet] became stuck in the barrel about half way down. [Next,] the iron ram rod stuck half way out of the muzzle of the gun. I hammered the ram rod against a tree to drive the cartridge down. The ram rod bent at [a] right angle and I could not straighten it out. I had to throw away the gun. But I picked up the musketoon of a man named [William H.] Stratton[62] in our company who had been killed. His gun had blood on the strap which was attached to hold it on the back of the cavalry when on horseback. I think I used Stratton's musketoon until I was shot off of my horse three weeks later [at Hawe's Shop on 28 May 1864.
>
> Brooke was also wounded in the left thigh at "Ft. Kennon" [Wilson's Wharf] on 24 May 1864].[63]

Brooke's "smoothbore musketoon" possibly was an early 19th century Virginia Manufactory flintlock musket that had been altered to percussion, had its barrel and forestock shortened, and was fitted with a leather sling.[64] Brooke soon used his "pick-up" and "indifferent" musketoon with deadly effect at about 13 yards—close range. He recalled:

> [A]s the two lines [of battle in the undergrowth] were perhaps within forty feet of each other ... a fierce fight commenced.... I was kneeling on one knee behind a tree, pressing the [musketoon] against the tree as a rest for the gun to steady my aim. The man next to me called to me, "Look out for that fellow behind that log; he is shooting at you." I took steady aim at the place and waited ... the blue cap rose slowly and cautiously above the log. Drawing sight fine I pulled my trigger. The cap fell; its wearer fired no more. This gallant fellow, lying flat on his stomach behind the log and resting his gun on the log had deliberately fired at me three times and had put three bullets in the tree not three inches above my head. I was the better shot.[65]

V

The Land-Naval "Action at Wilson's Wharf"

"From the accounts of every officer the negro troops behaved most splendidly."—Maj. Gen. Benjamin F. Butler to Secretary of War Edwin M. Stanton, 26 May 1864

After Brig. Gen. Edward A. Wild's U.S. Colored Troops landed on 5 May, the stage was set for the dramatic land-naval "Action at Wilson's Wharf" on 24 May 1864 ... where both forces of different types (infantry and cavalry), and different racial make-up, were led by experienced generals of vastly different backgrounds, experiences, politics, and temperaments. On 24 May, the officers and men on both sides who fought on land, and

U.S. Navy officers and sailors on gunboats, and civilians in transports on the James River, probably totaled about 4,500 in all. Accounts of the "Action" on 24 May from the Union side include reports of Generals Wild, Hinks, and Butler; U.S. Navy officers; two U.S. Army Signal Corps officers; correspondents from *Harper's Weekly* and the *New*

First Lieutenant John B. Moise was "present" with Co. A, 10th Regiment, U.S. Colored Troops, which was there all day of the Action on 24 May 1864 (Mass. Commandery, MOLLUS, United States Army Heritage and Education Center, Carlisle, PA).

York Times; a postwar paper by a Union officer, Edward Simonton, who commanded Company I of the 1st Regiment, U.S. Colored Troops; a postwar speech by William Davis Parlin, who commanded Company E, 1st U.S. Colored Troops; and unpublished notes by General Wild. Confederate accounts include official reports, newspaper accounts, and reminiscences by several individual participants in the Action.

Fitzhugh Lee's Movement from Atlee's Station to Wilson's Wharf

With the mission to "surprise and capture if possible a garrison of Negro Soldiers at Kennon's (Wilson's) Wharf," and his "object to break up *the nest* and stop them from uncivilized proceedings in the neighborhood," Lee left camp at Atlee's Station [northeast of Richmond] at 4 p.m. on 23 May. (There was no mention of establishing a post from which to interdict Union lines of communication on the James River.) Marching all night via Mechanicsville and Seven Pines to the Charles City Road, he reached Samaria (or St. Mary's) Church, a distance of 26 miles, after daylight. Lee wrote from "Samaria Church, May 24, 1864—5:30 a.m. General B. Bragg: I have reached this point and will push ahead to Kennon's on river. Reports from three different scouts report Sheridan's cavalry corps to have crossed Pamunkey near White House, going up through King William to Grant. I think it would be well to order *Lomax, commanding the remainder of my troops at Atlee's,* and all available cavalry at once up to General [R.E.] Lee, as a counteracting force. I can supply their places as I come back. Fitz. Lee, Major-General."[1] Later, Fitz Lee wrote that he "hoped to get in front of the [enemy] position by daylight, but the distance being much greater *than I had been led to expect*, my Advance did not get in sight of Kennon's [Wilson's Wharf] until 11 a.m. the next day" (24 May), after another march of "about 15 miles."[2]

Earlier, on the James River at 9:30 a.m. on Monday the 23rd, the gunboat USS *Dawn* "exercised crew at general quarters. Filled 17–100-Pdr and 10–20-Pdr shell."[3]

The Action Begins at Noon with Confederate Attacks on Pickets and Their Supports

Sergeant John Gill, Confederate Signal Corps, later wrote:

On May 23rd we were at Atlee's Station. In the afternoon we moved to Kenyon's [*sic*; Kennon's] farm, on the Lower James, opposite Brandon, for the purpose of breaking up an encampment of negro troops, who had fortified quite extensively [using later exaggeration] at a point known as Harrison's [*sic*; Wilson's] Landing. We reached the place about 1 o'clock. *I had command of* [Fitzhugh Lee's] *headquarters couriers in driving in the pickets and led the charge. Willie* [William Hamilton] *McFarland of Richmond, Va., a very warm personal friend of mine, and a member of my Signal Corps, killed a negro in this charge.* The rest surrendered without *further resistance.*[4] [Apparently, the pickets did "resist."]

On the 24th, "after marching all night and wading through swamps, [the Confederates] arrived in the vicinity of ['Fort Kennon'] about 11 o'clock in the morning."[5] The "Action at Wilson's Wharf" began about noon on 24 May with a mounted Confederate charge on the pickets and their supports posted some distance in front of the fort. Captain Stephen A. Boyden's Company F and Captain Giles H. Rich's Company C of the 1st Regiment, USCT were posted in support of the pickets and "decidedly checked" the Confederates, according to Wild,[6] or they were "immediately" (J.D. Ferguson, *Memoranda*) or "quickly" (Fitzhugh Lee, *Report*) driven in to the fortifications. Chaplain Henry M. Turner of the 1st Regiment, USCT watched what happened: [The officers] *"with their gallant companies, were at some distance in front [of the fort], skirmishing with the advance guard of the rebels. It was the grandest sight I ever beheld."* Chaplain Henry M. Turner also described what was happening at the fort:

> I was retiring from dinner, feeling very jolly … having eaten quite heartily of a fat chicken, &c., which is generally something special in camp, when my attention was called to the front of our works by a mighty rushing to arms, shouts of "The rebels! The Rebels! The Rebels are coming!" The long [drum] roll began to tell the doleful tale she never tells unless the enemy is about to invade our quarters. Then commenced another rush to arms, fearful in its aspect. Notwithstanding many were at dinner, down fell the plates, forks, and cups, and a few moments only were required to find every man, sick or well, drawn into the line of battle to dispute the advance of twice, if not thrice their number of rebels.[7]

Captain William Davis Parlin, like Captain Boyden a native of Natick, Massachusetts, later added more details about the earliest encounters on 24 May 1864:

> Capt. S.A. Boyden, formerly of Natick, commanded the left of the line [of the picket support]. His problem was to get his men into camp [i.e., inside the fortifications] after giving the alarm. We had no cavalry outposts. He [Boyden] says he had the feeling that we should be attacked that day and he went twice over his [picket] lines giving instructions [that morning, before the attack].
>   At the sight of the rebel advance, the outer post fired their guns and the whole line [of pickets] made for the camp [inside the fort]. But they were on foot where the rebels were mounted. Out came the rebel cavalry and away ran the men [of the pick-

ets] towards a common rendezvous about halfway to camp. They could not have reached it, but all at once out from a little body of woods covering [concealing] a ravine that made out into the plain, just at the right place [and at the right time] came a volley that checked the rebel advance. A dozen colored soldiers and one brave white officer (Capt. Boyden) had turned back to save their comrades. They made such a determined fight that the rebel advance halted, dismounted, & charged the thicket.

The time thus gained saved a score of lives. One man only was lost. Dempsey Maybee [or Maby, age 20, a farmer born in Elizabeth City, North Carolina, from Company F[7]], blackest of negroes, would not leave his post, saying no rebel should drive him, and he was killed. He was a hero. They were all heroes that day.[8]

Confederates Shoot Prisoners; One Is Returned to Slavery; Both Acts Are Atrocities in Violation of the Laws of War

Several Union soldiers of Company F, 1st Regiment, USCT on picket duty were cut off, captured and shot, and one prisoner returned to slavery. Fitzhugh Lee reported "prisoners," and Major J.D. Ferguson, Lee's assistant adjutant general, reported: "*A few negro prisoners were taken, some were shot attempting to escape, and but one was brought away and he was sent to his master in Richmond.*"[9] Col. John H. Holman, 1st Regiment, reported Private George Wilson, 19, Co. F: "Missing, was on picket at time of attack by rebels, never heard from," and a notation "Slave" appears on his regimental descriptive record, but he survived the war. Private James Connelly (or Conly), 21, Co. F, was shot in the "posterior right scapula" (back), but escaped. Privates Samuel Langley, Co. F, "shot in the head, skull fractured, died 1 August"; and Pvt. Dempsey Mabey (Maby), Co. F (above), "a brave soldier, shot through the breast,"[10] *apparently were shot at close range; i.e., possibly executed after capture.* Major Ferguson's matter-of-fact description "shot while trying to escape" probably is a cover-up of a Confederate atrocity in violation of the laws of war in effect even then. "Shot while trying to escape" has long been used by some soldiers and policemen as a euphemism to cover up their execution of prisoners. Ferguson's statement is especially suspect, considering that the prisoners were afoot at a distance from the fort, very unlikely to outrun mounted cavalrymen. Returning a captured soldier [Private George Wilson, 19 years old, Co. F, 1st Regiment, USCT who was on picket when captured] to slavery also was against the laws of war. Ferguson's *Memoranda* report confirms the worst fears of Wild and his officers and men about their possible treatment if captured individually, or surrendered *en masse.*

On 27 May 1864, the *Richmond Sentinel* reported: "We gather the

A Parrott 10-pounder rifled gun at the Chickamauga Battlefield Visitors Center, Georgia. Front view (top) and rear view (bottom). Two of these guns were used with deadly effect at Wilson's Wharf on 24 May 1864.

following particulars of the late affair in Charles City from a gentleman who accompanied the expedition…. *One or two negro soldiers* and *forty horses* [taken from farms and plantations?] *captured, with considerable loss in killed and wounded,* was all that was gained by the trip." The article ends with a list of names of 2 killed and 15 wounded in the 4th Virginia Cavalry.[11]

Thomas W. Colley, a former corporal in Company D, 1st Virginia Cavalry, which unit was probably first in Lee's force to approach the fort, recalled in a letter on 21 December 1904: "[O]n the 24th we went on [a] wild Goose Chase to Kennon's Landing on James River for the Purpose of capturing some *800 Negro Soldiers* who were reported to be there in a fort by *them selves,* when we made our attack on it we found it manned by *some 15000 white Soldiers*[!] … we made 3 assaults on it but were unsuccessful in our efforts … *we killed two negroes and captured one* [in the charge on the picket]."[12]

The Situation at Wilson's Wharf on 24 May 1864 from Both Sides' Perspectives

Wild's Federal garrison at the beginning of the Action consisted of the "1st (Infantry Regiment,) U.S. Colored Troops, four companies of the 10th U.S. Colored Troops, and a section [two guns] of the 3rd New York Artillery Regiment, about 1,100 men all told," according to 1st Lieutenant Edward Simonton of the 1st Regiment.[13] *General Wild reported he had 900 infantry*[14] (i.e., musket-armed "shooters") in the ten companies of the 1st Regiment, USCT and four companies of the 10th Regiment, USCT, which had replaced the 22nd Regiment, which had gone to Fort Powhatan during 17 or 18 May. According to company muster rolls for May–June, the 1st Infantry Regiment, USCT had 703 soldiers who carried muskets, but 64 of these men (9 percent) were sick (44), detached (16), or in confinement (4), which leaves *about 639 men* present for duty. The four companies of the 10th Regiment (A-82 men, C-84 men, D-70 men, and H-67 men) initially present had a total of 303 enlisted soldiers, of whom 4 were under arrest or in confinement, and at least 2 were sick, leaving about 297 men, to give General Wild *a total of about 936 musket-armed infantrymen in the two understrength regiments at noon on 24 May 1864,* not counting officers, artillerymen, signalmen, and perhaps a few attached pioneers.[15]

The 1st Regiment was armed with Springfield Model 1861/1863 .58 cal. rifle-muskets; the 10th Regiment had imported British Enfield Pattern 1853 .577 cal. rifle-muskets[16]; both weapons could fire the same ammunition.

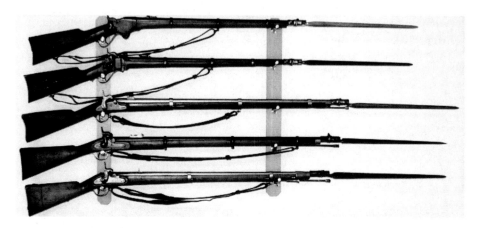

Weapons used by both sides during the Action on 24 May 1864, from top: (1) Spencer 7-shot repeating rifle; a captured one was carried by Pvt. Paul B. Means, Co. F, 5th North Carolina Cavalry. (2) Sharps breech-loading rifle; carbine versions and possibly some rifles were carried by Confederate cavalrymen. (3) Model 1861 .58 cal. rifle-musket, type issued to the 1st Infantry Regiment, USCT, this is a contract one manufactured in Trenton, New Jersey. (4) English Pattern 1853 .577 cal. rifle-musket, type issued to the 10th Infantry Regiment, USCT, and the 5th South Carolina Cavalry which also had carbine and rifle versions. (5) Austrian Lorenz Model 1854 .54 cal. rifle; captured or imported ones were used by some Confederate cavalry and infantry (from the Edwin W. and Donna S. Besch Collection).

Wild was supported by "efficient and undaunted" (Wild) Lieutenant Nicholas Hanson with his two Parrott 10-pounder rifled guns from Captain John H. Howell's Battery M, 3rd New York Light Artillery (which replaced a section of two 6-pounder howitzers from Battery B, 2nd U.S. Colored Light Artillery, which had landed on 5 May).[17] Wild reported on 25 May: "We might have slaughtered twice as many of them [by artillery fire], but we were at the time short of artillery ammunition (owing to the recent change of batteries at this post) of that particular caliber, and economized our stock, fearing a lengthened siege. This fault is since corrected."[18] The Signal Corps detachment led by 2nd Lt. Julius M. Swain would play key roles in communicating both with the gunboat USS *Dawn*, Navy Acting Lt. J.W. Simmons, and Fort Powhatan "under most discouraging circumstances," i.e., under fire from Confederate sharpshooters, and a thunderstorm.

The Action Begins in Earnest at Noon

In his immediate after-action report, General Wild stated: "I have the honor to report that this post was attacked yesterday at noon by a considerable force of the enemy, supposed to be cavalry, having three guns, probably horse artillery." He estimated Lee's cavalry force as being "at least double my own [i.e., about 2,000, only 30 off from Major Ferguson's total figure of 1,970 for the three Confederate brigades, but excluding the 5th South Carolina Regiment] and probably triple," or about 3,000, based on Confederate prisoners' statements about "detachments from three cavalry brigades, comprising all their available men."[19] The estimated total of about 2,620 Confederate cavalrymen (including an estimated 650 South Carolinians) actually present falls roughly between Wild's two estimated totals of Fitzhugh Lee's strength present.

An officer in the 1st Regiment, USCT who identified himself as "M.W.S."(probably 1st Lt. Myron W. Smith, the adjutant), penned a newspaper article on 26 May:

> We have had a fight with Fitzhugh Lee, and whipped him completely. He had 2,000 men.... We had *about 1,100 men* [in ten companies of the 1st Regiment, USCT, four companies of the 10th Regiment, USCT , and others]. He came down on our pickets, expecting to cut them off, and then surprise the camp. But he "reckoned without his host." The pickets [i.e., their support] fought them for half an hour and emptied several saddles. In the meantime, we, hearing the firing, formed line of battle in the trenches and waited for the pickets to come in. As soon as they were in the works we opened on the rebs. They then sent in a flag of truce demanding an immediate surrender.[20]

Fitzhugh Lee later downplayed his own strength and overestimated, or exaggerated, that of Wild's infantry garrison, his supporting artillery, one U.S. Navy gunboat initially, and transports:

> My total was about 1,600. It is proper to say that [Wild's] numbers were *represented to be* about 1,500 [a realistic total if all eighteen companies of the entire 1st and 10th Regiments, USCT were initially present, but four companies of the 10th Regiment were at Fort Powhatan and returned later during the Action at 4 p.m.] encamped only behind rifle pits [true, on two-thirds of the fort], and upon that data the expedition was planned.... The force of the enemy as reported by prisoners consisted of the *4th, 10th, and 22nd Regiments of Colored troops*, with one [entire 4- or 6-gun] battery (white) and two [*sic*; one] gunboats when I first arrived. They were reinforced before I could attack by a number [two] of transports (reported as five) *bearing white* [*sic*; black] *troops* from a neighboring fort *across* [*sic*; 7 miles up] the river. Their colored regiments were exceedingly large, the *three* I was informed numbering over 2,500 men.[21]

The Union "prisoners" may have assisted their comrades *if they identified three* USCT *regiments*, two of which had no troops at Wilson's Wharf, and thus exaggerating Wild's actual strength by two and a half times. The "white battery" was only a section of two guns, not six guns; there was only one gunboat, the USS *Dawn*, initially present. Although some *unarmed* white troops were taken off passing steamers, the armed reinforcements that arrived later were U.S. Colored Troops. It was clearly humiliating for Major General Fitzhugh Lee to admit that his proud cavalrymen, recruited from the cream of Southern chivalry, were beaten by black Union soldiers, many of whom were former slaves.

On 24 May, the Union fortifications at Wilson's Wharf were incomplete. Then-Lieutenant Edward Simonton, Co. I, 1st Regiment, USCT recalled: "*Along one-third of the line ran a ditch* 8 feet wide and 5–6 feet deep [but] *along the remaining part* [*there*] *was no ditch at all*; abatis constructed simply of felled trees with trimmed branches and limbs [was] placed outside the ditch. *Our intrenchments were only about one-third completed* when General Lee's force came upon us so suddenly. Along the unfinished portion of our line, the enemy could easily and successfully have charged upon [and over?] the works, but our men were ready for them."[22]

The *Richmond Sentinel* of 27 May 1864, however, exaggerated them: "Gen Fitz Lee then charged *their works*; but when, the men reached them, they could not enter, as they *were thrown up seven feet high, and surrounded with a deep ditch, which could not be crossed*, and our men had to retire over an open field, under a heavy fire from the gunboats, field artillery and small arms."[23]

Confederate Artillery Present; "Did Not Fire Any"

Wild reported on 25 May: [Confederates] "having three guns, probably horse artillery." But Admiral S.P. Lee wrote to the Secretary of the Navy: "Wild says enemy *used* (i.e., fired] *no artillery*"; perhaps Lee moved his one gun (see below) around so that Wild thought Lee brought three guns, but the cannon crew apparently couldn't find a suitable position to shoot from without hitting fellow Confederates. On 21 September 1864, Major John J. Shoemaker reported about his battery's participation: "On the 22nd [of May 1864] we moved to Atlers [Atlee's] Station, Va. Cen. RR & on the 23rd *one gun* under command of Lieut. [Marcellus] Moorman with a portion of Gen. Wickham's Brig. marched all that night & arrived near Fort Cannon [*sic*; Kennon—Wilson's Wharf] on James River at 10 a.m. the next day, a distance of 55 miles. It was under fire of the enemy's *batteries* [*a section of two* 10-pounder Parrott guns] for near 3 hours but *did not fire any*. No casualties. It started back about 2 p.m. and reached camp near Hanover C.H. the next day."[24]

The Action Continues

Fitzhugh Lee described the Action after the Federal pickets and advanced posts were driven in to the fortifications:

A close reconnaissance developed their main body strongly intrenched in a Fort. *A wide ditch ran along the entire front with steep scarp and counterscarp, & strong abatis in front.* Its wings rested on the river, upon which in close proximity floated *two* gunboats. Though a very different state of things existed than was *represented by citizens, upon whose accounts the Expedition had been sent,* I nevertheless resolved to make *an attempt* for the capture of the place, now that the march had been made.

My command had been divided into two detachments. The troops from Wickham's Brigade, being commanded by that officer, and those from Lomax's, Gordon's, and the 5th S.C. being placed under Col. Dunnovant [*sic*]. Gen. Lomax had been left at Atlee's [station] in command of the camp and remaining troops. I then moved up, dismounted my command, and invested the work. A staff officer was sent to demand a surrender.[25]

Major Ferguson's *Memoranda* states: "Deploy Wickham's and Dunovant's *commands* in line of skirmishers and advance on the works, but finding them too strong, dismount more men and make a demand for surrender of the place."[26]

After Lee initially divided his command into "two detachments ... Wickham's *Brigade*, being commanded by [Brig. Gen. William C. Wickham]; and *those from Lomax's* [and] *Gordon's* [Brigades], *and the Fifth South Carolina* [Regiment], being placed under Col. Dunovant ... and then moved up, dismounted my command, and invested the work.... After a parley ... Wickham's *detachment* under that officer moved ... to the eastern or lower side [of the fort], with orders to assault it." After Wild refused to surrender, Lee evidently decided to reinforce Wickham's Brigade with Gordon's Brigade, based especially on Private Paul B. Means's account of assaulting the fort with the 5th North Carolina Cavalry on the Confederate extreme left, nearest the James River. After one of every four or five men remained behind as horse-holders, Wickham's dismounted assault detachment probably numbered as follows:

Wickham's "command" or "detachment" minus horse-holders, consisted of:

Wickham's Brigade (800 men in all): *600 men*
Gordon's Brigade (420 men in all): *315 men*
Assault detachment total: *915 men* (of 1,220 present)

Col. Dunovant's "detachment" minus horse-holders, finally consisted of:

Lomax's Brigade (750 men in all): *562 men*
5th SC Cavalry (estimated 650 men): *488 men*
Diversionary Attack detachment total: *1,050 men* (of about 1,400 present)

Brigadier General William Carter Wickham, CSA, was the colonel of the 4th Virginia Cavalry Regiment. He commanded Fitzhugh Lee's left-wing "detachment," which assaulted Wild's strong right flank (Library of Congress, Washington, D.C.).

Wild initially had about 936 infantrymen to defend against Lee's approximately 1,965 dismounted cavalrymen of an estimated total of 2,620 men, minus men whose horses had broken down en route, and a few casualties, giving Lee about a 2:1 numerical superiority. Fitzhugh Lee later claimed *"My total force* was about *1,600."* Lee assigned his seven most experienced regiments, armed with short-ranged carbines or "musketoons," pistols, and sabres in the assault force under his most experienced and trusted officer, and he assigned his three other Virginia cavalry regiments, all led by captains, and the 5th South Carolina Cavalry under a senior but untried colonel to make the diversionary attack. General Wild: "A large portion of the [Confederate] force dismounted and made their approach more cautiously. They encompassed our front, and filling the wood on the river bluff to the north [west], tried to stop all communication with steamers [from below the fort or from Fort Powhatan upriver] coming to our aid, and harassed our landing place. They also made it uncomfortable for the gunners to serve their pieces [cannon] on our gunboats."[27]

The Gunboat USS Dawn *Provides Effective Naval Gunfire Support While Also Under Fire*

The key U.S. Navy player in the Action was the gunboat USS *Dawn*, commanded by Acting Volunteer Lieutenant J.W. Simmons. The *Dawn* was built in New York in 1857 as a screw steamer 154 feet long, with a 28-

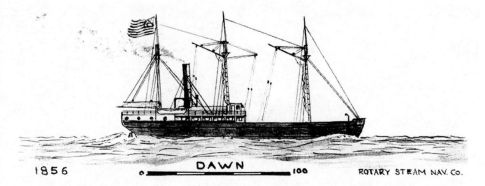

The civilian steamship *Dawn* (1856), later the gunboat USS *Dawn*. Watercolor by Erik Heyl (photograph #NH 66961, Naval Historical Center, Washington, D.C.).

foot beam, 12-foot draft, and 399 tons displacement. In an early drawing she appears ungainly, with a superstructure aft and forward cargo compartment. The *Dawn* was chartered, then later purchased by the U.S. Navy in 1861. She served with the Potomac Flotilla, the South Atlantic Blockading Squadron, and in coastal waters off South Carolina, Georgia, and Florida, assisting in capture of several Confederate blockade runners. She and her crew had captured three ships, exchanged fire with shore batteries, and participated in an attack on Fort McAllister, Georgia.[28]

On the James River, Tuesday, 24 May 1864, began uneventfully for the *Dawn*. Her Log states:

Tuesday, 24 May
12 to 4 AM heard firing upriver
4–8–8–12 at 9:30 inspected crew at quarters
9:50 Tug, "Young America" came alongside and delivered two barrels of beans from the "Atlanta" 11 Officers on a survey recommended that one barrel Flour, 114 lbs Pickels, two kegs 2 Bbls beans 50 lbs Butter 5 lbs Sugar to be thrown overboard.
12–6 Watch 12 to 1.30 an alarm...

At 1 p.m., J.A. Jackaway recorded weather conditions in the log of the USS *Dawn*: "Wind SW, Force 2 (kts), Weather B (Bright), Temperature 80 (degrees F.), Barometer 29.18" (at Noon)." He remarked: "12 to 1.30 an alarm from the fort at Wilsons Landing / hove up anchor and beat to quarters / then shell to westward of the fortification until 4 p.m. / received a galling fire from the enemys [*sic*] Sharpshooters on the bank of the river / shifted our position to the Eastward."[29]

Correspondent "M.W.S." continued his letter to the Washington *Daily Morning Chronicle*:

The ten-gun USS *Mendota*, looking forward, with the crew mustering by one of its two Parrott 100-pounder rifled guns. The USS *Dawn* carried one Parrott 100-pounder rifled gun and fired it with dramatic effect on 24 May 1864 (Mass. Commandery, MOLLUS, Vol. 15, p. 713; United States Army Heritage and Education Center, Carlisle, PA).

> General Wild answered the message [the surrender demand from Fitz Lee], "We will try it." While this parley was going on, the rebels were getting into position, and as soon as the flag was carried back, commenced a very lively firing. We opened with our artillery (two 10-pounder Parrotts), and, with the assistance of the guns on the steamer *Dawn*, drove the enemy back into the woods. They then began flank movements on both sides of us, so as to rake our line of works. It therefore became necessary to have the gunboat shift her position, so as to rake the rebs. General Wild sent me off in a small boat with the message, and as the river bank was lined with sharpshooters, I had a very hot sail.[30]

Lieutenant Simmons and his crew of some 62 Navymen (*of whom 30.5 percent of the 59 enlisted men were described as "Negro" or "Mulatto"*[31]) on the 154-foot gunboat USS *Dawn* actively supported Wild's troops from the river. The ship's gunners drove off sharpshooters (probably from the 5th SC Cavalry, armed with Enfield rifle-muskets or rifles) in the woods on the river bank west of Wild's position who had "showered with musketry" gunners on the exposed deck of the USS *Dawn*, and fired on the transport *Mayflower*. Then, Lt. Simmons reported: "The firing having almost ceased on our right [eastern] flank, I altered the position of this vessel, and commenced shelling the enemy just as they were making a charge, which drove them back, and, as Gen. Wild tells me, ended a sharp action of five and a half hours."

Lt. Simmons reported expending the following ammunition during the Action at Wilson's Wharf: "*100-pdr rifle:* 46 rds percussion shell; *20-pdr rifle:* 34 rds percussion shell, one 10-second shell; *rifled 12-pdr howitzer:* 11 rds percussion shell, 3 rds canister, 2 rds grape [shot]. Making 118 rds expended.... I have only 17 rds remaining." Simmons "very respectfully request[ed] that if I had two 32-pdrs in addition to my present battery, I could do much more service.... I am anxious to get a supply [of ammunition] as soon as possible."[32] Lieutenant Simmons clearly was a Naval Officer in the mold of John Paul Jones, wanting only more guns and ammunition so he could do more damage to the enemy. He also noted the heroic performance of his other officers and the crew:

> The officers and crew behaved finely, Acting Ensigns William B. Avery, E.T. Sears, and P.W. Morgan serving their different guns with great coolness and energy, although the enemy's sharpshooters were throwing musket shot over and at us continually. I take great pleasure in reporting to you the noble and gallant conduct of my executive officer, Acting Master J.A. Jackaway, in shifting my position to follow the enemy. The vessel got very near a shoal in the river and was compelled to turn by backing for the purpose of getting my guns to bear on the sharpshooters, who were completely showering us with musketry. Mr. Jackaway did the duties of pilot, thus getting the vessel in position, and eventually driving the enemy away and saving that [left or western] flank of our troops. I do think he deserves promotion if noble and gallant conduct and strict attention to duty merit such a reward. I am happy to report no casualties on board.[33]

A Virginia cavalryman described effects of 100-pounder naval gunfire: "Each of four [*sic*; of one, later two] gunboats threw large caliber shells that were great black masses, as big as nail kegs, hurling in the air and making the earth tremble under us and the atmosphere jar and quake around us where they burst."[34]

Confederate Major Ferguson stated, however, that: "*Two [sic; one] gunboats were found in support of the place when we arrived, but did no damage, their firing being too high.*"[35] Whether or not the naval guns of the USS *Dawn*, and later, the USS *Young America*, inflicted any Confederate casualties cannot be resolved from conflicting reports. But the screeching shells passing overhead or exploding nearby must have been very discouraging to those Confederates attacking near the river who were also receiving small arms fire, and very encouraging to Wild's outnumbered soldiers.

Communication between Wild's garrison on shore and the U.S. Navy gunboat on the river was essential to providing effective naval gunfire, and coordination with Fort Powhatan seven miles upriver by signal was necessary to request other support. Lieutenant Swain, Wild's Signal Officer, stated:

> My [Signal] station is on the bank of the river, within ten yards of our rifle pits, and during three hours of the attack served as a prominent mark for the enemy. I sent Private Mott with one man on the gunboat [USS *Dawn*], and until 5 o'clock we were enabled to direct the fire of the [*Dawn*'s] guns and communicate with Fort Powhatan. Our [signal] flag was in sight, but we were screened from view [of the Confederates] by a projection from the river bank.
>
> [About 5 PM,] A detachment of the enemy, about 100, gained possession of the heavy-timbered point on [above] the river, not more than 70 yards from the [signal] station, and opened fire on us so fiercely that we were forced to abandon our post and seek protection behind the earthworks. After half an hour's delay, I opened station on board a transport near the wharf, and was enabled to direct the fire from the gunboat [USS *Dawn*] in the river so successfully that they materially checked the enemy's movements on our right [eastern side].[36]

Soon after the Action began, the mailboat steamer *Thomas Powell*, on its way from Fort Monroe to Bermuda Hundred, was stopped by Wild's adjutant on the wharf. Wild:

> During the afternoon we stopped passing steamers, claiming their aid, and calling ashore all troops aboard them, took them into our service, arming some with guns of our wounded men and other spare guns [possibly as many as 130 muskets *may* have been "spare"], and working them in various ways. We were greatly indebted to volunteers—artillerymen of the First Connecticut Heavy Artillery—for taking the place of several men who had dropped from the heat, and one who was shot [Pvt. John Taylor, who was wounded in the face], under the direction of the efficient and undaunted Lieutenant Nicholas Hanson, of Howell's Battery [M, 3rd New York Light Artillery Regiment].[37]

Among the men on the *Thomas Powell*, which had a capacity of 1,000 men,[38] were: "6 enlisted men of the First Connecticut Artillery, returning from volunteer furlough. Although no officers were present, these men volunteered to serve a 10-pdr Parrott then silenced, and did so, so effectively as to contribute materially to the repulse of the rebels. They fired about 80 rounds, some being double-shotted canister, at about 200 yards range, and their gun was the only one not silenced by the enemy."[39] The Friday, 27 May, *New York Times* reported that the *Thomas Powell* added 150 men under a lieutenant colonel to Wild's garrison. They "were on their way to join various regiments to which they belonged ... *the women and children of the post, about 50,* then came on board the *Powell* to go to Bermuda Landing."[40] The cowardly white chaplain from the 10th Regiment, USCT also hopped aboard the steamer.[41]

Fitzhugh Lee's Two Surrender Demands and General Wild's Final Defiant Reply: "Present my compliments to General Fitz Lee and tell him to go to hell."

Chaplain Turner, 1st Regiment, USCT: "By the time our pickets [and their support] had been driven in, a flag of truce was seen waving in the distance, when General Wild gave orders to cease firing. Lieutenant Colonel Wright was immediately dispatched to meet it."[42] About 1:30 p.m., General Fitzhugh Lee sent forward a surrender demand under a flag of truce. General Wild retained the surrender note and forwarded it to Butler's Headquarters; Wild wrote:

> [A]fter fighting an hour and a half, they sent forward a Flag of Truce with a note containing a summons to surrender, in the name of Maj. Gen. Fitz Lee. (This note and the reply are appended below.) This note was forwarded to Dept. Headquarters yesterday....
>
> *Lee' Note.* May 24th 1864.
> By command of Major-General Fitz Lee, I am sent to demand the surrender of the Federal Troops at Wilson's Wharf. He (Genl Lee) thinks he has troops enough to carry the position. Should they surrender, they will be turned over to Authorities at Richmond, and treated as prisoners of war. Should they refuse, Genl. Lee will not be responsible for the consequences.
>
> Very respectfully your obedient servant,
> To R.J.* Mason. Major & A.I.G. [assistant inspector general]
> Brig. Gen. Wild, Com' Federal Troops
> [*Wild mistakenly transcribed Major Mason's middle initial "F." as "J."]
> *My Reply.* We will try it.
> Edwd A. Wild. Brig. Gen. Vols.[43]

Lieutenant Hiram W. Allen, on Wild's staff, copied the surrender note as above, with the exception of "R.*F.* Mason" (Major Robert French Mason was from Charlottesville, and Quartermaster to Brig. Gen. Wickham). Fitzhugh Lee simply reported: "A staff officer was sent to demand a Surrender. After a parley, its commander, Genl. Wilde [*sic*], decided, as he expressed it, 'to try and hold it.' This occurred about 1:30 p.m."[44] The actual circumstances were considerably more dramatic and threatening than Fitzhugh Lee reported. Memories on the Federal side were exact and vivid.

Lee's threat: "If the surrender of the Federal forces is made, the soldiers will be taken to Richmond and treated as prisoners of war. But if they do not surrender, Gen. Lee will not be answerable for the consequences." Union 1st Lt. Simonton later noted that no promises were made concerning the (white) officers, and he stated "which language [of Lee's surrender summons] was interpreted by us to mean that *their success and our failure meant another Fort Pillow massacre.*"[45]

Lieutenant Allen stood beside General Wild and copied his reply: "Without a moment's hesitation, Gen. Wild took from his pocket a used envelope, tearing a piece therefrom wrote with a pencil: '*We will try it*' [a phrase he used as a student at Harvard before attempting a difficult problem], and signing same, sent it back as his answer." General Wild also reported officially: "I declined."[46]

The 11 June 1864 *Harper's Weekly* stated: "Lee sent a flag, stating that he had enough force to take the place, demanded its surrender, and in that case the garrison should be turned over to the authorities at Richmond as prisoners of war; but if this proposition would be rejected he would not be answerable for the consequences when he took the place. General Wild replied, 'We will try *that*.'"

Lieutenant Allen's letter to then-1st Lieutenant, later Brevet Lt. Col. Simonton, written "38 years" after (in 1902) states: "[O]ne's memory can rarely be depended upon for that length of time.... The quotations from the letter accompanying the flag of truce [in a preceding paragraph] from the enemy may be depended upon as literally correct, for I copied the same from that letter, as also the reply of Gen. Wild 'to try and hold it,' by whose side I was standing as he wrote the reply, and I made a note of the exact phraseology of both."[47]

New York Times correspondent "HJW" wrote that he also "...saw [Lt. Allen's] copy of the note Lee sent to Wild demanding the surrender of the garrison. It was deceptively worded, but Wild saw through it at once. Instead of saying the garrison, in case of surrender, *should be treated as prisoners of war*, Lee said they *should be handed over to the authorities at Richmond as prisoners of war.* The 'as' is a neat little subterfuge ... the loop-hole out of which the Richmond authorities would have crawled if Wild had been foolish enough [to surrender]."[48] Before results of the Action were known there, the *New York Times* of 27 May stated: "The colored soldiers don't expect quarter, and are not likely to give it."[49]

According to a postwar Southern source, Irving P. Whitehead, son of Major Thomas Whitehead, who commanded the 5th Squadron, "composed of Companies E and G," of the 2nd Virginia Cavalry, and who wrote "I know so many of my father's old squadron [members] intimately [and probably also Col. Thomas T. Munford], and I have talked with them so much about the war," wrote about Fitzhugh Lee's *two demands for surrender*:

> On the 24th, Gen. Fitz Lee conducted an expedition of a select body of men against Fort Kennon…. Fitz Lee sent Major Mason of his staff forward under a flag of truce with a demand for immediate surrender of the Fort. The Federal officer in command [Wild] received Major Mason and detained him in the Fort for some time and then dismissed him with a reply that the Confederate General must give him better terms. In the meantime the Federal officer had been signaling the gunboats [*sic; one* gunboat] in the river to come to his assistance and they [only the USS *Dawn*] were now moving up the stream [the *Young America* came *down* the river at 4 p.m.].
>
> Upon receiving this report, *Gen. Fitz Lee became very angry and sent Major Mason back with a reply that unless the Fort was surrendered in ten minutes, he would capture it and put its garrison to the sword.* The Federal officer [Wild] in turn said to Major Mason: *"Present my compliments to Gen. Fitz Lee and tell him to go to hell."* … Upon receiving this message, Fitz Lee ordered his troops [i.e., Wickham's and Gordon's brigades to assault] against the eastern side of the Fort and when they came in sight, the negro soldiers speedily hid themselves from view [behind the fortifications existing on that side]. The Confederates rushed forward, but alas, when they reached the fort, they found it surrounded by a deep moat filled with water [there had been a thunderstorm] which barred their way.[50]

Not mentioning Major Robert French Mason, Signal Corps Sergeant John Gill wrote later:

> I carried a message from General Lee, under flag of truce [the first time], to the commander of the fort, to surrender. This was refused by Brigadier General Wild, in command, and I was told to say to General Lee, "Take the fort if you can."
>
> The garrison consisted of three [at this time one and a half] regiments of colored troops, and a number of transports and gunboats [which he couldn't have seen or counted] were in the river in reserve.
>
> On my return I was asked if the fort could be taken, and I replied that it could not. I had been so close to it, surrounded as it was by a moat[?], that my mind was quickly made up that any attempt, even to attack, would prove disastrous. However, the order was given to dismount, and *two lines* were formed. [Wickham's on the left and Dunovant's on the right, or one line behind the other for the assault on Wild's right?] As we approached the fort, *the negroes with uncovered heads,* rose above the intrenchments and leveled their guns upon us. *I could see the glint of the sun reflected on their teeth* [that's really close to them!] and their polished rifle barrels. Then came a cloud of smoke, [and] *bullets whizzed through our ranks, and the men in our lines tumbled over each other, some forward, some backward. Our fire was ineffective, and they poured volley after volley into our waning ranks.* Finally, our lines broke and retreated, and we *left many dead and wounded on the field.*[51] [Most probably were removed by the Confederates under a flag of truce at the end of the action.]

Naval Drama: Senior Officers at Fort Powhatan Delay Sending Support to Wilson's Wharf; a U.S. Navy Ensign Takes Charge on the James River

Dramatic events occurred on the James River during the land Action on the bluffs above. First one, then later two U.S. Navy gunboats provided naval gunfire support while Army transports brought reinforcements to Wild's garrison at Wilson's Wharf. At Fort Powhatan, Navy Lt. Cdr. Stephen P. Quackenbush, captain of the USS *Pequot*, was ashore when the post commander (Col. Kiddoo) received a signal at 12:30 p.m. from General Wild that Wilson's Wharf was being attacked. But the two officers cautiously "supposed that the attack on Wilson's Wharf was a feint to draw forces from this place while an attack should be made in force here" [at Fort Powhatan], as [signal] communication was prevented [by an "interrupting thunderstorm"]. Lieutenant Commander Quackenbush delayed sending assistance until 3 p.m., when he sent the Army tug *Johnson* to tow the armed tug USS *Young America*, with its disabled engine, to the scene of action so her guns might be used if needed.[52]

The former Confederate tug *Young America* was captured by the Union Navy sloop-of-war *Cumberland* in Hampton Roads on 24 April 1861 as the tug attempted to help a blockade-running schooner enter the James River. The prize tug was a screw steamer built in 1855 at New York City, and the *Cumberland* used her as a tender. *Young America* performed invaluable service during engagements with CSS *Virginia* in March 1862. On 7 January 1864 the armed tug finally was purchased by the Navy from the Boston prize court. *Young America* was assigned to captured Confederate ironclad ram *Atlanta* for use as a tug on 9 April 1864 and it "assisted troops under General Wild in repulsing a Confederate attack upon Wilson's Wharf, James River, Va. On 24 May 1864." The 173-tonnage steamer tug had a draft of 10 feet, 6 inches, and was armed with one 30-pdr Parrot rifle, one 32-pdr gun, and one 12-pdr rifle.[53] The USS *Young America* carried an enlisted crew of 18 men, of whom 5 (28 percent) were listed as former "Contrabands" (runaway slaves), but the terms were later marked out with an "X."[54]

The log of the U.S. tug *Young America* states:

May 23rd Weather Clear wind East 7 p.m.
   Went on Picket off Fort Powhatan Wharf.
   T.S. Sullivan

May 24th Weather Misty wind S.E. at 11.30 a.m.
blew down all steam and water at 3 p.m.
got orders to proseed [*sic*] to Wilson's Wharf to shell the woods with the Dawn
T.S. Sullivan
May 25th Weather Clear Westerly wind at 7 a.m.
left Wilson's Landing and came to our Station off Fort Powhatan.
T.S. Sullivan[55]

A cautious Quackenbush also sent Acting Ensign William F. Chase from the USS *Pequot* on the transport *Mayflower* (or *May Flower*) to Wilson's Wharf "to learn from the general [Wild] if the attack was in force, and if *Dawn* needed aid." Ensign Chase performed admirably. Lieutenant Commander Quackenbush: "I take pleasure in mentioning the gallant conduct of Acting Ensign William F. Chase, of this vessel. When the captain and pilot of the *Mayflower* were struck down helpless with wounds at his side he took the wheel, went in to the wharf, and went on shore in obedience to orders, although a storm of bullets was rained on the vessel and wharf from the enemy's line [of 5th South Carolina Cavalry sharpshooters] near by." Ensign Chase also hailed the *Dawn*, whose captain wanted assistance in providing fire support to Wild's garrison. Chase then went on shore and learned that Wild had repeatedly signaled to Fort Powhatan for gunboats, and that he needed help at once. When Ensign Chase returned later aboard the *Mayflower*, which was commandeered to carry wounded, at 6 p.m., Lt. Cdr. Quackenbush "immediately" [i.e., finally] got the *Pequot* underway for Wilson's Wharf, "but the enemy had disappeared about an hour before my arrival."[56]

In his second report, to Admiral S.P. Lee on 26 May, Quackenbush claimed his warning to post commanders and arrangements in positioning the gunboats "I understand tended in a great measure to the repulse of the enemy," in a lame effort to excuse himself for his own powerful ship's (the USS *Pequot*) missing the entire action and an attempt to claim credit.[57]

Paymaster Calvin Gibbs Hutchinson wrote in his diary aboard the *Pequot*: "The Pequot was a new screw propeller [ship] of a beautiful model & built at the Charleston Navy Yard fitting out at Boston Sept 1863, also had 2 masts, rigged like a topsail schnr, 539 tons OU, carried two pivot and ten broadside guns (1x 150-pdr, 1x 30-pdr Parrott rifle, 6x 32-pdrs, 2x 24-pdrs, and 1x 12-pdr rifle), crew 180 men—one of the fastest sailors of her class." The *Pequot* carried a 116-man enlisted crew of whom 23 men (19.8 percent) were described as "Negro."[58] Paymaster Hutchinson continued: "[O]n May 24th, Fitzhugh Lee's rebel cavalry attacked the post at Wilson's Landing on the north side and lower down the river, but were beaten off by Genl Wild's negro troops *before the Pequot arrived*. [Earlier,] Ensign Chase of the Pequot was sent in a tug [or "transport *Mayflower*"] to communicate with Genl Wild and in doing so *the Cap't and Mate of the tug were shot by the enemy whose fire enfiladed the wharf* but Mr Chase steered the boat to it; walked ashore through the fire unharmed and *was promoted to Master*."[59]

Reinforcements (4 Companies of the 10th Regiment, USCT) Finally Are Sent from Powhatan

Wild: "Afterwards, '*at 4 o'clock,*'[60] *a steamer* [the *George Washington*] *came down from Fort Powhatan, bringing back to us 4 companies* [of the 10th Regiment, USCT] *whom we had sent up some hours before* [the attack] on order of Hinks. These troops, sailing along in front of the bank [upriver from Wilson's Wharf] peppering the rebels handsomely, and in conjunction with a few more shells from the gunboat *Dawn* drove them out."[61] Lieutenant Colonel E. Henry Powell, who had been sent to Fort Powhatan with the four companies, later recalled: "Wilson's Landing, which we had just left, was attacked by Fitzhugh Lee's whole division. Having marched up the hill [to Fort Powhatan, located on a high, steep bank on the south side of the James River] we at once marched down again, and embarked for home *just as the second charge was being successfully repulsed*. As usual, 'the Colored Troops fought nobly,' but to a large extent we were not 'in it.'"[62]

After the remaining four companies of the 10th Regiment, USCT arrived "at 4 o' clock" and were deployed in the fort, Wild's musket-armed "shooters" would have consisted of the original "900" or about 936 men of the 1st Regiment, USCT and 4 companies (A, C, D, and H) of the 10th Regiment who were at Wilson's Wharf all day, plus about 130 men who came off the *Thomas Powell* sometime after noon of whom "some [100?] were armed with spare guns" (Wild), and about 253 more men in the remaining four companies (B-90 men, E-64 men, F-65 men, and G-34 men)[63] of the 10th Regiment, USCT who arrived after 4 p.m., bringing the new total to about 1,289 "shooters" armed with muskets, minus casualties, and a possible total altogether of about 1,400 to 1,450 white officers and black and white enlisted Union soldiers.

A Fight to the Finish: Lee Assaults on Wild's Stronger Right and Feints on Wild's Weaker Left; Personal Accounts by Confederate Veterans

Goaded by Wild's reply to his surrender demand, Lee sent Wickham with his own men and Gordon's North Carolina Brigade (seven regiments in all) to assault Wild's strongest position on his right, while Dunovant with Lomax's Brigade and his own 5th South Carolina Cavalry created a diversion against the weakest portion on Wild's left and fired on vessels on the James River. Lee reported: "Keeping up constant skirmishing, Wickham's detachment moved by a circuitous, wooded, and concealed route to the Eastern side (along Kennon Creek), with orders to assault it…. Dunovant was directed to make a demonstration upon the upper and opposite side, with a view to drawing the garrison in his front whilst Wickham got in. The orders were admirably carried out." When deployed, the Confederate line, starting at the extreme left (Wild's right), consisted of Gordon's Brigade (with the 5th North Carolina Cavalry closest to the James River), Wickham's Brigade, then Lomax's Brigade (5th, 6th, and 15th Virginia Cavalry Regiments) in the center or possibly one in reserve, and the 5th South Carolina Cavalry on the extreme right. The regiments of each brigade customarily were posted with its "1st," or senior regiment on the right, and its highest numbered or junior regiment on the left. Wickham's men were well-armed with carbine or "musketoon," pistol, and 125 cartridges. Normally, their sabres would have been left attached to their saddles, but Corporal Charles T. Price, Co. C, 2nd Virginia Cavalry, wrote: "*The reason we carried our sabres when we dismounted* [to attack], *was that the Yankees ran on a high pole a black flag. We had orders to kill every man in the fort if we had taken them. There were negro troops as well as white in the fort.*"[64]

A black flag usually meant "no quarter"—but this one, if taken as such by the Confederates, probably was another signal to Fort Powhatan upriver to send reinforcements, since Wild noted a thunderstorm (and Confederate sharpshooters) had interrupted communications between the two signal stations. Furthermore, Wild had issued detailed instructions four days earlier that prohibited executions of enemy soldiers, including even guerrillas, without a trial[65]; and Wild's troops did take as many as 19 wounded and unwounded Confederates prisoner after the Action ended. Since Wild and his troops expected no quarter anyway, a "no quarter" flag on a high pole would have been redundant. However, Corporal Charles T. Price's chilling statement "We had orders to kill every man in the fort if we had taken them" indicates that Fitzhugh Lee gave that order himself, not only because General Wild refused to surrender, but also Wild's delaying tactics and defiant replies enraged him.

Whatever lofty motives of preserving the Union and/or abolishing slavery impelled Wild, his white officers, and his black soldiers to enlist or seek a commission in the USCT, they now were fighting not only for their personal freedom from captivity, but for their very lives. The final Action began with Lee's careful preparations, movements of his units to their final attack positions, continued skirmishing, a diversionary secondary attack, and the main assault on the Wild's right flank. Fitzhugh Lee later reported:

> Keeping up constant skirmishing, Wickham's detachment [Wickham's and Gordon's *two brigades*] under that officer [General Wickham] was moved by a circuitous, wooded, and concealed route to the Eastern or lower side, with orders to assault it. Whilst he was getting into position, Dunovant [with Lomax's Virginia brigade and his 5th South Carolina Regiment] was directed to make a demonstration upon the upper and opposite side, with a view to drawing the garrison to his front whilst Wickham got in....
>
> The orders were admirably carried out. Wickham's men made a most gallant charge under a hot-fire, across an open space, but after getting to the very ditch itself were forced to retire: *the nature and thickness of the intertwined abatis and width of ditch being in themselves insurmountable obstacles to an ingress.* His loss, principally in retiring when the fire was more confidently delivered, was heavy, being *ten killed and forty two wounded, with four missing. Dunovant's loss was only six wounded.* Among the killed was Lieut. [Rudolphus W.] Cecil, Co. "K," 1st Va Cavalry, an officer frequently mentioned in my previous official reports as possessing daring bravery which I have rarely seen equaled.[66]

Private Henry St. George Tucker Brooke, Co. B, 2nd VA Cavalry, recalled in great detail his participation in the first dismounted assault on the fort, later attacks, and being wounded:

> Of course, we could not attack the Fort on horseback. Accordingly, the command, which had become painfully monotonous, "Halt; Prepare to fight on foot; Dismount"; was given. We first attacked the Fort from the front ... on the other side from the [James] river front. I ... was in a line that advanced across an open field to attack the Fort. Here for the first time we had the experience of having fire opened upon us by gun boats lying in the river. They shot such enormous elongated shells that one man said there was no sense in shooting lamp-posts at people. While in this field a bullet struck me on the shin six inches above the ankle. It hurt me badly. I thought my leg was smashed and turning around walked off the field. When I got out of the way of the bullets I sat down and pulled off my boot. Unfolding the leg of my trousers to get at my sock, the bullet dropped out. It had been a .45 calibre [?] elongated Minnie [*sic*; Minié] bullet. It was so much flattened that I think it must have gone through something before it struck me. My cavalry boot was made from the heaviest kind of hide....

The bullet had passed through it and thicknesses of my folded heavy trousers and had smashed a hole in my sock against my shin bone. I began to feel ashamed of myself.... I put the bullet in my pocket, pulled on my boot and went back to my company in the field.

Private Brooke described a second attack after the first one was repulsed:

I found that [Wickham's] brigade had returned from the field and was massing in the woods for [a second] assault. It marched through the woods to the river ["Swan neck" Creek on an 1864 map, now Kennon Creek] below the [eastern side of the] Fort. It was a most difficult march. The undergrowth was thick and the land was swampy. We drew up in line of battle facing the Fort. There was a field between us and the Fort. [We] charged across a field and suddenly came to a deep ravine ... 50 yards across. The trees had been cut down so as to fall lengthwise along the sides of the ravine and the branches left on the trees. This formed an impenetrable thicket on each side of the ravine. *When the charging column reached the ravine it came to an abrupt halt.* The enemy had poured a *destructive fire* into the column as it charged across the field. When the column came to the ravine and halted [and then facing to the right to form a skirmish line], I found standing next to me on my right Color Sergeant [Peachy Gilmer] Breckinridge, a brother of Major [Cary] Breckinridge and also of Capt. [James] Breckinridge, all of my regiment. Next to me on my left, and close enough to touch elbows, stood young (Sergeant) "Trip" Nelson of Company K. *As we stood there firing at the enemy who was behind breastworks, I felt a sharp sting on my ankle.* I knew a bullet had done it. I remarked to Breckinridge that I was struck again. [P. Gilmer] *Breckinridge said, "I hope you are not seriously hurt"' and then fell dead. I heard the bullet strike him.*[67]

Almost immediately afterwards ... "Trip" Nelson was shot and mortally wounded. There was [now] a considerable interval between me and the next man on each side. I am sure I was singled out and shot at individually. Several bullets whistled exceedingly close to my ears. I wore a broad brimmed light colored felt hat. I think everybody else had black hats. I had on a light colored Woolsey jacket. Confederate gray had given out. A bullet went through my hat. Another went through my boot leg. It was evident I was conspicuous although standing still. I was beginning to feel lonesome and help-less. I could not get at the enemy and he was decidedly getting at me. *At this time the whole column retreated precipitately across the field. I do not know whether any command was given or whether the men realizing the nonsense of standing there and being killed without doing any killing took the matter in their own hands.* Probably the command to fall back was given as it was not the manner of Confederate soldiers to take such matters into their own hands....

This is ... only the personal recollections of an insignificant private soldier, but I may be permitted to remark that I have never thought of that fight in the past forty years that I did not feel certain that "Somebody had blundered." Gen'l. Fitz Lee had been made Maj. General. I am sure he was not with us [he *was there!*] because *I did not see him and he was always much in evidence on the field of battle.* General Wickham ... was in command in this fight. I saw him ... when I was going from the field after being wounded the first time. He asked me where I was going. I told him I was wounded. He said nothing more. When the column got back over the open field [after the first assault] into the woods it reformed. I saw Gen'l. Wickham on foot among the soldiers wading ankle deep in mud and water through the thick undergrowth. He was doubtless with the column when it charged over the open field to the ravine [during the second attack]. He was a gallant officer and a true man and I would not like to think he was responsible for that attack upon a Fort by cavalry without artillery.[68]

Four days later, after receiving two light wounds (ankle and left thigh) at "Fort Kennon," i.e., Wilson's Wharf, Private Brooke was again wounded, this time seriously, at Hawes Shop, Virginia, where he was "wounded, (left thigh, compound fracture with deformity), and horse killed." He was captured in a Richmond hospital on 3 April 1865. After the war, he became a school teacher, lawyer, and professor of law at West Virginia University. He died 16 May 1914 at Charlestown, West Virginia, and was buried in Zion Episcopal Church Cemetery.[69]

General Wild later reported that in "the abatis, the scene of the assault … we found a captain (unidentified) and a major…. A memorandum book in the pocket of *the dead major (Cary Breckinridge, Sixth* [*sic*; Second] *Virginia Cavalry*)." Possibly Gilmer Breckinridge had written his name as "G. Breckinridge" and the "G." was smudged and/or mistaken for "C." Ironically, Cary, later promoted to colonel, was one of only two Breckinridge brothers to survive the war.

Corporal Charles T. Price, Company C, 2nd Virginia Cavalry, wrote that after the first charge was repulsed, he brought a wounded man back to the surgeon:

> [W]e went back and was in *the third charge*. I well remember of Sergeant F.H. (Francis K., "Trip") Nelson, of Company K, Albemarle Troop. He and myself were standing on a log watching the gunboats, which were not over 300 yards off, firing chained shots and shrapnel into the tree tops over us, as they could not lower their aim as they fired over the fort. He says, "Price, I am going to be killed in the next charge," and he was [see Private Brooke's account, above]. Out of the ten men detailed from our company, two held the horses, and the rest was in the fight and I was the only one not killed or wounded or taken prisoner, and I attributed it to lying behind a big tree stump when we reached the breastworks and other soldiers packed around me like sardines. We had but little chance to use our carbines, as we could not see the Yankees in the fort, as they shot through port-holes[?]. We charged through abbatis [*sic*] and sharpened limbs of fallen trees, [and] through an old field. *We carried the wounded back to Richmond that night, under a flag of truce.*[70]

Fitzhugh Lee claimed, "Wickham's loss [occurred] *principally in retiring* when the [enemy's] fire was more confidently delivered." Irving P.W. Whitehead later wrote: "Judge [former 2nd Sgt. John] J. Thompson Brown of Co. E [2nd Virginia Cavalry] has stated to me that as he went out, he found another wounded comrade, who begged to be carried to the rear. Accordingly he and another trooper picked the poor fellow up and between them they were struggling on, but before reaching a place of safety, the wounded man was killed by a second shot."[71]

Lieutenant J.A. Hotzman, Company D, 4th Virginia Cavalry, wrote in his diary: "1864; May 24. A memorable day in my life fighting negroes, and *we charged their breastworks under* a *galling fire.*" Author Kenneth L. Stiles: "*Charging the heavily defended breastworks* [on Wild's right] *three times,* the 4th [Virginia Cavalry] lost nineteen killed and wounded. The brigade [Wickham's] received a 'galling fire' each time it attacked."[72]

From his perspective of being on the Confederate far left (Wild's far right), nearest the James River before, during, and after the attack, Private Paul B. Means, Company F, 5th North Carolina Cavalry, later recalled:

Kennon's Landing, or Wilson's Wharf
  The attack on Kennon's Landing was the most useless sacrifice of time and men and horses made during the war.
  The [North Carolina Cavalry Brigade: 1st, 2nd, and 5th North Carolina Cavalry Regiments] was camped 23 May near Hanover Junction, recuperating a little from the terrible ride and fighting of Sheridan['s] Raid [during 11–12 May]. Late that afternoon an order came to each Captain for a "detail of picked men for specially dangerous work." The Sixty-third [5th Cavalry] furnished about 225 men and officers under command of Major [James H.] McNeill [420 men total from the three regiments in the Brigade, according to Major Ferguson's Report]. Wilson's Wharf was a fortified post of great natural strength on the James River ... forty seven miles in a *straight* line, by best military maps, from Hanover Junction. It was built on a fort built in semi-circle form on a bluff ... with each end resting on the James, with heavy parapets[?–see Lt. Simonton's description] and a canal of water[?] the entire front of the half circle. There was open ground for several hundred yards all around the fort covered with abattis [*sic*] and large fallen pine trees to impede assailants. If we could ever have taken it we never could have held it. The expedition was under the command of General Fitzhugh Lee, and originated with him, it was said at the time, to drive some negro soldiers off Virginia soil. We left Hanover Junction about 6 p.m. on the 23rd and rode all night and much of the time at a gallop. Early on the morning of the 24th we were near the fort, but for some inexplicable reasons the attack was delayed.

Means then quotes "Vol. 68, p. 269" of an unspecified source: "A note, by flag of truce, was sent to General Wild, commanding the post, demanding immediate surrender, and saying if not complied with, that *General Lee would not be responsible for action of his men when the fort was taken.* Wild answered; 'We will try that.'"

  Means continues:

It was 11 o'clock before we began to get into position; in the meantime the gunboats [*Dawn,* which did not get the alarm and get into firing position "until 12–1:30 p.m.," and *Young America,* which was towed by an Army tug starting from off Fort Powhatan at 3 p.m.], *Pequot* [which did not arrive until an hour after the Action ended] and the *Atlanta* (ironclad) [which had a disabled engine and did come into action at all] were shelling us fiercely[?] and the fort was filling with reinforcements[?]. The enemy also had a small vessel named the *Mayflower.* Some of our forces wounded the captain and pilot of this boat [true].... We had no artillery [one gun came along, but it "didn't fire any"]; but with or without artillery, "no regiment of our cavalry was afraid of those things." [Despite a few errors, Paul Means's perceptions years later are interesting.]

The shells [from USS *Dawn*] were chiefly 100-pounders. We could see them plainly coming at and over us; great black masses, as big as nail kegs, hurtling in the air and making the earth tremble under us and the atmosphere jar and quake around us when they burst. They certainly were terrifying. And under their effect I compared the "details" from the Ninth [1st NC Cavalry] and Sixty-third [5th NC Cavalry]. The former were dismounted and ours mounted, each in column of fours [before moving to the position where they would assault the fort] near together under those awful missiles. As one came towards us and burst over us, I saw those old veterans of the Ninth looking up at them with horror, lean back slightly and out of line. Just such a look and backward incline of their bodies as I imagine the immortal sentinel at Pompeii made, momentarily, when that dark, ashen death fixed him erect at his post for the admiration of future ages. Captain N.P. Foard saw their movement and, under the bursting, crashing sound and mass, he said[:] "Steady ... men, steady!" Possibly before the words were uttered they were erect as statues. At the same second I glanced along the Sixty-third, in the same line of my vision, and *every man* sat in his saddle motionless. It was no discredit to the Ninth [1st NC Cavalry], but the contrast was glorious for the Sixty-third [5th NC Cavalry]. [Mixed humor and pride probably helped to steady Means's own nerves while under fire.]

We were soon put in line of battle around that fort, *our regiment on the extreme left, the enemy's right.* We were to charge, at the firing of a signal gun on our left. We lay there for an hour or more waiting [for] that signal, eating strawberries in the fence corners and quietly talking of the scene in front of us; and all the while we could plainly see platoon after platoon of reinforcements [the four companies of the 10th Infantry Regiment, USCT returning from Fort Powhatan upriver at about 4 p.m.] coming over the bluff into the fort on the decline next to us. The shells from 100-pounders, 20-pounders, and 12-pounders [from the U.S. Navy gunboat *Dawn*] were still bursting over us and other parts of the line. Our regiment [5th North Carolina Cavalry] and some others

Postwar photograph of Major Thomas White-head, father of historian Irving P. W. White-head. He commanded the 2nd Virginia Cavalry's 5th squadron: companies E, which lost 1 killed and 3 wounded on 24 May 1864, and G, which reported no losses. His eyes seem to reflect having "seen the elephant" [brutal combat] (courtesy Mrs. Elvira Whitehead Morse, Amherst, Virginia).

[1st and 2nd North Carolina Cavalry, and Wickham's 1st, 2nd, 3rd, and 4th Virginia Cavalry Regiments—seven regiments in all] on our immediate right in the line were to make the charge, while those in front [the 5th, 6th, and 15th Virginia Cavalry Regiments of Lomax's Brigade?] and on the left of the fort [5th South Carolina Cavalry Regiment] were to fire incessantly on the fort when the charge began.

About 2:30 or 3 p.m.[?], the signal gun fired and the Sixty-third [5th North Carolina Cavalry] arose with a mighty yell for that terrible charge. We mounted the high rail fence in our front and went straight and fast, as obstructions would permit, for that fort—yelling and firing [Means carried a captured Spencer 7-shot repeating rifle[73]] as we went and receiving fierce front and cross fires into our ranks from rifles and artillery in the fort and the gunboats; we were within thirty feet of the fort when we saw the utter hopelessness of the attack. The line halted a moment; the order to retreat was given and *we retired under that awful fire from the most useless and unwise attack and the most signal failure we were ever engaged in.* Out of the detail of ten or twelve men from Company F, W.S. Prather and Green L. [*sic*; William S.] Bingham were killed outright; Worth McDonald and I were wounded. I was shot through the left shoulder within thirty feet of the fort, firing at the moment, I am sure, at the very identical white man [either a USCT officer, or a soldier landed from the *Thomas Powell?*] who shot me. Worth McDonald was wounded by one of those 100-pounders. It passed at least ten feet from him and paralyzed his right arm by concussion of air. There was no visible injury, but it fell useless to his side, quickly turned black its entire length, and he never recovered the use of it during his life time. He got an honorable discharge for the war and I got a furlough, 5 June, from Chimborazo Hospital in Richmond, for three months, with great joy at the thought of going home.[74]

Paul Means continues:

Some Virginians charged immediately on the right of our [three North Carolina] regiment[s]. As we retreated we came to a long, wide lagoon in a ravine, back of where we began the charge. The water was three to four feet deep. In some way, unknown to me, I attracted the attention of one of those Virginians, a giant of a fellow. I knew he was a Virginian by his regimental designation[?] on his coat sleeve. Of his own motion, he kindly and tenderly offered to carry me over that water. I thankfully declined and said to him: "I think I can make it all right." He looked down at me and said: "Oh! Boy get on my shoulders." And suiting his action to his words, he stooped down in front of me. I put my arms around his neck, he put his right hand under my right knee, his left holding his gun, and thus, like we used to play when children, he carried me over that water and almost to the top of the slope beyond....

After he let me down, I walked a short distance and, from loss of blood, lay down in some young corn. I heard some one tell Major McNeill of my condition. The Major came to me and asked me to ride out on his horse, which had just been brought to him after he had led our charge, and from which he dismounted. I refused, he insisted. I refused positively, and he sent a man on his horse for mine and stood by me until the horse came, put me on it and sent the man with me to the surgeon, while he directed the men of the regiment how to move out ready for the expected attack from our rear. And it was acts like this, of gentleness and love for *all* his men, which he was constantly doing, that caused the men of the Sixty-third all *to love* him.[75]

On 25 May, Wild reported from his perspective inside the fortifications:

Private Paul B. Means (upper right), Co. F, 5th North Carolina Cavalry Regiment, "wounded in action at Kennon's Landing, VA, by gunshot wound left shoulder" (courtesy John M. Bigham, Curator of Education, South Carolina Confederate Relic Room & Museum, Columbia).

We then went at it again. They massed troops [Wickham's and Gordon's brigades] on our extreme right, concealed by wooded ravines, and made a determined charge, at the same time keeping up a steady attack all along our front and left flank. *This charge approached our parapet, but failed under our severe cross-fires.* They fled back into the ravines and after another hour gradually drew off out of sight. I sent out three sallying parties who found them still drawn up in skirmishing array beyond the woods. We left the picket to watch them, and *brought in a few rebel wounded and prisoners.* The enemy built camp-fires, and passed a portion of the night in our front, but when at sunrise we advanced again to feel of them, they had disappeared. Contrabands to-day tell us they went to Bottoms Bridge to resist the crossing of our troops at that point.[76]

After the Action ended, the Federal troops probably took care of their wounded, distributed ammunition in case of another attack, repaired any damage to their fortifications, and worked feverishly to improve the incomplete ditch and fortifications. The three "sallying parties" (patrols) scoured the immediate area to search for their missing comrades (whom Major Ferguson reported were "shot trying to escape," and the one later "returned to his master in Richmond"), to gather any Confederate wounded left behind (as many as 19 wounded and unwounded were brought in), and to pick up weapons the Confederates had dropped.

Captain William Davis Parlin, Company E, 1st Regiment, USCT stated in a speech during the early 1890s:

Then came the rebel yell and a charge on our right flank. Then the men showed their metal [*sic*]. No cringing behind breastworks. No cowardly skulking nor hugging the ground—but *boldly, defiantly leaping on top of the breastworks* they gave that "flower of the rebel army" such a reception that the [final] charge was cut short almost before it began.... Fitzhugh Lee drew off without another attempt[,] leaving the[ir] dead on the field [on Wild's right flank].... The next day the houses a short distance away were filled with rebel wounded....

How dark and rainy it was that night as we pushed out in the blackness to reestablish our pickets. I believe it was the blackest night I ever knew. You could not see your hand before your face, when we were ordered out to find the rebels or to find them gone. At any rate we must reestablish our posts. We must feel out in the blackness where each step might uncover an alert foe.... They had gone, even leaving their dead for us to bury.[77]

In 1902, Captain, Brevet Lt. Col. Edward Simonton, a 1st Lieutenant in Company I on 24 May 1864, gave his own "brief account of the action, in which I participated, and where I had the opportunity to observe the principal events[:]"

The enemy began their attack on our position. Dismounting, they first made a *feint attack* [Dunovant's detachment] on the left and center of our line and then a direct charge on our right [by Wickham's and Gordon's brigades]. The surrounding woods favored the enemy so that they were able to advance quite near our works before the fire from our line could have much effect on them. But as the "Johnnies" showed themselves, they received a destructive fire from our line....

Still the enemy charged on with a yell, firing all the time as they advanced; [they] seemed confident of their ability to drive all our force into the river. *Then it was that our sable warriors showed their fighting qualities. They stood their ground firmly, firing volley after volley into the ranks of the advancing foe.* Many of the "Johnnies" ["Johnny Reb," a term Union troops used during the war] succeeded in approaching quite near our line. The artillery [two Parrott 10-pdr rifled cannon] stationed in our works then threw grape[shot] and canister into their ranks. Again *the brave and determined foe* rallied under the frantic efforts of their officers; again their ranks were scattered and torn by our deadly fire.[78]

Correspondent "M.W.S."/1st Lt. Myron W. Smith, the 1st Regiment adjutant, concluded his article for the *Washington Daily Morning Chronicle*:

A feint was made on one flank and a charge on the other. They came in with a yell, but our boys gave a louder yell (which must have been heard to be appreciated), and poured so much lead among them that they broke and ran like sheep, leaving numbers of dead and wounded on the field.... We lost in our regiment (1st Regiment, USCT) two men killed, one officer and fourteen men wounded, and one man missing....

That the black men will fight is an established fact.

We had a section of the 3rd New York volunteer artillery here, and the lieutenant in charge told me, after the fight, that no men in the world could do better than those [black soldiers] who supported his gun....

We have taken a number of prisoners, some wounded and some not. *We have treated them well, but woe to them if we find that our missing man has been unfairly dealt with.*[79]

What Colonel Dunovant's "detachment" (three Virginia regiments and the 5th South Carolina Cavalry) accomplished in their "feint attack" on the left and center of Wild's line is a mystery. Except for accounts from the Federal side about sharpshooters firing on the signal station, the gunboat *Dawn*, and transports on the river, from the bank east of the fort, any other efforts remain unknown. The author found no mention in regimental histories or a few personal accounts from the Virginia soldiers in the 5th, 6th, and 15th Virginia cavalry regiments of Lomax's Brigade.

However, in 1903, former Captain Zimmerman Davis, Company D, 5th South Carolina Cavalry Regiment, recounted: "On the 24th at Charles City [Wilson's Wharf] under Fitzhugh Lee, *we fought severely past noon* on one of the hottest days, and *were shelled very hard by gunboats* [USS *Dawn* and USS *Young America*], *losing 400 men* [???] *but killed and wounded about 600 Yankees* [???], mostly by firing into their transports from the banks of the James River, as they brought in reinforcements."[80] Zimmerman's casualty figures for both sides are ridiculous, but his words confirm that the 5th South Carolina Cavalry fought on the Confederate extreme right, partly on the river bank on the western side of the Federal fort. The unnamed captain and mate or pilot of the steamer *May Flower* (or *May-*

flower) were reported "badly wounded on the James River above Wilson's Wharf," and "two Robinson brothers [civilian crewmen?] were wounded." The captain of the gunboat USS *Dawn* reported no casualties. The 5th South Carolina Cavalry reportedly suffered only seven wounded[81]; however, these included the regiment's lieutenant colonel, in temporary command while Col. Dunovant commanded his "detachment," the sergeant major, and a staff captain, and only four lower enlisted men, hardly indicating a "severe fight." The ratio (3:4) of leader casualties to enlisted men (a corporal and three privates) is very unusual, indicating that the 5th South Carolina Cavalry Regiment's troopers either were holding back and needed prodding, or that there were more casualties on Fitzhugh Lee's right, as reported on the Federal side. That the Union soldiers were able to "pick off" three key leaders also is significant.

Lieutenant Swain, the signal officer, reported that about 5 p.m.: "I opened station on board a transport near the wharf, and was enabled to direct the fire from the gunboat [USS Dawn] in the river so successfully that they materially checked the enemy's movements on our right" [eastern side].[82] Lieutenant Simonton's account: "Next the gunboat [*Dawn*] in the river began to throw shells into their already demoralized ranks, when they broke and fled to the rear. Our soldiers poured into their ranks a final volley; this was the last of the fight."[83]

On 31 May from Wilson's Landing, Lt. Swain reported to Captain L.B. Norton:

> 24th instant, Maj. Gen. Fitz Lee, with 3,000 cavalry, attacked this post fiercely, but after *six hours of continuous firing* were repulsed with serious loss. During the attack I directed the fire of the gun-boats, and *for over three hours of the* ["six hours"] *time we kept communications open, under fire, with* [Fort] *Powhatan*, and were enabled to send all messages ordering re-enforcements from City Point and gun-boats from Powhatan. The enemy withdrew about 7 p.m., and the attack was not renewed. Most of the messages sent this day were received verbally from the general or his staff, and no record kept of them. We have continued communication between this point and Powhatan, but the distance, about 8 miles, all over water, renders it very necessary to have good glasses [telescopes]. Sergeant Walker [at Fort Powhatan] has but an indifferent one, and I would respectfully apply for a good telescope for him, as many times he cannot distinguish my [signal] flag when his can be seen [at "Wilson's Landing"].[84]
>
> The difference between "six hours of continuous firing" and only "over three hours of the time we kept communications open," and Sergeant Walker's "indifferent" glass, may account for General Wild's flying a "black flag on a high pole," probably to signal Fort Powhatan during stormy weather when Lt. Swain's signal flag wasn't seen.

Major General Fitzhugh Lee Grudgingly Accepts Defeat

After Wickham's three attacks were repulsed on Wild's right, Lee was

> determined to assault with my whole force, and made the necessary dispositions, hoping to get in at some point, but a *subsequent close personal reconnaissance* [contrary to Pvt. H. St. George Tucker Brooke's comments] showed the [Federal] work to be too elaborate and the orders were countermanded. Accordingly I withdrew my command, encamping for the night at Charles City Court House…. [The expedition] had the good effect, though unsuccessful, of keeping the negro troops more within the fort and lessening their outrages upon wandering outside.[85]

Major Ferguson: "Withdrew the command at dark and made Hd. Qrts. [Headquarters] at Dr. Christian's house. Depredations [had occurred] at Messrs. Vaden, Clopton [whom Wild had his ex-slaves whip], and Ferguson's places. In Dr. Christian's place [was] broken furniture, etc. Great distress of the inhabitants and their dread of Yankee soldiers."[86]

Fitzhugh Lee continued: "Upon the 25th, the march back to Atlee's was resumed, reaching [there] on the 26th. It was joined there by the Divisions of [Wade] Hampton and W.H.F. Lee, and on the 28th of May the three divisions marched under the command of Hampton, the senior Major General, in the direction of Hawe's Shop [where a large engagement was fought with Union cavalry on 28 May]."[87]

Major Ferguson further described the return march:

> May 25th. March from Charles City C.H. (Court House) to the vicinity of Riddles Shop 10 miles and halt during the heat of the day. Resume march during the afternoon and encamp on the Charles City Road near White's Tavern and receive rations and corn [for the horses] from Richmond. Learn of the passage of army of Grant over the North Anna [River] and of our position [of R.E. Lee's Army of Northern Virginia] in the vicinity of Hanover Junction. [General Joseph E.] Johns[t]on reported to have fallen back within 6 miles of Atlanta….
> May 26th. [Fitzhugh Lee's] Command marches from White's Tavern across to vicinity of Mechanicsville Pike and graze. Dine with Mr. Watts and go with Cavendish to call on Trenholm … March on to Atlee's Station and encamp. Find that detachment under Lomax had gone to Hanover C.H. in consequence of the enemy's cavalry having moved up.[88]

More Naval Drama on the James River: Four Civilian Casualties, and a Cowardly

Captain and a Military Mutiny
on the Steamer Thomas Powell

At Fort Monroe on May 25, 1864, Lt. Col. H. Biggs scrawled: "Dear Colonel. The rebel cusses fired into some of [our] transports near Wilson's Wharf which of course has been reported to you—: they did considerable harm to the Stˢ [steamers] "May Flower"–shot Captain & Mate and cut steam pipe later…. The steamers "Geo. Washington," "Suwanee" & "May Flower" are *the only ones fired into* that have reported here…. [Illegible] & a few bales of hay to put around pilot house [illegible].⁸⁹ The Sunday, May 29, 1864, *New York Times* stated: "Steamers Fired Into…. The steamers *George Washington*, *Mayflower* and *Suwanee* were fired into, and the Captain and mate of the *Mayflower*, and *two brothers, named Robinson* [civilian crew members?], *were wounded*."⁹⁰

Correspondent "H.J.W." described what happened after troops were taken off the steamer at Wilson's Wharf:

[After the *Thomas Powell* had] scarcely gone three lengths distance [upriver], the small propeller [transport] *Mayflower* was met. The [wounded] pilot of the *Mayflower* hailed Captain Lyons of the *Powell*, and said that a few minutes before, they had been fired upon by sharpshooters on the bank, and that his captain had been seriously wounded…. The captain of the *Powell* took the responsibility of heading his boat *down* the river without consulting any of the military gentlemen remaining on board. After running two miles below Wilson's Wharf, Capt. Lyons was waited on by Major Ackerly, 11th Pennsylvania [Cavalry Regiment], who was the senior military officer left on board, and had the right to give orders, and who requested to go again upstream, at least as far as the *Dawn*….

The captain positively refused compliance, making all manner of excuses about his not coming into the department to fight…. Further forbearance with this weak-minded individual ceased to be a virtue, and Major Ackerly ordered him to be placed in irons, which was done. The first engineer also refused to do [his] duty, and was furnished with iron bracelets. The second engineer, [his] brother, was likewise obstreperous, declined to work the engines, but was finally brought to his senses by Lt. Mahon, 11th Pennsylvania Cavalry, *who persuaded him by placing a cocked and loaded revolver at his head* … the *Dawn* was hailed and circumstances reported…. [Lieutenant Simmons] promptly replied, "Put the cowardly rascals in irons, and I will send you officers, then you can crowd on steam and run up to Fort Powhatan" … the *Powell*, true to her reputation for speed obtained on the Hudson, again went up the river, "passing the dangerous point like a streak of greased lightning." … There was a civilian who used his influence with the second engineer to prevent him from doing his duty…. Asked to give an account of himself, he at first said, "Bob Lincoln," son of the President. He was fitted to a pair of irons, when he changed his cognomen to Hancock.⁹¹

The *New York Times* correspondent reported on 26 May:

The captain of the *Thomas Powell* and his two engineers were Yesterday examined by Gen. Butler about their refusal to run the risk of rebel fire. Their answers were not satisfactory. Capt. Lyons was sentenced to 30 days' imprisonment and forfeiture of his vessel's charter money for 30 days. The first engineer was sentenced to two months' labor upon the fortifications at Hatteras. The second engineer was reprimanded and returned to duty; the young gentleman Hancock was expelled from the department. It is seldom that our steamboat men show the white feather. My experience with the officers of our transports everywhere since the war began, serves them to be brave and ready enough to risk any rebel fire in prosecution of their duty.[92]

Aftermath of the Action at Higher Federal Headquarters

Meanwhile, Brig. Gen. Hinks reported to Maj. Gen. Butler from City Point at 8 p.m. on the evening of the Action:

Reports from Wilson's Wharf state that Fitzhugh Lee demanded surrender of the post at 2 p.m. At 5 o'clock his [main] attack [by Wickham's and Gordon's Brigades]. I have sent the 37th Regiment [USCT] to reinforce the post, and shall proceed, as soon as I can obtain transport with [Capt. Francis C.] Choates's battery [B, 2nd U.S. Colored light Artillery] and the 5th Regiment [USCT] to join him.

This leaves the 5th Massachusetts (Colored) Cavalry, dismounted, and a battalion of the 4th Massachusetts Cavalry at City Point. Will you send a regiment to City Point?[93]

The next day, 25 May, Hinks directed Wild to "order the 37th U.S. Colored Troops to Col. Kiddoo [at Fort Powhatan, where Kiddoo had his 22nd Regiment, USCT] and other organizations that do not belong to you back to their proper post at once."[94]

At 7:30 a.m. on 25 May, General Butler telegraphed Secretary of War Stanton:

Maj. Gen. Fitzhugh Lee, lately promoted [*sic*], made, with cavalry, Infantry [possibly the 5th South Carolina Cavalry, some carrying rifles and rifle-muskets, and wearing brown "homespun" uniforms rather than gray ones, and fighting dismounted, was mistaken as "infantry"], and artillery, an attack upon my post at Wilson's Wharf ... garrisoned by two regiments, all negro troops, Brigadier-General Wild commanding, and was handsomely repulsed. Before the [main] attack Lee sent a flag, stating that he had force enough to take the place, demanded its surrender, and in that case the garrison should be turned over to the authorities in Richmond as prisoners of war, but if this proposition was rejected, he would not be answerable for consequences when he took the place. General Wild replied, "We will try that." Re-enforcements were at once sent, but fight was over before their arrival. Loss not yet reported....[95]

At Wilson's Wharf, Private Ruphus Wright, 23 years old, born in Edenton, North Carolina, of Company G, 1st Regiment, USCT, proudly and lovingly wrote to his wife:

wilson Creek Va May 25th 1864

 dear wife I take the pleasant opportunity of writeing to you a few lines to inform you of the Late Battle we have had we was in a fight on Tuesday five hours we whipp the rebels out *we Killed $200 & captured many Prisener out of our Regiment we lost 13 Thirteen* Sergent Stephenson killed & private out of Company H & about 8 or 10 wounded we was in line Wednesday for a battle But the rebels Did not Appear we expect an Attack every hour give my love to all & to my sisters give my love to Miss Emerline tell John Skinner is well & sends much love to her. Joseph Grinnel is well & he is as brave [as] a lion all the Boys sends there love [to] them give my love to Miss Missenger You must excuse my short Letter we are most getting ready to go on Picket No more from your Husband

Ruphus Wright[96]

Reported Execution of Two Black Union Soldiers in Petersburg; General Hinks Requests Confederate Prisoners Be Held for Execution in Retaliation, if Report Proves to Be True

On 27 May, General Hinks directed General Wild: "You will send to these Headquarters a list of all men captured by the enemy from your command to date." On 7 June, Hinks also "request[ed a] roll of the prisoners captured by you in the engagement at Wilson's Wharf, in addition to the roll of those already sent to this headquarters."[97] The requests were related to an ominous dispatch Hinks sent to Butler on 28 May:

General: It is reported that on Sunday, the 22nd instant [22 May], 2 men of the 22nd U.S. Colored Infantry, who were captured by the enemy on the 22nd instant, in the attack on Fort Powhatan, were shot to death in Petersburg at a place called the "Gallows," designated for the execution of criminals. *Five other prisoners have been captured since it has been in occupation of points along the James River, of whose fate nothing is known....* I respectfully request that Private Heaton, Twenty-fourth Virginia Regiment, who was captured on the 18th instant, and *all the prisoners captured from Fitzhugh Lee at Wilson's Wharf, on the 18th* [*sic*; 24th or 25th] *instant, be held for execution for the murder of the soldiers of the Twenty-second Regiment, and any of the other soldiers of this division who have met a like fate, if the above report is proved to be true.*[98]

On 30 May, Captain James H. Wickes, provost marshal, wrote General Wild: "*You will please require all arms captured from the enemy at Wilson's Wharf, to be collected, including rifled muskets, shotguns, carbines, and revolvers,*" and forwarded to these Headquarters at the earliest opportunity."[99]

A soldier who fought during the Action on 24 May, Private George R. Minor, a 25-year-old school teacher from Charlottesville who served in Company K, 2nd Virginia Cavalry, wrote:

"My dear Mother" (Mrs. Mary Ann Carr Minor) on 30 May 1864: ...

Two squadrons of our regiment were along (on the Charles City expedition). Our boys charged very strong breastworks—so strong that Captain [James C.] Breckinridge said it would have taken us some time to have gotten into them, even if there had been no Yankees there. We lost two of our best men—poor James Carr and Frank Nelson. Nelson was wounded in the thigh, and the fire was so hot they could not bring him off. No one in the company can give any account of Jim; whether he was taken prisoner, badly wounded or killed, we do not know. I stayed along the line of sharpshooters in hopes that he might be wounded and came out after dark.... Gilmer Breckinridge was left mortally wounded on the same field. We had another man badly wounded in our Company—Grayson. He was shot through the neck.

Death stalked soldiers of both sides as the armies experienced horrendous casualties during the spring campaign of 1864. During May, the 1st Virginia Cavalry, for example, had lost 34 men killed, 122 wounded, and 12 captured, total 168, its heaviest *monthly loss* for the first half of 1864. Very many soldiers—and their mothers—were concerned whether or not they were prepared to die. George Minor grappled with his own faith as he added in his letter:

My dear mother ... I will try to answer your important question, and one which I have so often asked myself, but have never been able to answer satisfactorily to myself—whether or not I am a Christian. I have a hope that I am. Christ has promised in His word that whosoever cometh to Him, He will in no wise cast off; I do strive to come to Him through prayer. When I look at myself to see what I have to recommend me to Christ, I despair, but when I read in His word, it is not by works, but by grace ye are saved, I feel very much comforted. I hope, I trust alone in the righteousness of Christ. His is a perfect righteousness with which God is pleased, and why should poor, sinful man not be satisfied. My dear mother I have no time to write more. I thank you for your prayers, and you do not know how much I value them—I always remember you in mine. My dear mother, I do hope if we if we shall meet no more in this "vale of tears," to meet you in Heaven; if I can die in such a hope I will welcome death....

Your affectionate son,

Geo. R. Minor[100]

VI

Conflicting Casualty Reports

Federal Casualties Incomplete;
Confederate Losses Covered Up
by Fitzhugh Lee and Richmond Papers

Reporting friendly losses and determining or estimating enemy losses after a battle is not an optional academic exercise for historical purposes. Accounting for personnel ("present for duty, absent sick, absent wounded, absent without leave," etc.) was accomplished on bi-monthly company muster rolls and was necessary for pay purposes and for ordering replacement men and horses, resupply of arms and ammunition, food rations, and fodder for horses, etc., in order to restore combat strength for the next battle. After the Action on 24 May, Fitzhugh Lee's staff had to arrange for wagon transportation of seriously wounded to Richmond hospitals, while less severely wounded cavalrymen could ride their horses. Estimating Confederate losses during the Action at Wilson's Wharf was particularly important for General Butler and the Northern public because U.S. Colored Troops were controversial in the North and hated in the South. For Fitzhugh Lee, being defeated by U.S. Colored Troops was personally humiliating, and a matter of concern to Southerners. Thus, Fitzhugh Lee reported only 62 total losses compared to "between 200 & 300 [Confederates] killed" reported in two Northern newspapers. See Table 1, below, for "Federal Casualties" and Table 2, for "Confederate Casualties."

At 11 a.m. on the 25th, General Butler reported to Secretary of War Stanton: "General Fitzhugh Lee abandoned his attack on our post at Wilson's Wharf during the night, having completely failed. *He lost 20 killed, whom he left on the ground in our hands.* Among these is reported Major Breckinridge of the Second Virginia Cavalry. *We took 19 prisoners from him.*

Our own loss is 1 man killed, 20 wounded, and 2 missing. The defense was commanded by Brigadier-General Wild in person, commanding a force of 1,800 men, *all of whom were negroes*" [not entirely true].[1] General Hinks had earlier reported to Butler the casualty figures for both sides from City Point, including "19 prisoners. Their wounded were removed."[2]

At 10:45 a.m. on 26 May, Maj. Gen. Butler again telegraphed Secretary of War Stanton: "Further official reports show that the repulse at Wilson's Wharf was even more complete than I telegraphed. The enemy retreated during the night, *leaving 25 of their dead in our hands, and showed a loss of killed and wounded of more than 200. From the accounts of every officer the negro troops behaved most splendidly.*"[3]

The *Richmond Sentinel* published that same day, 26 May 1864, had a very different version of events and the numbers and kinds of Wild's soldiers and of Confederate casualties:

> From The Peninsula
>
> We learn that on Tuesday General Fitz Lee made a reconnaissance through Charles City County, without discovering the enemy until he reached Kennon's farm, on the James River, a few miles below the Court House—He here found the enemy strongly fortified, with a deep ditch in front and protected by abattis. Their force consisted of *two regiments of white, two* [regiments] *of negroes*, and *a detachment of marines from the gunboats*[!]—After *skirmishing* with the enemy for a short time, during which we lost *some fifteen men killed and wounded*, the cavalry withdrew from before the works. It was not known what was the loss of the enemy.[4]

The disparity in casualty claims required the author to research about 50,000 names in microfilm muster rolls, regimental rosters, and hospital records for both sides. It still resulted in only partial identification of casualties by number or name, because about half the Confederate muster rolls were lost or are missing. Identifying soldiers now who made the ultimate sacrifice or were maimed, is important to honor them and for their posterity's sake. Names of officers and soldiers on both sides who were killed and wounded, and are known, are listed in Appendix A, "Action at Wilson's Wharf: Casualties' Names, Types of Wounds, Etc."; and the numbers of other losses during the period May 1864–June 1865 at Fort Pocahontas— so named on 6 August 1864—are summarized in Appendix B.

Federal Casualties

On 25 May, after praising officers and men from other units and the gunboat USS *Dawn*, General Wild reported: "Within my own command, all behaved steadily and well. Especially the conduct of the pickets and skirmishers under Capt. Giles H. Rich, First U.S. Colored Troops, was very fine. Our loss is 2 killed, 19 wounded, and 1 missing."[5] Chaplain Henry M. Turner: "I must tell you, the First Regiment of United States Colored Troops, with a very small exception, did all the fighting"[6] [and suffered nearly all the Federal casualties].

Table 1. Casualty Reports and Estimates for the Action at Wilson's Wharf on 24 May 1864

Union Casualties:

Date/Reporter	No. Killed	Wounded	Captured / Missing	Total
25 May—Wild	2	19	1	22
25 May—Hinks	1	20	2	23
25 May—Butler's HQ	1	20	—	21
26 May—Butler	1	20	—	21
27 May—*NY Times*	1	40 (1 mortally)	—	41
*11 June—*Harper's Weekly*	7	40	—	47
1902—Capt. Simonton	2	14	—	16
1908—Dyer, *Compendium*	2	24	—	26

*Possibly most accurate, but "one negro prisoner returned to his master in Richmond" is not listed as "missing," but he probably was presumed dead.

The Federal "Return of Casualties in the Union Forces, & etc. cmded by MG Butler" shows 18 battle casualties for the 1st Regiment, USCT: 2 enlisted killed, 1 officer and 14 enlisted wounded, and 1 enlisted soldier captured or missing, 4 short of the casualties identified by name in Appendix A. The Federal "Return" also lists 2 enlisted mortally wounded in the 10th Regiment, USCT, and 1 enlisted wounded for "3d New York Light (Artillery), Battery M."[7] Excluded are the four civilians wounded aboard the steamer *Mayflower*. The total of 26 military and 4 civilian casualties, total 30, is still short of the 7 killed and (approximately?) 40 wounded stated in the 11 June *Harper's Weekly*. The author found the names of 2 men killed and 4 who died of wounds, total six, but one died in August. Private George Wilson of Company F, 1st Regiment, USCT, who was earlier reported "Missing," but was "captured and returned to his master in Richmond," according to Confederate Major Ferguson, may have been presumed dead and included in the newspaper's "7 killed," for six of the total of "7 Killed" by 11 June. Major Ferguson also stated *"several prisoners* on picket were shot while trying to escape," leaving the final number of "killed" unresolved.

Nearly all the Federal military casualties were black enlisted men, but three whites, including two officers, were also wounded:

- Captain Walter H. Wild, the General's brother and a member of his staff, was wounded in the forehead by a spent ball, but he returned to duty;
- 1st Lt. Elam C. Beeman, Co. A, 1st Regiment, USCT, was "shot in the right hand & wrist by [a] Minie ball," and he also returned to duty;
- Private John Taylor, Lt. Hanson's section of Battery M, 3rd N.Y Light Artillery, "Gunshot Wound of face-Minie ball ... returned to duty."

Two black Union soldiers from the 1st Regiment, USCT were killed, and two were mortally wounded:

- 5th Sergeant Moses Stevenson or Stephenson, 25, VA, Co. G, "*killed*, shot through the head";
- Private William Butler, 26, MD, Co. E, "fracture of skull by cannon fire ["friendly fire?"—the Confederate artillery piece "didn't fire any"], *died* 27 May";
- Private Samuel Langley or Langway, 40 or 48, NC, Co. F, "shot in head, *died* 1 August";
- Private Dempsey Maby or Mabey, 20, NC, Co. F, "*killed*, shot through the breast. He was a brave soldier." (He either fought to the death or was executed after capture.)

Two black soldiers from the 10th Regiment, USCT were mortally wounded:

- Private William Upture, 21, VA, Co. D, "Seriously wounded (in abdomen) at Wilson's Landing, VA; *died* on board Steamer *Mayflower* in Hampton Roads on May 25th enroute to Fort Monroe."
- Private Isaac West, 20, VA, Co. D, ""Dangerously wounded in abdomen; *died* Hampton Hospital 6/4/64."

Nineteen Army wounded in all are listed in Appendix A, leaving an unexplained 21 or so unidentified wounded of the 40 claimed in *Harper's Weekly*, but "soldiers with mild wounds (the "walking wounded") were treated in the field, not carried to field or general hospitals, and thus not registered as wounded in hospital statistics."[8] Having been a surgeon in the Turkish army, General Wild probably saw to the proper treatment of their wounds at the fort, and thus their names were not recorded. Chaplain Henry M. Turner, 1st Regiment, USCT, who also would have tended the wounded, wrote: "Our loss, considering the terribleness of this conflict [on 24 May] was *incredibly small.*"[9]

Confederate Casualties

Chaplain Henry M. Turner, 1st Regiment, USCT also wrote:

I am sorry that it is inexpedient to give you a full description of that terrific battle, which lasted several hours, but the coolness and cheerfulness of the men [of the 1st Regiment, USCT], the precision with which they shot, and the vast number of rebels they unmercifully slaughtered, won for them the highest regard of both the General [Wild] and his staff, and *every white soldier that was on the field....*

Allow me to say that the rebels were handsomely whipped. They fled before our men, *carrying a large number of their dead, and leaving a great many on the field for us to bury. They* [prisoners] *declared our regiment were sharpshooters.*[10]

Table 2. Casualty Reports and Estimates for the Action at Wilson's Wharf on 24 May 1864

Confederate Casualties:

Date/Reporter	No. Killed	Wounded	Captured / Missing	Total
25 May—Wild	"about 24"	—	10 (6 wounded)	34
25 May—Lt Swain	20	"several wounded"		20+
25 May—Hinks	"about 21"	"removed"	19	40+
25 May—Butler	20	—	"19 prisoners"	39
25 May—Butler's HQ	20–30	(101–111)	19	150
26 May—Butler>Stanton	25	—	—	"total k & w more than: 200"
26 May—Richmond *Examiner* "only some 18 killed & wounded"				18
27 May—*NY Times* "between 200 & 300 killed & wounded"				about 250+/- ?
28 May—*Richmond Examiner* "60 killed & wounded"				60
11 June—*Harper's Weekly* "between 200 & 300 k & w on field"[11]				about 250+/- ?

**Sept. Report—Fitzhugh Lee: 10 48–4 62
**Oct.—Maj. Ferguson, CSA 10 48–4 62
*1902—Capt. Simonton "over 100 dead and wounded" 100+
**These reports exclude Gordon's and Lomax's brigades' casualties.

In reports dated in September and October 1864, respectively, *Maj. Gen. Fitzhugh Lee and Major J.D. Ferguson reported Confederate casualties on 24 May to have been 10 killed, 48 wounded, and 4 missing; a total of 62; repeated as "60 killed and wounded" in the Richmond Examiner of 28 May. These figures clearly understate the casualties.* Casualties in Wickham's Brigade, which along with Gordon's North Carolina Brigade made the main assault, were admittedly heavy, and Major Ferguson reported: "One officer and five men wounded in the 5th So. Ca[rolina] Regiment." *There are no casualty reports for Gordon's North Carolina Cavalry Brigade, attached from W.H.F. Lee's Division, and Lomax's Virginia Cavalry Brigade.* Major J.D. Ferguson, Lee's assistant adjutant general, had obtained totals of men detached from Wickham's, Lomax's, and Gordon's brigades (but not the attached 5th South Carolina Cavalry). He had time to get casualty and strength reports from these units during the two-day return trip to Atlee's Station, especially while Lee's command rested at Seven Pines and grazed their horses "in the vicinity of Mechanicsville Pike." He found time to "dine with Mr. Watts ... go with Cavendish to call on Trenholm," etc. The great disparity between 62 officially reported, but understated, Confederate casualties and the estimated "between 200 & 300 killed and wounded on the field" required extensive research to identify as many Confederate casualties by name as possible. See results in Appendix A.

The *101 casualties identified by name in Appendix A, and 5 unnamed others, total 106 Confederate casualties from Confederate sources.* This count reveals significant discrepancies in Fitzhugh Lee's and Major J.D. Ferguson's official reports of casualties, but they are still very incomplete.

Irving P.W. Whitehead: "There is no official report of this affair, but I have learned from those who participated in this 'wild goose chase' as they term it, that *about 75 Confederates* [in Wickham's brigade alone] *were killed or wounded.*"[12]

Federal officers counted *24, later 25 bodies* from Wickham's "detachment" left behind in abatis on the eastern side of the fort, but *only 20* have been identified by name. Three of the four regiments in Wickham's brigade may have left nearly complete records of their casualties at "Fort Kennon" (Wilson's Wharf). Names of 1st Virginia Cavalry casualties (4 killed and, 16 wounded, 1 mortally) are listed in Appendix A; its total losses are unknown. Author Robert J. Driver, Jr., reported a total of 29 casualties (7 killed, 19 wounded, and 3 captured) from the 2nd Virginia Cavalry commanded by Col. Thomas T. Munford.[13] Of the 29, names of 5 killed, 16 wounded (1 mortally), and 3 captured, total 24, are listed in Appendix A. Private Horatio ("Horace") Nelson, Company A, 4th Virginia Cavalry, wrote in his diary: "May 24, 1864 Tuesday: Our Brigade in front attacked the enemy at 1 o'clock. Made *three charges* [later] on their Breastworks but was repulsed with *19 killed and wounded in Regt.*"[14] Seventeen names of killed and wounded from the 4th Virginia Cavalry were reported in the *Richmond Sentinel* on 27 May; two additional names are known from other sources (see Appendix A). Casualty figures for the 3rd Virginia Cavalry are probably incomplete; names of 4 killed, 1 died of wounds and 5 others wounded, a total of 10 compared to 8 reported losses, are listed in Appendix A.

Twenty-seven companies out of forty companies in Wickham's brigade reported their casualties, as identified in Appendix A: 1st Virginia: 9 of 10; 2nd Virginia: 7 of 10; 3rd Virginia: only 4 of 10; and 4th Virginia: 7 of 10. It's unlikely that the other 13 companies didn't suffer any losses on 24 May 1864. And of *"19 captured,"* only *9 prisoners* (including 3 wounded—2 mortally) are identified by name. Heavy attrition of officers and men during early May and at Trevilian Station, the bloodiest cavalry battle of the war, in June 1864 made for poor record-keeping, and later loss of muster rolls, etc., are some reasons for our inability to accurately count, or identify by name, all Confederate casualties incurred by each unit at Wilson's Wharf.

On 6 June 1864, Captain W.W. Tebbs, Company K, 1st Virginia Cavalry, wrote to Dr. William G. Carr, Albemarle County, regarding the possible fate of his son, Corporal James Garland Carr, Company K, 1st Virginia Cavalry ("captured at Fort Kennon 5/2464 and never heard from after leaving Fortress Monroe"—see Appendix A for details): "I would not raise any unreasonable hope in your bosom ... [but] We are thrown upon the proportion of killed and wounded. *The killed are about one to six or seven wounded.*" At Fort Pillow, where dismounted Confederate cavalrymen successfully assaulted a fort, Brig. Gen. Chalmers reported their losses as 14 men killed and 86 wounded, a ratio of slightly more than 1 killed: 6 wounded. According to postwar medical research: "After a battle, whenever specific figures are given totaling killed and wounded, the *ratio of wounded to killed is almost always 4:1 or 5:1 and sometimes even higher.* This is the number of men who needed medical care after a battle."[15]

Applying ratios of 4:1 and 5:1 to the "25" bodies *only left in the abatis* on Wild's right, gives the following:

No. of bodies:	25	25
Ratio:	x4	x5
No. of wounded:	100	125
Total, KIA & WIA:	125	150

Listed in Appendix A are 20 named killed and 75 named wounded, including those mortally wounded, compared to 125 to 150 total killed and wounded for 25 bodies found only in the abatis on the right of the fort.

An unknown correspondent dated his report May 25, 1864, at the headquarters of General Butler, which was published in 1868 in Volume XI of *Rebellion Record, 1861–65*, states:

The fight commenced. At first [the diversion by the 5th South Carolina Cavalry Regiment and Lomax's Virginia Brigade] *raged fiercely* on [Wild's] left. The woods were riddled with bullets. *The dead and wounded* [Lee and Ferguson reported only six wounded] of the rebels *were taken away from the field*, but I am informed by one accustomed to judge [perhaps one of Butler's staff officers] and who went over the field today [the day after the battle] that *from the pools of blood and other evidences the loss must have been severe.*[16]

It isn't likely that Col. Dunovant's force of about, 1,050 veteran dismounted cavalrymen ("750 in Lomax's Brigade" plus an estimated 650 men in the 5th South Carolina Regiment, a total of about 1,400 men, minus one-quarter, or 350 men serving as horse-holders, and any men whose horses gave out en route), would have been deterred or repulsed even in a secondary attack on Wild's left by the loss of only six wounded! Fitz Lee reported: "Dunovant's loss was only six wounded," an implied total for his whole "detachment," and Major Ferguson stated: "*In the Fifth South Carolina, 1 officer* and 5 men wounded"; however, the *Charleston Daily Courier* listed *two officers* (Lt. Col. Jeffords and Captain Green, Quartermaster), and 4 men, including the regimental sergeant-major, as wounded, an unusual ratio (3:3) of senior personnel to junior enlisted men. Of the six, five were listed as having a "light wound," but Federal reports of dead carried off and "pools of blood" (above) on Lee's right indicate a higher loss by Dunovant's "detachment" as a whole. "Lightly wounded" men don't leave "pools of blood" visible the next day.

The unidentified correspondent continued:

Finding [Wild's] left could not be broken [the attack here was actually intended to draw Wild's troops here from his right], Fitzhugh Lee hurled his chivalry [Wickham's Virginians and the North Carolinians]—dismounted of course, upon the right. *Steadily they came on, through obstructions, past abatis, without wavering.* Here one of the advantages of negro troops was made apparent. They obeyed orders, and bided their time. When [the Confederates were] *well tangled in the abatis, the death-warrant "Fire" went forth.* Southern chivalry quailed before Northern balls. Volley after volley was rained upon the superior by the inferior race [sarcasm], and chivalry broke and tried to run. The fight lasted till about 5 o'clock....

On the right of [Wild's] *line*, at Wilson's Wharf, *between 20 and 30 dead rebels were found … their total loss was one hundred and fifty;* [and?] *nineteen prisoners were taken.*"[17]

General Wild reported on 25 May that he "sent out three sallying parties who found them still drawn up in skirmishing array beyond the woods ... and brought in a few rebel wounded and prisoners" (six wounded and four not wounded, or as many as 19 according to later reports by Hinks and Butler). On the morning of 26 May (two days after the battle), Butler telegraphed Secretary of War Edwin M. Stanton: "The enemy retreated during the night, *leaving 25 of their dead in our hands, and showed a loss of killed and wounded of more than 200.*"[18]

Further examination of casualty reports and circumstances, and comparing figures and names with postwar accounts and regimental rolls, not surprisingly reveals more discrepancies with Lee's figures. Wild noted:

> *The enemy had ample opportunities for removing all their dead and wounded from every part of the field, except from the abatis, the scene of the assault* [on Wild's right by Wickham's and Gordon's brigades]. There we found about two dozen killed, including a captain and a major. We brought in 6 wounded rebels and 4 prisoners [from Wickham's Brigade?].... A memorandum book in the pocket of the dead major (Cary Breckinridge, Sixth [*sic*; Second] Virginia Cavalry) gives us a clue on pages 41 and 42 to the parties, but not the numbers.[19]

The 27 May *New York Times* published a 25 May report from Fortress Monroe that claimed "one rebel major was killed, a rebel colonel was made prisoner, and ten privates were also captured." If a "rebel Colonel [was] made prisoner," it didn't happen at Wilson's Wharf on 24 May. The *New York Times* of 29 May published a report from "H.J.W. In Camp, Bermuda Hundred" that mentions "Major Breckinridge, of the Second Virginia Cavalry [being] among the ['about two dozen'] corpses left on the field." *Major Cary Breckinridge* was not killed or wounded, but his older brother, *Acting Captain P. Gilmer Breckinridge,* was "killed at Fort Kennon" [i.e., Wilson's wharf—formerly "Kennon's Landing"] on May 24, 1864.

The postwar roll of the 2nd Virginia Cavalry states that *Cary Breckinridge* was "twice severely wounded, with a sabre-cut at Second Manassas, and on the Opequon, near Winchester on Sept. 20, 1864, and in the thigh on October 20, 1864; had been captured at Kelly's Ford on March [*sic*; April] 17, 1863; and wounded at Raccoon Ford." He had been 1st lieutenant, then captain of Company C, and was successively promoted to major, lieutenant colonel, and finally colonel of the 2nd Virginia Cavalry.[20]

Ironically, Lieutenant Rudolphus W. Cecil, the officer whose loss Fitzhugh Lee lamented in his report, and whose bravery he praised, was listed in the roll of the 1st Virginia Cavalry as a private in Company K, "composed of Marylanders" with the remarks: "promoted Lieutenant; killed at James City [*sic*] Landing."[21] Perhaps the most tragic of the Confederate casualties was Private Walter Kilbey, Company D, 4th Virginia Cavalry, "shot through the hips at Kennon farm [*sic*], Charles City County, died from wounds 5/26/64. *The last of seven sons killed.*"[22]

Some companies lost more men than others. Corporal Charles T. Price, Company C, 2nd Virginia Cavalry, wrote that he was "the only one [of eight dismounted men] in the fight not killed, wounded, or captured"; all are identified in Appendix A. Since Color-Sergeant P. Gilmer Breckinridge, who was assigned from Company C to act as acting captain of Company B, was killed, Price was the only one of nine men from Company C who was not a casualty.[23]

An insert "Bury horses" on Wild's draft note to "Sir" of May 28 may be an indicator that some projectiles fired high by the gunboat *Dawn* exploded among the Confederates' horses and horse-holders in the rear of the fighting. Sergeant John Gill, a courier with Fitz Lee's staff, who probably was in the rear after participating in the first dismounted attack on the fort, later wrote: "In addition to the effective firing from the fort, several gunboats opened on us, and *stampeded our horses.*"[24] James Michael Barr, Company I, 5th South Carolina Cavalry, wrote: "W*e lost two horses killed in Capt. Whilden's Company* [E] *by a shell* [fired by Wild's artillery or the gunboats that exploded among the horse-holders and horses]. It is a wonder that more were not killed." Perhaps more horses held in the rear were killed elsewhere on the battlefield. Officers' and other horses belonging to Wild's command would have been sheltered in defilade below the bluff near the river during the Action. If any had been hit, they would have been buried or thrown into the river soon after the fighting ended, not left unburied for four days in the hot weather. If not, the stench would have been unbearable inside the fort.

On 28 May 1864, Fitzhugh Lee's division encountered Gregg's Federal cavalry and "immediately engaged them." During the ensuing battle of Hawe's Shop-Enon Church, Custer's brigade reinforced Gregg and drove the Confederate troopers from the field after a bloody seven-hour encounter. The Federals suffered 350 casualties, including 44 killed; Custer reported: "From an examination of the ground, the [Confederate] loss was far heavier than during any previous engagement of the same extent and duration. The havoc was particularly great in the South Carolina brigade." (The 5th South Carolina Cavalry and half of the 4th Cavalry Regiment fought here.) On 30 May, Sheridan reported: "Extracts from Richmond newspapers, Hawe's Shop: Col. Dunovant of SC wounded by pistol shot through left hand." On 1 June, Sheridan reported: "Butler's brigade of South Carolina was with Fitz Lee's division & is well represented in prisoners."[25] Losses of the 5th South Carolina Cavalry on 24 May at Wilson's Wharf may have been combined on muster rolls, etc., with the heavier losses at Hawe's Shop.

Because the Action at Wilson's Wharf lasted 5 or 6 hours, the Federal infantry "shooters" initially numbered about 936 and finally increased to as many as 1,350–1450; the veteran Confederate cavalry numbered about 2,620 present (excluding horse-holders and some men whose horses gave out en route); at least 80 rds of artillery and 118 rds of naval ammunition were fired from the USS *Dawn* and an unknown number were fired by the USS *Young America*; very determined efforts by both sides; and Lee's and Ferguson's reports did not include losses for Gordon's and Lomax's brigades, and are otherwise inaccurate; these factors indicate *a reasonable estimate of about 175 total Confederate casualties, including 25 bodies left behind and perhaps 19 prisoners; compared to 6 Federal soldiers killed or mortally wounded and one black soldier captured and returned to slavery but perhaps presumed dead, total 7; and about 36 military and 4 civilian wounded.* The high estimate of 200 Confederate casualties represents only about 7.6 percent of Lee's total Confederate force of about 2,620 men.

Numbers and even names of casualties derived from muster rolls and hospital reports do not convey the trauma and suffering that wounded soldiers on both sides endured. Private James Michael Barr, 5th South Carolina Cavalry, a 36-year-old prosperous farmer and businessman from near Leesville in central South Carolina and who owned 12 slaves, did not get to the Action on 24 May because his horse became very lame, but he was wounded eighteen days later, on 11 June 1864, during the bloody two-day Battle of Trevilian Station in central Virginia. On 14 June, he wrote the first of several letters from the hospital at Charlottesville, Virginia:

My Dear Rebecca…. I was wounded in the leg last Saturday, the 11th. I was shot in the leg about one inch below the knee cap of my right knee on the inside. The ball I think went down the bone and around, coming out some four inches below where it went in, coming out on the other side of the leg.

I was on my knees when the ball hit me. I could not walk off the battlefield. In about an hour, I was carried to the rear, was put in an ambulance. There I fared bad as the Yankees were trying to flank us and did succeed in getting 3 ambulances and some of our wounded for a short while when they were recaptured…. I have no use of my leg. If I want to move it, I have to call for help, but I have gotten good attention so far.

I hope to be able to go home soon, yet the Dr. said I could not go in three or four weeks unless someone came for me…. I would like to go to Richmond. I have no clothing here, all back near Richmond.

I will write again soon. I am doing tolerably well.

I get plenty to eat here. Tell Johnny that Pa had strawberries for dinner…. The doctor says my wound is eight inches long. It is plenty sore and will be for some four or six weeks.

No one could come for me as I am too far from Richmond.

Morning of the 15th of June 1864:

I feel quite pert this morning. I have just washed and combed and had my wound dressed, my leg is still in my way. I hope I may soon be able to move it about.

Evening: I feel much as I did this morning. You can't come here and I can't go away on account of the Rail Road. The Yankees have burned and torn up the tracks....

Morning, 16 June:

My Dear, I suffered pain all night, but feel easier this morning. I am sitting up....

Your True Husband, James M. Barr

Delvan Hospital, Charlottesville, Va., June 22, 1864, My Beloved Wife: ... I cannot get into any position that I can write. My leg is swagged down[?] a good deal. They poultice it twice a day. It has run considerably. I still have no use of my leg, but the Doctor says the ball passed through the bone. You don't wonder that I have no use of it.... I think my leg is safe now. I think it will get well. It pained me so for two or three nights that I thought it would have to come off, but I think now that I am doing as well as I possibly can. The wound looks healthy and my leg is nearly down to its usual size. My foot and ankle are swelled a good deal.... I have no idea when I will be able to leave here and I am out of money.

July 1st, 1864.... Tomorrow will be three weeks since I have been wounded and I am not much if any better off.... Pains me a great deal, a continual burning pain for the last three or four days. I know you would like to be with me, but it can't be. If I had some one to stay and look after me, I would do better. A good many little attentions I miss. My appetite is not very good. They have plenty here, but it is not half cooked, no salt in anything.... I am still quite weak, can't sit up yet. I can move my leg now myself. The wound at the knee and thigh is doing very well. I think it is healing. The flies bother me a great deal, also the green ones. They want to blow my leg. [Blowflies and other insects deposit eggs in rotting meat in a process known as "blowing."] I am afraid they will, but I am conscious to keep the [bed] spread well tucked down....

I cannot go home now as my wound is too bad. It is sluffing off instead of healing. I hope it will turn for the better in a short time. I feel as if I would like to get up and walk about. If I had the strength and it would not hurt my leg I would try. It would do me good, but I could not manage crutches.

My Dear, I must close. I wish you could be with me. I cannot write for anyone to come for me. I don't know who would come.

Your Husband, J.M. Barr

On 8 July, Captain George W. Meetz, 13th South Carolina Infantry, wrote:

Mrs. James M. Barr:

By request of my friend, Major [Barr's 1853 rank in the Upper Battalion, 15th Infantry Regiment of the State Militia, a title he used also as a private in the Confederate Army] Barr, I write a few lines to inform you of his condition. His wound has not done well since here and day before yesterday it took a change for the worse, so much so that his leg had to be amputated. His leg was taken off above the knee. The operation was performed yesterday about ten o'clock. I spent the night with him. This morning he is doing very well. He desires that you come at once. Said you must get your Brother, the Doctor, to come with you. I can assure you that he has the best of attention and seems to be in good spirits. He is a warm friend of mine and anything I can do will be done. Hoping that you may soon be with him and that he will soon be well enough to return Home with you.

Upon learning of her husband's condition, Rebecca Barr, about five months pregnant, made the difficult decision to travel from their South Carolina home to Charlottesville, Virginia. Her infant son Charlie was so ill that she feared the child would not survive, and she laid out clothes for him to be buried in. Rebecca's brother, Dr. Elijah Henry Dowling, escorted her to Virginia. During much of the trip they rode on open flat cars with Rebecca sitting on a chair. Where sections of the rail line were blocked, they rented or borrowed horses to get them to a rail link to Virginia. At the Charlottesville Hospital they found that James Barr's condition had deteriorated, with infection spreading up the stump of his leg, requiring another amputation. Rebecca was able to spend several days nursing her husband, but Private James M. Barr died on 29 August 1864.[26]

Rather than leave her husband's body in Virginia, she boarded a flat car with his remains and began the trip back to South Carolina in the hot August sun. She sent word ahead and had two of her slaves meet her at the train station at Columbia, from where they traveled the last 30 miles by wagon to Leesville. Rebecca Barr held a service and laid her husband to rest in the Barr Family Cemetery. On 6 December 1864, Rebecca gave birth to a daughter who died the following day and was buried near her father. Rebecca later returned with her brother and sons to reclaim the overgrown fields of her farm and establish a grain mill and sawmill. In 1883, she married a veteran who had served in the 1st South Carolina Infantry during the war.[27]

VII

Covering Up a Dismal Confederate Failure

"The attack on Kennon's Landing was the most useless sacrifice of time and men and horses made during the war."—Private Paul B. Means, Co. F, 5th North Carolina Cavalry

While Maj. Gen. Fitzhugh Lee's and Maj. J.D. Ferguson's covering up of Confederate losses was sad and disrespectful to the valor of his soldiers who attacked Wilson's Wharf on 24 May 1864, their exaggeration of General Wild's force and of the number of U.S. Navy gunboats was ludicrous. The *Richmond Examiner*, which had clamored for military action against Wild's garrison, stated on 26 May:

A force of the enemy, *supposedly* [?] *negro troops*, had been committing atrocious outrages on the people. So bad had become their conduct it was determined to break up the *nest of them*. Accordingly, General Fitzhugh Lee, with a force considered adequate for the occasion, on Tuesday night approached their position. Before attacking, he made a *reconnaissance in force* to ascertain their strength, nature of defences, etc., when he found them *and a large number of marines from the fleet* [i.e., well-disciplined and trained U.S. Marines, not black Union Army soldiers or white volunteers] *so strongly intrenched and fortified that he deemed it impracticable* [to attack]....
   Their earthworks were formidable, and before them was a ditch some fifteen or sixteen feet wide, making an attack by [mounted?] cavalry out of the question ... the enemy landed reinforcements from their gunboats [No!], when Fitzhugh Lee, finding the position could not be carried by cavalry, retired; *losing only some 18 killed and wounded in the whole affair.* There were many exaggerated rumors afloat last night of the affair, but we are assured, *on official authority*, that the above is the correct version.[1]

Two days later, 28 May, the *Richmond Examiner* elaborated:

[T]he affair in Charles City County, in which General Fitzhugh Lee *ventured a partial attack* on an enemy intrenched near the James River. *The statements of the great strength of the enemy's fortifications are fully corroborated ... a ditch ten or twelve feet deep, and some fifteen to eighteen feet wide,* and *an abatis made more intricate and impenetrable by the*

174

intertwining of wire [telegraph wire, a device employed by Federal troops at Drewry's bluff on 15–16 May but *not* at Wilson's Wharf] with the limbs and branches of felled trees. *So formidable and complete were the fortifications that we are told by an officer, who participated in the affair, that it would have taken our men two hours to get into their works, had there not been a man inside them...* [!]

The force of the enemy, too, was considerably larger than first supposed.... There were *six gunboats* in the river *playing upon our men all the time with grape and canister.* Under the circumstances, Gen. Fitzhugh Lee thought it unwise to make the sacrifice it would have cost to carry the position, and retired after an unsuccessful assault [by Wickham's and Gordon's brigades] upon a portion of the work *in which we had some sixty men killed and wounded.*[2]

Fitzhugh Lee's *"partial attack"* consisted of a charge on the advanced picket, an attack and skirmish with two companies of the picket support in front of the fort, a frontal dismounted attack on the fort, feint attacks on the front and west side of the fort, and two or probably three determined assaults with "orders to kill every man" on the east side of the fort (six or seven "attacks" in all) during a period of 5 or 6 hours.

Ironically, in his postwar handwritten "Report of the Military Services of Edward A. Wild, Brig. Gen. U.S. Vols. (concluded)," *Wild or someone else made several errors himself.* It states:

1864 ... May 24. Battle of Wilson's Wharf. We were at that date protected only by [as noted above: "a long line of"] rifle pits and some abbattis [*not entirely true; see Edward Simonton's postwar account*]; and manned *solely* by Colored Troops [not entirely true, either], viz: about one regiment and a half of infantry [*true, but in small notes "(10th. USCT)" above "one regiment" and "(1st . USCT)" above "a half* [the opposite was true] of infantry," and one section of light battery = two 6-pounders, with note "(Battery B, U.S.C.T.)." [This, too, is incorrect; Wild actually was supported by "efficient and undaunted" (Wild) Lieutenant Nicholas Hanson with his two 10-pounder Parrott rifled guns from Howell's Battery M, 3rd New York Light Artillery," which had replaced the section of two 6-pounder howitzers from Captain Francis C. Choate's Battery B, 2nd U.S. Colored Light Artillery Regiment.][3]

Wild's "Report," above, was apparently the basis for "Military Life of Edward A. Wild, Brig. Genl., Vol.," a copy of which is at the Massachusetts Historical Society at Boston. These errors, whether noted in Wild's own hand or by another person, were perpetuated by: Frances H. Casstevens in her otherwise outstanding biography, *Edward A. Wild and the African Brigade in the Civil War:* "May 24, 1864—Wilson's Wharf—Fort Pocahontas," pp. 171–172; Leonne Hudson, "Valor at Wilson's Wharf," *Civil War Times Illustrated*, March 1998, pp. 48–49; and perhaps others.

First Lieutenant (on 24 May 1864), later Captain and Brevet Lt. Col., Edward Simonton states in his postwar account:

I saw no mention made in the northern newspapers of this action at Wilson's Landing [which was overshadowed by the Battle of North Anna River, 21–26 May, involving approximately 93,000 total Federal and Confederate troops, and resulting in some 4,000 total casualties on both sides[4]]. The only account I noticed at the time was in the *Richmond Examiner* [of May 28, 1864] which was *a gross exaggeration of the actual facts* and *which amused us not a little at the time.* Of course, Gen. Fitzhugh Lee and his command desired to make as good a showing as possible from a Confederate standpoint for their defeat and loss of men, without results....

[Simonton then quotes the *Richmond Examiner* account verbatim.]

So much for the enemy's side of the case. Now the actual truth as evidenced by one who saw the intrenchments as they were constructed is this: The Union line of intrenchments started from a point above the landing and ran in the shape of a horseshoe to a point a short distance below the landing. *Along about one-third distance of this line ran a ditch about 8 feet wide and 5 to 6 feet deep; along the remaining part of our line there was no ditch at all*; the earth being thrown up from the inside; *the abatis constructed simply of felled trees with trimmed branches and limbs placed outside of the ditch as* [far as] *completed, and no farther. The alleged wire entwined* among the tree branches *existed only in the lively imagination of the enemy or the writer of the newspaper article.* The fact is that *our intrenchments were only about one-third completed when Gen. Lee's force came upon us so suddenly....*

As for the unfinished part of our intrenched line, *where there was no abatis or ditch, the enemy could easily and successfully have charged upon the works there,* had we no forces to oppose them, *but our men were ready for them. The enemy tried that to their discomfiture and sorrow. As to the gunboats* in the river, *so far from there being six or seven at that* time, *there was only one gunboat, the Fawn* [sic; *Dawn*]....

No mention was made in the [Richmond] newspaper that *Gen. Lee was defeated and driven back by Union forces consisting nearly all of colored troops.*[5]

Captain William Davis Parlin, whose Company E, 1st Regiment, USCT probably was posted "where there was no abatis or ditch," and breastworks were unfinished; he later stated: *"Cattle ran over the breastworks that very morning in my company's front* and in one of the most exposed position on the line & we had only about 1,000 men in our whole force [when the Action began]. *It was the brave* [and] *fearless stand made by those negro soldiers that made it impregnable."*[6] The exaggeration of Wild's fortifications, numbers of black Federal troops (and the transformation of some into two white regiments and U.S. Marines from the fleet), numbers of gunboats and transports, fabrication about wire entanglements, and downplaying the size of Fitzhugh Lee's Confederate forces and their determined assaults, and their losses, by Confederate officers who briefed Richmond newspaper correspondents, reflect humiliation of having been "defeated and driven back by *Union forces consisting nearly all of colored troops.*"

In 2006, William Gladstone wrote: "[At Wilson's Wharf] the 1st Regiment, USCT played the leading part. 1,100 black troops defeated a rebel cavalry force of 2,500. It was possibly the largest single victory during the Civil War won by a force comprised mostly of African American soldiers. They could [also] attack a fortification [later] as well as defend them."[7]

Major General Fitzhugh Lee had two very special reasons for covering up his failure by understating his losses and exaggerating Federal fortifications, numbers of U.S. Navy gunboats, etc. The first and most obvious reason was expressed by Union veteran Edward Simonton: "No mention was made in the *Richmond Examiner* that Gen. Lee was defeated and driven back by ... *colored troops.*" The second reason was Fitzhugh Lee's aspiration to command the cavalry corps of his uncle's Army of Northern Virginia. The "Virginia clique" favored Fitz Lee, but Maj. Gen. Wade Hampton, a wealthy patrician from South Carolina, was senior and demonstrated his competence for corps command at Trevilian Station, Samaria (St. Mary's) Church, and First Reams Station, and he was appointed to the coveted corps command on 1 August 1864,[8] perhaps partly to avoid a charge of nepotism if Fitz Lee had been chosen. Fitz Lee eventually replaced Hampton in early 1865 when Hampton was sent to the Carolinas to help defend against Sherman.

Civil War Cavalry Historian Eric J. Whittenberg summarized Fitzhugh Lee's military traits: "Articulate and witty, Fitz Lee had a personality that mirrored Stuarts's, and he was the commander's favorite subordinate. Although Fitz had prewar military experience, his early war performance consisted of flashes of brilliance leavened with sometimes lackluster actions and disappointing miscues."[9] Fitz Lee certainly had one of his "disappointing miscues" on 24 May 1864, when he suffered a humiliating defeat inflicted by, of all enemies, United States Colored Troops.

Later, Maj. Gen. Fitzhugh Lee took his cavalry to support Maj. Gen. Jubal Early's army in the Shenandoah Valley in August 1864. He was seriously wounded at Winchester on 19 September and was out of action until January 1865, when he returned to command the cavalry on the north side of the James River. Although he succeeded Wade Hampton as the senior cavalry commander in the Army of Northern Virginia, he did not act as chief of the decimated cavalry corps until near the end of the Petersburg siege. He was absent during the Battle of Five Forks, but in command at Appomattox on 9 April. Riding through Federal lines with part of his troops, he surrendered two days later. After the war he farmed, was elected Democratic governor of Virginia during 1885–1889, and was consul general to Havana during 1896–1898, displaying firmness and tact in the difficult times preceding the Spanish-American War. In 1898 he became a major general, U.S. Volunteers and commanded the VII Corps in Cuba before retiring as a U.S. Army brigadier general, having commanded the Department of Missouri. He wrote a biography of his uncle Robert E. Lee and other historical works about the war. He died in the District of Columbia on 28 April 1905.[10]

The Union Generals Who Commanded U.S. Colored Troops at Wilson's Wharf in May 1864

Two newspaper correspondents described General Wild at Wilson's Wharf and his earlier leadership style in North Carolina. The correspondent whose account was published in 1868 wrote a very complimentary article about Wild and his division commander, Brig. Gen. Hinks:

> Gen. Wilde [sic] directed the fight in person. [He] is an *ENTHUSIAST* on the subject of colored troops. *He firmly believes that a white man*, in course of time and by strict discipline, *can be made as good a soldier* [as a black man]. He has the most implicit confidence in his troops, and so have they in him. General Hinks, who commands the colored division, took it by preference. There are those who affect to despise negro troops, and say they cannot be trusted in positions of responsibility, or in an emergency. A Regular Army officer, who entertains many of the prejudices, admitted that *with good officers the negroes would make good soldiers. An old adage, and true of any men of any color.*[11]

That correspondent, possibly an Army officer, was well ahead of his time. It would take almost 100 years or so before the U.S. Armed Forces would truly assimilate that "old adage," despite positive experiences with non-white soldiers dating back to the American War for Independence and prior colonial conflicts.

Wild's Division Commander, Brig. Gen. Edward Winslow Hinks (or Hincks—he dropped the "c" early in life and reinstated it in 1871) was born in Bucksport, Maine, in 1830. He moved from Bangor to Boston and became a Massachusetts legislator in 1855. When the Civil War began, he was commissioned a 2nd lieutenant in the 2nd U.S. Cavalry Regiment; then lieutenant colonel and colonel of the 8th Massachusetts Infantry; and colonel of the 19th Massachusetts Infantry on 3 August 1861. He saw combat at Ball's Bluff on 3 August 1861, was wounded at White Oak Swamp on 30 June 1862, and wounded again at Antietam and disabled for six months; he suffered pain and debility for the rest of his life.

Promoted to brigadier general in 1862, Hinks took command of the Division of U.S. Colored Troops on 20 April 1864, two weeks before it led Butler's army up the James River and made three amphibious landings. He "served credibly" despite often being ill or prostrated by his wounds. His afflictions helped persuade General Butler to suspend a promising assault by Hinks's division against Petersburg on 9 May. Hinks was forced to relinquish his command and quit active service on 1 July 1864 and return to recruiting duty.[12]

Hinks's Colored (later 3rd) Division was part of the XVIII Army Corps commanded by Maj. Gen. William Farrar ("Baldy") Smith from 2 May through 10 July 1864. From Vermont, Smith graduated from West Point in 1845. He was a "contentious controversalist who spent most of his time criticizing plans of other generals." Grant summarized Smith: "Whilst a very able officer, [he] is obstinate, and likely to condemn whatever is not suggested by himself."[13] Smith had expected an independent command and was disappointed to serve under Butler, of whom he asked Grant: "I want to ask how you can place a man in command of two army corps, who is as helpless as a child on the field of battle, and as visionary as an opium eater in council?"[14]

Major General Benjamin Franklin Butler, Commander of the Department of Virginia and North Carolina since November 1863, and of the Army of the James, was a complex man of many contradictions. He became Massachusetts's most famous and infamous Civil War politician and general, acquiring nicknames as "Old Cock-eye" for his appearance; "Beast" for his treatment of New Orleans civilians as military governor; and "Spoons" for allegedly stealing the Twiggs family silverware, but which he always insisted he paid for.

Gerard Patterson provided a succinct sketch of Butler in the May–June 1993 issue of *Civil War Times Illustrated*:

> Butler was a man of lofty intellect, clever and insightful legally, politically, and, one can conclude, financially. He was amazingly enterprising, always busy with imaginative projects. His energy and persistence were boundless. In his career, he was a man of utter fearlessness, ready to champion the most unpopular causes or challenge authority at any level if an issue stirred him....
>
> At the same time, Butler could be cruel, a man of strong, unyielding prejudices, willing to hurt anyone who got in his way or upset his plans. Some of his actions were utterly outrageous and probably intended to have that effect.... There is little doubt he misused his positions of power to enrich himself and those around him. [No wonder he tolerated Edward A. Wild's idiosyncrasies.]

Butler was born in Deerfield, Massachusetts, in 1818, but his widowed mother moved the family to Lowell, Massachusetts, where she operated a very respectable boarding house for young women who worked in cotton mills there. Ben, a brilliant student, could not gain an appointment to West Point, an experience which contributed to his lasting disdain for the Military Academy's graduates, who would later disdain him as an incompetent political general. He attended Colby College and read law, building his practice by taking at low fees cases of factory girls who had complaints against the mill, grievances with which he was familiar from his early days at home. He won a seat in the Massachusetts legislature in 1852 on a platform calling for a 10-hour work day, and by 1860 he owned a fine mansion and was regarded as one of the wealthiest men in his district. In 1844, he had married a cultivated young actress, Sarah Hildreth, who bore him three sons and a daughter.

Butler was a delegate to the 1860 Democratic Convention in Charleston, South Carolina, pledged to support Stephen A. Douglas for the presidential nomination. He shocked his constituents back home by voting for Jefferson Davis of Mississippi on 57 ballots. Davis, as Secretary of War, had appointed Butler, an unlikely choice, as a member of the West Point Board of Visitors. In Lowell, Butler defended his support of Davis by arguing his nomination would appease the South and hold the Union together. After Butler's later conduct in New Orleans in 1862, Confederate President Davis declared, "In the event of [Butler's] capture, the officer in charge do cause him to be immediately executed by hanging."[15]

In May 1861, Butler, the first volunteer officer promoted to major general by President Lincoln, refused to return fugitive slaves belonging to a Confederate colonel and coined the term "contraband." At New Orleans, Butler took another major step. Louisiana was the only state where black men served in the militia. The Louisiana Native Guards, recruited from the free colored population of New Orleans, became part of the State Militia of Louisiana, Confederate States of America, on 23 April 1861. The Native Guards had their own black officers. By early 1862, there were 2,000 to 3,000 members of colored military organizations in the state. When the Confederates evacuated New Orleans in March, the Native Guards were ordered to disband. On 22 August 1862, Butler, as Union commander and military governor, issued General Order No. 63, which established four regiments of Louisiana Native Guards, three of which had some black officers, as volunteer soldiers of the United States. In June 1863, these became the 1st through 4th Regiments of Infantry, Corps d'Afrique; in April 1864, they would be redesignated the 73rd, 74th, 75th, and 76th Regiments, U.S. Colored Troops.[16]

Unfortunately, Butler's military skills did not match his political and other talents, and he shared blame with his two West Point–educated corps commanders, Gilmore and Smith, for dawdling and failing to exploit their surprise movement up the James River by aggressively assaulting Petersburg and Richmond when they were lightly defended. Instead, he allowed their forces to be bottled up on the narrow-necked Bermuda Hundred Peninsula.

The three Union generals, Wild, Hinks, and Butler, who commanded U.S. Colored Troops at Wilson's Wharf, Fort Powhatan, and other places during May 1864 certainly had their personal shortcomings as senior military officers. But these Union generals believed African Americans were not mere property, but human beings who deserved to be free and become more than enslaved field hands or house servants. They were devoted to their black soldiers and did their utmost to ensure their success and survival in battle. And their subordinate white officers and black soldiers demonstrated that their generals' trust and confidence were not misplaced.

VIII

United States Colored Troops, Black Sailors and Black Confederates

Many Body Servants and Cooks, Very Few Soldiers

Nearly all 7,122 officers (except for some 100 black officers) ranking from 2nd lieutenant to colonel who commanded the 178,975 black men (and a few Native Americans and whites) who enlisted in 135 infantry regiments, 12 regiments of heavy artillery, ten batteries of light artillery, and six cavalry regiments that comprised the United States Colored Troops (USCT) were white. White officers also commanded the approximately 17,000 black men who served in the U.S. Navy,[1] some of them during the Action at Wilson's Wharf on 24 May 1864.

A "War Graph" states that, of a total of "172,984 African American USCT Recruits" (not counting about 4,500 additional black soldiers who enlisted in four state colored regiments), 93,542 came from "Confederate Slave States"; 41,719 were from "Border Slave States"; and 37,723 from "Northern Free States." States providing over 4,000 recruits each were: Louisiana, 24,502; Kentucky, 23,703; Tennessee, 20,703; Mississippi, 17,869; Pennsylvania, 8,612; Ohio, 5,092; and New York, 4,125. Strength levels of USCT units reached 37,482 troops in October 1863, and 101,950 troops by October 1864.[2]

Seventy-five black officers, including a major, in two Louisiana regiments recruited by Butler at New Orleans in 1862, comprised about two-thirds of all black officers who served in the Civil War. Butler's successor forced out most of them under the guise of their "incompetence." Most of the other black officers were chaplains or surgeons.[3] Joseph T. Glatthar states: "The basic premise for an exclusively white officer corps was that blacks lacked the qualities to become good soldiers. The assumption was that only the best white officers could convert them into passable soldiers."[4] A recruiting advertisement described the type of officers sought for the U.S. Colored Troops:

> NO PERSON IS WANTED [as an officer] who feels that he is making a sacrifice in accepting a position in a Colored Regiment, or who desires the place simply for higher rank and pay. It is the aim of those having this organization in charge to make Colored Troops equal to the best of White Troops, in Drill, Discipline, and Officers. It is more than possible that Colored Troops will hereafter form no inconsiderable portion of the permanent army of the United States, and it should be the aim of every officer of Colored Troops to make himself and his men fit for such an honorable position…. *It can be no "sacrifice" to any man in command in a service which gives Liberty to Slaves, and Manhood to Chattels, as well as Soldiers to the Union.*"[5]

Strong motivation, indeed!

But Can They Fight?

In an oft-quoted statement, Frederick Douglass, prominent black abolitionist and staunch advocate for enlisting black soldiers in the Union Army, said: "Once let the black man get upon his person the brass letters 'U.S.,' let him get an eagle on his button and a musket on his shoulder and bullets in his pockets and there is no power on earth which can deny that he has earned the right to citizenship in the United States." Confederate Major General Howell Cobb of Georgia, former chairman of the 1861 Secession Convention at Montgomery, Alabama, and a staunch *opponent* of enlisting black soldiers for the Confederate army, essentially agreed with Douglass when he wrote to Secretary of War Seddon on 10 January 1865: "The day you make soldiers of them [slaves] is

"Frederick Douglass, 1818–1895, born a slave on the Eastern shore of Maryland, but ran away to become a great anti-slavery leader" (postcard, Leib Image Archives, York, PA).

the beginning of the end of the [Confederate States'] revolution. *If slaves will make good soldiers, our whole theory of slavery is wrong.*"[6]

Slavery, emancipation, and citizenship for African Americans were political and economic issues that could be debated, but they left unanswered a key military question: "Can black men make good enough soldiers to fight veteran white Confederate troops?" The answer could only come from the battlefield. After his overwhelming victory against black and white Union troops at Fort Pillow, Maj. Gen. Nathan Bedford Forrest gave *his* answer when he reported on 15 April 1864 to Lt. Gen. Leonidas Polk, concluding: "*It is hoped that these facts will demonstrate to the Northern people that negro soldiers cannot cope with Southerners.*"[7]

Prior to the Action at Wilson's Wharf on 24 May 1864, Federal black military units had fought in 77 battles, actions, and skirmishes significant enough to be listed in the *Official Army Register of the Volunteer Force of the United States Army*, Part VIII, as compiled by William A. Gladstone.[8] But only nine of these, mostly minor skirmishes involving only one USCT regiment or detachment, had occurred in Virginia during March and early May 1864.

Despite having "good officers" and "good material," it took time and experience to discipline and train U.S. Colored Troops into cohesive and effective fighting units. As late as 26 June 1864, Brig. Gen. Hinks reported on the mixed readiness of the ten regiments in his Colored division:

> Of these ten, I consider but five to be effective for duty in line of battle; to wit, the First, Fourth, Fifth, Sixth, and Twenty-second. These are the regiments of infantry that were engaged on the 15th [at Petersburg]. The Tenth and Thirty-seventh Regiments of Infantry are largely composed of new recruits, and but partially organized; the Fifth Massachusetts Cavalry (dismounted) is also composed of new recruits, and not drilled in infantry formations; the First and Second U.S. Colored

Major General, later Lt. Gen. Nathan Bedford Forrest, CSA (Library of Congress).

Cavalry (dismounted) are unskilled in the use of arms, untaught in infantry formations, and without drill and proper discipline.

Justice to these troops, as well as regard for the true interests of the service, would seem to require that the five regiments last named be sent to a camp of instruction, and be prepared for effective service. As they now are I am unwilling to risk them in battle.[9]

William A. Gladstone summarized the history of the black soldier in the Civil War, which involved more than the soldier alone: "[His] participation was due to the efforts of *both white and black men*: politicians, abolitionists, military and religious leaders, and simple, concerned citizens of the Nation ... their numbers increased [despite] problems of pay, bounty, fatigue, education, health, cooperation with white soldiers, family considerations, etc., [most of which] had been rectified by the time black soldiers were discharged. By the end of the war, black soldiers constituted 11 percent of the Union Army; by fall of 1865, after most white units had been disbanded, black soldiers made up 36 percent of the U.S. Army. Most USCT units then belonged to the XXV Army Corps commanded by Maj. Gen. Godfrey Weitzel. It was formed in December 1864 by combining black units from the old X and XVIII Corps that had served under Butler, and later it was sent to Texas to counter French influence in Mexico. The last USCT regiment, the 125th Infantry, was disbanded in December 1867. *In addition to 13 white officers in the USCT, 16 black soldiers and eight black sailors received the Medal of Honor for their heroism during the Civil War.*[10]

Some Union Colored Units That Suffered the Most Casualties

The Union Army black unit that suffered the highest percentage of killed and died of wounds began as a battalion of fugitive slaves from Arkansas and Missouri and was organized without presidential authority at Fort Scott, Kansas, in August 1862. In a skirmish at Island Mound, Missouri, on 29 October 1862, some 450 Confederate guerrillas attacked 225 black Kansas soldiers and their white officers on a scouting expedition. The 1st Kansas suffered 22 casualties, including *10 killed—the first black Union soldiers to die in battle.* The Rebels suffered three times as many casualties, and Confederate prisoners were gathered up by wagonloads. In January 1863, this unit mustered into Federal service as the 1st Kansas Colored Volunteers; in December 1864 it was redesignated the 79th (New) Infantry Regiment, USCT. It fought in fifteen engagements. Of a total enrollment of 1,249, the 79th Regiment, USCT lost 5 officers and 183 enlisted men killed or mortally wounded; the total of 188 combat deaths, 15.0 percent, ranked it 21st among all Union regiments (the first-ranked 2nd Wisconsin Infantry Regiment lost 238, or 19.7 percent of its 1,203 enrolled.) The 79th Regiment, USCT also lost 1 officer and 165 men felled by disease, for a total of 354 deaths.[11]

The first major engagement after the Emancipation Proclamation took effect on 1 January 1863 that involved black Union soldiers *and black officers,* occurred at Port Hudson, Louisiana, on 27 May 1863. The First Louisiana Native Guards (ex-Confederate Louisiana State Militia composed of free black men from New Orleans and redesignated 1st Regiment, Corps d'Afrique, and later the 73rd Infantry Regiment, USCT), and the Third Louisiana Native Guards (3rd Regiment, Corps d'Afrique, and later 75th Regiment, USCT) made brave but futile charges across open ground against a strongly fortified Confederate position. Captain Andre Cailloux, a free black from New Orleans, shouted orders in English and French as he led the advance until he was killed by an artillery shell. The First Regiment's color bearer replied to his colonel's order to "Protect, defend, die for, but do not surrender these colors" with: "Colonel, I will bring back these colors to you in honor, or report to God with the reasons why." Sergeant Plancianos "reported to God" during the battle. The regiment charged six times with desperate valor, despite a deep bayou between them and the enemy, to a useless sacrifice of brave men.[12] The First Louisiana Native Guards/73rd Regiment, USCT also fought in the last major battle of the Civil War, assaulting Fort Blakeley on 9 April 1865; in all, eleven regiments of U.S. Colored Troops served in the land campaign for Mobile.

Joseph T. Glatthaar noted: "Fortunately for the black enlistment movement, neither the northern government nor public learned that the black attackers inflicted no casualties on the Confederate defenders" during the assault on Port Hudson. But a *New York Times* correspondent observed: "The men, white or black, who will not flinch from that will flinch from nothing…. It is no longer possible to doubt the bravery and steadiness of the colored race, when rightly led." In failure, they earned glory, and more importantly, respect.[13]

On 15 June 1864, the 1st Infantry Regiment, USCT, which had fought during the Action at Wilson's Wharf three weeks earlier, was among a "cloud of skirmishers" that overran the Dimmock Line works "defended by only a skirmish line of infantry," but the XVIII Corps commander, W.F. "Baldy" Smith, hesitated and an initial success was not exploited.[14] The 1st Regiment, USCT tied for having suffered the highest loss with 156 casu-

"Colored Troops after the Disaster of the Mine," Battle of the Crater, 30 July 1864. These were some of the troops in cowardly Brig. Gen. James M. Ledlie's 1st Division, Burnside's IXth Corps. Ledlie was drinking with another general in bombproof quarters while his troops were being slaughtered in the Crater (Library of Congress).

alties (17 killed, 114 wounded, and 25 missing) with the 55th Pennsylvania Volunteer Infantry; the 22nd Regiment, USCT, which had fought at Fort Powhatan on 21 May 1864, was third with 138 casualties.[15] Lieutenant Edward Simonton, 1st USCT Regiment, was seriously wounded during the attack.

The Bloody Failure in the Crater After the Mine
*   Explosion at Petersburg on 30 July 1864;*
*   the Colored Troops Are Blamed, Rather*
*   Than the Union Generals Who Blundered,*

but a Harper's Weekly Editorial Rebuts Critics of "Black Troops"

Perhaps the greatest opportunity for U.S. Colored Troops to excel and to end the war in mid–1864 came with the explosion of a mine tunneled under a section of Petersburg defenses on 30 July. Lieutenant General Ulysses S. Grant stated afterward what happened:

> So fair an opportunity will probably never occur again for carrying fortifications; preparations were good, orders ample, and everything subsequent to the explosion of the mine, shows that almost without loss the [objective] crest beyond could have been carried....
>
> General Burnside wanted to put his colored division [which had been trained for the assault] in front, and I believe if he had done so it would have been a success. Still I agree with General Meade as to his objections to the plan. General Meade said that if we put the colored troops in front ... and it should prove a failure, it would then be said, and very properly, that we were shoving those people ahead to get killed because we did not care anything about them....
>
> I blame myself for one thing. I was informed that General Burnside ... trusted to *the pulling of straws* which division should lead. It happened to fall on what I thought was the worst commander in his corps.... I mean General [James Hewitt] Ledlie [who had drunkenly sacrificed his brigade of white troops at Ox Ford during the Battle of North Anna on 24 May but had succeeded to division command]. It was the saddest affair I have ever witnessed in the war ... if the troops had been properly commanded ... we would have captured Petersburg with all the artillery and a good portion of its support, without the loss of 500 men.[16]

Instead of leading the attack as they had been prepared to do, the black regiments followed white regiments that had allowed themselves to be trapped inside the mine crater, where fighting was extremely chaotic and violent. The confused retreat under fire added to the Union disaster that resulted in 3,800 Federal and only 1,500 Confederate casualties as well as a lost opportunity to possibly end the war. Again, black prisoners were murdered. A Georgia soldier wrote home: "Some four [captured] negroes went to the rear as we could not kill them as fast as they passed us."[17]

Black Union troops were criticized by some Northern newspapers in a national debate after the Battle of the Crater, prompting a very angry and blunt reply in a long, unsigned editorial, "The Black Troops," in the 20 August 1864 issue of *Harper's Weekly*:

> There can be nothing more pitiful than the malevolent eagerness with which certain newspapers deride the colored troops for being no braver than the white troops at Petersburg. Did the unhappy panic at Bull Run three years ago, prove that white men were cowards? [The author then lists several failures of white Union troops.] ... When we read of McCook's [cavalry's] misfortune we remember Sheridan's, and Kautz's, and

Grierson's, and Averill's daring and victorious excursions, and we acknowledge with pride and gratitude the valor of our cavalry while we regret every mischance that befalls them....

And every sensible and true American citizen, when he reads of the faltering and retreat of the colored troops at Petersburg, recollects Fort Wagner, South Carolina [where Col. Shaw and the 54th Massachusetts made their famed charge]; Olustee, Florida [where the 54th fought an unsupported rear guard action]; Milliken's Bend, Louisiana [where black units repulsed Confederates after white troops fled]; and Baldy Smith's charge upon the same ground at Petersburg [on 15 June 1864]; and knows that failure is not the proof of cowardice or incompetency, but is one of the painful events from which no record of no corps and no army can be entirely free....

We have always insisted that colored men should have the same chance of fighting in this war that white men have; and we have always believed that, battle for battle, they would show the same spirit and pluck. Nor has the history of the war, the last assault at Petersburg included, belied our belief. And we may fairly ask whether any class of men—white, black, red, or yellow—whose services had been so grudgingly received and so reluctantly rewarded; who knew that their capture was equivalent to torture, massacre, or slavery, and for whose wrongs retaliation so loudly promised was as yet not inflicted; who were so maligned, rebuffed, and insulted as the colored men in this country are—we may fairly ask whether any soldiers would have fought more steadfastly and bravely and willingly than the colored troops in the Union army?

The mental and moral condition of those who begrudge fair play to the unfortunate, but by no means the least meritorious class of our population, is one of the most melancholy phenomena of the times. *The want of that fair play has produced the war.... The most brutal part of our population, deluded by "Conservative" demagogues, incessantly declare that "niggers are only fit for slaves"....*

The most intelligent American citizens, and the conscience of all Christian civilization rejects the foul injustice. It is the conflict of that enlightened sense of equity and right with the ferocious determination of class privilege and prejudice which is reddening our soil everywhere. Whoever panders to that injustice prolongs the war. Whoever cherishes it postpones the peace which can be permanently established upon Justice only.

One wonders whether or not the writer realized that he also was speaking to generations living now who still struggle with racial and political conflict in America and the world, between an "enlightened sense of equity and right" and "class privilege and prejudice."

The editorial continued:

The more thoughtful among those ... fostering the unmanly refusal to allow the black race fair play in this country must sometimes clearly see the hopelessness of their cause.... They know the word slavery expresses some form of injustice, disguise it as they may; and are aware that they are fighting against the human heart, against the instinct of civilization, and against the peace of the world ... they are doomed to defeat and ignominy....

They know that General [Nathaniel] Greene, in commending the valor of colored troops in the revolutionary [war] battle of Rhode Island [or Newport] on 29 August 1778, in which a newly raised Rhode Island regiment of Negroes [and whites] under Col. Christopher Greene showed "desperate valor" in repulsing three "furious assaults" by Hessian regulars[18] is more humane and enabling than he would have been had he sneered at them as unfit for soldiers because they were "niggers." For that is not the spirit which makes honorable men or great nations....

    We, too, are passing into history. In our children's eyes, which will seem nobler, the men who died bravely fighting on the slopes at Wagner and Petersburg, and on the plains of Olustee and Milliken's Bend, or those who contemptuously cried as they read [of] the last Petersburg assault, "Pshaw! Niggers will never make soldiers?"[19]

Black Sailors Who Served in Civil War Navies: Proportionately, More Blacks Served in the U.S. Navy Than in the U.S. Army

    The study of African American sailors in the Civil War must begin with the numbers who are known to have served. Joseph P. Reidy wrote:

> Over the past decade [the 1990s], a research partnership among Howard University, the Department of the Navy, and the National Park Service has made possible an examination of a fuller array of records than earlier researchers, working as individuals, were unable to explore. As a result, *nearly eighteen thousand men of African descent (and eleven women) who served in the U.S. Navy during the Civil War have been identified by name.* At 20 percent of the navy's total enlisted force, black sailors constituted a significant segment of naval manpower, and *nearly double the proportion* [11 percent] *of black soldiers who served in the U.S. Army during the Civil War.*[20]

Based on the Federal Militia Act of 1792, the U.S. Army and most state militias (except Louisiana) excluded black men until the summer of 1862, but the U.S. Navy never barred black men from serving, although from 1840 onward, regulations limited their numbers to 5 percent of the enlisted force.[21] After the war began, at enlistment centers at major Atlantic ports from Chesapeake Bay up through New England, Navy recruiters drew from the international seafaring fraternity to supplement recruits from seaboard states. By the end of the war, some 7,700 of the roughly 17,000 men whose place of nativity is recorded had been born in states remaining loyal to the Union. Many men had been mariners before the war, and others had worked on docks or at shipping-related businesses. The largest number of black men from any northern state—over 2,300 in all—came from Maryland, with its maritime culture of Chesapeake Bay and the port of Baltimore, and an 1864 agreement that transferred 800 black Marylanders from incomplete units of U.S. Colored Troops into the Navy. Another 1,500 black enlistees were born outside the United States, mostly in Canada and the Caribbean Islands. The remainder of the 17,000 men whose place of nativity is recorded—some 7,800 in all—were born in seceded Confederate states. The first-hand experience with slavery that these men had, distinguished them from their free-born shipmates. Men held in bondage often had to rely on circumstances of war for the opportunity to escape and enlist. By September 1861, the volume of requests from commanders of naval vessels to enlist fugitive slaves, originally termed "contrabands" by General Butler at Fort Monroe, reached such proportions that Secretary of the Navy Gideon Welles, a Connecticut native of antislavery bent, felt obliged to act. He permitted enlistment of former slaves whose "services can be useful," but he stipulated that all "contrabands," regardless of age, be classified as "boys," the lowest rating and pay scales, and otherwise reserved for young men under the age of eighteen.[22]

Concentrations of enslaved Africans on plantations along the Mississippi River had special relevance to the U.S. Navy's Mississippi Squadron, commanded by Flag Officer David D. Porter, who enlisted more than 2,000 "acclimated men" for his Vicksburg Campaign. Refugee camps in Union-occupied areas were a rich source of recruits. In coastal North Carolina, recruiters from the North Atlantic Blockading Squadron displayed posters promising good pay and amenities, and urging volunteers to "Come forward and serve your Country." Thus, largely composed of free men at the start of the war, over time the force included growing numbers of recently enslaved men from states where Union forces operated: the Carolinas, Mississippi, and Louisiana. But the largest contingent of Southern-born men were Virginians, more than 2,800 strong, numbers of whom had been sold to plantation regions further south. Thus, nearly 6,000 (35 percent) of the black sailors whose nativity is known, came from the Chesapeake Bay region. "Even more striking is that more than 11,000 men were born in the slave states as against 4,000 in the free states. Even allowing for a small fraction of men born free, nearly three men born into slavery served for every man born free. This demographic division profoundly affected the black naval experience during the war."[23]

From spring of 1861 through fall of 1864, the percentage of black sailors increased steadily from less than 5 percent to a peak of 23 percent. Racial demographics of the enlisted force varied by squadron and by vessel. In the European Squadron, where a few ships pursued Confederate commerce raiders and blockade runners in the North Atlantic, black sailors were few in number; e.g., on the USS *Kearsarge* black men made up 5 to 10 percent of the crew. In the North Atlantic Blockading Squadron, which drew men from both the northeast seaboard and coastal regions of Virginia and the Carolinas, the percentage was 25 percent. David Farragut's West Gulf Blockading Squadron reached 20 percent, but the Mississippi Squadron reached a high of 34 percent.[24]

Black Confederate Navymen: Most Were Slaves; a Few Were Free Men

The Confederate Navy's maximum enlisted strength was barely 4,500 men during the entire Civil War, and at any given time, probably fewer than 3,000 men. Free blacks could enlist with approval of the local squadron commander or the Navy Department, and *slaves were permitted to serve*

"Palmetto Artillery Battery, South Carolina State Troops (upper right, playing cards, etc.) near Charleston, August 1861." Four cooks/body servants (slaves), one of whom holds a tambourine, appear about to prepare a meal. Behind and above them, a corporal has his hand thrust into his jacket, Napoleon-style (Library of Congress).

with their master's consent. No draft of seamen to a newly commissioned vessel could have more than 5 percent of blacks (following old U.S. Navy regulations). "Though figures are lacking, a fair number of blacks served as coal heavers, officers' stewards, or at the top end, as highly skilled tidewater pilots."[25] Michael Foster adds:

> In the [Confederate] South, things were different. Most blacks employed by the Confederate Navy were slaves used as cooks or pilots. There weren't many freedmen who wanted to serve in the Confederate Navy ... but there is evidence of a few who did. According to tradition, three freedmen—Charles Cleaper, James Hicks and Joe Johnson, voluntarily served aboard CSS *Palmetto State*, and were the only free African Americans to surrender under arms with General Robert E. Lee at Appomattox.[26]

David White, a slave from Delaware (a border slave state) had been traveling to Europe with his master on the packet *Tonawanda* when it was captured by the CSS *Alabama*. Captain Raphael Semmes freed him and put him on the rolls of *Alabama* as a wardroom "boy." Tragically, David White drowned when the *Alabama* sank during her battle with the USS *Kearsarge* on 19 June 1864.[27]

Joseph T. Glatthaar suggests that "Blacks alone did not win the war, but their timely and extensive support contributed significantly and may have made the difference between a Union victory and stalemate or defeat." President Abraham Lincoln admitted this himself in late 1864: "Any different policy in regard to the colored man, deprives us of his help, and this is more than we can bear. We can not spare the hundred and forty or fifty thousand now serving as soldiers, seamen, and laborers. This is not a sentiment or taste, but one of physical force which may be measured and estimated as horse-power and steam-power are measured and estimated. Keep it and you can save the Union. Throw it away, and the Union goes with it."[28]

Black Confederates: Those Who Served with, but Not in the Confederate Army, and the Very Few Who Served in the C.S. Army at the End of the War

Following are extracts from an early manuscript (121 pages, single-spaced) on the subject of blacks—many slaves and some free—who served as *civilian* body servants, cooks, teamsters, etc.; and the very few who served in Confederate ranks as soldiers.

Wednesday, 10 September (1862):

At 4 o'clock this morning the Rebel army began to move from [Frederick, Maryland], [Stonewall] Jackson's force taking the advance. The movement continued until 8 o'clock p.m., occupying 16 hours. [They had] not more than 64,000 men. Over 3,000 negroes must be included in the number.... They had arms, rifles, muskets, sabers, bowie knives, dirks, etc. [Many] were supplied with knapsacks, haversacks, canteens ... and they were manifestly an integral portion of the Southern Confederacy army. They were riding horses and mules, driving wagons, riding on [artillery] caissons, in ambulances, with the staff of generals and *promiscuously mixed up with all the Rebel horde.*

Diary of Dr. Lewis Steiner,

U.S. Sanitary Commission[29]

The blacks carrying arms (for their masters? ... or extra arms) *were not soldiers*! They were not in ranks of a military unit but "promiscuously mixed up."

About the possibility of recruiting blacks *as soldiers in* the Confederate Army, a British officer-observer with the Army of Northern Virginia, wrote (as recruiting of U.S. Colored Troops in the North had barely begun):

I am of the opinion that the Confederates could, if they chose, convert a great number [of the black population] into soldiers.... *But I do not imagine such an experiment will be tried, except as a very last resort."*

Journal of Lt. Col. James Arthur Lyon Fremantle,
Coldstream Guards, on the Retreat from Gettysburg,
July 1863[30]

Colonel Freemantle's words, particularly "except as a very last resort," proved prescient. These two contemporary statements essentially summarize participation by black males in the Confederate armies during most of the war: thousands served in *civilian* capacities since early in the war, but official sanction would not be given to organizing slaves and/or free blacks *as soldiers* until March 1865 when the Confederate military situation was hopeless.

Two issues were obstacles to large-scale use of blacks in ranks of Southern combat units. The "Theory of Slavery," as Maj. Gen. Howell Cobb of Georgia, who owned over 1,000 slaves, noted, was that Africans were part of an inferior race and could not become good soldiers because they lacked pride, courage, self-reliance, and other qualities essential to success in battle. The other issue was a longstanding fear of slave revolts, exacerbated by John Brown's 1859 Raid on Harpers Ferry to seize the U.S. Armory and arm slaves for a massive insurrection, an uprising that didn't occur. But blacks, especially ubiquitous "body servants," were an integral part of Confederate armies from the beginning.[31] And a few may have been present during the Action at Wilson's Wharf.

On 7 November 1863, Maj. Gen. Dabney H. Maury, a Virginian and West Point graduate who commanded the Department of the Gulf at Mobile, wrote General Samuel Cooper at Richmond: "General: I again call your attention to *my request to accept into the Confederate service the company of Creoles at Mobile.*" On 20 November, Secretary of War James A. Seddon replied: "*Our position with the North and before the world will not allow the employment as armed soldiers of negroes.* If these creoles can be naturally and properly discriminated from negroes, the authority may be considered as conferred; otherwise not, unless you can enlist them as 'navies' [the English term] *or for subordinate working purposes.*"[32]

Eventually, four small units of Creoles or free Negroes under white officers were raised by Maury at Mobile, after Admiral David Glasgow Farragut's stunning victory at the Battle of Mobile Bay on 5 August 1864 and Federal capture of the forts at the bay entrance added urgency to Maury's recruiting efforts.[33]

To Maj. Gen. Patrick R. Cleburne in winter quarters at Dalton, Georgia, in January 1864, it seemed natural to suggest *recruiting of negroes as soldiers.* Recognizing the impracticality of having an army half slave and half free, he thought it logical to simply *emancipate all the slaves.* He submitted his ideas in a written document, signed by most of the officers in his division, which he read during a meeting at Army of Tennessee Headquarters. Cleburne's document, which also stated the war was being lost, created a sensation immediately. There were strong expressions of dissent, and no officer present favored it. Major General W.H.T. Walker sent a copy to Richmond. Secretary of War James A. Seddon wrote General Joseph E. Johnston, "[W]hile no doubt or mistrust was for a moment entertained of the patriotic intents of the gallant author," *President Davis thought*

"**Major General Patrick Cleburne, engraving from a wartime photograph.**" He was killed while leading a charge at Franklin, Tennessee on 30 November 1864 (postcard, American Heritage Engravings, Alexandria, Virginia).

that "promulgation or dissemination" of the paper would produce "discouragement, destruction, and dissension" and asked that it be suppressed.[34]

On 24 January 1865, Robert Garlich Hill Kean, Head of the Confederate Bureau of War, confided to his diary: "Rives [A.L.] showed me a copy of a letter from General [R.E.] Lee to Mr. Andrew Hunter on the subject of negro enlistment, at the sentiments of which I am astonished. *He favors emancipation per se; advocates large enlistments accompanied by the promise of prospective emancipation of the families of the negro soldier as a reward of good conduct; overlooks entirely all the difficulties,* legal, constitutional and physical; *and urges that negroes be enlisted at once.*"[35]

On 4 March 1865, the Virginia House of Delegates resolved:

> ...that the General Assembly of Virginia do hereby authorize Confederate authorities to call upon Virginia, through the Governor of the commonwealth, *for all her able bodied male free negroes* between the ages of eighteen and forty-five, *and as many of her male slaves* between the ages aforesaid, *as may be deemed necessary for the public defense, not exceeding twenty-five per centum of said slaves, to be called for on requisition of the General-in-Chief* [Robert E. Lee] *of the Confederate Armies,* as he may deem most expedient for the public service ... not more than one slave in every four shall be taken from one owner.... But nothing in the foregoing resolution shall be construed into a restriction upon the President or General-in-Chief ... or a prohibition to the *employment of the slaves and free negroes* for the public defense in such manner, *as soldiers* or otherwise. As the General-in-Chief may deem most expedient."[36]

Virginia was the only Confederate state to do so.

On 7 March, General Lee gave General Longstreet detailed instructions about which routes to take when the time came to retreat from Richmond and Petersburg.[37]

On 13 March, the Confederate Congress enacted:

> That in order to provide additional forces to repel invasion, maintain the rightful possession of the Confederate States, secure their independence, *and preserve their institutions,* the *President* be, and he *is hereby, authorized to ask for and accept from the owners of slaves, the services of such number of able-bodied negro men as he may deem expedient, for and during the war, to perform military service in whatever capacity he may direct....*
>
> Section 2. That *the General-in-Chief be authorized to organize the said slaves into companies, battalions, regiments, and brigades.*
>
> Section 3. That while employed in the service the said troops shall receive the same rations, clothing, and compensation as are allowed to other [i.e., white] troops in the same branch of service.
>
> Section 4. ...the President is hereby authorized to call on *each state,* whenever he thinks it expedient, *for her quota of 300,000* troops ... *irrespective of color....* That not more than twenty-five per cent of the male slaves ... shall be called....
>
> Section 5. *That nothing in this act shall be construed to authorize a change in the relation the said slaves shall bear toward their owners, except by consent of the owners and of the States in which they reside,* and in pursuance of the laws thereof."[38]

In short, slaves who fought for the Confederacy would remain slaves, unless their owners and the states in which they lived, decided otherwise! But soon that was changed.

On 15 March 1865, the War Department authorized "Majors J.W. Pegram and Thomas P. Turner (through General Ewell) ... to raise *a company or companies of negro soldiers* under provisions of the act of Congress approved March 13, 1865.[39]

General Orders No. 14 was issued at Richmond on *23 March 1865, ten days after Congress passed the Act of 13 March "to increase the military force of the Confederate States."* Paragraph IV provided: "The enlistment of colored persons under this act will be made on *printed forms, to be furnished,* similar to those established for the regular service." Paragraph VIII stated: "It is not the intention of the President to grant any authority for raising regiments or brigades. *The only organizations* to be perfected at the depots or camps of instruction *are those of companies* (and in exceptional cases where slaves are [from] one [large] estate) of battalions consisting of four companies.... *All larger organizations will be left for future action as experience may determine.*"[40] This was written 3½ months after the Union Army's XXV *Corps* was created by assigning *32 infantry regiments* and *one cavalry regiment* of experienced U.S. Colored Troops in *three divisions made up of several brigades each*!

On 21 March 1865, the *Richmond Sentinel* observed: "The Battalion [of three companies, two of them white] from Camps Winder and Jackson, under the command of Dr. Chambliss, will parade on the square on Wednesday evening at 4½ o'clock. This is the first company of Negro Troops raised in Virginia. It was organized about a month [ago], by Dr. Chambliss, from the employees of the hospitals." Another company of blacks, this one raised by Major J.W. Turner, was drilled daily in Richmond by Lt. Virginius Bossieux. On 27 March, the *Richmond Examiner* reported that the company numbered 35 men (12 free blacks, 23 slaves). "They moved with evident pride and satisfaction to themselves.... Their rations are cooked in Libby Prison."[41]

On 1 April, as "the final curtain was beginning to drop on closing acts of Lee's Army of Northern Virginia and the Confederate Government," President Davis wrote a long letter regarding "the raising of negro troops":

General Robert E. Lee, Commanding Armies, &c.:

Sir: *I have been laboring without much progress, to advance the raising of negro troops....* [After describing many difficulties, Davis concludes:] The question is often asked of me "Will we hold Richmond?" to which my answer is, "If we can; it is purely a question of military power." *The distrust is increasing, and embarrasses in many ways.*[42]

About 9 p.m. on 1 April, General Grant rejoined his staff after scribbling out dispatches in his tent and said ("as coolly as if remarking on the state of the weather"): "I have ordered a general assault along the lines."[43]

On 2 April 1865, as the Federal VI, IX, and XXIV Corps gained their objectives in bloody fighting against determined resistance at Petersburg, General-in-Chief Robert E. Lee at first remained calm. He later confided to one of his officers: "Well, Colonel, it has happened as I told them it would in Richmond. *The line has stretched until it has broken.*"[44]

On 4 April, Private R.M. Doswell, a Confederate courier, witnessed a skirmish near Amelia Court House on Lee's retreat from Richmond: "I saw *a wagon train guarded by Confederate negro soldiers, a novel sight for me.*" The wagon train was manned by a company of black infantry, who repulsed a charge by overconfident Federal cavalry. The Yankees reformed on a hillside, then charged down, overran the train, and captured or scattered the black Confederate soldiers. On 4 (or 6) April, the courier saw black Confederates who were wearing "good gray uniforms" and working on fortifications. He was "informed 'they belonged to the *only company of colored troops in the Confederate service,*' having been enlisted by Major Turner in Richmond. *Their muskets* were stacked, and it was evident that they regarded their present employment in no unfavorable light."[45] The company of "Confederate negro soldiers" guarding a wagon train, and "the only company of colored troops (left of several companies?) in the Confederate service" apparently were the remnant of Major Thomas T. Turner's so-called "Negro Brigade."[46]

The author also found names of 129 "Negros," "Mulattos," etc., one a slave, each of whom was

General Robert E. Lee, Commander, Army of Northern Virginia, and then General-in-Chief of all Confederate Armies, advocated emancipation and enlistment of slaves as soldiers in late 1864 ... too late (The Virginia Historical Society).

President Jefferson Davis. He lamented his inability to recruit slaves as Confederate soldiers (courtesy Cary Delery, Metairie, Louisiana).

enlisted as a "Private" in *white* Confederate units, in a microfilm roll at the National Archives and Records Administration, and "14 negroes" who were enlisted in white Louisiana units, besides others previously mentioned. So the uncounted total number of "Confederate colored soldiers" *may number a few hundred*, but certainly *not* "thousands" as some modern "Confederate-Americans" claim as part of their "Lost Cause" mythology. Uncounted thousands of blacks, mostly slaves, *did serve* in *civilian* support roles *with*, *but not in*, Confederate armies.

Unfortunately, entrenched prejudices die hard, even during wartime. Lessons about excellent performance by U.S. Colored Troops and state colored regiments during the Civil War, and by their counterparts in previous and subsequent wars, were lost again as America entered World War II. U.S. Marine Major Darrell L. Choat states:

Future generations of Marines will view the "Moving forward" article [about accepting openly gay and lesbian Marines in the Corps] much as Marines today view the racist comments made

by our [Marines'] 17th Commandant, Gen. Thomas Holcomb. In 1941, before the Navy's General Board, which was considering the question of desegregation, Holcomb stated, "Negroes did not have the 'right' to demand a place in the corps.... If it were a question of having a Marine Corps of 5,000 whites or 250,000 Negroes, I would rather have the whites." ... Gen. Holcomb's statements, and similar ones made at the time by Army Chief of Staff GEN George C. Marshall, and ADM Chester Nimitz and GEN Hap Arnold, demonstrate a collective inability of conservative and traditional military leadership to reflect on long-held prejudicial beliefs and reject them.[47]

IX

Fort Pocahontas,
June 1864–June 1865

A 1 June Sketch Plan for "Fort Pocahontas,"
So Named Officially on 6 August 1864

On 1 June 1864, Brig. Gen. Godfrey Weitzel, Chief Engineer Officer, (Butler's) Department of Virginia and North Carolina, signed *"Sketch(es)" of the fortifications at "Wilson's Wharf or Landing" and "Fort Powhattan"* [*sic*] *that were prepared "By* [i.e., at Weitzel's] *Order" by Capt. John W. Donn, Coast Survey.*[1] On 6 August 1864, Sergeant George L. Brooks, 143rd Infantry Regiment, Ohio National Guard, wrote in his diary: "We to day rec'd notice that 'the Post' on the north side of James River known as Wilson's Landing is hereby named 'Fort Pocahontas'—By order of Maj. Genl B.F. Butler— a *very* important change—but I do not believe it will be felt much. Wish we were *out* of said Fort and at home."[2]

The outline of the breastworks on the sketch map of Wilson's Wharf matches remains still visible today. The sketch was the *plan* for completing the fort with abatis all around, etc., rather than the actual fortifications that existed prior to, or on 1 June. The *official naming* of the fort occurred on or slightly before 6 August, more than two months after the Action on 24 May.

The map also shows two raised bastions, "Wilde's [*sic*] Hd. qr's" in the L-shaped Wilson house, two or three outbuildings, probably barns, and an entrance with a possible sentry post. Jagged lines at the base of two planned bastions may be the original line of the fort at the time of the Action on 24 May 1864. A 1995 aerial photo shows the trace of the fortifications after their completion, which are in an excellent state of preservation. Promoted to Major General, Godfrey Weitzel later commanded the XXVth Army Corps, composed of all U.S. Colored Troops, some of whom under Brig. Gen. Edward A. Wild were among the first to enter Richmond on 3 April 1865. The Wilson house burned sometime after the war, and a sand quarry was established at the house site sometime in the 20th century.

Union Movements Along the James River After the Action on 24 May 1864

On 26 May, on orders from General Butler, Brig. Gen. Edward W. Hinks "leapfrogged" the 1st and 22nd Infantry Regiments, USCT forward to City Point before withdrawing the 37th Regiment, USCT back to Wilson's Wharf, now supposedly his least threatened post. When moves were completed, Wild had the 10th and 37th Regiments, USCT, neither of which had completed organizing, at Wilson's Wharf. On 27 May, Hinks sent Wild a company of U.S. Colored Cavalry and asked him to "please organize [an] expedition to break up the [Confederate] signal station at Harrison's Landing."[3]

On 2 June, Wild ordered Col. John H. Holman to report at City Point with his 1st Infantry Regiment, USCT (sent to Fort Powhatan on 26 or 27 May), and Hinks directed Wild to "send one of your remaining regiments at your disposal [at Wilson's Wharf] to Fort Powhatan, retaining the other at Wilson's Wharf."[4] Wild sent the 10th Infantry Regiment, USCT to Fort Powhatan where it remained until 6 July, when it was sent to City Point. Wild retained the 37th Regiment, USCT at Wilson's Wharf. It remained there until 28 September, when it moved to Deep Bottom and then fought at Chaffin's Farm, New Market Heights, and Fair Oaks, and served in the Petersburg siege trenches before participating in assaults on Fort Fisher and the capture of Wilmington, North Carolina.[5]

The Federal Garrison at Wilson's Wharf Is Reinforced; Its Artillery Increased

By 11 June, artillery at Wilson's Wharf was increased to *four* Parrott 10-pdr rifled cannon from Captain John H. Howell's Battery M, 3rd New York Light Artillery Regiment. Artillery ammunition consisted of 852 shell rds, 237 canister rds, 161 case rds, and 54 percussion rds, for a total of 1,304 mixed rounds. Detachments of 15 engineers and 30 pioneers assisted in laying out and digging fortifications and gun platforms in the two new bastions, etc. The New York artillerymen and engineers were armed with Enfield rifle-muskets; the pioneers with "mixed" small arms. Companies E and I of the 1st U.S. Colored Cavalry Regiment arrived about 21 June.[6]

U.S. Colored Troops Attack on the Petersburg Front on 15 June 1864

On 15 June, Col. Samuel A. Duncan's 2nd Brigade: 4th, 5th, 6th, 22nd Infantry Regiments; USCT, Hinks's 3rd Division, XVIIIth Army Corps, supported by Col. John H. Holman's command, which consisted of the 1st Infantry Regiment, USCT, under Lt. Col. Elias Wright; the 5th Massachusetts Cavalry (dismounted), a colored unit; two companies of the 4th Massachusetts Cavalry (a white unit); and Captain Francis B. Choate's Battery B, 2nd Light Artillery Regiment, attacked a part of the Petersburg trenches occupied by Brig. Gen. Henry A. Wise's Confederate brigade and local militia. Duncan's brigade, and Wise's brigade and militia, numbered about 2,200 men each. Duncan's brigade formed the first line in the assault; Holman's troops (including dismounted cavalry) formed the second line. The 1st Regiment also assaulted later that day. Both Union forces performed very well under heavy artillery and small arms fire and on difficult terrain. Duncan's brigade suffered 378 casualties, but it "captured six pieces of artillery, the works and line of rifle-pits at Baylor's farm, and five of the strongly fortified works on the line of defenses around Petersburg."

Hinks's colored division had demonstrated for the first time in Virginia that U.S. Colored Troops could assault and capture Confederate fortified positions defended by artillery and sharpshooters as well as defend them, which they had already proven at Fort Powhatan and Wilson's Wharf during May 1864. Colonel Duncan summarized the performance of his brigade:

> While deploring the loss of so many valued officers and brave men, the colonel commanding finds abundant occasion for rejoicing over the important successes of the day and the splendid behavior of the troops. The troops [of Duncan's brigade, except for the 22nd Regiment] were all untried in battle, and *by many it was still a problem whether the negro would fight*. The events of the day justify the most sanguine expectations for the future. Skirmishers pushed forward with boldness; lines advanced firmly; hours of inaction under fire were endured with fortitude; assaults were made with gallantry; and wounds endured heroically."[7]

General Edward A. Wild Arrested and Court-Martialed; He Was Found Guilty but the Verdict Was Disapproved on a Technicality

On 16 June, Wild's brigade headquarters moved from Wilson's Wharf to Point of Rocks to make room for Brig. Gen. Gilman Marston, whose brigade of Ohio National Guard "100 Days" troops was coming the other way from Bermuda Hundred to occupy Wilson's Wharf, Fort Powhatan, and City Point in place of Wild's brigade of U.S. Colored Troops. By 19 June, friction between Generals Hinks and Wild had reached a boiling point. On 23 June, Hinks ordered Wild arrested and confined to limits of his 1st Brigade for refusing to obey orders to replace his brigade quartermaster, and then he had Wild court-martialed for "stripping a citizen" (William H. Clopton) and having his ex-slaves whip him, for intimating he would do it again, and for defiant and disrespectful language to Hinks.[8] Wild defended himself in a letter on 25 June to the assistant adjutant general of XVIIIth Corps, stating in a draft that his arrest was: "1. Unjust— an unlawful order, 2. [It was] *oppressive, intentionally so* ... being one of a series of oppressive and insulting acts ... designed to entrap me to my harm."[9]

Wild's court-martial by 11 officers lasted from 29 June through 1 July 1864. The Court found Wild guilty, but on 30 July, Butler issued General Order No. 86, which stated: "*Proceedings disapproved.*" Frances H. Casstevens: "Thus, *although found guilty*, Wild was freed on a technicality." Butler's action was approved by the Judge Advocate General.[10]

Ohio National Guard "100 Days" Troops Garrison Wilson's Wharf/Fort Pocahontas from Mid-June through August 1864; Diaries and Letters Describe Life at the Fort

On 16 June, the 143rd and 163rd Infantry Regiments, Ohio National Guard, were ordered by General Hinks "to proceed to Wilson's Wharf to hold that point and relieve General Wild, who will report at City Point in the same steamers that carry the Ohio troops." Both Ohio regiments would remain at Wilson's Wharf until 29 August; the 163rd Ohio (and the 143rd

Ohio as well) participated in "fatigue duty building a portion of the works [fortifications] known [after 6 August] as Fort Pocahontas."[11] On 12 June, Col. William H. Vodray's 143rd Ohio had only 415 men in six companies; Col. Hiram Miller's 163rd Ohio had 29 officers and 679 enlisted men, total 708. The enlisted men were armed with new Enfield rifle-muskets. Brigadier General John Wesley Turner, Commander, 2nd Division, Xth Corps reported: "The 100-days men I do not think are yet [reliable]. They have scarcely had a musket [for] three weeks and many are reported who do not even know how to load." Nevertheless, 250 men of the 163rd Ohio participated in a "severe skirmish" during a "reconnaissance on the Petersburg & Richmond Railroad" on 14 June and "comported themselves like veterans."[12]

On 19 June, Brig. Gen. Gilman ("Old Gil") Marston replaced Brig. Gen. Edward A. Wild, who awaited his court-martial. Marston, a 53-year-old lawyer from New Hampshire, had commanded the 10th New Hampshire Infantry Regiment at First Bull Run, in the Peninsular Campaign, and at Fredericksburg; as a brigadier general he had commanded the Department of Virginia and North Carolina and established the Point Lookout, Maryland, P.O.W. camp. Marston now commanded the 1st Brigade, 3rd Division, Xth Army Corps.[13]

Captain Albert R. Arter's Letter of 23 June 1864 to "Dear Friend"

Wilson's Landing

June 23 1864

Dear Friend

The boys are all out on duty, and I am the only one in the tent and having nothing particular on hand to day, I thought I might be wrighting [sic] a small history of my campaign as well as be loafing in my quarters and at the same time knowing that it will be interesting to you.... [1st] Lieut. [Davis] Burson [42 years old] is out on picket. Our Picket lines extends about 1 1/2 miles outside of the fortification, and is very strongly man[ne]d. I was put on Picket on last Sunday and remained until monday evening. I had control of the Picket Line. The circumstances in which I went out made me feel a little squally [apprehensive?] on Sunday morning a dispatch came into camp that there was a heavy Force of Rebs making their way towards our works. Consequently every man that could shoulder his gun was at his post and should we of been attacked we would not of gave them a very kind reception as *we have one of the best arranged breastworks I have seen. And had about one thousand men armed with the sharps Rifles[?], and one full artillery company composed of some 12 or15[?] heavy cannon* in addition there is *Two large gun Boats laying at the landing*[.]

This point was taken by our men from the Rebs some four weeks ago, and there is no dou[b]t they would like to have it back again. This point is the most prominent on the James River & is said to be the highest ... it is about Fifty feet above the river, so you will see that the country on the Jas. River cant be very high. Mr. [Doctor John C.] Wilson, the man that owned this farm, had put out this spring some 300 acres of corn. there has never been a plow or how [hoe] put in it. it is growing up in weeds. it is said he owned some 2,000 acres—and well stocked with Negros [he had 60 slaves in 1860]–when our army came in he started out [escaped] and had the Rebs to attack our forces [on 24 May]. they were entirely defeated. *Mr.* [Doctor] *Wilson with many other Rebs were kil[l]ed, and can be seen lying around outside the camp yet* [and] his negros were all set free. [Dr. Wilson was not present or killed.]

There is a man right across the [James] River—Reb who ownes [*sic*] some seventeen thousand acres of land and any amount of Negroes. & since our troops got possession here they have [been] taking all his negroes & everything else. This whole country is owned by heavy land holders owning from one to Twenty thousand acres— a poor man cant own any land. All the men on the approach of our forces leave their homes and our men destroy [vandalize their homes]. The boys bring in lots of stuff every day that they take from deserted houses. A lot of the boys went out yesterday and *broke into President Tyler[']s house* [Sherwood Forest—the gouges from their bayonets on the door frames are still visible today!] *and took and destroyed lots of stuff.* They say he [the late former President John Tyler] has the nicest kind of a mansion—the house furnished in the best of style. They [Ohio soldiers] bro[ugh]t in some very nice furniture, such as sofas, lo[o]king glasses [mirrors], [candle or wash?] stands, carpeting, etc., of the very costliest kind and destroyed the pyana [piano] & large looking glasses [they left one large mirror behind, which is still there today] & such other stuff they could not bring in ... there was a foringing [*sic*; foraging] Party went out from this post yesterday on a steamer and came back last night with a full load they Brot in 80 head of sheep, some 20 or 30 head of cattle, [a] lot of mules & Horses & *among the rest eighty negroes* they were mostly women & children, [a] good many of them young women, [and] one old nig 105 years old. so he says, there [*sic*; they] were all took from one family; they also took all the furniture they had. the family they said went on a great rail at the idea of loosing their all and well they might. Just think [how] we would feel if we had everything took. our men shows the rebs in this section no mercy. [They] take everything. we are getting up another party to start out tomorrow to clean out an old Reb [who] lives out some six miles [from Wilson's Wharf]. They say he has lots of Niggers & stock. they will bring them in—*the negroes we sent* [send] *to Fortress Monroe. There they have a large lot of land which they make them work. There is about 25,000 there.*

Besides the theft and vandalism of items obviously of no military value, except chairs and perhaps china used as "comfort items" at Wild's headquarters in the Wilson house and in officers' or hospital tents, some of the confiscated food and animals could be used to feed or transport Grant's and Butler's large armies. The "liberated" slaves were gainfully employed to produce food for Union forces, and soldiers were recruited from among them. Areas along the James River were a "no man's land" where Confederate conscription and foraging parties also operated. Cruel as they were to the white inhabitants, Federal operations denied the same resources to the Confederacy, especially General Robert E. Lee's Army of Northern Virginia.

Captain Arter continues:

[S]ome of our captains are selecting young darkeys to take home. They want me to take one. I can get any kind I want—they are more of a drug [drag?] than anything else. I see young darkies—all kinds of colors from nearly white to as Black as Black. I thought I had better counsel [consult] with you before I risk to bring one [back home]. *Now if you think you would like to have a little darky and that if you would undertake to raise one let me know and also what kind you would like to have, for I can get any kind of one.* they are a perfect drug here there is a great many things I might wright [*sic*; write to] you that would be of interest to you but time wont permit. when I get home I will be able to give you a good deal of news and many interesting details. That is if you can get me in a good mood for talking for you know I am quite a talker.[14]

Four other Arters served in the 143rd Ohio Regiment: Lt. Theodore Arter, 30, served as regimental adjutant; three privates: Alpheus, 22, and Richardson Arter, 20, served in Company K; and Leonard Arter, 18, served in Company C.[15]

On Saturday, 25 June, Private John Brownhill Linn, Company H, 143rd Ohio Infantry Regiment, wrote in his diary: "There was a great excitement last night of the enemy. All of our men were up in arms. But nothing seen. *We have 2 Regiments of Infantry* [143rd and 163rd Ohio National Guard Regiments, *8* [not "15 or 16" as Captain Arter claimed in his letter two days earlier] *pieces of artillery* [probably mounted in the two raised bastions which still have four cannon platforms each], 2 gun boats [USS *Dawn* and USS *Young America*?] on the river in the rear."[16] The eight artillery pieces consisted of two sections (four Parrott 10-pdr rifled guns) of Battery M, 3rd New York Light Artillery Regiment, and four guns of unknown type of the 33rd New York Independent Light Artillery Battery, which arrived about 19 June.

By now, within two weeks of the two Ohio regiments' arrival at Wilson's Wharf, sickness, too often fatal, was taking its toll of the soldiers. On Monday, 27 June, Linn wrote: "Reuben Jennings of Com. E, 143, died this morning making 3 out of the Com[pany]. Within last two weeks, of Co. H, 7 in the Hospital…. For last two days it has rained & the air is much cooler & will be healthier. *34 men in our hospital for 143ᵈ at 7 p.m.* Reuben Jennings was buried in military [ceremony]."[17] On Tuesday, 28 June, Linn wrote: "Still in hospital. Will get well yet in a few days. Colonel [Hiram] Miller of 168 [*sic*; 163rd Ohio] commander of the post, has ordered a shanty built for cooking for the hospital. We are stationed in a barn, a very good place, lays high from the river."[18]

On Wednesday, 29 June, Sgt. George L. Brooks, Co. D, 143rd Ohio

Infantry, wrote at "Wilson's Wharf": *"Was out yesterday & saw the Skull and some Bones of Rebels bleaching in the sun. They were killed during the attack on this place by Fitzhugh Lee some weeks ago & were buried—but being slightly covered, the rains in some cases washed the dirt away and left them to view."*[19]

On 1 July, Private Linn reported to the doctor and "took a dose of castor oil. It worked me." Also, "two Rebel prisoners [were] brought in by Colored Cavalry troop, also some wounded men" [and] "7 p.m. preaching by a chaplain [Samuel D. Bates, age 35] from 163rd" [Regiment].[20]

Orders on 2 July specified that "half a gill of whiskey per man, night & morning, combined with quinine, will be issued ... [and also] 2 hours of "School of the Soldier: Manual of Arms, Loading, and Firing to be conducted daily. After proficiency [is] attained, one hour to be devoted to battalion drill."[21]

On 8 July, Linn wrote: "Today 30 men in the hospital. An old Rebel flag found here."[22]

On 11 July, Monday, Linn noted: "Colored Cavalry got in a fight with some Rebel scouts. Cavalry lost one killed & one wounded." The men were Privates William Morris and Richard White, Co. I, 1st U.S. Colored Cavalry. The next day, he wrote: "The wounded Cavalry[man] has since died. *The one killed had nine balls shot in him."*[23]

On 31 July, Brig. Gen. Gilman Marston's 1st Brigade of Hinks's 3rd Division, Xth Army Corps, was deployed at three posts, as follows:

Wilson's Landing

143rd Ohio Regt. (Col. William H. Vodray);
163rd Ohio Regt. (Lt. Col. John Dempsey);
Co.'s. E & H, 16th NY Heavy Artillery Regt.—(Capt. Henry C. Thompson);
33rd NY Independent Battery, Lt. Artillery—(Capt. Alger M. Wheeler)
Co. E, 1st U.S. Colored Cavalry Regt—(Capt. Charles W. Emerson);
Co. I, 1st U.S. Colored Cavalry Regt.—(Capt. Orville L. Howard)

Fort Powhatan

133rd Ohio Regt. (Lt. Col. Wm. Ewing)—564 men;
Co. L, 1st NY Vol. Engineers—59 men—(Lt. Wm. H. Baldwin);
Detachment, 3rd PA Hvy Artillery Regt.-79 men- (Lt. Frederick Grill)
(Of 642 available men, 120 served daily on picket at or near the fort.)

Marston's HQ at City Point
148th Ohio Regiment (Col. Thomas W. Moore)[24]

Not listed, but also present at Wilson's Landing since 26 May was Lt. Col. A.G. Chamberlain's 37th Infantry Regiment, USCT, about 700 men.

The Ohio National Guard infantry regiments—133rd, 143rd, 148th

Private John Falconer, Co. B, 143rd
Infantry Regiment, Ohio National
Guard (Timothy Brooks Collection,
Mass. Commandery, MOLLUS, United
States Army Heritage and Education
Center, Carlisle, PA).

(at City Point), and 163rd—probably all had been issued imported British Enfield .577 caliber rifle-muskets, as were the New York regiments: 1st Engineers, 16th Heavy Artillery, and probably the 33rd Independent Battery. The 3rd Pennsylvania Heavy Artillery Regiment was armed with Springfield .58 cal. rifle-muskets. The mounted colored cavalrymen were armed with Colt M1860 Army .44 cal. revolvers, sabres, and possibly Merrill .54 cal. breech-loading carbines.[25]

Sergeant Brooks reported the *"deaths of 25 Ohio soldiers from disease* [due to a combination of factors, but poor sanitation from occupancy by large numbers of troops at Wilson's Wharf was probably one of them] *or accidents,"* including one soldier from the 143rd Ohio who died from too large a dose of opium (probably at the hospital there). Records show that 33 members of the 143rd Regiment, and 31 members of the 163rd Regiment died from disease probably contracted at Wilson's Wharf/Fort Pocahontas. The 163rd Ohio lost another member by accident. Most died in hospitals elsewhere, but 13 members of the 143rd Ohio and 9 members of the 163rd Ohio were buried at Wilson's Wharf. At least 56 Union soldiers, including both white and black soldiers, were initially buried at Wilson's Wharf through the end of the war; however, most of the bodies were reinterred at Glendale National Cemetery in 1866.[26]

On 17 August, Private Linn wrote: "A scout[ing party was] sent out this morning: 20 men [each?] of (Linn's) Co. H, (143rd Ohio) & 16th light [*sic*; heavy] Artillery & 33rd heavy [*sic*; light] Artillery N. York Battery, 50 Colored Cavalry … went up [the James River]. Two Colored Cavalry were shot—one killed, the other wounded in the right shoulder. One [5th Sgt Elias B. Flexer, Co. K] of the 163rd (Ohio) was accidentally shot & instantly killed, shot through the left breast."[27]

On "Thursday, Aug 18th," Sgt. Brooks wrote: "Have no relief yet from this miserable country. Dont know why we are not started for Ohio, but suppose our great generals know all about it. Will try to be patient. Our 100 days [men] finish their course tomorrow evening."[28]

On 23 August, Linn wrote: "*Gen. Grant was here to see the post*, but he did not stay long."[29]

On "Wednesday Aug 24, 9 a.m. … (Sgt. Brooks wrote:) I forgot to mention in my memo of the 23rd that *I had the pleasure of taking a good look at Lieut. Gen Grant & staff on board the Sanitary Boat. He was the plainest looking man in the whole party.*"[30]

New Units Arrive to Garrison Fort Pocahontas Until June 1865

In Special Orders No. 237 dated 31 August, General B.F. Butler ordered: "XI. Brig.-Gen. Gilman Marston, U.S. Volunteers, is hereby assigned to the command of all U.S. troops on the James river, east of City Point and west of Fort Monroe. He will establish his headquarters at Wilson's Wharf." Marston's "Separate Brigade" was charged with policing the army's line of communications on the James River and protecting it from interference by rebel raiding parties.[31]

Top: **Unidentified Sergeant, Co. D, 143rd Infantry Regiment, Ohio National Guard (Mass. Commandery, MOLLUS, United States Army Heritage and Education Center, Carlisle, PA).** *Bottom:* **Captain William Fletcher Curtis, Co. E, 163rd Infantry Regiment, Ohio National Guard (Mass. Commandery, MOLLUS, United States Army Heritage and Education Center, Carlisle, PA).**

Regiments That Served at Wilson's Wharf/Fort Pocahontas, Fort Powhatan, and Harrison's Landing During and/or After the Four Ohio National Guard Regiments Left on 29 August 1864

37th Infantry Regiment, USCT

This unit was sent 26–27 May to Wilson's Wharf and served there until 28 September 1864, when it moved to Deep Bottom. Not listed as part of Gilman Marston's brigade, perhaps it was part of Wild's, now Col. Holman's brigade, or unattached.[32]

Companies E (145 men) & H (130 men), 16th New Heavy Artillery Regiment

No artillery weapons are reported; the artillerymen may have been employed only as infantry. They served there from June to Dec. 1864 assigned to 1st Brigade, 3rd Division, Xth Corps; then to the Separate Brigade until June 1865.[33]

33rd New York Independent Battery, Light Artillery

Organized at Buffalo in Sept. 1863; their cannon type unknown; "assigned to duty as *Garrison Artillery* (after supporting assaults at Petersburg 15–18 June) from August 1864 until January 1865, when it served in defenses at Bermuda Hundred." It lost 12 men by disease, etc.[34]

2nd New Hampshire Vol. Infantry Regiment

Armed with Springfield rifle-muskets and 20 Sharps rifles; served 1 Sept.–1 Oct. 1864 when it moved to Aiken's Landing.[35]
Other units:

38th New Jersey Vol. Infantry Regiment

Organized at Newark in October 1864; was armed with Enfield rifle-muskets; sent to City Point and Fort Powhatan where it served Oct. 1864–June 1865. *Four companies served at Fort Pocahontas until 31 Dec. 1864.* Its commander, Col. William J. Sewell, partially recovered from prostration due to exposure during Wilderness campaign in May, had a prior distinguished record. The regiment lost by death 11 men, by desertion 59.[36]

89th New York Volunteer Infantry Regiment ("Dickinson Guard")

A veteran regiment organized at Elmira in Dec. 1861; armed with 199 Springfield M1863 rifle-muskets on 30 Sept. 1864; it briefly garrisoned Harrison's Landing during September(?) 1864.[37]

184th New York Vol. Infantry Regiment ("M'Clellan's")

Mustered at Elmira, New York, in Sept. 1864; armed with Enfield & Springfield rifle-muskets. "Co's. A, B, D, & F served in Shenandoah Valley; Co's. C, E, G, and H served in the Separate Brigade at Harrison's Landing Dec. 1864–June 1865; *Co. I served at Fort Pocahontas Dec. 1864– June 1865.*"[38]

Companies E & I, 1st Regiment Cavalry, USCT

Both companies were reported at Wilson's Landing on 31 July 1864, then "Co's. 'E' & 'I' detached at Fort Powhatan and Harrison's Landing during August 1864–May 1865."[39]

Companies D & F, 20th New York Cavalry Regiment ("McClellan's Cavalry")

Armed with Starr .54 cal. carbines, Colt Army .44 cal. revolvers, and M1840 and M1860 sabres; *Captain Wayland F. Ford's Company D was detached at Fort Pocahontas*, and Company F at Fort Powhatan during *late Dec. 1864–June 1865.*[40]

On 9 October, Butler ordered Brig. Gen. Joseph B. Carr, a New Yorker who had commanded divisions in the XVIIIth Corps, to replace Brig. Gen. Gilman Marston as commander of the Separate Brigade, Army of the James, parts of which garrisoned Fort Pocahontas, Fort Powhatan, and Harrison's Landing until June 1865.[41]

Reorganization of the Army of the James into the XXIVth and XXVth Army Corps; Brig. Gen. Edward A. Wild Restored to Command of U.S. Colored Troops, Then Demoted

In December 1864, Butler's Army of the James was reorganized. The Xth and XVIIIth Army Corps were disbanded, with white units consolidated into a new XXIVth Corps, and all colored troops consolidated into a new XXVth Corps commanded by Maj. Gen. Godfrey Weitzel. During mid–December, Brig. Gen. Edward A. Wild was assigned to command the First (formerly Third) Division of *the XXVth Corps, the "first and only American army corps composed entirely of black units."* Wild reported 3 days after "Butler's fiasco at Fort Fisher" near Wilmington, North Carolina, which resulted in Butler's being relieved from command and replaced by Maj. Gen. Edward Otho Cresap Ord.[42] In March 1865, Maj. Gen. Weitzel ordered Brevet Maj. Gen. Augustus V. Kautz to relieve Brig. Gen. Wild of command of the Corps' 1st Division; Kautz assigned Wild to command his division's 2nd brigade. Wild was bitter at being demoted to brigade command. He was highly critical of Maj. Gen. Ord, a favorite of Grant. Ord commanded most of the Union army in front of Petersburg, and he left less-favored units, including Wild's brigade, back at Bermuda Hundred. Wild was sure Ord disliked him and was determined to deprive black soldiers of honors due them.[43]

The Fall of Richmond, 3 April 1865: Wild's Troops Among the Very First to Enter City

President Davis and his cabinet had fled, along with funds from the Treasury and Richmond banks. Wild's brigade of U.S. Colored Troops was among the first Federal soldiers to enter the now former Confederate capital, arriving before sunrise. Because of Maj. Gen. Ord's assignments, Wild entered Richmond at the head of his colored troops, which gave Wild "great satisfaction." He reported the city was "occupied and guarded by provost guards and patriots of our cavalry," who all were busy trying to put out fires set by "Rebel soldiers, and even by Rebel owners."[44]

Ord quickly put a damper on Wild's satisfaction. Soon after Robert E. Lee surrendered his Army of Northern Virginia at Appomattox on 9 April, Ord ordered Wild: *"You must get these damned niggers of yours out of Richmond as fast as you can!"* Wild and his brigade then occupied forts and lines around Richmond until 12 April, when they went to Petersburg to occupy camps there. On 13 April, Ord relieved Wild of his duties in the XXVth Corps and directed him to report to Lt. Gen. Ulysses S. Grant. Wild complied.[45]

Brigadier General Edward A. Wild marched in the grand review of approximately 150,000 Union men by President Andrew Johnson, other government officials, and commanding generals in Washington during May 23–24, 1865, exactly one year after his victory during the Action at Wilson's Wharf on 24 May 1864. Then he headed home with his two colored servants and arrived at Brookline by 26 May 1865.[46]

After numerous adventures, Edward Augustus Wild died early on the morning of Friday, 28 August 1891 in Medillin, Department of Antioquia, Colombia, South America, while on a railroad surveying trip. In 1861 he had summed up his feelings about death to his wife: "As for me, when I am shot down, let no one put on mourning for me. Rather hang out the stars and stripes and be proud. Say what you will, I am not a rash person, neither am I so brave as a hundred thousand others; I mean naturally and constitutionally brave. What courage I have comes from force of reason and of faith and of self-discipline and determination. I pray heaven that when I see the need of sacrificing myself, no weakness of mine shall deter me."[47]

X

Rediscovery and Preservation of Fort Pocahontas

Genesis

The rediscovery, survey of its condition, research and analysis, purchase, preservation, archaeology, and interpretation of Fort Pocahontas began at the U.S. Army Intelligence and Threat Analysis Center in the Navy Yard in Washington, D.C., in 1986. There, two civilian intelligence analysts, Kenneth A. (Ken) Bako and Edwin W. (Ed) Besch (the author) had strong interests in the American Civil War and preservation of historic military sites. They are members of the Company of Military Historians; Ed became a Fellow in 1989. Captain (later Retired Lieutenant Colonel) Ken Bako, U.S. Air Force Reserve, supported military preservation efforts by the Reserve Officers Association (ROA), and he established Battlefield Chapter 10, ROA, at Manassas, Virginia, with Ed Besch as secretary for the chapter, which grew to 65 members.

Battlefield Surveys for the Civil War Sites Advisory Commission

A Civil War Sites Advisory Commission was established in November 1990 because of national concern over increasing loss of Civil War sites. The Commission, appointed by Congress and the Secretary of the Interior, was asked to identify the nation's historically significant Civil War sites; determine their relative importance and condition; assess threats to their integrity; and recommend alternatives for preserving and interpreting them.[1]

After the congressional commission was established, Ken Bako decided that he and Ed Besch, with members of ROA Battlefield Chapter 10, could volunteer to survey threatened battlefields. Ken approached the National Park Service's American Battlefield Protection Program in Washington, D.C., with his idea, which was accepted. Captain Edwin W. Besch, U.S. Marine Corps (Ret.), a U.S. Naval Academy graduate, and an infantry officer who had participated in ten ground combat operations in Vietnam during 1966, and Captain Kenneth A. Bako, an enlisted aerial observer in O-1 "Bird Dog" light aircraft during U.S. Air Force Forward Air Controller (FAC) combat operations in Vietnam during 1968–1969, were considered excellent candidates to survey Civil War battlefields because of their familiarity with military use of terrain.

Bako and Besch recruited volunteers to conduct Civil War site studies of battlefields assigned them by the National Park Service (NPS). During October 1991–October 1992, they organized 22 reserve officers and civilian volunteers to conduct studies for the National Park Service's Interagency Resources Division. They surveyed 48 sites at five battlefields: North Anna River, Hawe's Shop–Enon Church, Old Church–Matadequin Creek, Totopotomoy Creek, and the Trevilian Raid. The studies totaled 101 pages, including maps, and contained 123 photos. David Lowe, National Park Service (NPS), commented that these battlefield site studies were *the best ones done in Virginia and by the only group of volunteers who participated in the fourteen-state effort.* On 24 September 1992, NPS Chief Historian Ed Bearss and U.S. Secretary of the Interior Manuel Lujan, Jr., expressed their appreciation to Ken Bako and Ed Besch at a congressional seminar on "Preserving Civil War Battlefields." They were also told they had been assigned difficult battlefields that "professionals" didn't want to survey.

During April–August 1993, Ken Bako and Ed Besch worked under contract as independent consultants to the National Conference of State Historic Preservation Officers for the Civil War Sites Advisory Commission and the NPS. They conducted seven Civil War battlefield surveys: Dranesville, Fair Oaks Station–Darbytown Road, Lee's Retreat from Gettysburg (in Maryland), Rappahannock Station, St. Mary's Church–Nance's Shop, Walkerton–Mantapike Hill, and *Wilson's Wharf*. They contacted 54 persons; their seven reports totaled 279 pages and contained 31 maps and 165 illustrations. Ken Bako and Ed Besch also co-authored a draft handbook for the NPS titled *Civil War Heritage Preservation: A Handbook for Establishing Cooperative Relationships with Landowners*, 42 pages. Besides submitting their reports to the NPS, the authors gave copies to *everyone* who had been contacted during their surveys. Giving them copies was the "right thing to do," as well as means of gaining their interest and possible cooperation for later preservation efforts.

When they were assigned to survey Wilson's Wharf, the only information given Ken Bako and Ed Besch was that "black Union soldiers had fought there" and it was "located on the James River midway between Richmond and Williamsburg." Their survey of Wilson's Wharf entailed contacting ten persons; their report contained 24 pages with four maps and two illustrations. In April, while Ken Bako continued to work, Ed Besch retired from the Department of the Army (DA) after 37 years' Federal military and CIA, DIA, and DA civilian intelligence service. This enabled him to concentrate on the battlefield surveys until he and his family moved to Mobile, Alabama, in November 1993, but it also imposed a deadline.

The Civil War Sites Advisory Commission's *Report* dated July 1993 states: "Some 10,500 armed conflicts occurred during the Civil War, ranging from battles to minor skirmishes; 384 conflicts (3.7 percent) were identified as principal battles and classified according to their historic significance." Neither Wilson's Wharf (nor Fort Pocahontas) were among 368 sites listed in the July 1993 *Report* because information on 17 sites was still missing. A telling caption for an image of some U.S. Colored Infantry states: "The story of African Americans in the Civil War often remains untold to battlefield visitors."[2]

Finding Wilson's Wharf and Determining If There's Anything There to Preserve

Ed Besch's first foray from Reston in northern Virginia to locate "Wilson's Wharf somewhere on the James River" brought him to a driveway with a "No Trespassing" sign. Ed felt walking up to a homeowner's door to inquire was *not* "trespassing." The owner initially became hostile after Ed explained his purpose. He growled, "You're a preservationist!" and turned on his heel and started walking away. Ed asked, "What's wrong?" The construction engineer explained that he had been denied a permit at Richmond to build a seawall on a neighbor's property because an eagles' nest with baby eagles was located about a mile across the James River. He said his machinery made loud noises every day, which had not disturbed the eagles. Ed replied that he understood the man's feelings because he had often felt frustrated dealing with Federal bureaucrats. The man relented, took him in, provided the general location of Wilson's Wharf, and suggested Ed visit two prominent men who might be of more help: Hill Carter, owner of the

Harrison Ruffin Tyler, a true Virginia gentleman and historic preservationist, proudly stands next to one of three "Fort Pocahontas" signs on VA Rte 5 that he sponsored. This one tells about the Action of Wilson's Wharf on 24 May 1864.

historic "Shirley" home and plantation, and descendant of famed "King Carter," a 17th-century land baron who amassed over 300,000 acres; and Harrison Ruffin Tyler, owner of the "Sherwood Forest" plantation and a descendant of President John Tyler. These encounters provided lessons for Ed Besch: *Be bold*; learn landowners' concerns and try to understand their viewpoint; and gain their trust to achieve your own and their objectives.

Ed visited Hill Carter on the steps of "Shirley," and Harrison Ruffin Tyler at "Sherwood Forest," where he pointed out marks on a doorframe left by bayonets of Federal soldiers who broke into the home when it had been abandoned in June 1864. Mr. Carter could not help, but Mr. Tyler did help. Meeting these distinguished Virginia gentlemen at their beautiful and very historic homes was a major highlight of conducting the battlefield surveys. Ken Bako and Ed Besch often knocked on doors at more humble, isolated rural homes to inquire about battlefield sites; they were always welcomed, once by a young mother with a baby in her arms. History is not only about soldiers and civilians long gone, or artifacts and battlefields, but also about interesting, living people encountered by chance in pursuit of that history.

"We don't want history to be discovered there"

After locating the approximate site of Wilson's Wharf, Ed Besch called
the landowner, a developer in Chevy Chase, Maryland, who intended to
clear the site, which would have removed any traces of fortifications, etc.,
that might still be there, and build a community for senior citizens. He
told Besch: *"We don't want history to be discovered there."* Militarily strategic
terrain accessed by major roads or rivers and where battles were fought and
forts built, are also great locations for commercial development, hence conflicts between developers and preservationists often occur. Methods other
than walking onto the "No Trespassing" site were used first to "survey" the
forested battlefield area. In April 1993, Ed and his daughter Cathy flew
over the area in a light plane piloted by Mitchell (Mitch) Bowman, a former
U.S. Air Force pilot who later became executive director of *Civil War Trails*.
Unfortunately, trees had blossomed and obscured traces of any existing
fortifications. Later, Mitch Bowman took very useful photos when snow
background showed the outline of what had been Fort Pocahontas. Harrison Tyler remembered he took Ed Besch on his pontoon boat to make
an amphibious reconnaissance of the fort itself.

In their Wilson's Wharf report for the National Park Service dated
July 25, 1993, Ed Besch and Ken Bako concluded:

...Description of current condition: Good.
Current condition of the battlefield was good, [learned from] interviewing three
local, life-long residents who were very familiar with the location of the entrenchments at Wilson's Wharf and affirmed they were in good condition:
"...Earthworks are 9 feet high in places, but some of the ditch is partially filled in,
the entire works are visible from the air when the foliage is gone...." Trees were growing on the entrenchments, and the site of Dr. Wilson's home (which "he died defending as a Confederate Home Guard"—*incorrect hearsay*), and which served as BG
Wild's HQ) is an old sand quarry. Part of the Kennon Tract, the site, was entirely
wooded.
Threats to the Integrity of the Resource:
Short-term threats:
...The Kennon Tract ... zoned M-1 (Medium Industry), and a sale was being nego-
tiated as of mid–June 1993, according to Mr. W___, the Trustee. *He did not want any
discovery of historical remains to jeopardize the sale; he said "Let the next owner find out."*
The "next owner's" intended use of the property and his/their attitude toward histori-
cal preservation are unknown....
Long-term threats:
...Unknown; but the broken nature of the terrain and extent of the Kennon Tract
might allow for balanced commercial, light industrial, or residential development while
preserving existing earthworks/entrenchments pertaining to the Action at Wilson's
Wharf as a small park. *A marker* to this small, but possibly unique combat between a
Union force of almost entirely Black troops and numerically superior, veteran Confed-

"Charles City Court-House (built 1733, 5 miles from Wilson's Wharf), VA, June 1864. Negative by T.H. O'Sullivan & Positive by A. Gardner." A colored Union infantryman (37th Regiment, USCT?) with his rifle-musket at left "shoulder arms" stands picket duty in foreground; a colored cavalry trooper (?) wearing hat and boots, stands next to another man in doorway at rear (Plate 68, Mass. Commandery, MOLLUS, United States Army Heritage and Education Center, Carlisle, PA).

erate cavalry *should be placed on Route 5 as soon as possible. The entrenchments and area of combat, at least, clearly deserve preservation....*

History of "Kennons/Wilson's Wharf/Fort Pocahontas"

Fort Pocahontas is situated about 1.5 miles south of Route 5 in Charles City County, Virginia, on the north shore of the James River; Kennons Creek bounds it on the east. The fortification is located less than 5 miles east of Sherwood Forest, plantation home of the late President John Tyler. Archaeological surveys reveal traces of prehistoric occupation by Native Americans during the Late Archaic, Middle Woodland, and Late Woodland periods.[3]

Early Virginia colonial documents reveal that in July 1635, David Jones

"Sherwood Forest," home of President John Tyler and his second wife, Julia Gardiner Tyler. It was vandalized by Ohio National Guard troops in June 1864. (By Pi3.124 [Own work] [CC BY-SA 4.0 (http://creativecommons.org/licenses/by-sa/4.0)], via Wikimedia Commons 58).

obtained his first land patent in Charles City County, a 300-acre tract "a little below the point [later known as Sturgeon Point], butting South Southwest upon the maine [James] river, being bounded between 2 Creeks, the second & third Creeks between Matisoe Creek" [probably now Mapisco Creek]. By the early 1650s, David Jones had sold a 450-acre tract to Col. Guy Molesworth. Molesworth's 17th-century plantation became the 18th-century seat of the Kennon family of Charles City. By the late 1730s, Richard and Anne Hunt Kennon had established their home at "Kennons." In 1742, the Virginia Assembly selected "'Kennons,' where warehouses are now kept," as one of two tobacco inspection warehouses in Charles City County.[4]

In 1738, Richard Kennon was elected to the House of Burgesses, where he served until 1755. In July 1758, the Charles City County clerk recorded a "deed of gift," likely Kennon property in that county, from Richard Kennon to his son William, who was elected to the House of Burgesses. in 1760 William was colonel of the Charles City County militia. In 1765, William Kennon emigrated to North Carolina. Financial difficulties may have prompted his move.[5]

Benedict Arnold's British Raid Up the James River in January 1781

During January 1781, the American traitor Benedict Arnold, now a British brigadier general, conducted a raid up the James River to Richmond and beyond, where his men wreaked destruction and gained huge amounts of tobacco and other pillage as prizes. Arnold left Portsmouth with about 1,000 men, a heterogeneous mixture of American Loyalist, Scottish, and German officers and troops who included some white and black Virginians who had served in Virginia Colonial Governor Lord Dunmore's "Ethiopian Regiment" in 1775; all were commanded by English officers under the notorious American traitor. Transports carried artillery and provisions. Black men, most of them fugitive slaves, manned barges and skiffs that raided coastlines.[6]

While sailing up the James, after Virginians fired on British boats trying to seize a vessel driven ashore and its cargo, Arnold sent a letter warning he would burn the nearby village if they didn't cease firing. The senior American officer, possibly Virginia Militia Brig. Gen. Thomas Nelson, Jr., who had 150 state troops, received Arnold's letter and replied that he would defend Williamsburg. Then, according to Captain Johann Ewald, a Hessian Jaeger officer, Nelson or another officer asked whether he was the traitor Arnold. If this was the case, he requested him to tell the next ranking English officer that he would like his name, for the American officer would not and could not give up to a traitor. *But if he were to get hold of Arnold, he would hang him up by the heels, according to the orders of the Congress.* Captain Ewald: "The English naval officer delivered the message word for word, and Arnold was obliged to make a wry face."[7] Governor Thomas Jefferson offered a reward of 5,000 guineas for Arnold's capture; Washington, who had ordered Arnold to be taken alive in New York, ordered Lafayette, who was sent to Virginia to oppose Arnold, to summarily put him to death if captured.[8]

On 2 January, as Arnold's fleet sailed upriver, Arnold received intelligence that Americans had fortified the heights of Hood's Point upriver and posted 50 Virginia militia and cannon there to bombard the fleet as it passed in the narrow channel. While a detachment under Lt. Col. John Graves Simcoe and Captain Ewald landed and seized Hood's Point (later the site of Civil War Fort Powhatan), Arnold's main fleet anchored seven miles downriver, *off Kennon's Landing*, where some of Arnold's troops disembarked at the tobacco inspection station once owned by the Kennon family. Historian D. Gardiner Tyler wrote: "On January 4, 1781, Arnold landed at Westover in Charles City County with 900 men. On that same day *others of his men ascended to Kennon's Landing* (a point just below Sturgeon Point on the James River, not far south of the intersection of Rt 615 and Rt 5 in Charles City County today) *where they disembarked.* The demeanor of the British soldiers was far from exemplary, and inhabitants along the riverfront were forced to flee before them."[9] The British military unit(s) were not identified (Captain Ewald was not there to record the event in his diary), but Arnold's soldiers probably searched and plundered the plantation and warehouses, and secured the height over the landing to ensure no Virginia militia were there to fire down on his anchored vessels,[10] much as Brig. Gen. Edward A. Wild's U.S. Colored Troops landed there on 5 May 1864 to prevent Confederates from attacking Union vessels on the James River. On 9 January 1781, General Nelson wrote Governor Jefferson: "I have ordered two Pieces of Cannon to be planted *at Kennons*, where I am told we may do them Mischief [on Arnold's return downriver]. These cannon I propose to defend by infantry as long as I can. Should they overpower us, it is better to lose the Guns than not to attack them somewhere."[11] It's unknown whether or not General Nelson's order was carried out. It may have been overtaken by events, but it demonstrates his frustration and determination to attack Arnold.

By 1782, Kennons was a 679-acre tract owned by Henry Edloe, and "the wharf and warehouses at Kennons seem to have survived. In 1783, two years after Arnold's visit, the Assembly again designated Kennons as site of a tobacco inspection warehouse." After a long succession of owners, in late 1835 the Lightfoot Family *sold Kennons, described as an 863-acre estate, to Josiah C. Wilson for $3,000.* In 1829, Wilson, who was from Surry County, seems to have taken up residence in Charles City County, later possibly at Kennons. Kennon's Landing (or *Wilson's Wharf,* as it became known) seems to have been a quasi-public facility. In 1857, Edmund Ruffin traveled from his plantation in Prince George County to visit former President John Tyler, taking a passenger steamer to "Kennon's wharf," as he called it. From there he walked "three and a half miles to Sherwood Forest, the residence of Ex-President Tyler, carrying his very light carpet bag" (the suitcase of his day).[12] During March 1862, Maj. Gen. George B. McClellan landed his huge Union army at Fort Monroe to begin his Peninsular Campaign (March–July 1862). Josiah C. Wilson's death date is not known, but his will went to probate in December 1862.[13] After the Civil War ended, "Kennons/Wilson's Wharf" came under a long succession of private and commercial owners as property values fluctuated.

Harrison Ruffin Tyler Purchases and Clears Fort Pocahontas in 1996

In the fall of 1996, Harrison Ruffin Tyler purchased some 800 acres on the James River that included Fort Pocahontas, site of the Action at Wilson's Wharf, approaches to the fort, and surrounding areas back to Virginia Route 5, crediting "Besch [as] the military historian who rediscovered Fort Pocahontas and bringing its history to the attention" [of Tyler]. Then, in conjunction with the Center for Archaeological Research at the College of William and Mary, and the Virginia Department of Human Resources, Harrison Tyler worked to clear (often by himself), preserve, and interpret the fort for the future. Clearing 100 years of accumulated trees and brush from the site was itself a herculean task. He also had the site identified for visitors passing by on Route 5, having three Virginia historical markers placed there to locate the site and explain its significance. In 2000, he had beautiful Binford House, a c.1740 residence, moved from Southampton County to the interior of Fort Pocahontas. It is of similar age and construction to the Kennon/Wilson house that had served as General Wild's headquarters in 1864, but which burned in 1876. It was restored to provide a small museum for artifacts from prehistoric times, the 18th century, and the Civil War, and it was expanded. Besides Binford House, well-preserved earthworks that include two bastions that each have ramps for four cannon, and some rare firing steps on the earthworks, are features worth seeing, although many portions were constructed after the 24 May 1864 Action. Harrison Ruffin Tyler states that the Action that occurred there "proved African Americans could fight effectively without extensive support from white (Union) troops." A historic site, indeed! "Virtually untouched for over 130 years, the Virginia Department of Historic Resources views Fort Pocahontas as 'one of the best preserved fort sites.' It has been placed on the National Register of Historic Places." The Fort Pocahontas site is under a Tyler family trust, with William B. Tyler as president.[14]

Harrison Ruffin Tyler, the Tyler Family Lineage and Their Accomplishments

Harrison Ruffin Tyler, the benefactor and preserver of Fort Pocahontas, and his older brother Lyon Gardiner, Jr., are descendants of Paramount Chief, the Mighty Powhatan, who built a Native-American empire in

Southeast Virginia, through his daughter Pocahontas, baptized Rebecca; and her English settler husband John Rolfe, who brought prosperity to the failing Jamestown Colony by introducing a strain of mild tobacco he called "Varina" that became a huge commercial success in Europe; and their son Thomas Rolfe. Harrison's and Lyon's most prominent ancestor was their grandfather, John Tyler, who served as president of the United States during 1840–1844. John Tyler served as a militia captain during the War of 1812, in the Virginia House of Delegates, and as U.S. congressman and senator from Virginia, before he ascended to the presidency as first to do so through succession as vice-president. President Tyler is probably best remembered for helping push the annexation of Texas in 1845.[15]

The election of Abraham Lincoln as president in 1860 cast John Tyler into gloom. After heading the failed Washington Peace Conference, John Tyler joined Southern secession efforts and was elected to the Confederate House of Representatives before his death in 1862. Due to his Confederate ties, John Tyler's death was not officially mourned for some years.[16] Asked to consider his grandfather John Tyler's presidency, Harrison Ruffin Tyler stated:

> He's been maligned in some ways, because he was elected to the Confederate Congress, so people say he was a traitor. But actually, he should be known for his efforts as organizer of the Peace Conference in Washington in [February] 1861. He tried to get the uncommitted states to all agree on a program, then get the other states to join in, and get everybody back together. That's not generally recognized. That's the thing he really should be known for. And he *did not serve* in the Confederate Congress. He was elected, he went to Richmond, where the Confederate Congress moved [from Montgomery, Alabama], in January of 1862. He went to take his seat, but unfortunately [he] had a stroke and died a week later…. No, he *didn't serve*.[17]

Harrison Ruffin Tyler also is descended from his great-grandfather Edmund Ruffin, who was a distinguished agriculturist and one of the three most prominent secessionist "Fire-eaters," through his mother Susan Harrison Ruffin Tyler (1889–1953).

After John Tyler's presidency, the Tylers retired to "Sherwood Forest," where they lived tranquilly until the Civil War. Although a northerner by birth (on Gardiner's Island off the eastern tip of Long Island, New York, in 1820), Mrs. Julia Gardiner Tyler "soon grew accustomed to owning slaves and enjoying a leisurely life as wife of a wealthy plantation owner. Defending slavery as a humane and even enlightened institution [as many Southerners believed, and even some ministers there taught], she soon became an ardent supporter of the principles of the South." After her husband's death in 1862, Julia moved north to Staten Island, where her sympathy for the Confederates strained relations with her Unionist family. Later, she returned to Virginia to live and died from a stroke suffered at Richmond on 10 July 1889.[18]

Through their grandmother Julia Gardiner Tyler, Lyon Gardiner Tyler, Jr., and Harrison Ruffin Tyler are descended from Lion Gardiner, an English adventurer and military engineer under contract to the Connecticut Company, who arrived in Boston from Rotterdam, the Netherlands, in 1635 and built a fort at Saybrook; he slaughtered Indians and was wounded by arrows during the Pequot War, 1636–1637. He learned the Indian tongue and befriended Montauk Chief Waiandance; and he purchased Manchonake (Gardiner's Island) in Long Island Sound from the Montauks. In 1639, he was granted Gardiner's Island and became the first English settler in what is now New York State. Of Massachusetts Bay Colony officials who had provoked the Pequot War, he wrote: "The Lord be merciful to us for our extreme pride and base security, which cannot but stink before the Lord."[19] Timeless words, indeed! On Gardiner's Island, the Gardiner family eventually owned as many as 352 black and Indian slaves.[20]

Harrison Ruffin Tyler never gave much thought to his grandfather, President Tyler. Instead, what drove young Harrison was a desire to make his own way in the world without relying on his ancestry. He was home-schooled by his mother, spent three years in Charles City County schools, and briefly studied at St. Christopher's in Richmond. At 16, he was awarded a scholarship by Lady Astor to the College of William and Mary, graduating in 1949 with a degree in chemistry. There were no jobs in chemistry, and he was told "all the action was in chemical engineering," so after excelling in his studies he graduated from Virginia Tech in 1951 with a degree in chemical engineering. Hired as project manager at Virginia-Carolina Chemical Corporation, he was put in charge of starting a plant in Charleston, South Carolina. His success there led to assignment as start-up engineer for a plant in Cincinnati, Ohio. There he faced a challenge: he had worked with soft water at Charleston, but the plant at Cincinnati was going to use hard water from a well, which meant a change in the engineering process. Tyler: "I got a crash course in water treatment," but he distinguished himself and received a patent for an improvement to shiny aluminum.[21]

In 1963, after Mobil Oil bought Virginia-Carolina Chemical Corporation, Harrison R. Tyler discerned a change in corporate culture. He thought about starting his own water treatment company of a different kind: "I vowed [that] if I had a company, each employee would be judged on results and not on how they made the manager look." In 1968, Tyler and a partner, William P. Simmons, founded ChemTreat, Inc., headquartered at Glen Allen, Virginia. By 2007, it had become "the largest and fastest growing independent firm dedicated to industrial water treatment." ChemTreat provides vital services to many hospitals, and it entered the pulp and paper industry and became international in scope. Tyler and Simmons achieved their original goals: "sell a product that works, hire good employees, and take care of those employees."[22]

Always very busy, Harrison Tyler devoted a great deal of his energy, financial support, and time to ensure that the site of the "Action at Wilson's Wharf on 24 May 1864" and completed Fort Pocahontas was cleared, interpreted by historical markers, archaeology conducted, and a museum-house moved to the site. It is fair to say that without Harrison Ruffin Tyler, there would be No "Fort Pocahontas" in the 21st century to memorialize the victorious U.S. Colored Troops and Confederates who fought and died there on 24 May 1864, and white and black Union soldiers who completed and garrisoned the fort until the end of the Civil War, many of whom died of disease or other causes.

Harrison Tyler married Payne (Paynie) Bouknight Tyler in July 1957. They have three children: Julia Gardiner Tyler Samaniego, born 1958; Harrison Ruffin Tyler, Jr., born 1960; and William Bouknight Tyler, born 1961; and eight grandchildren.[23]

Archaeology at Fort Pocahontas

Both Tylers—Harrison and his presidential forebear—are graduates of the College of William & Mary, and Harrison's father served as president of the institution from 1888 to 1919, so Harrison Tyler naturally looked to the William & Mary Center for Archaeological Research.[24] During 1997, the Center began to conduct annual archaeological assessments at the site of Fort Pocahontas. The first project involved seventeen persons who did shovel testing, surface collection, test unit excavation, controlled metal detector survey, and historical research. Results in the initial report are summarized:

> In addition to traces of prehistoric occupation, the most prominent elements were remains from Civil War activity. Besides extant earthworks of Fort Pocahontas and surface features related to the fort's defenses, subsurface archaeological evidence related to the likely headquarters of General Wild during his initial occupation, and an area of possible military shelters. The likely headquarters corresponds to location of an antebellum domestic area presumably occupied before the war by the Wilson family. Outside the fort enclosure, very well preserved evidence of a Union military encampment was identified. Features likely representing traces of shelters and associated debris were documented.[25]

During fall 2000, the William and Mary Center for Archaeological Research conducted an archaeological investigation at Fort Pocahontas funded through a grant from the National Park Service's American Battlefield Protection Program. The objective was to identify and document the American Civil War battle known as Wilson's Wharf in order to evaluate and preserve archaeological evidence of the May 24, 1864, conflict. Ten archaeologists and other specialists mapped the site and recovered artifacts. The report has sections including "Historical Background" and "Interpretation and Recommendations."[26] The American Battlefield Protection Program sponsored some subsequent archaeological studies.

Reenactments and Living History Events Create a "Sense of History" at Fort Pocahontas

Harrison Ruffin Tyler sponsored annual Civil War reenactments on weekends nearest the date of the "Action at Wilson's Wharf" on 24 May, beginning in 1997. Reenactments involve soldiers or ladies in period clothing, and dedicated persons who organize and publicize events, maintain Fort Pocahontas, and recruit and coordinate reenactors, food vendors, etc. Events are managed by Harrison R. Tyler and his daughter-in-law, Kay Montgomery Tyler, who also is the manager of Fort Pocahontas. The coordinator of reenactors is T. Joseph ("Joe") Funk, great-nephew and "spitting image" of Maj. Gen. Godfrey Weitzel, General Benjamin F. Butler's chief engineer and later commander of the Union XXVth Corps, composed of U.S. Colored Troops. Joe's wife Patricia Ann ("Patty") Finegan coordinated "Ladies' Fashions" Civil War demonstrations. African Americans participate as "U.S. Colored Troops" and their camp followers.[27]

In summary, the successful rediscovery, survey of condition, research and analysis, purchase, preservation, archaeology, and interpretation of the site of the 24 May 1864 Action at Wilson's Wharf/Fort Pocahontas combined dedicated efforts of the Congressional Civil War Sites Advisory Commission, NPS American Battlefield Protection Program personnel, archaeologists from the College of William & Mary, reenactors, behind-the-scenes coordinators, the initiative and efforts of two private individuals—Ken Bako and Ed Besch—and *above all the tireless efforts and resources of Harrison Ruffin Tyler.*

Appendix A
Federal and Confederate Casualties at Wilson's Wharf

Dates are 24 May, unless otherwise indicated. Numbers only are ages. Abbreviations are GSW = gunshot wound; RTD = returned to duty; WW = Wilson's Wharf. Soldiers' native states are indicated. Microfilm muster roll records of the 1st and 10th Regts., USCT and Confederate units are at the National Archives & Records Administration (NARA).

Federal Casualties

Brigade Staff

Captain Walter H. Wild, MA; Inspector & Adjutant General—"wounded in forehead," RTD. Walter was hit in the head by a spent bullet, and "a plate of silver the size of a half dollar" was inserted into his skull and remained there the rest of his life. (Frances H. Casstevens, *Edward A. Wild and the African Brigade in the Civil War*, p. 177.)

1st Regiment Infantry, USCT

Killed or mortally wounded:

Pvt. William Butler, 26, Charles Co., MD; Co. E—"Shot in head; fracture of skull by *cannon ball* at WW. Died in USA General Hospital, Hampton, VA 27 May 1864."

Pvt. Samuel Langley (Langway), 40 or 48, NC; Co. F—"Shot in head and neck, skull fractured May 25 [*sic*]." Died 16 August at hospital at Ft. Monroe.

Pvt. Dempsey Maby, 20, NC, Co. F—Killed: "shot through the breast. He was brave soldier."

5th Sgt. Moses Stevenson or Stephenson, 25, VA; Co. G—"Killed, musket shot through head."

Wounded:

1st Lt. Elam C. Beeman, 27, former Sgt., 148th NY Vol. Infantry, Co. A—"Shot in the right hand & wrist by Minie ball at WW." RTD 8/26/64.

Pvt. Robert Burt, 19; Co. B—"GSW left leg; sent USA General Hospital, Hampton. RTD 8/25/64."

Pvt. Peter Calhoun, 19, Baltimore, Co. C—"GSW left forearm; Summit USA Hospital, Philadelphia; RTD 2/6/65."

Pvt. James Connelly (Conley), 21, DC, Co. F—"GSW Minie ball posterior part of right scapula (right shoulder) passing down; simple dressings." RTD 11/23/64.

1st Cpl. James H. Douglas, 38, DC, Co. K—"GSW in right arm (biceps muscle), simple dressings. *Disabled & Discharged* 10/17/64."

Pvt. Humphrey Drewett or Duett, 23, VA; Co. K—"Shot in left hand by Minie ball." RTD 8/26/64.

Pvt. Edmund Gatlin, 28, NC, Co. B—"Wounded."

Pvt. William H. Grant, 18, Lenox, MA, Co. C—"GSW right wrist, treated at Fort Monroe; RTD 5/24/64."

Pvt. John Gray, 25, VA; Co. G—"Shot in right side." RTD and wounded again on 8/29/64.

Pvt. Richard Jones, 26, MD, Co. E—"GS flesh wound by Minie ball right thigh." RTD 7/23/64.

? Pvt. Edward Keeland, 20, VA, Co. B—"GSW right hand by Minie Missile." Reported "wounded" during attack on Confederate signal station on 6 May; possibly wounded then and on, or instead of, 24 May. RTD 8/1/64.

Pvt. William E. Smith, 23, VA; Co. B or Co. K—"GSW in mouth passing out side of neck, no special treatment, sent USA General Hospital, Hampton." RTD 8/17/64.

Pvt. William Strother (or Strater), 21, VA; Co. I—"Wounded right arm and leg 27 May" [*sic*—incorrect hospital record?].

Pvt. George Taylor, 22, MD; Co. F—"Wounded (no place or date on muster roll) right elbow by [cavalry] carbine ball, fracture Hummus [*sic*; humerous], treatment: Potass(ium) permang(anate) to wound." *Disabled.*

Pvt. Daniel (David) Webster, 22, DE, Co. C—"GSW, Minie ball, middle third of left thigh; simple dressings; *deserted* 12/11/64 from Summit House USA Gen. Hospital, Philadelphia.

Pvt. William Alexander Webster, 25, VA, Co. C—"Shot in right leg; *deserted* in December, 1864." Only muster roll record states "Wounded."

Pvt. Benjamin Williams, 17, VA; Co. H—"GSW of right hand" and/or "shot in left wrist. RTD 2/10/65."

Captured and enslaved:

Pvt. George Wilson, 20, Norfolk, VA; Co. F—"*Missing*, was on picket at time of attack by the rebels, never heard from" (Col. John H. Holman). Notation "Slave" appears in the 1st Reg't. *Descriptive List*, NARA. He escaped 4/7/65 and rejoined Co. F on 5/6/65.

Sources: 1st Regiment, USCT Soldiers' Descriptive Books for Companies A–K, and Microfilm Rolls, Record Group 94, 9W3, Row 11, at the NARA; "Rosters," C.R. Gibbs, Black, Copper, & Bright (Silver Spring, MD: Three Dimensional Publishing, 2002), 225, 228–259.

10th Regiment Infantry, USCT

Pvt. William Upture, 21, farmer from Upshur Co. VA; Co. D—"Seriously wounded
(in abdomen) at Wilson's Landing, VA on 24 May 1864; died on board Steamer
Mayflower in Hampton Roads on May 25th while enroute to Fort Monroe."
Pvt. Isaac West, 20, Sailor from VA; Co. D—"Dangerously wounded in abdomen;
died at Hampton Hospital 6/4/64 from wounds rec'd at Wilson's Landing,
Va."

*Sources: 10th Regiment, USCT Morning Reports; Letters, Order, & Detail Book at
the NARA.*

Lt. Hanson's Two-Gun Section from Battery M,
3rd New York Light Artillery

Pvt. John Taylor, 18, MD—"GSW of face-Minie ball-at WW May 24, 1864; RTD
8/30/64."

Others

Unnamed captain and mate or pilot of Steamer *May Flower* (or *Mayflower*)—
"Badly wounded on James River above Wilson's Wharf."
"Two brothers, named Robinson [civilian crew?], were wounded."

Federal Casualty Summary

Unit	Killed	Died of Wounds	Wounded	Captured	Total
Brigade Staff			1		1
1st Regiment, USCT	2	2	17(1?)	1	22*
10th Regiment, USCT		2	0		2
Battery M, 3rd NY LA			1		1
Others (Steamer *Mayflower*)			4		4
TOTALS:	2	4	23	1	30

* Federal Return for 1–31 May shows 18 total battle casualties.

Tenth Infantry Regiment, USCT company daily reports also list the following
men, *all sick*, who were sent to the General Hospital at Hampton Roads on 24 May.
Co. E (returned to WW at 4 p.m.) reported: "Battle at Wilson's Landing. Levin
Bloxom & Josiah Deans sent to General Hospital." Co. H (present at WW all day)
reported: "Charles Drummond and Samuel Beach sent to General Hospital at
Hampton, VA."

*Sources: After-action reports, regimental books, carded medical records; microfilm, RG 94,
9W3, NARA; "The Attack on Wilson's Wharf…. Steamers Fired Into," New York Times,
Vol. XIII, No. 2955(?), Friday, May 27, 1864, page 1, col. 2, bottom. Same article states:
"Our loss was forty wounded, one killed, and one died on the way down the river."*

Reenactors' tents inside Fort Pocahontas. Behind them are well-preserved fortifications, on the other side of which Virginians and North Carolinians vainly
attempted to assault the fort (Ed Besch photograph).

Confederate Casualties

*Sources: Personnel rosters in regimental histories, microfilm records, unit record folders for
Virginia cavalry regiments at the Library of Virginia and Museum of the Confederacy,
soldiers' letters, postwar rosters, etc. Well over half of the muster rolls for May–June 1864
are missing, lost, or incomplete due to heavy attrition during battles, horses disabled and
their owners absent, absent sick, etc. Some muster rolls for May–June were compiled in
September 1864, mainly for pay purposes. Wartime rolls and postwar rosters note many
"killed" or "prisoner" or just "May" or "1864." Microfilm records for the 5th SC Cavalry
fail, but names of casualties published in the Charleston Daily Courier, and extracted by
Mr. Randolph W. Kirkland of Charleston from his data base, were an invaluable resource
for identifying the six wounded reported for that unit. Confusing identification of Confederate casualties from the "Action at Wilson's Wharf" are the Confederates' use of "Fort Kennon, Kennon's (or "Cannon's" or "Kennen's") Farm" or "Charles City County"; a different
date from May 24; or a mix-up with Fort Powhatan.*

Wickham's Brigade (800 Men)

**1st Virginia Cavalry (4 killed, 16 wounded [1 mortally], total 20 identified
below.)**

Pvt. Frank H. Bayne, Co. E—"Wounded at Kennon's Landing 5/24/64." RTD;
wounded twice; *deserted.*

3rd Lt. Rudolphus W. Cecil, MD, Co. K—"Wounded left foot at Kennon's Landing 5/24/64. Foot amputated at Richmond hospital. Died there 6/22/64; buried Hollywood Cemetery."

Pvt. John W. Cross, 19, Co. A—"Wounded right shoulder at Kennon's Landing 5/24/64."

Pvt. John Crossett, Co. B—"Wounded at Kennon's Landing 5/24/64. Casualty list [is his] only record."

Pvt. Alexander Nathaniel Dalhouse, 30, Co. E—"Wounded (contusion from shell above ankle joint) at Kennon's Landing 5/24/64." Hospitalized at Richmond and Farmville. RTD.

1st Lt. David Brainerd ("Brent") Devier, Co. I—"Wounded left hand—fractured 1st metacarpal, at Kennon's Landing 5/24/64." RTD.

Pvt. James Henry Eakle, age 17, Co. E—"Killed Kennon's Landing 5/24/64. Buried in same blanket with Pvt. Caspar Koiner; reinterred at New hope Methodist Church Cemetery, Augusta Co. after War."

Pvt. Ezekial Gilbert, Co. C—"Killed Kennon's Farm 5/26/64" [*sic*].

4th Sgt. William A. Gresham, Co. G—"Wounded at Kennon's Landing 5/24/64; hospitalized at Richmond and Lynchburg. RTD; captured 9/12/64."

? Pvt. Augustus T. Hanger, Co. C—"Wounded right hand 5/21[*sic*]/64. Absent wounded in Richmond hospital 5/26 [*sic*]/64; transferred to Lexington, VA hospital 5/30/64."

2nd Lt. Nathan Chew Hobbs, Co. K—"Wounded at Kennon's Landing 5/24/64. Promoted to captain 8/15/64."

African American enlisted men and white officers represent U.S. Colored Troops at an annual reenactment at Fort Pocahontas (Ed Besch photograph).

Pvt. Thomas C. Johnston, Co. C—"Wounded right leg at Kennon's Landing 5/24/64; transferred to Lexington, VA hospital 5/30/64."

Pvt. John Pierceall Kearfott, Co. B—"Wounded through the breast at Kennon's Landing 5/24/64." RTD.

Pvt. William H. Keyes, Co. F—"Killed at Kennon's Farm 5/24/64."

Pvt. Caspar (or Casper) M. Koiner (or Coiner), Co. E—"Wounded 3/17/64, RTD. Killed at Kennon's Landing 5/24/64. Buried in same blanket with Pvt. Eakle; reburied at his church near Waynesboro after the War."

Pvt. George Michael Koiner, Co. E—"Wounded Kennon's Landing 5/24/64."

Pvt. William Madison Monroe, Co. H—"Wounded in stomach at Kennon's Landing 5/24/64. Survived."

1st Corporal George Robert Roadcap, Co. I—"Wounded left hand at Kennon's Landing 5/24/64; RTD."

Pvt. Benjamin Franklin Smith, Co. F—"Wounded right testicle at Kennon's Landing 5/24/64. Admitted to hospital 5/26/64."

Pvt. John William Zollman, Co. C—"Wounded in shoulder at Kennon's Farm 5/24/64. Carried bullet to his grave." RTD.

2nd Virginia Cavalry ("7 killed, 19 wounded, 3 missing"; 29 total at "Ft. Kennon" [Driver, *2nd Virginia Cavalry*, 179]—24 identified below.)

Pvt. T.W. Allen, Co. B—"Wounded in hand at Fort Powhatan [*sic*], sometimes called Fort Kennon, on James River, Charles City County, Va., May 14 [*sic*], 1864."

Captain James Breckinridge, 27; Co. C—"Wounded in arm at Fort Kennon 5/24/64; *killed* at Five Forks on 4/1/65." (He was the younger brother of P. Gilmer [below], a VMI graduate, and a UVA law student 1859–60. Ref.: Johnson, *The University Memorial.* [UVA], 1871.)

Color Sgt.–Acting Captain Peachy Gilmer Breckinridge, 29; Co. C—"Assigned for gallantry as captain of Co. B in absence of all commissioned officers, who were wounded; killed at Fort Kennon on May 24, 1864, having mounted the parapet when he fell." (Captain James Breckinridge gives a different version; See Note, below.) Burial "not known" in 1884. (He was a VMI graduate, a student at W&M College and UVA [law], and member of the Pacific Railroad Exploring Expedition in 1858. A Unionist in 1861, he became a captain in the 28th VA Infantry, but was not re-elected; then a major in the VA State Line, but he resigned and enlisted as a private in his brother's Co. C. Ref.: *The University Memorial.*)

Pvt. Henry St. George Tucker Brooke, Co. B—"Wounded left thigh (or "ankle"-Brooke) at Fort Powhatan [*sic*], May 24 1864; WIA (left thigh), compound fracture with deformity—permanently disabled, and horse killed, at Hawe's Shop, May 28, 1864. "The bravest of the brave."

4th Cpl. James Garland Carr, 21, a UVA student in 1861; Co. K—"Captured at Fort Kennon 5/24/64 *and never heard from after leaving Fortress Monroe*." (Pvt. J.W. Hatcher, also taken prisoner at WW [below], wrote that Carr was sent from Belle Plain, Virginia, to Fort Delaware [prisoner of war camp]. Ref.: Johnson, *The University Memorial.*)

Pvt. George W. Denton, Co. C—"Wounded in both legs at Fort Kennon 5/24/64."

Pvt. James W. Denton, Co. C—"Flesh wound in leg at Fort Kennon 5/24/64."

Pvt. Miles P. Dollman, Co. C—"Wounded at Fort Kennon 5/24/64." RTD.

Pvt. Jefferson D. Furbush, Co. H—"Killed at Fort Kennon 5/24/64."

Pvt. Joseph H. Grayson, Co. K—"Mortally wounded (ball entered neck and exited into back) at Fort Kennon 5/24/64. Died Orangeburg Hospital, Richmond 6/14/64."

? Pvt. James Wellington Hatcher, Co. A—Captured—"taken prisoner with Pvt. James G. Carr" and sent to Point Lookout, Maryland, prisoner of war camp. Ref.: Johnson, Memorial. (Or captured at Spottsylvania Court House 5/12/64?)

Pvt. William S. Head, Co. K—"Wounded at Fort Kennon 5/24/64."

Pvt. Thomas D. Keene, Co. I—"Wounded (slightly) at Fort Kennon 5/24/64. Wounded again 6/12/64."

Pvt. Marcellus H. Knight, Co. E—"Wounded at Fort Kennon 5/24/64." RTD.

Pvt. W. Hazlett Kyle, Co. C—"Wounded left thigh at Fort Kennon 5/24/64. A splendid soldier." RTD.

Pvt. John W. Meade (or Mead), Co. A—"Killed at Fort Kennon, also called Fort Powhatan."

4th Sgt. Francis K. ("Trip") Nelson, Co. K—"Killed (or "mortally wounded" ["in the thigh"]—Pvt. H.St.G.T. Brooke's and Pvt. George R. Minor's postwar accounts—and captured?) at Fort Kennon 5/24/64. Buried Fort Monroe Cemetery."

Pvt. William Richard Rucker, Co. E—"Wounded at Ft. Kennon 5/24/64."

Pvt. George H. Smith, Co. E—"Killed at Fort Kennon 5/24/64."

Pvt. Cephus P. Switzer, Co. C—"Wounded at Fort Kennon 5/24/64. A good soldier."

Pvt. Joseph Taylor, Co. E—"Wounded at Fort Kennon 5/24/64."

Pvt. Alexander ("Sandy") White, Co. C—"Wounded (slightly) at Fort Kennon 5/24/64." RTD.

Pvt. Samuel White, Co. C—"Captured at Fort Kennon 5/24/64." Sent to Fort Monroe and was "held hostage (for captured U.S. Colored Troops) by order of Gen. Butler for a month before being sent to Point Lookout" prisoner-of-war camp, Maryland. Exchanged 3/65.

Pvt. James Henry Woodson, 24, Co. H—"Wounded (abdomen) at Fort Kennon 5/24/64." RTD.

Note: P. Gilmer's sister, Lucy Breckinridge, received a letter from "Brother (Captain) James" on 1 June 1864: "Gilmer had just been promoted to a Lieutenancy *and assigned to the command of Company B. The same day (23 May) we received orders to go to … Kennon's Landing (where the enemy was) in a strongly entrenched camp with gunboats and land batteries. We dismounted and made the (initial) assault and were repulsed.* Gilmer was grazed by a ball on the wrist. *We then changed our position and charged again through some obstructions of fallen trees and sharpened limbs (abatis). Gilmer pushed on … under heavy fire.* He got within 50 yards of the parapet, when he was seen to fall, struck somewhere in the body … every man near him being either killed or wounded … he did not speak after he fell" *(Lucy Breckinridge, Journal, 1862–1864. See Bibliography).*

3rd Virginia Cavalry ("3 killed, 5 wounded," 8 total—names of 4 men killed, and 6 wounded (one mortally), 10 total, are listed below.)

Lt. Clement Carrington, Co. C—"wounded 5/24/64, Fort Kennon; promoted captain 12/64."

Pvt. William Ellington, Co. C—"Wounded in left shoulder at Fort Kennon" 5/24/64.

1st Cpl. John L. Fraser, Co. I—"Killed (or "mortally wounded") on James River, Charles City Co. 5/24/64.

Pvt. Thomas D. Glass, Co. H—"Killed, Fort Kennon."

Sgt. John A. Green, Co. H—"wounded, 'scalp, flesh wound,' 5/24/64, Fort Kennon."

Pvt. Jacob C. Ham, Co. B—"died of wounds received 21 [*sic*; 24] May 1864" (the 3rd Virginia Cavalry did not fight on 21 May).

Pvt. Benjamin J. Jolly, Co. I—"Killed at [the single Confederate] cannon, Fort Kennon on James River, Charles City Co. May 24, 1864."

Pvt. William J. Jordan, Co. C—"Wounded at Fort Kennon."

Pvt. Charles Henry Phillips, Co. B—"Wounded at Kennon's Wharf 5/24/64."

Pvt. Lorenzo Tucker, Co. C—"Killed May 20 [*sic*; 24] 1864" (the regiment did not fight on 20 May).

(Author's review of 3rd Virginia Cavalry company folders at the Library of Virginia, Thomas P. Nanzig, 3rd Virginia Cavalry (Lynchburg, VA: H.E. Howard, 1989), 50–51, 85, 100, 109, 122.)

4th Virginia Cavalry ("19 killed and wounded."—Pvt. Horatio Nelson, *Diary*; 17 names are listed in the 27 May 1864 *Richmond Sentinel* [RS]; two are from other sources.)

Sgt. R.J. Baldwin, Co. K—"Wounded left arm and side" (RS); Chimborazo Hospital 5/24/64. Assigned to Invalid Corps 12/22/64.

Pvt. John Warden Davis, Co. A—"Wounded badly" (Pvt. Horatio Nelson, *Diary*); "severely" (RS).

Pvt. J.W. Garth, Co. C—"Killed, shot through the head" (RS).

Pvt. Montgomery George, Co. I—"Wounded in thigh and arm" (RS). He lost an arm at High Bridge in 1865.

Pvt. P.M. Gregg, Co. K—"Killed" (RS).

Pvt. Edmund Wilcox Hubard, Co. K—(Slightly) "wounded 5/23/64" [*sic*] (RS).

Pvt. Joab C. Jackson, Co. C—"Wounded slightly in the foot" (RS).

Pvt. William R. Jaurman, Co. F—"Wounded slightly in the breast" (RS).

Pvt. Walter Kilbey, Co. D—"Shot though the hips at Kennon's Farm, Charles City Co." (RS). Died 5/26/64. "The last of seven sons killed."

Pvt. Shadrach Alvin Lewis, Co. K—"Wounded in right leg" (RS).

Pvt. George Woodson Logan, was a VMI cadet; Co. F—"Wounded and captured 5/24/64 at Wilson's Wharf, Charles City County" (RS). Exchanged 11/1/64.

Pvt. W.M. (or: Emmet) McGraw, Co. K—"Wounded in right knee" (RS).

Pvt. Richard C. Messenger, Co. F—"Wounded slightly in right thigh" (RS).

Pvt. Albert T. Mitchell, Co. C—"Wounded slightly in knee" (RS).

Pvt. James Garnett Priest, Co. H—"Wounded in arm" (RS).

Pvt. Marcellus Stallard, Co. D—"Wounded in the arm" (RS).

Pvt. George W. Utz, Co. C—"Killed, shot in abdomen ("through the bowels, since dead"—RS) 5/25/64 [*sic*] in Charles City Co."

Pvt. Townsend D. Vass, Co. H—"Killed, shot in right side (or "in chest"—RS) 5/26/64 [*sic*] Kennon's Farm, Charles City Co."

Pvt. George A. Washington, Co. C—"Killed 5/25/64 [*sic*] Kennon's Farm, Charles City Co."

Lomax's Brigade (750 Men)

5th Virginia Cavalry (no casualties identified except 1 possibly wounded at WW)

At Yellow Tavern, 11 May: "losses in the regiment are estimated at between 150 and 200 killed, wounded and 'many' captured, about half our number. Col. Henry Clay Pate and 3 captains were killed.... Of five captains, only Captain Boston and myself were left.... The regiment took part *in all subsequent engagements up to Cold Harbor, 30 May.*"—Capt. Thaddeus Fitzhugh & P.J. White. No casualties for the Action on 24 May 1864 were found.

? Pvt. William Edward Payne, Co. E—"In hospital 5/25/64." Wounded? (*Not counted.*)

6th Virginia Cavalry (3 probably wounded at WW on 5/24/64 are identified.)

("Fitz Lee led an expedition to Kennon's wharf from May 23–26 with large contingents from each of his regiments.... If it was barren of success, it was also barren of further significant losses in the regiment, i.e., compared to 4 May–13 May, when Chaplain Davis wrote that the 6th VA "lost 14 killed, 58 wounded, 35 missing, total 107." He added: "Of our 10 captains, only 2 are with their companies. One has been under arrest & 7 are killed or wounded.")

Pvt. Dabney Adams, Co. I—"Wounded (or hospitalized?) 5/26/64," probably at Wilson's Wharf. RTD.

Pvt. John M. Bickers, Co. I—"Wound(ed) in left thigh" (or hospitalized?) 5/26/64. RTD.

Pvt. Henry Dodge Kerfoot, Co. D—"Wounded in right forearm and sent to Charlottesville hospital 5/26–6/20/64."

No other data or names of casualties for "Fort Kennon, etc. on 24 May" have been found.

15th Virginia Cavalry (1 who was probably wounded on 5/24/64 is identified below.)

? Pvt. Kedar W. Old (or Cato W. Olds, or Kadar Olds), Co. I—"GSW right side, hospitalized 5/23[*sic*]/64; furloughed 6/7/64."

Gordon's Brigade (420 Men commanded by Col. Clinton M. Andrews)

1st North Carolina Cavalry (5 wounded; 4 are identified from hospital records.)

Pvt. George W. Harrison, Co. E—"Admitted to hospital at Richmond 5/26/64 with GSW "scalp slight." RTD 6/2/64."

Pvt. Joseph Marlowe, Co. D—"Admitted 5/25/64 to a Richmond general hospital with a gunshot wound to the chest" (probably on 24 May).

Pvt. Jacob W. Misenheimer, Co. F—"Wounded in action at Cannon's [*sic*; Kennon's] Landing May 21 [*sic*; May 24] 1864. Promoted to corporal 7/1/64."

Pvt. Nathaniel Price, Co. A—"Admitted 5/25 or 5/27/64 to a Richmond general hospital. Furloughed 7/17/64 due to a gunshot wound in the thigh"[at Wilson's Wharf or Hanover Court House on 27 May?].

Pvt. James Proffit, 37; Co. D—"Admitted to hospital at Richmond 5/26/64 with GSW 'right arm, flesh'; (retired to) Invalid Corps 11/25/64."

Company muster rolls for May through August 1864 are lost, but the above names were listed in the "Roster of 1st North Carolina Cavalry Regiment (9th Regiment, North Carolina State Troops), in: Chris J. Hartley, Stuart's Tarheels: James B. Gordon and His 1st North Carolina Cavalry in the Civil War *(Jefferson, NC: McFarland, 2011).*

2nd North Carolina Cavalry (1 captured and 1 wounded are identified. No company muster rolls.)

Pvt. James Thomas Armstrong, Co. G—"Captured at Wilson's Landing 5/24/64."

2nd Lt. James R. Harris, Co. K—"Wounded in action 5/24/64 and admitted to hospital 9/27/64 at Raleigh, NC with GSW 'middle finger, hand fractured.'"

5th North Carolina Cavalry (225 men; 4 killed, 5 wounded, 1 wounded and captured, total 10, are identified. No muster rolls for nine of ten companies.)

Pvt. Caswell B. Askew, Co. K—"Admitted to hospital at Richmond 5/26/64 with GSW, right arm, flesh; retired to Invalid Corps 12/15/64."

Pvt. Andrew J. Bethune, Co. A—"Admitted to hospital at Richmond 5/25/64 with GSW; captured 8/21/64 at Weldon Railroad."

Pvt. Green L. Bingham, Co. F—"Killed outright." (Pvt. Paul B. Means's postwar account.)

Pvt. Haywood Hargrove, Co. A—"Admitted to hospital at Richmond with GSW, right leg, flesh, on 5/26/64. *Discharged as a minor 8/25/64.*"

Pvt. Worth J. McDonald, Co. F—"Wounded in action at Kennon's Landing 5/24/64 with contused wound, side." Transferred to Farmville, VA, 6/2/64, where condition was recorded as: "Temporary paralysis of right arm caused by explosion of shell 5/29/64 [*sic*]." Sent to a hospital at Charlotte, NC, 1/19/65 with "paralysis" and transferred to another hospital on 4/29/65." Pvt. Means wrote: "[H]e never recovered its use during his lifetime."

Pvt. Kenneth McIver, Co. A—"Killed at Kinison's [*sic*] Landing, VA, on 5/24/64."

Pvt. Neill McLeod, Co. A—"Killed at Kennon's Landing, VA, 5/24/64."

Pvt. Paul B. Means, Co. F (quoted in text)—"Wounded in action at Kennon's Landing, VA, 5/24/64 by GSW left shoulder. RTD. Wounded again at Chamberlain Run, VA on 3/31/65 and at Namozine Church, VA, on 4/3/65. Admitted to hospital with GSW, heel and RTD 4/11/65."

Pvt. William S. Prather, 36; Co. F—"Killed in battle 5/24/64 at Kennon's Landing, VA."

Pvt. John W. Siler, Co. E—"Wounded—supposedly mortally—in action near Kennen's [*sic*] Landing 5/24/64 and captured. No Federal provost marshal records found relative to his capture or imprisonment."

Sources: Louis H. Manarin, North Carolina Troops 1861–1865, A Roster, v. 2, *Cavalry; and Paul B. Means's two accounts of the 5th NC Cavalry published in 1901—see Bibliography. Pvt. Means wrote that Co. F of the 5th NC Cavalry lost 2 killed and*

2 wounded out of 10 or 12 men detailed for the attack on WW. Company muster rolls for most companies not available.

5th South Carolina Cavalry (Attached—about 650 men, estimated; 7 wounded are identified below.)

Maj. J.D. Ferguson, AAG to Maj. Gen. Fitzhugh Lee, reported that the 5th SC Cavalry lost "one officer and five men wounded." The Charleston Daily Courier *of 3 June 1864 listed the following two officers and five men who became casualties on 24 May at "Charles City Court House," i.e., WW.*

Sgt. Maj. V. C. Dibble—"Light wound, face."

Pvt. ___ Fogle, Co. E—"Wounded, arm amputated." (He may be Pvt. W.A. Fogle, who was also wounded [slightly?] at "Drury's [Drewry's] Bluff on 5/16/64.)

Captain, Regimental Quartermaster, E.C. Green—"Light wound, forehead."

Pvt. M. Hagan (or Hogan), Co. G—GSW "left shoulder," and "sent to hospital from Battle of Charles City May 24, 1864." RTD (Company G, Muster Roll).

Pvt. Theodore Thaddeus Hames, Co. K—"WIA, Charles City C.H., VA 24 May 1864." "5th South Carolina Cavalry, Company K, Mountain Rangers," freepages.genealogy.rootweb. ancestry.com/~york/5thSCC/K.html.

Cpl. J.J. Hucks, Co. E—"Light wound, forehead" or GSW "left arm, Jackson Hospital, Richmond, 5/26."

Lt. Col. Robert J. Jeffords—"Light wound, leg." (He temporarily commanded the 5th SC Cavalry while Col. Dunovant commanded the right wing at WW. Jeffords was *killed* at Burgess' Mill on 10/27/64.)

Other sources: (1) Capt. A.B. Mulligan, Co. B, 5th SC Cavalry did not go to WW, but he wrote on 26 May: "On Monday last all the effective force of my Regt went out on a raid ... after a lot of negro cavalry [sic] in the neighborhood of Charles City." On 28 May he wrote: "[T]hat portion of our Regt which went towards Charles City Court House the other day ... all returned safely with the exception [of] a few wounded (none from my company)." (See O.F. Hutchinson, Jr., ed., My Dear Mother & Sisters—Civil War Letters *... in Bibliography.) (2) Roll of the Dead, South Carolina Troops, Confederate States Service, manuscript c. 1870, published by the SC Dep't. of Archives & History, lists no deaths by place or date for the Action at Wilson's Wharf.*

Appendix B
Casualties At or Near
Wilson's Wharf–Fort Pocahontas
During 5 May 1864–June 1865

The Table below summarizes data: names and/or known numbers of casualties from both sides listed in Appendix A, including soldiers who were recorded as buried at "Wilson's Landing (or) Wharf," or "Fort Pocahontas." The Table is not complete, since records for some Federal units are incomplete; and Confederate losses, if any, during some skirmishes have not been reported. Many soldiers became ill and were taken to hospitals elsewhere; some died on boats even before they reached a hospital. Most of the sick recovered. DOW = died of wounds. Numbers in ( ) below are soldiers who were initially buried at "Wilson's Wharf–Fort Pocahontas."

	COMBAT-RELATED					OTHER CAUSES		
Units	Killed/ DOW	Wounded	Cap- tured	Miss- ing	Deser- tions	Disease	Acci- dents	Total
Operations, 5–23 May 1864								
UNION:								
1st Regiment, USCT						2(1)		2
22nd Reg't. USCT							1	1
CONFEDERATE:								
CSA Signal Corps	4	2	2					8
Armed Citizens	2+3?	2	1					8?
Scouts, Soldiers	1		5					6

Units	COMBAT-RELATED				OTHER CAUSES			
	Killed/ DOW	Wounded	Cap-tured	Miss-ing	Deser-tions	Disease	Acci-dents	Total
Action at Wilson's Wharf, 24 May 1864								
UNION:								
Wild's Brigade Staff		1						1
1st Regiment, USCT	4	17	1 (Enslaved)					22
10th Regiment, USCT	2	0?						2
Battery M, 3rd NY Lt. Art'y		1						1
Civilians on steamer		4						4
CONFEDERATE:								
Fitzhugh Lee's Cavalry (Estimated total loss of 175 killed, wounded, & captured; 101 names are known.)								
LEFT BEHIND:	25(25)	?	19					175
Operations, 25 May 1864–June 1865								
2nd New Hampshire Vol. Infantry						1		1
38th New Jersey Vol. Infantry						2(2)		2
143rd Ohio Vol. Infantry, NG						34(12)		34
163rd Ohio Vol. Infantry, NG						31(10)	1(1)	32
Co. I; 1st U.S. Col'd Cavalry	6(2)					1	1(1)	8
E, 16th NY Heavy Artillery			2	2	1	2(1)		7
H, 16th NY Heavy Artillery					1	5(4)		6
33rd NY Lt. Artillery Battery					7	1(1)		8
37th Regiment, USCT					2		1	3
2nd NH Vol. Infantry						1		1
38th NJ Vol. Infantry						2		2
89th NY Vol. Infantry (no info)								
184th NY Vol. Infantry						4(4)		4
Co. D, 20th NY Cavalry (no info)								
"Negroes" (Civilians?)						2		2
Confederates			6		7+			13+
FEDERAL LOSSES	12(2)	23	3	2	11	86(34)	6(2)	143(38)
CONFEDERATE LOSSES	32+(25)	154(est.)	33		7+			226(25)

Incomplete records reveal that at least 369 Americans—143 Federal and 226 Confederate officers, soldiers, and civilians, of white, black, and mixed races—were killed, mortally wounded, or captured, died of disease or wounds, or were accidentally shot or drowned, or deserted their units posted at Fort Pocahontas during May 1864 through June 1865. Many other Federal soldiers who were wounded or took sick there recovered, as did most wounded Confederates.

The twelve Federal soldiers who were killed or mortally wounded were evenly divided between infantrymen of the 1st and 10th Regiments, USCT who fought on 24 May 1864; and cavalrymen of Company I, 1st U.S. Colored Cavalry who later became casualties during minor skirmishes. An officer of the 22nd Infantry Regiment, USCT and a 1st Sergeant of Company I, 1st U.S. Colored Cavalry were accidentally shot and killed. Other members of U.S. Colored units died of disease; one soldier (37th Regiment, USCT) and a "negro" civilian(?) drowned; and another (soldier or civilian?) was shot.

Two soldiers of the 1st Regiment, USCT on advance picket on 24 May 1864 may have been executed after capture. Another soldier, captured at the same time, was returned to slavery but he escaped and rejoined his unit in 1865. Had Maj. Gen. Fitzhugh Lee's force captured the fort on 24 May and carried out his orders "to kill every man in the fort," the Federal death toll would have far exceeded that of the Fort Pillow "massacre" six weeks earlier. Confederate losses also would have been much higher.

Approximately 226 Confederate cavalrymen, men of the Confederate Signal Corps, scouts, and armed citizens became casualties. Possibly about 50 Confederates were killed or mortally wounded on 24 May; 25 bodies were left behind. Another 7 were known killed at other times; 33 Confederates were captured; and another 7 deserted.

Disease alone probably took the lives of 86 Federal soldiers; six more men died in accidents. The total of 92 non-combat deaths is nearly 8 times the number of combat-related deaths. Two Ohio National Guard "100 days" regiments lost no men in battle, but they suffered the highest casualties, 34 and 32 deaths, respectively; probably all were by disease except for one sergeant who was accidentally shot while "on a scout upriver." Several Ohio soldiers died on their way home.

Cemetery records state that 33 bodies (but list only 28 names) of Federal soldiers were removed from "Wilson's Landing" in 1866 and reinterred in Glendale National Cemetery. However, 38 Federal soldiers who were initially buried at "Wilson's Wharf (or) Landing/Fort Pocahontas" and later reinterred at the Glendale Cemetery are in most cases located by section letter and grave number in the cemetery. Federal soldiers may have been reinterred at Glendale Cemetery or elsewhere under "Unknown" headstones.

Twenty-five bodies of Confederates left in the abatis on the east side of the fort on 24 May 1864 were buried outside the fort; at least two of them were removed and re-interred near their homes.

Chapter Notes

Prelude

1. Mark M. Neely, Jr., "One Country, One Destiny-Abraham Lincoln's First Inaugural Address," *North & South*, Vol. 13, No. 5, January 2012, p. 22.
2. "Elections, United States," and "Lincoln, Abraham," in Patricia Faust, ed., *Historical Times Illustrated Encyclopedia of the Civil War* (New York: Harper & Row, 1986), pp. 238, 439.
3. "Lincoln, Abraham," in Faust, *ibid.*, p. 439.
4. James M. McPherson, *Battle Cry of Freedom: The Civil War Era*, (New York: Oxford University Press, 1988), pp. 253–257, 272–273; Historian McPherson comments: "Did this mean that Republicans killed the last, best hope to avert disunion? Probably not. Neither Crittenden's nor any other compromise could have stopped secession in the lower South. No compromise could undo the event that triggered disunion: Lincoln's election by a solid North."
5. McPherson, *ibid.*, p. 254.
6. "Secession Sequence and Dates," in: Mark M. Boatner III, *The Civil War Dictionary, Revised Edition* (New York: David McKay Co., 1988), pp. 729–730.
7. *Ibid.*
8. "Slavery," in: Patricia L. Faust, *Historical Times Illustrated Encyclopedia of the Civil War* (New York: Harper & Row, 1986), p. 692; "Slavery," in: Boatner, Dictionary, p. 764.
9. Gordon Rhea, "Fellow Southerners!" *North & South*, Vol. 13, No. 5, pp. 14–15.
10. *Ibid.*, pp. 13–14.
11. McPherson, *Battle Cry of Freedom*, pp. 557–558.
12. A compilation from numerous sources in "Emancipation Proclamation," in Wikipedia.
13. McPherson, *Battle Cry of Freedom*, pp. 558–559.
14. "Emancipation Proclamation," in Wikipedia.

Chapter I

1. Frances H. Casstevens, *Edward A. Wild and the African Brigade in the Civil War* (Jefferson, NC: McFarland, 2003), pp. 6, 7. William Connery, "Outline of the Lives of General Edward Wild and General Fitzhugh Lee, Presented at the Fort Pocahontas Reenactment on May 21, 2005," sent by William.connery@verizon.net to EBesch@aol.com on 5/26/2005.
2. Casstevens, pp. 14–16; Connery, p. 1.
3. Casstevens, pp. 22–25, 27–29; Edward A. Wild, "Military Life of Edward A. Wild, Brig. Genl. Vol[unteers]," (Massachusetts Historical Society, Boston).
4. Casstevens, pp. 30–31, 35–38, 40–42; Connery, "Outline," p. 1.
5. Casstevens, pp. 45–46.
6. *Ibid.*, pp. 49–50.
7. *Ibid.*, pp. 52–54.
8. *Ibid.*, p. 61; Hari Jones, "The Color of Bravery, United States Colored Troops in the Civil War," *Hallowed Ground*, Civil War Trust, Vol. 14, No. 2, Summer 2013, p. 30.
9. Editor Dana B. Shoaf, "Sea Change, Thoughts & Comments," *Civil War Times*, Vol. 52, No. 1, February 2013, p. 31.
10. Casstevens, *Edward A. Wild*, p. 61; "Freedmen," in: www.civilwarhome.com/freedmen.htm. On 3 March 1865, President Lincoln signed a bill that established the American Freedmen's Bureau of Refugees, Freedmen, and Abandoned Lands, known simply as the Freedmen's Bureau, to assist more than four million former slaves after the war ended. ("3 March 1865," in: www.history.

com/this-day-in-history/freedmans-bureau-created.)

11. Casstevens, p. 55.

12. *Ibid.*, pp. 56–57.

13. William Gladstone Letter to Ed Besch dated 26 August 2003, p. 7.

14. Casstevens, pp. 62–63. Chris Howland, "Foiled at Fort Wagner," *America's Civil War*, Vol. 26, No. 5, November 2013, pp. 58–61; excellent full-page Color Maps: "Charleston's War 1861–1863" on p. 59, and 2 Maps "Assault on Fort Wagner July 18, 1863" on p. 60.

15. Casstevens, p. 63; Connery, "Outline," p. 2.

16. Casstevens, p. 63; Faust, p. 282.

17. Casstevens, pp. 65–66; Connery, "Outline," p. 2.

18. Casstevens, pp. 68–70.

19. Casstevens, pp. 70–71; Connery, "Outline," p. 2.

20. Casstevens, p. 74; Connery, 2.

21. Casstevens, pp. 74, 76–79, 80–84.

22. "Gabions" were "cylindrical baskets with open ends, made of brush or metal ribbons woven on pickets, used as a revetment in constructing field fortifications," Boatner, *Dictionary*.

23. Casstevens, pp. 85–86, 92.

24. The 55th Massachusetts and the 1st and 3rd NCCV Regiments were issued Enfield Pattern (P) 1853 .577 cal. rifle-muskets, which also were issued to white units such as the 144th New York Volunteer Infantry Regiment. The 1st and 3rd NCCV Regiments, later re-designated the 35th and 37th Infantry Regiments, USCT, were issued Springfield M1863 .58 cal. rifle-muskets in 1864. Frederick P. Todd, et al; *American Military Equipage*, 1851–1872, Vol. II, State Forces (Chatham Square Press, 1983), pp. 909, 1075, 1053. The U.S. Ordnance Department considered Enfield rifle-muskets produced in England to be equivalent to U.S. M1861/1863 Springfield or contract rifle-muskets. However, most of the Enfield rifle-muskets imported in large quantities by both the North and South were made by contractors of the Birmingham gun trade and varied in quality.

25. Casstevens, pp. 88–89.

26. *Ibid.*, pp. 89–90.

27. *Ibid.*, p. 93.

28. *Ibid.*, pp. 89–90.

29. *Guerrillas* were "bands of armed men engaged in conducting irregular warfare because of their irregular origin." *Partisan rangers* were armed units organized "to injure the enemy by actions separate from that of their own main army." The latter, in contrast to guerrillas, were a genuine part of an army and "entitled to privileges afforded them by the laws of land war-

fare" if captured. Casstevens, p. 94. Sometimes, guerrilla bands behaved more like self-serving bandits, but sometimes so did regular troops on both sides.

30. Casstevens, pp. 89–90.

31. *Ibid.*, pp. 94–95. There was much controversy about guerrilla warfare in the South as well as in the North, particularly the kind practiced by William Clarke Quantrill in Missouri and Kansas. The Confederate Congress passed an act on 21 April 1862 that legalized partisan units "to have the same pay, rations, and quarters during their term of service, and be subject to the same regulations as other soldiers." Confederate partisan ranger units operated in Alabama, Georgia, Florida, Louisiana, Mississippi, North Carolina, South Carolina, and Virginia (where John Singleton Mosby gained fame). (*Ibid.*, p. 95.)

32. "Report of Brig. Gen. Edward A. Wild, U.S. Army, commanding expedition," Dec. 28, 1863; *O.R.*, Ser. I, Vol. 29, Pt. I, pp. 911–917; cited in Casstevens, p. 96. (Hereafter: "Wild, Report, 28 Dec. 1863.")

33. Casstevens, *Edward A. Wild*, pp. 98–99.

34. Wild, Report, 28 Dec. 1863, in *O.R.*, Ser. I, Vol. 29, Pt. I, p. 911; cited in Casstevens, pp. 100–101.

35. Benjamin F. Butler, "General Order No. 46," Dec. 5, 1863, *O. R.*, Ser. III, Vol. 3, p. 1139; portions cited in Casstevens, p. 102.

36. Wild, Report, 28 Dec. 1863, in *O.R.*, Ser. I, Vol. 29, Pt. I, p. 912.

37. Wild, "Report," in *ibid.*, p. 911; Casstevens, *Edward A. Wild*, p. 103.

38. Casstevens, pp. 103–104.

39. *Ibid.*, 105–106.

40. Casstevens, pp. 142–143. Webb Garrison, "Scores of hostages were pawns in the power struggle of the American Civil War," *Military History*, Vol. 12, No. 2, June 1995, p. 79; "Lee, William Henry Fitzhugh, CSA, b. Arlington, Va., 31 March 1837," Faust, *Encyclopedia*, p. 431. W.H.F. Lee had suffered a severe leg wound at Brandy Station on 9 June 1863 and was captured by Federal raiders while recuperating. He was Maj. Gen. Fitzhugh Lee's first cousin.

41. Casstevens, pp. 106–108; "Tewksbury," *New York Times*, 9 January 1864, cited in Casstevens, pp. 107–108.

42. Wild, Report, 28 Dec. 1863, in *O.R.*, Ser. I, Vol. 29, Part I, pp. 912–913. Having experienced, tactically proficient white officers leading Wild's relatively inexperienced black soldiers consistently paid off when fighting Confederate guerrillas on their home grounds.

43. Casstevens, *Edward A. Wild*, pp. 108–111, 127.

44. Wild's Letter from Northwest Landing,

in *O.R.*, Ser. II, Vol. 6, p. 1130; Lt. Munden's affidavit to the special committee, no date, in *ibid.*, pp. 1129–1130.

45. Casstevens, *Edward A. Wild*, pp. 111–112.

46. *Ibid.*, p. 114, Appendix—Table II—"Results of Wild's Raid into North Carolina," with "Results of Colonel Alonzo Draper's Detail, December 17–20, 1863"; and Table III, "Wild's Losses during Raid into North Carolina"; both tables compiled from: "Reports of Brig. Gen. Edward A. Wild, U.S. Army, commanding expedition," Edward A. Wild, Brigadier General of Volunteers to Capt. George H. Johnston, Assistant Adjutant General, Norfolk, Va., *O.R.*, Ser. I, Vol. 29, Pt. I, pp. 911–917; and "Report of Alonzo G. Draper, to Lieutenant Hiram W. Allen, A.A.A.G., Colored Troops, District of Norfolk and Portsmouth, Va.," *Edward A. Wild Papers*, Southern Historical Collection, University of North Carolina, Chapel Hill, North Carolina; p. 269. Col. Draper's Report was combined in Wild's Report; hence it is not included in the *O.R.*; Casstevens, p. 269, Notes 6, 7, 8 on p. 309.

47. "Tewksbury," "Gen. Butler's Department; Invasion of North Carolina by Gen. Wild's Colored Battalions," *New York Times*, 9 Jan. 1864, p. 1, col. 6.

48. Casstevens, *Edward A. Wild*, pp. 113, 122.

49. "Tewksbury," "Gen. Butler's Department; Invasion of North Carolina by Gen. Wild's Colored Battalions," *New York Times*, 9 Jan. 1864, p. 1, col. 6.

50. W.H.N. Smith, Chairman, "Report of the special committee to inquire into certain outrages of the enemy," *O.R.*, Ser. II, Vol. 6, pp. 1127–1129; a part quoted in Casstevens, *Edward A. Wild*, p. 108.

51. Colonel Griffin's letter to Wild was published as "Recent Expedition to Elizabeth City," in the Milledgeville, Georgia *Southern Recorder* on 19 Jan. 1864; cited in Casstevens, Ch. VII, Note 2 on p. 289.

52. Casstevens, pp. 117–119. Letters from Maj. Gen. Butler to Maj. Gen. Halleck; Col. Samuel Spears to Butler; citizens of Pasquotank County, NC to General George W. Getty; Col. James W. Hinton, commanding North Carolina State Forces, to Butler; Butler to Col. Hinton; Butler to Lt. W.J. Munden and Mr. Pender Weeks, etc., pertaining to hangings; written during 15–26 January 1864, are in *O.R.*, Ser. II, Vol. 6, pp. 845–847, 858, 877–878, 883–884.

53. Casstevens, pp. 115–116. While looking for artifacts relating to General Wild and his colored soldiers at a major museum in North Carolina, the Author found "General Wild's

(pistol) cartridge box" listed, but the curator couldn't find it.

54. E.A. Hitchcock, "Letter to the Editor" of the *New York Times*, 28 Nov. 1863; in Casstevens, *Edward A. Wild*, p. 117, Note 1 on p. 289.

55. Casstevens, pp. 140–142. Webb Garrison, "Scores of Hostages..." *Military History*, June 1995, p. 79.

56. Casstevens, p. 42.

57. Hondon B. Hargrove, *Black Union Soldiers in the Civil War* (Jefferson, NC: McFarland, 1988), pp. 106–107. The "Regiments or Companies" and their "Aggregate Strength" of each of General Thomas's listed organizations he raised, are on p. 107.

58. *O.R.*, Ser. II, Vol. 6, p. 1190; cited in: Hargrove, *ibid.*, p. 108.

59. James L. Nichols, *General Fitzhugh Lee, A Biography*, 2nd ed. (Lynchburg, VA: H.E. Howard, Inc., 1989), pp. 1, 4, 5; Edward G. Longacre, "Fitzhugh Lee (1835–1905)," www.encyclopedia virginia.org/Lee_Fitzhugh_1835–1905; "Fitzhugh Lee," en.wikipedia.org/Wiki/Fitzhugh_Lee.

60. Nichols, *General Fitzhugh Lee*, pp. 5, 6.

61. *Ibid.*, pp. 7, 8. Former Cadet, then Secretary of War and later Confederate President, Jefferson Davis, was himself a frequent visitor to Benny Havens' Tavern. On 31 July 1825 he was caught there, court-martialed, and nearly dismissed. (James A. Beckman, "A visit to a notorious tavern, nearly ended the West Point career of a young cadet named Jefferson Davis," *America's Civil War*, Vol. 13, No. 5, November 2000, pp. 34, 62–63.)

62. Nichols, *General Fitzhugh Lee*, p. 8.

63. *Ibid.* The U.S. Army officers mentioned later became prominent Confederate generals.

64. *Ibid.*, pp. 10–11.

65. *Ibid.*, pp. 12–13.

66. *Ibid.*, pp. 14–15.

67. Nichols, *ibid.*, p. 16.

68. Longacre, "Fitzhugh Lee," p. 2.

69. Nichols, *General Fitzhugh Lee*, pp. 18–19.

70. *Ibid.*, p. 20.

71. Nichols, *ibid.*, p. 21. "Confederate Cavalry," in Michael Blake, *American Civil War Cavalry* (London: Almark Publishing, 1973), p. 7.

72. Philip Katcher, *Confederate Cavalryman 1861–1865* (Oxford, UK & New York: Osprey Publishing, 2002), p. 7.

73. Nichols, *General Fitzhugh Lee*, p. 21.

74. *Ibid.*, pp. 21–22.

75. *Ibid.*, pp. 22, 23–24.

76. *Ibid.*, pp. 25–26.

77. *Ibid.*, pp. 26–29.

78. *Ibid.*, pp. 31–32.
79. *Ibid.*, pp. 32–33.
80. *Ibid.*, p. 34.
81. *Ibid.*, pp. 34–35.
82. *Ibid.*, p. 35.
83. *Ibid.*, pp. 35–36.
84. *Ibid.*, pp. 37–38.
85. *Ibid.*, pp. 39, 42, 43–44. "Killed at Antietam," "Antietam (Sharpsburg)," Boatner, *Dictionary*, p. 21.
86. Nichols, *ibid.*, p. 44.
87. *Ibid.*, 45–46.
88. *Ibid.*, pp. 45–47.
89. *Ibid.*, pp. 46–47. "Kelly's Ford (Kellysville), Va. 17 Mar. '63"; Boatner, *Dictionary*, p. 451.
90. Nichols, *General Fitzhugh Lee*, pp. 47–48.; Boatner, *ibid.*
91. Nichols, *ibid.*, pp. 47–48; Boatner, *ibid.* Fitzhugh Lee's Report in the *O.R. of the War of the Rebellion*, cited in www.civilwar.org/battlefiields/kelly's_ford_history_articles/fitzhugh_; lees_report.html.
92. Nichols, *ibid.*, p. 48.
93. *Ibid.*, p. 50.
94. *Ibid.*, p. 51. Casualties in "Chancellorsville Campaign, Apr.–May 1–6, '63"; Boatner, *Dictionary*, p. 140.
95. Nichols, *ibid.*, pp. 51–52.
96. *Ibid.*, pp. 52–53; "Brandy Station, Va. 9 June '63 (Gettysburg Campaign)," Boatner, *Dictionary*, pp. 80–81.
97. Boatner, *ibid.*, p. 333.
98. Nichols, *General Fitzhugh Lee*, pp. 53–54.
99. *Ibid.*, p. 54.
100. *Ibid.*, pp. 55–56.
101. Earl B. McElfresh, "Fighting on Strange Ground, Can poor planning and bad maps explain the Confederate defeat at Gettysburg," *Civil War Times*, Vol. 52, No. 4, August 2013, pp. 34, 37.
102. "Cavalry Action, Gettysburg Campaign," Boatner, *Dictionary*, p. 339; "Battle of Gettysburg, Third Day cavalry battles," en.wikipedia.org/wiki/Battle_of_Gettysburg_Third_Day_cavalry_battles, p. 3.
103. Nichols, *General Fitzhugh Lee*, pp. 56–57; "Battle of Gettysburg, Third Day cavalry battles," *ibid.*
104. Nichols, *ibid.*, pp. 56–57; "Battle of Gettysburg, Third Day cavalry battles," *ibid.*
105. Nichols, *ibid.*, pp. 57–58.
106. Larry Tagg, *The Generals of Gettysburg* (Campbell, CA: Zapas Publishing, 1999), p. 364; cited in "Fitzhugh Lee," en.wikipedia.org/wiki/Fitzhugh_Lee.
107. Nichols, *General Fitzhugh Lee*, p. 59.
108. *Ibid.*, pp. 59–61.
109. *Ibid.*, pp. 62–64.

110. James L. Nichols states that Sheridan's "over 12,000 men [were] armed with breechloading, repeating Spencer carbines," but far less than even a quarter of them were armed with 7-shot Spencer rifles and carbines at this time.
111. Nichols, *General Fitzhugh Lee*, pp. 64–65.
112. *Ibid.*, p. 74.
113. *Ibid.*, 66–67; Thomas P. Nanzig, *3rd Virginia Cavalry* (Lynchburg, VA: H.E. Howard, 1989), pp. 47–50; John Fortier, *15th Virginia Cavalry* (Lynchburg, VA: H.E. Howard, 1993), p. 53; Sheridan's Report, in: *O.R.*, Ser. I, Vol. 36, Pt. II, p. 516.
114. Nanzig, *ibid.*, p. 50. Maj. Gen. James H. Wilson's Report, in: *O.R.*, *ibid.*, pp. 554–555.
115. Nichols, *General Fitzhugh Lee*, pp. 67–68.
116. *Ibid.*, pp. 68–69.
117. Thom Hatch, "Custer," *America's Civil War*, Vol. 26, No. 5, November 2013, p. 56.
118. Nichols, *General Fitzhugh Lee*, p. 69.
119. John Gill, *Reminiscences of Four Years as a Private in the Confederate Army* (Baltimore: Sun Printing Office, 1904), Preston Library, V.M.I., Lexington, VA, pp. 92–93. John Gill, who was born at Annapolis, MD in 1841, later wrote: "Capt. Henry Lee, brother of Gen. Fitz Lee, [was] a classmate of mine at the University of Virginia prior to the war. From the beginning I formed a most agreeable association with Gen. Lee, his staff, couriers and members of the Signal Corps, which has lasted these many years. General Lee ... promoted me after the Culpeper [or Kelly's Ford] fight, to rank of sergeant of the Signal Corps." (Gill, *ibid.*, pp. 92–93.)
120. Nichols, *General Fitzhugh Lee*, pp. 69–70.
121. Robert J. Driver, *2nd Virginia Cavalry* (Lynchburg, VA: H.E. Howard, 1995), p. 120.
122. Chris J. Hartley, *Stuart's Tarheels-James B. Gordon and His North Carolina Cavalry in the Civil War*, 2nd ed., (Jefferson, NC: McFarland, 2011), p. 234.
123. Nichols, *General Fitzhugh Lee*, p. 70.
124. James L. Nichols cited Fitz Lee from his comprehensive report of his activities from May 4, 1864, to the end of the war, in his postwar report to Robert E. Lee, Dec. 20, 1866, in Robert E. Lee, Headquarters Papers, Virginia Historical Society, Mss 3 L515a; Notes 36, 49 in *ibid.*, p. 194.
125. Driver, *2nd Virginia Cavalry*, p. 120.
126. Nichols, *General Fitzhugh Lee*, p. 70.

Chapter II

1. A Chorus of the Rally Song for the 1st Regiment of Colored Volunteers, District of Columbia, written and dedicated 25 May 1863; John H. Holman Papers, Western Historical Manuscript Collection, Columbia University of Missouri, cited in: C.R. Gibbs, *Black, Copper & Bright* (Silver Spring, MD: Three Dimensional Publishing, 2002), p. 2. (Hereafter: "C.R. Gibbs.")

2. C.R. Gibbs, *ibid.*, p. 3.

3. *Ibid.*, pp. 4–5.

4. *Ibid.*, pp. 6–8.

5. *Ibid.*, p. 8.

6. *Ibid.*, p. 10.

7. *Ibid.*, pp. 12, 14, 15, the published law cited on p. 13.

8. *Ibid.*, pp. 20, 21, 24–25, 27.

9. *Ibid.*, pp. 27–28.

10. *Ibid.*, pp. 30–32.

11. *Ibid.*, pp. 32, 111–112.

12. *Ibid.*, p. 104. Sources disagree over whether Turner was born in 1833 or1834; his military record says "1833." His birth date also is stated as "February, 1831," in Robert Ewell Graves, *Black Defenders of America, 1775–1973* (Chicago: Johnson Publishing, 1974), p. 94.

13. C.R. Gibbs, p. 104, Note 1 on pp. 215–216.

14. *Ibid.*, pp. 104–105.

15. *Ibid.*, pp. 105–106.

16. *Ibid.*, pp. 105–107. "Henry M. Turner," in William Simmons, *Men of Mark: Eminent, Progressive, Rising* (1887), p. 109; cited in C.R. Gibbs, pp. 107–108.

17. C.R. Gibbs, *ibid.*, pp. 108–109.

18. *Ibid.*, p. 112.

19. C.R. Gibbs called it the "1st Regiment of Colored Volunteers, DC"; William A. Gladstone wrote "I have found it to be properly identified as the '1st District of Columbia [Regiment] Infantry, African Descent.'" Gladstone omitted "Regiment." William Gladstone Letter to Ed (Besch) dated 26 August 2006, p. 2.

20. C.R. Gibbs, pp. 34–35.

21. *Ibid.*, pp. 34–35.

22. *Ibid.*, pp. 40–41. "Colonel William Birney," mentioned in C.W. Foster's Letter to Secretary of War Edwin M. Stanton dated 31 October 1863, in *O.R.*, Ser. III, Vol. 3, p. 1112.

23. C.R. Gibbs, p. 43.

24. *Ibid.*

25. *Ibid.*, pp. 44–45; description of clothing issue from "Clothing Account" of Corporal John Ross, illustrated on page 51.

26. *Ibid.*, p. 46.

27. *Ibid.*, pp. 49–50.

28. C.W. Foster, Assistant Adjutant General of Volunteers, Letter about the 2nd Regiment, USCT to Secretary of War Stanton dated 31 Oct. 1863, in *O.R.*, Ser. III, Vol. 3, p. 1112; William A. Gladstone Letter to Ed Besch dated 26 August 2003, p. 6.

29. C.R. Gibbs, pp. 52, 53.

30. *Ibid.*, pp. 46–47.

31. *Ibid.*, pp. 55, 58.

32. *Ibid.*, pp. 61–62.

33. *Ibid.*, p. 57.

34. *Ibid.*, pp. 64–65, 67.

35. *Ibid.*, pp. 120, 122–123, 130. Besides hospital and post chaplains, there were a total of 930 regimental chaplains in the Union Army. Of these, 133 served in the U.S. Colored Troops, and only 14 of them were African Americans. (*ibid.*)

36. Letter to Brig. Gen. Palmer from Fort Monroe dated April 20, 1863, in *O.R.*, Ser. III, Vol. 3, p. 1288.

37. *O.R.*, Ser. I, Vol. 33, pp. 374–375.

38. "10th Regiment Infantry, U.S. Colored Troops, Regimental Histories," Frederick H. Dyer, *A Compendium of the War of the Rebellion* (Des Moines, IA: F.H. Dyer, 1908; Reprint: Morningside Bookshop, 1978), p. 1725; E. Henry Powell, Lieut. Col. 10th U.S.C.T., "The Colored Soldier in the War of the Rebellion," Read before the Vermont Commandery of the Loyal Legion, Vermont War Papers for The Military Order of the Loyal Legion of the United States (Wilmington, NC: Broadfoot Publishing, 1994), p. 42; *Morning Reports; Regimental Letter, Order, and Detail Book,* 10th Regiment, USCT; NARA, Washington, DC.

39. "Plymouth, N.C., 17–20 Apr. '64," Boatner, *Dictionary, p.* 656; "Battle of Plymouth (1864): Order of Battle," en.wikipedia.org/wiki/Battle_of_Plymouth(1864)#Order_of_Battle; "African Americans During the Civil War," "Go Wild in Washington County," www.gowildnc.org/ history-african_americans.aspx.

40. Quoted from another source by James W. Loewen in Letter to Edwin W. Besch dated May 24, 1999, attachment, no page no.

41. *Ibid.*

42. "10th Regiment Infantry, U.S. Colored Troops, Regimental Histories," Dyer, *A Compendium of the War of the Rebellion,* p. 1725; E. Henry Powell, Lieut. Col. 10th U.S.C.T., "The Colored Soldier in the War of the Rebellion," p. 42; *Morning Reports; Regimental Letter, Order, and Detail Book,* 10th Regiment, USCT, NARA, Washington, DC. "Escape from the Confederacy, Robert Smalls," en.wikipedia.org/wiki/Robert_Smalls; Stephen T. Foster, *Robert Smalls, From Slave To Politician, 1839–1915* (Card, USA: Atlas Editions, 1993).

43. E. Henry Powell, Lieut. Col. 10th U.S.C.T., "The Colored Soldier in the War of the Rebellion," *ibid.*, pp. 45–46. Chaplain Alvah R. Jones was placed in arrest on 12 July 1864 and released from arrest sometime in August 1864. (Ancestry.com—"Alvah R. Jones," U.S. Colored Troops Military Service Records, 1861–1865, Courtesy Henry H. McCawley, Jr., of Mobile, AL.)

44. All documents and Letters quoted, are from the Military Records of Alvah R. Jones, in *ibid.*

45. Sources include correspondence at the National Archives: Office of the Adjutant General, RG 94; Office of the Quartermaster General, RG 92; the Regimental Record Book of the 10th U.S. Colored Troops; and various others cited in: Roger Sturcke & Anthony Gero, "Zouave Dress for the 10th United states Colored Troops, 1863–1864: A Probability," *Military Collector & Historian*, Vol. 49, No. 3, Fall 1997, pp. 132–133.

46. "10th Regiment, USCT," Microfilm Record Group 94, NARA.

47. "U.S. Colored Troops—The Regiments," http://www.ideas-classroom.org/IDEAS/civil war/189-colregts.html.

48. Casstevens, *Edward A. Wild*, p. 109.

49. Dyer, *Compendium*, p. 1730; "Sharps rifles," Earl J. Coates & John D. McAulay, *Civil War Sharps Carbines & Rifles* (Gettysburg, PA: Thomas Publications, 1996), p. 27.

50. Dyer, *ibid.*, p. 1722.

51. *Ibid.*, pp. 937, 1395, 1434; Henry Hall & James Hall, *Cayuga in the Field, A record of the 18th N.Y. Volunteers, All the Batteries of the 3rd New York Artillery, and 75th New York Volunteers....* (Auburn, NY: 1873), pp. 114, 115, 225, 237–238.

52. Boatner, *Dictionary*, pp. 917–918; Faust, *Encyclopedia*, p. 823.

53. Driver, *2nd Virginia Cavalry*, pp. 110–112.

54. Nanzig, *3rd Virginia Cavalry*, pp. 46, 50.

55. Kenneth L. Stiles, *4th Virginia Cavalry* (Lynchburg, VA: H.E. Howard, 1995). Also referenced: Lee A. Wallace, 2nd ed., *A Guide to Virginia Military Organizations 1861–1865* (Lynchburg, VA: H.E. Howard, 1986), pp. 40, 41, 42, 43. (H.E. Howard published an excellent series of regimental histories of all Virginia artillery batteries, cavalry and infantry regiments, etc. that provide a detailed history and roster of each unit.)

56. Wallace, *A Guide to Virginia Military Organizations 1861–1865, ibid.*, pp. 45, 46, 55, 56, 71; Robert J. Driver, Jr., *5th Virginia Cavalry* (Lynchburg, VA: H.E. Howard, 1997), pp. 78, 79, 80, 186; Michael P. Musick, *6th Virginia Cavalry* (H.E. Howard, 1990), 59–60; John

Fortier, *15th Virginia Cavalry* (H.E. Howard, 1993), pp. 55, 71, 127–128.

57. Greg Mast, *State Troops and Volunteers, A Photographic Record of North Carolina's Civil War Soldiers*, Vol. One (Raleigh: NC Department of Cultural Resources, 1995), pp. 118–121.

58. Todd, *Military Equipage*, Vol. III, p. 1070.

59. *O.R.*, Ser. I, Vol. 33, Pt. II, p. 940.

60. Paul B. Means, "Additional Sketch, Sixty-third Regiment (Fifth Cavalry)," Louis H. Manarin, *North Carolina Troops, 1861–1865, A Roster*, Vol. III, pp. 529–545. Gen. William P. Roberts, "Additional Sketch, Ninth Regiment (Second Cavalry)," *North Carolina Troops...*, vol. II, p. 767.

61. Todd, *Military Equipage*, Vol. III, p. 1070.

62. Mast, *State Troops and Volunteers, ibid.*, pp. 118–121; Chris B. Hartley, *Stuart's Tarheels: James B. Gordon and His 1st North Carolina Cavalry in the Civil War* (Jefferson, NC: McFarland, 2010), pp. 175, 326, 362.

63. "Introduction," Lewis F. Knudsen, "The Official Records of Company D (South Carolina Rangers), 5th South Carolina Cavalry Regiment, 1861–1865," Draft, pp. 1–2; Richard J. Sommers, "John Dunovant," William C. Davis, ed., *The Confederate Generals*, Vol. II, (National Historical Society, 1991), p. 86; "South Carolina 5th Cavalry Regiment" in Stewart Sifakis, *Compendium of Confederate Armies, South Carolina and Georgia* (Facts on File, 1995), pp. 43, 45; Edwin W. Besch, John M. Bingham, & Robert L. Brown, "The Confederate Fifth South Carolina Cavalry and Its Battle Flag and Enfield Arms," MS c. 1997, p. 1. (Hereafter: "Besch et al, The Confederate Fifth.")

64. *O.R.*, Series I, Vol. 33, Pt. III: General R.E. Lee to Jefferson Davis, p. 1097; S.O. No. 65, p. 1232; movements, reduce company strengths, p. 1258.

65. Captain A.B. Mulligan's Letter of 26 June 1864, in: Olin Fulmer Hutchinson, Jr., *"My Dear Mother & Sisters"—Civil War Letters of Capt. A.B. Mulligan, Co. B, 5th South Carolina Cavalry—Butler's Division—Hampton's Corps 1861–1865* (Spartanburg, SC: The Reprint Company, Publishers, 1992), p. 126; Besch, et al, "The Confederate Fifth," p. 1.

66. John D. Brown's *Orderly Book*, South Carolina Dept. of Archives & History, Columbia, SC.

67. Browne's *Orderly Book, ibid.*

68. Thomas D. Mays, ed., *Let Us Meet In Heaven, The Civil War Letters of James Michael Barr, 5th South Carolina Cavalry* (Abilene, TX: McWhiney Foundation Press, McMurray University, 2001), p. 17, Note 192.

69. *O.R.*, Ser. I, Vol. 36, Pt. III, pp. 812, 813.
70. *Ibid.*, p. 1258.
71. Edward L. Wells, *A Sketch of the Charleston Light Dragoons from the Earliest of the Corps* (Charleston, SC: 1888), p. 29.
72. *Ibid.*, p. 35.
73. *O.R.*, Ser. I, Vol. 12, Pt. III, pp. 1021, 1301.
74. Wells, *A Sketch of the Charleston Light Dragoons...*, p. 36.
75. *O.R.*, Ser. I, Vol. 33, Pt. III, pp. 1021, 1301.
76. Edward A. Wild papers, Box: "Wild's Correspondence," USAMHI, Carlisle, PA; Captain Mulligan's Letter in "My Dear Mother & Sisters," pp. 126–127; "SC Prisoners of War Disposition," p. 2, List provided the Author by Randolph W. Kirkland from his 5th SCVC records in his DBASE files on 31 May 1997.
77. *O.R.*, Ser. I, Vol. 36, Pt. II: pp. 202, 223; cited in: Herbert M. Schiller, *The Bermuda Hundred Campaign* (Dayton, OH: Morningside House, Inc., 1988), p. 241, map on p. 242.
78. *The Official Records of Company D (South Carolina Rangers)*, p. 1.
79. Captain A.B. Mulligan Letter of 18 May 1864, in: Hutchinson, "*My Dear Mother & Sisters,*" p. 116; quoted in: Besch, et al., p. 2.
80. U.R. (Ulysses Robert) Brooks, *Butler and his cavalry in the War of Secession 1861–1865* (Camden, SC: J.J. Fox {Reprinted at Oxford, MS: Guild Bindry Press, 1989}), p. 338.
81. Sommers, "John Dunovant," *The Confederate Generals*, Vol. II, pp. 86–87.
82. Report of Col. Thomas C. Devin, commanding brigade, dated 4 July 1864, *O.R., Ser. I*, Vol. 36, Pt. I, "Reports," p. 841; Walbrook Davis Swank, *Battle of Trevilian Station* (Shippensburg, PA: 1994), p. 38, cited by Lewis F. Knudsen, Jr., "The Official Records of Company D," Note 3 on p. 2.
83. "5th SC Cavalry Regiment Engagements 1861–1865," *ehistory.osu.edu*; Letter to the Author from Robert L. Brown, USC at Sumter dated 17 October 1996. Some regimental histories omit any reference to its participation at "Charles City Court House, Kenner's Point, Wilson's Wharf," etc. (because it was an embarrassing defeat?).
84. Letter in: Hutchinson, "*My Dear Mother & Sisters*", p. 119.
85. "Report of Maj. Gen. Fitzhugh Lee, C.S. Army, of operations May 9–13, 1864," in *O.R., Ser. I, Vol. 36, Pt. II, p. 250.* "Baltimore Light Artillery," in Musick, *6th Virginia Cavalry*, p. 58.

Chapter III

1. Lieutenant General Ulysses S. Grant, "Final Report of Operations, March 1864-May 1865," cited in Noah Andre Trudeau, *The Last Citadel,* (Boston: Little, Brown, 1991), p. 3.
2. Frances H. Casstevens, *Edward A. Wild* (Jefferson, NC: McFarland, 2003), p. 165.
3. Herbert M. Schiller, M.D., *The Bermuda Hundred Campaign* (Dayton, OH: Morningside, 1988), p. 37.
4. *Official Records of the Union & Confederate Navies in the War of the Rebellion (O.R.N.),* Ser. I. (Washington, DC: U.S. Government Printing Office, 1894–1922), Vol. 9, p. 698. Frances H. Casstevens states on page 168 of *Edward A. Wild* that "Fort Pocahontas [Wilson's Wharf, but so-named only after completion of the fort there in early August 1864] *served as a Federal supply depot,*" without providing a source for her assertion. Other writers have repeated the erroneous "supply depot" comment. In fact, all the Federal garrisons who occupied Wilson's Wharf/Fort Pocahontas were "supply consumers" whose mission and function were to guard the James River line of communications.
5. Col. J.W. Shaffer, Chief of Staff, "Circular," Headquarters, Hink's Division, Hamilton, Va., Edward A. Wild Papers,' U.S. Army Military History Institute (USAMHI), cited in Casstevens, *Edward A. Wild*, pp. 167–168; and in Schiller, *The Bermuda Hundred Campaign*, p. 61.
6. *O.R.*, Ser. I, Vol. 33, p. 1020; *O.R.*, Ser. I, Vol. 37, Part I, pp. 71–72; *A History of Negro Troops in the War of the Rebellion*, p. 238; cited in: Bruce Catton, *A Stillness at Appomattox* (Garden City, NY: Doubleday, 1953), p. 233.
7. Schiller, *The Bermuda Hundred Campaign*, pp. 62–65; "Report of Julius M. Swain to Chief Signal Officer," dated 31 May 1864, in *O.R.* Ser. I, Vol. 36, Pt. II, p. 30; "Report of Capt. Lemuel B. Norton, Chief Signal Officer, Dept. of VA & NC," dated 2 Sept., 1864, in *O.R.*, Ser. I, Vol. 36, Pt. II, p. 21; Letter of 1st Lt. Lewis B. Rice to "Dear Friends at Home," dated 16 May 1864 from "Chesapeake Hospital," JPEG Files, no page no., sent via e-mail by his descendants William Kerry and Stephen Kerry to Ed Besch on 24 May 2006. (Hereafter: "Lewis B. Rice Letter of 16 May 1864.")
8. Part of very detailed instructions from "Acting Rear-Admiral S.P. Lee, Commanding North Atlantic Blockading Squadron, From Flagship Malvern at Newport News, May 4, 1864," in *O.R.N.*, Ser. I, Vol. 9, pp. 724–726.
9. Hand written, undated copy of "Report

of the Military Services of Edward A. Wild, Brig. Gen. U.S. Vols"; p. 125; Folder 2149, "First Use of Black Troops in the Union," Massachusetts MOLUS Paper- General Wild; Archives, U.S. Army Military History Institute, Carlisle Barracks, PA.

10. Report of Brig. Gen. Edward W. Hinks from City Point dated 13 May 1864; in *O.R.*, Ser. I, Vol. 36, Pt. II, pp. 165–166; and Vol. 36, Pt. III, p. 430. Excerpt from Captain William Davis Parlin's speech to a civic group at Natick, MA during the early 1890s, MS copy, pp. 14–15, Courtesy The Eaton Family of Watchung, NJ and sent to the Author by Douglas Eaton of Pala, CA in February 2014.

11. "The Expedition up the James....," *New York Times*, 8 May 1864, Vol. XIII, No. 3938, p. 1.

12. Butler to Grant, 5 and 6 May 1864, *O.R.*, Ser. I, Vol. 36, Pt. II, p. 430.

13. Benj. Butler, *Butler's Book, Autobiography and Personal Reminiscences of Benj. Butler* (Boston: A.M. Thayer, 1892), p. 670.

14. Solon A. Carter Papers, Letter of 1 May 1864, U.S. Army Military History Institute, Carlisle, PA (USAMHI).

15. Report of Brig. Gen. Edward W. Hinks to Maj. Gen. B.F. Butler about operations during 5–18 May 1864, in *O.R.*, Ser. I, Vol. 36, Pt. II, pp. 165–166.

16. *O.R.*, Ser. II, Vol. 5, pp. 795–797.

17. *Journal of the Congress of the Confederate States of America, 1861–1865*, Ninetieth Day, Friday, May 1, 1865, Closed Session, pp. 486–488; online version at: http://memory.loc; cited in: Casstevens, *Edward A. Wild*, p. 57; C.R. Gibbs, *Black, Copper & Bright*, p. 33.

18. *O.R.*, Ser. I, Vol. 4, p. 599; and Series II, Vol. VI, pp. 17–18; Ira Berlin, et al., Editors; *Freedom: A Documentary History of Emancipation, 1861–1867*, Series II, (London: Cambridge University Press, 1982), p. 568; the above quotations and comment are from: William A. Gladstone, *Men of Color* (Gettysburg: Thomas Publications, 1993), pp. 117–118. (Hereafter: Gladstone, *"Men of Color."*)

19. "Fort Pillow 'Massacre,'" Boatner, *Dictionary*, pp. 295–296; "Fort Pillow, Tenn."; Battle of"; Faust, *Encyclopedia*), pp. 277, 278.

20. Daniel Tyler's chilling account of events at Fort Pillow titled "Buried Alive" is in the 7 May 1864 *Harper's Weekly*, p. 302.

21. George Huston, report of, April 30, 1864, *O.R.*, Ser. I, Vol. 32, Pt. I, pp. 536–537; and James Lewis, report of, April 30, 1864, in *O.R.*, Ser. I, Vol. 32, Pt. I, p. 537; both are cited in Casstevens, *Edward A. Wild*, p. 165.

22. Daniel Tyler, "Buried Alive," 7 May 1864 *Harper's Weekly*, p. 302.

23. Daniel Tyler's Military Records, including his "Memorandum From Prisoner of War Records," researched by Henry H. McCawley, Jr. of Mobile, AL.

24. Catton, *A Stillness at Appomattox*, p. 233.

25. *Montgomery Daily Advertiser* microfilm file, AL Dept. of Archives & History, Montgomery.

26. For example, wounded German-American Union soldiers of Company H, 17th Missouri Volunteers were shot, sabered, or cut down after surrendering by "Texas Rangers" near Searcy, Arkansas on 19 May 1862, in *O.R.* Ser. I, Vol. 3, pp. 558, 559.

27. Casstevens, *Edward A. Wild*, p. 164.

28. Both incidents, and similar ones are related in: Trudeau, *Like Men of War*, p. 214; Byrd Charles Willis Papers, 1864–1865, Accession 23975, Papers, 1961–1908, of Byrd C. Willis, (1847–1911) of Orange County and Alexandria, Virginia, while serving with the 9th Virginia Cavalry, includes a diary, 7 April 1864–23 May 1865...., Library of Virginia, Richmond.

29. General Kirby Smith, in *O.R.*, Ser. II, Vol. 6, pp. 21–22; cited in Trudeau, *ibid.*, p. 203.

30. Joseph T. Glatthaar, "5. Black Glory: The African-American Role in Victory," Gabor S. Boritt, *Why the Confederacy Lost* (New York: Oxford University Press, 1992), p. 157.

Chapter IV

1. Reports of: 1) Edward A. Wild to General Robert S. Davis, Headquarters, 1st Brigade, 3rd Division, 18th A.C., Wilson's Wharf, James River, May 12, 1864; 2) Wild, "List of wounded prisoners captured at Sandy Point Signal Station, May 6, 1864, and sent to Fort Monroe May 8, 1864"; both are in the Wild Papers at USAMHI, Carlisle, PA; 3) 2nd Lt. Julius Swain, 31 May 1864; Capt. Lemuel B. Norton, U.S. Army Chief Signal Officer, Dept. of VA & NC, 2 Sept. 1864, *O.R.* Ser. I, Vol. 36, Pt. II, pp. 22, 31; and 4) Casstevens, *Edward A. Wild*, p. 151, Notes 26 & 27, p. 293; Lewis B. Rice's participation in the Raid, from Lt. Lewis B. Rice's Letter of 16 May 1864 from Chesapeake Hospital, courtesy William Kerry & Stephen Kerry; A "huge mahogany tree ... 'The Rowe'" in: Mary Ruffin Copeland, *Confederate History of Charles City County, Virginia*, (Harrison Harwood Chapter, UDC, 1959), p. 20, a book in the Library of North Bend Plantation, shown to the author in 1993 by Owner Mrs. Ridgely Copland. The giant, multi-limbed tree at "The Rowe," described variously as a French walnut, a French chestnut, a butternut, and a mahogany tree, was cut down and sold for $600 to a furniture maker in Maryland in 1927.

The trunk of the tree had a diameter of 12 feet. It was used by both sides as a signal station during the Civil War. "Dr. Lyon G. Tyler, president emeritus of the College of William and Mary, today confirmed the statement that the tree had a place on John Smith's Map of Virginia...." "Fell Tree Marked on Map by Smith, Historic French Chestnut will be Sawed and Used for Furniture," undated *News Leader* clipping provided by Judy Ledbettor, Charles City County Historical Center.

2. "Edward Keelan," Medical Records, 1st Regiment, USCT, NARA, Washington, DC.

3. Untitled, Edward A. Wild papers, Box: "Wild's Correspondence," Mass. Commander of the Military Order of the Loyal Legion of the U.S. Collection, Archives, USAMHI.

4. Wild to Butler, 9 May 1864, Butler Papers, Library of Congress, quoted in Schiller, *The Bermuda Hundred Campaign*, p. 142.

5. "Kilpatrick-Dahlgren Raid to Richmond, 28 Feb.–4 Mar. 1864," Boatner, *Dictionary*, pp. 460–461; "Dahlgren Papers," Boatner, *ibid.*, pp. 218–219.

6. Quoted by Mary Ruffin Copland in *History of Charles City County, Virginia*, p. 20.

7. *Ibid.*

8. "List of Prisoners, May 8, 1864," Edward A. Wild papers, Box: "Wild's Correspondence," Mass. Commandery of the Military Order of the Loyal Legion of the U.S. Collection, Archives, USAMHI; Charles City County, Virginia Censuses of 1860 and 1870.

9. Calvin Gibbs Hutchinson, Acting Assistant Paymaster from USS *Commodore Morris*, assigned to USS *Pequot*, Pequot No. 2 Diary, pp. 129, 130. (Ronald E. Fischer Collection.)

10. "Report of Lieut. Col. Wyatt M. Elliott, Twenty-fifth Virginia Battalion, Hunton's brigade, of the capture of the U.S. gun-boat Shawsheen, at Turkey Island, May 7"; *O.R.,* Ser. I, Vol. 36, Pt. II, p. 268. A gunboat, the *Commodore Jones*, was also destroyed, but by a "torpedo," i.e., a mine.

11. First Lieutenant William C. Dutton reported for duty 9 December 1863 and was assigned to Co. B, 22nd Regiment, USCT. He was appointed Adjutant by the Secretary of War on 11 February 1864. He was "accidentally shot by pickets of the 1st U.S.C.T. on 7 May 1864." (ancestry.com-U.S. Colored Troops Military Service Records, 1861–1865. Courtesy Henry H. McCawley, Jr.)

12. Excerpt of a Letter by 1st Lt. Marion Patterson, 22nd Infantry Regiment, USCT, from Rick Leswing, *Facebook*, Wednesday, 13 April 2011.

13. From fragmentary notes made by the Author from the "Wild Papers" at USAMHI, c. 1999.

14. John M. Coski, Essay 9: "'All Confusion on the Plantations': Civil War in Charles City County," in: James P. Whittenberg & John M. Coski, *Charles City County Virginia, An Official History* (Salem, WV: Don Mills, Inc., 1989), pp. 70, 72.

15. Casstevens, *Edward A. Wild*, p. 155, Note 45 on p. 294.

16. Unsigned "List of Prisoners" dated May 8, 1864, and Letter to Capt. Cassells dated May 11, 1864; in Box: "Wild's Correspondence, Edward Wild Papers," Massachusetts Commander of the Military Order of the Loyal Legion of the United states Collection, Archives, USAMHI; Census Records for Charles City County, Virginia in 1860 and 1870.

17. Copland, *Confederate History of Charles City County Virginia*, p. 20.

18. *The Sentinel*, Richmond, Tuesday morning, May 19, 1864, front page; from microfilm at The Library of Virginia, Richmond.

19. *Ibid.*, for May 20, 1864.

20. Casstevens, *Edward A. Wild*, p. 152.

21. *Ibid.*, pp. 153–154.

22. John M. Daniel 16 April 1861 cited in Lester J. Cappon, Ph.D., *Virginia Newspapers, 1821–1835* (New York: Appleton-Century Co. for University of Virginia, 1936), p. 17. John Moncure Daniel (1825–1865) returned from Italy in February 1861 after serving as U.S. Minister to Italy. He resumed the editorship to urge secession of Virginia in order to unite the whole South. (Cappon, *ibid.*, Note on p. 174.)

23. "States Furnishing Men," Gladstone, *Men of Color*, pp. 214, 215.

24. Column "From the Peninsula—Outrages by the Yankees in New Kent [Sheridan's raiders] and [Wild's men in] Charles City Counties," Wednesday, 25 May 1864 Richmond *Examiner*, p. 1, column 1, Microfilm File, Library of Congress.

25. Letter of General Hinks to Gen. Wild dated 11 May 1864, and Wild's draft reply on the back of the same letter dated 12 May 1864, Box "Correspondence," Wild Papers, Archives, USAMHI.

26. Cited in Casstevens, *Edward A. Wild*, p. 158.

27. Gladstone, *Men of Color*, pp. 193, 194.

28. Casstevens, *Edward A. Wild*, p. 156.

29. *Ibid.*, pp. 159–160.

30. The author found the two original letters in a file at the Library of Congress. A copy of the Letter from Julia Gardner Tyler to President Lincoln dated May 21, 1864, is in the Tyler Family Papers. It reads: "William Clopton went to Kennon's [Wilson's] Wharf to be paroled & be enabled to stay w/ his family,

when 'some of my negro women had gone down and told him that I was a most cruel master & consequently I was stripped and whipped most cruelly by negroes.'—Mrs. Clopton & Marie (President Tyler's niece] are left alone. Not a negro left." (Tyler Family Papers, Group I, Box 9, J_G_T, 1861–1865, Folder 9, William & Mary University Library, Clear 6/30/64, Margaret Cook Special Collection.)

31. Casstevens, *Edward A. Wild*, pp. 156, 158.

32. Copland, *Confederate History of Charles City County, Virginia*, no page no.

33. The "Volunteer Enlistment" form for Robert P. Brown, and the other soldiers' military records; C.R. Gibbs, *Black, Copper, & Bright*, p. 71, and "Roster." The author had conversations regarding Robert P. Brown with Richard Bowman at his home and during annual Civil War reenactments at Fort Pocahontas.

34. Cited in Trudeau, *The Last Citadel*, pp. 3, 4.

35. "Brig. Gen. Edward A. Wild to Maj. Gen. B.F. Butler, Wilson's Wharf, May 13, 1864"; cited in Casstevens, *Edward A. Wild*, p. 168, Note 50 on p. 295.

36. Letter from Butler "in the Field," 13 May 1864, to Hinks, in: *O.R.*, Ser. I, Vol. 36, Pt. II, p. 744; Letter from Capt. Solon A. Carter, A.A.G., directed by General Hinks, dated 13 May 1864, Wild Papers, USAMHI; *O.R.*, Ser. I, Vol. 36, Pt. II, p. 744.

37. Copy in Wild Papers, *ibid.*

38. Report of Col. Samuel Duncan, 4th U.S. Colored Infantry, "commanding Hinks's 2nd Brigade," dated 19 May 1864, *O.R.*, Ser. I, Vol. 36, Pt. II, pp. 169–170.

39. "Edward A. Wild to [each] Company at Wilson's Wharf, Va., May 20, 1864," in Edward A. Wild Papers, Southern Historical Collection, University of North Carolina at Chapel Hill; also cited in Casstevens, *Edward A. Wild*, p. 170.

40. *O.R.*, Ser. I, Vol. 51, Pt. II, p. 872.

41. P.G.T. Beauregard Letter to General Braxton Bragg dated May 19, 1864, *O.R.*, Ser. I, Vol. 51, Pt. II, "Correspondence," p. 947.

42. P.G.T. Beauregard Letter to President Davis from Chester, VA dated 21 May 1864; *O.R.* Ser. I, Vol. 36, Pt. III, pp. 818–819.

43. *O.R.*, Ser. I, Vol. 36, Pt. III, pp. 208, 958.

44. *Ibid.*, pp. 819, 833.

45. *Ibid.*, pp. 43, 820, 833. In 1997, Edward G. Longacre stated: "Following his repulse at Fort Powhatan, Fitz Lee crossed his division to the north bank of the James...." (Edward G. Longacre, *Army of Amateurs, General Benjamin F. Butler and the Army of the James, 1863–1865* (Mechanicsburg, PA: Stackpole Books,

1997), page 110 about the Action at Wilson's Wharf on 24 May 1864.) *Fitz Lee didn't attack Fort Powhatan nor did he cross the James River to attack Wilson's Wharf on 24 May; he came from Atlee's Station northeast of Richmond.*

46. Colonel J.B. Kiddoo's Report, 22 May 1864, in *O.R.*, Ser. I, Vol. 36, Pt. II, pp. 166, 168.

47. Special Order No. 26, 2nd Division, XVIIIth Army Corps, City Point, VA, dated 22 May 1864, states: "Leave two sections [4 guns] of Captain Howell's battery [M], Third New York Artillery, at Fort Powhatan, and one section at Wilson's Wharf." "10-pdr Parrotts" in partial Ordnance List for Hinks's Division, in Wild Papers, USAMHI.

48. General Wild's Letter with General Hinks's endorsement dated 23 May 1864; General Butler's endorsement referring to Wild's request, dated 25 May "in the field"; and General Weitzel's recommendation, which includes: contracting defenses, getting the men under good bombproofs, and using skirmishers in rifle pits to keep enemy sharpshooters from "annoying our gunners; and then if necessary reinforce with artillery"; in Wild Papers, USAMHI.

49. Brig. Gen. Hinks to Maj. R.S. Davis, Asst. Adjt. Gen., Dept. of Va. and N.C., in the Field on 13 May 1864, in *O.R.*, Ser. I, Vol. 36, Pt. II, pp. 165–166.

50. *O.R.*, Ser. I, Vol. 36, Pt. III, p. 25.

51. Captain, later Brevet Lt. Col. (but a 1st Lt. on 24 May 1864) Edward Simonton, a Company Officer, First U.S. Colored Infantry; "The Campaign Up the James River to Petersburg," a Paper read 11 November 1902 and published in: *Glimpses of the Nation's Struggle*, Fifth Series, "Papers Read before the Minnesota Commandery of the Military Order of the Loyal Legion of the United States, 1897–1902"; St. Paul, MN: Review Publishing, 1903, p. 482. (Afterwards: Simonton, "Campaign Up the James River.")

52. *O.R.N.*, Ser. I, Vol. 10, pp. 87–92.

53. Post-war "Report of Fitzhugh Lee, Dec. 20, 1866," *Supplement, Army Official Records*, Vol. 6, p. 796.

54. Fitzhugh Lee, *Report of Major General Fitzhugh Lee of the Operations of His Cavalry Division, A.N.V. (Army of Northern Virginia) from May 4, 1864 to September 19, 1864*; Collection of the Eleanor S. Brockenbrough Library, Museum of the Confederacy. (Afterward, "*Fitzhugh Lee Report*."); Major, Ass't. Adj. Gen., J.D. (James Du Gue) Ferguson (a Charleston lawyer), *Memoranda of the Itinerary and Operations of Major General Fitzhugh Lee's Cavalry Division of the A.N.V.—from May 4th to October 19th, 1864, inclusive*; p. 4; provided the Author by J. Michael Miller (Author of *The North Anna Campaign*). (Afterward, "J.D.

Ferguson, *Memoranda.*") (Ferguson) Roll 49, Hotchkiss Papers, Library of Congress; *North Carolina Troops, 1861–865, A Roster*, Vol. II, *Cavalry*.

55. Mary Ruffin Copland: "Our cavalry, under the command of General Fitz Lee, made an assault on the forces at Kennon's, *in which the Charles City Troop participated.*" Copland, *Confederate History of Charles City County, Virginia*, p. 20.

56. J.D. Ferguson, entry for "May 23rd" in his *Memoranda*, p. 4.

57. Driver, *2nd Virginia Cavalry*, p. 120.

58. Douglas Southall Freeman, *Lee's Lieutenants—A Study in Command*, Vol. 3, *Gettysburg to Appomattox* (1944—a Taiwan copy purchased in Taipei during his R & R while the Author was serving as C.O. of Headquarters Company, 4th Marines in Vietnam in 1966), p. 499.

59. *Civil War Letters of James Michael Barr*, p. 225.

60. Captain W.F. Hullehen message to Col. Critcher dated 23 May 1864, *O.R.*, Ser. I, Vol. 51, Pt. II, p. 956.

61. Wells, *Charleston Light Dragoons*, pp. 29, 30, 38.

62. Private (former 2nd Lt.) William H. Stratton was "KIA [at] Spotsylvania C.H. 5/6/64 [and] buried at Lynchburg Cemetery." ("Roster," Driver, *2nd Virginia Cavalry*, p. 73.)

63. Typewritten "Autobiography of H. St. George Tucker Brooke written for his children, 2nd Virginia Cavalry, Company B, Fitzhugh Lee's Brigade," provided by Mrs. Sara W.H. Saunders in 1997, pp. 35–36.

64. "In altering percussioned [i.e., converted from flintlock] muskets to musketoons, the effort seems to have been made to save as much of the original [long] barrel and still have a maneuverable longarm for horseback service. Barrel lengths have been noted from 34 inches to as short as 25 5/8 inches. ... and the forestock was shortened" in one of two ways for either the "artillery configuration" or the "cavalry configuration" so that the arm could be fitted with a sling. Examples of "Virginia Manufactory Musketoons" ranging in calibers from .69 to .75; having locks dated 1818,1820,1804, and 1824, respectively; altered to percussion; and having barrel lengths of 28½, 30⅛, 25⅝, and 27¾ inches, respectively, are described and illustrated in: Chapter XX, "Virginia Manufactory And Other Confederate Muskets Altered to Cavalry Musketoons," John M. Murphy, M.D., *Confederate Carbines and Musketoons* (Dallas, TX: Taylor Publishing, 1986), pp. 226–233.

65. Autobiography of H. St. George Tucker Brooke, 37. Brooke described when the cavalry

dismounted to fight and the men counted out by fours to determine the number three man who would be hold all four horses. Brooke: "It was sometimes amusing to see the keen desire of some men to be the number three." (*Ibid.*, p. 38.)

Chapter V

1. Fitzhugh Lee Message to Braxton Bragg from Samaria Church, 5:30 a.m., 24 May 1864, *O.R.*, Ser. I, Vol. 51, Pt. II, p. 957.

2. Fitzhugh Lee, *Report*, pp. 21, 22; "May 23rd & 24th," Ferguson, *Memoranda*, p. 4.

3. Log of the USS *Dawn*, microfilm copy RG 24, Stack 18W4 Row 2, NARA.

4. John Gill, *Reminiscences of Four Years as a Private Soldier in the Confederate Army* (Baltimore: Sun Printing Office, 1904), p. 97; Preston Library, V.M.I., Lexington, VA. (Hereafter: "Gill, *Reminiscences*.") Also published as "Chapter VIII, Spotsylvania C.H., Trevilian Station to City Point," in Walbrook D. Swank, Col. USAF Ret., *Courier for Lee and Jackson 1861–1865* (____, Burd Street Press, 1993), pp. 47–49.

5. Irving P.W. Whitehead, "Meadow Bridge and Fort Kennon," *The Campaigns of Thomas T. Whitehead and the 2nd Virginia Cavalry*, Author's hand-written copy of typed manuscript on microfilm, no. 90, Deposit 1940, page 96, University of Virginia Library, Charlottesville.

6. Report of General Wild, 25 May 1864, in *O.R.*, Ser. I, Vol. 36, Pt. II, p. 270.

7. Chaplain Henry M. Turner's letter to the *Christian Recorder*, the official organ of the African Methodist Episcopal (AME) Church, published in Philadelphia on 25 June 1864; quoted in: C.R. Gibbs, *Black, Copper, & Bright*, p. 125.

8. Captain William Davis Parlin's account is from a speech he gave at Natick, MA in the early 1890s, manuscript copy, pp. 18–19, Courtesy the Eaton Family of Watchung, NJ. Parlin was born at Natick in 1839, enlisted as a sergeant in the 39th Massachusetts Volunteer Infantry Regiment on 7/22/1862, and was commissioned captain of Company E on 6/26/1863. Captain Stephen A. Boyden, also from Natick, MA, was a former corporal in the 39th Massachusetts Infantry Regiment. Captain Giles H. Rich was promoted to Lieutenant Colonel on 12 October 1864. (*Descriptive Book, 1st USCT Regiment*, NARA, Washington, D.C.)

9. J.D. Ferguson, *Memoranda*, P. 4.

10. See "Federal Casualties," Appendix A.

11. The Richmond *Sentinel* dated 27 May

1864, microfilm file, Library of Virginia, Richmond.

12. Thomas W. Colley Letter to "Mrs. Jas Dunlop at Richmond," in 1st Virginia Cavalry File, Eleanor S. Brockenbrough Library, Museum of the Confederacy, Richmond, VA.

13. Simonton, "The Campaign Up the James River," 1902, p. 482.

14. Report of Acting rear Admiral S.P. Lee, to Hon. Gideon Wells, Secretary of the Navy, dated 29 May 1864, in: *O.R.N.*, Vol. 10, p. 101.

15. Original Company Muster Rolls and *Morning Reports* for the 1st and 10th Regiments, USCT examined by the Author at the NARA, Washington, DC.

16. Gladstone, *Men of Color*, p. 214.

17. An undated ordnance list in the Wild Papers, USAMHI, states: "3rd New York, 4 guns, 10-pdr Parrotts," and "10th USCT, Co[mpanie]s G, H,—Enfields." But Admiral S.P. Lee's Report to Secretary of the Navy Gideon Welles dated 29 May incorrectly states "two *20-pdr* Parrotts, no other artillery"; in *O.R.N.*, Vol. 10, p. 101.

18. "Report of Brig. Gen. Edward A. Wild, U.S. Army, commanding First Brigade, Third Div., 18th Army Corps, Wilson's Wharf, Va. May 25, 1864," to Capt. Solon A. Carter, Brig. Gen. Hinks's Acting Assistant Adjutant General, in *O.R.*, Ser. I, Vol. 36, Pt. II, p. 71. (Hereafter: Wild's Report of 25 May 1864.)

19. Wild's Report of 25 May 1864, pp. 270–271.

20. "M.W.S." Letter to the Washington *Daily Morning Chronicle*, cited by Trudeau, *Like Men of War*, p. 217.

21. Fitzhugh Lee, *Report of Operations*, pp. 24, 25.

22. Simonton, "Campaign Up the James River," pp. 490–491.

23. The Richmond *Sentinel* of 27 May 1864, microfilm file, Library of Virginia.

24. VMI Archives Manuscript #015, William J. Black Diary (Maj. John J. Shoemaker's) Operations Report for Shoemaker's Battery, Horse Artillery Battalion, Sept. 1, 1864, no page no.

25. Fitzhugh Lee, *Report*, pp. 22, 23.

26. J.D. Ferguson, *Memoranda*, p. 4.

27. Wild's Report of 25 May 1864, p. 271. ("Gunboats," *after* the USS *Young America* arrives at 4 p.m.)

28. USS *Dawn* data at the NARA; her side drawing is in the files at the U.S. Naval Historical Center, Washington Naval Yard, Washington, DC.

29. "Report of, with Enclosure, Acting Volunteer Lieutenant J.W. Simmons, Commanding *Dawn* off Wilson's Wharf, 25 May 1864," *O.R.N.*, Vol. 10, "Operations," pp. 90, 91.

30. Cited in Trudeau, *Like Men of War*, pp. 218–219.

31. "Complete Descriptive Roll of the Crew of the U.S. Steamer 'Dawn' on 30 June 1864," NARA.

32. "Enclosure. Report of Ammunition Expended," "Report of, with Enclosure, Acting Volunteer Lieutenant J.W. Simmons, Commanding *Dawn* off Wilson's Wharf, 25 May 1864," *O.R.N.*, Vol. 10, p. 91.

33. *Ibid.*, p. 90.

34. Nanzig, *3rd Virginia Cavalry*, p. 51.

35. J.D. Ferguson, *Memoranda*, p. 4.

36. Report of Lt. Julius Swain, Signal Officer, 25 May 1864, in *O.R.*, Ser. I, Vol. 36, Pt. II, p. 272.

37. Wild, Report of 25 May 1864, *O.R.*, Ser. I, Vol. 36, Pt. II, p. 271.

38. "...capacity of 1,000 men," Captain Geo. S. Dodge Letter to Colonel Shaffer dated May 26, 1864, in *O.R.*, Ser. I, Vol. 36, Pt. III, "Correspondence," p. 235.

39. "Report of Col. Henry L. Abbott, 1st Connecticut Artillery Regiment, Commanding Siege Artillery," in *O.R.*, Ser. I, Vol. 6, Pt. II, p. 93.

40. "H.J.W.," "The Rebel Attack on Wilson's Wharf ... In Camp, May 25, 1864," *New York Times*, May 27, 1864, p. 1, column 2, top.

41. E. Henry Powell, Lieut. Col. 10th U.S.C.T., "The Colored Soldier in the War of the Rebellion," Read before the Vermont Commandery of the Loyal Legion, pp. 45–46.

42. Chaplain Henry M. Turner's letter in the *Christian Recorder* on 25 June 1864; in C.R. Gibbs, p. 125.

43. Hand written, undated copy of "Report of the Military Services of Edward A. Wild, Brig. Gen. U.S. Vols"; pp. 125–126; Folder 2149, "First Use of Black Troops in the Union," Massachusetts MOLUS Paper—General Wild; Archives, USAMHI.

44. Fitzhugh Lee, *Report*, p. 23.

45. Simonton, "Campaign Up the James River," pp. 483, 484.

46. *Ibid.*, 484; "We will try that," reported by General Butler, in his Report of 25 May 1864; in *O.R.*, Ser. I, Vol. 36, Pt. II, p. 269; "I declined," General Wild, Report of 25 May 1864.

47. Simonton, *ibid.*, p. 484.

48. "HJW," "General Butler's Army," *New York Times*, Sunday, May 29, 1864, p. 1.

49. *New York Times*, Friday, May 27, 1864, p. 1.

50. Combined from: Irving P.W. Whitehead, "Meadow Bridge and Fort Kennon," *The Campaign of Thomas T. Munford and the 2nd Virginia Cavalry*, p. 96; Irving Whitehead, "Meadow Bridge and Fort Kennon," in: "His-

tory of the Second Virginia Cavalry," × 90, pp. 95–96, Microfilm M-111 p. 4, Special Collections Department, Alderman Library, University of Virginia, Charlottesville.

51. Gill, *Reminiscences,* pp. 98–99.

52. Report of Lt. Cdr. S.P. Quackenbush, USN, aboard USS *Pequot,* to Acting Rear Admiral S.P. Lee, Comdg North Atlantic Blockading Squadron, dated 25 May 1864, in: *O.R.N.,* Vol. 10, p. 88; Wild states "My signaling with Fort Powhatan was interrupted by an intervening thunderstorm" in his draft letter dated 28 May 1864, Wild Papers, USAMHI.

53. *Young America,* description in: *Directory of American Naval Ships,* vol. 8, 548; Naval Historical Center, Washington, DC, p. 548.

54. "Complete Descriptive Roll of the U.S. Steamer 'Young America' on 30 June 1864," NARA.

55. *Young America* Logbook, microfilm, RG 24, 18W4, Row 13, Comp. 19, NARA.

56. Report of Lt. Cdr. Quackenbush to Rear Admiral S.P. Lee dated 25 May 1864, *O.R.N.,* Vol. 10, p. 88.

57. *Ibid.,* p. 89.

58. Calvin Gibbs Hutchinson, Acting Assistant Paymaster from USS *Commodore Morris,* assigned to USS *Pequot, Diary 1,* pp. 124, 135. (Ronald E. Fischer Collection, Charlottesville, VA.) Crew composition in "Complete Descriptive Roll of the U.S. Steamer 'Pequot' on the Thirtieth of June 1864," NARA.

59. Hutchinson, *Pequot Diary 2,* pp. 129, 130.

60. "The Attack on Wilson's Wharf..." by an unnamed correspondent from "Fortress Monroe, Wednesday, May 25," in the *New York Times,* 27 May 1864, p. 1, second column. The Friday, May 27 *New York Times* states: "At 4 o'clock the *George Washington* arrived with reinforcements from Fort Powhatan and *landed them immediately,*" "The Attack on Wilson's Wharf," *The New York Times,* Vol. XIII, No. 2955, Friday, 27 May 1864, p. 1, col. 2, bottom.

61. Wild's Draft Note to "Sir," from "Wilson's Wharf—May 28th, 1864": in Wild Papers, USAMHI Library Collection.

62. Lt. Col. E. Henry Powell, "The Colored Soldier in the War of the Rebellion," p. 44.

63. Descriptive Lists and "Morning Reports" of the 10th Regiment, USCT examined by the Author at NARA.

64. Charles T. Price, *An Account and Brief History of Company C, 2nd Virginia Cavalry* (Fincastle, VA: George Honts III, 1907?) copy provided in 1998 by Mrs. Walter Morse of Amherst, VA in July 1998; and quoted in: Driver, *2nd Virginia Cavalry,* p. 121. "Price, Charles Thomas, 3rd Corporal, Co. C., born

Fincastle 3/19/44, attended V.M.I. 1 year, 5 mos., Class of 1864. Drillmaster, Btry 9, Camp Lee, Richmond, 4/61–5/1/62. Enlisted Co. C, 2nd Va Cavalry at Fincastle 8/1/62 as private. Present ... promoted 3rd Cpl. Horse captured Stafford Co. 2/20/63. Paid $225.00. Present 3–4 and 7–8/63, captured near Cashtown, Pa 7/63 but escaped. Present or absence not stated 11/63–2/64, served as Courier for Gen. J.E.B. Stuart. Present 3–6/64, however, *WIA Louisa C.H. 6/10/64.* No further record. Hotel Owner, Fincastle 1865–1900. Farmer, Mbr, Peachy Gilmer Camp, CV, Fincastle. Died 11/20/21, Bur. Galatia Presb. Cem., Botetourt Co. Brother of Pvt., Lt. Geo. S. Price, Co. C, V.M.I. 1859–61, *KIA* Hartwood Church 2/24/63 in a charge; and 2nd Lt. William J. Price, Co. C." ("Muster Rolls, 2nd Virginia Cavalry," Driver, *2nd Virginia Cavalry,* p. 262.)

65. General Wild had issued a detailed "Code of Conduct" 20 May, which he ordered to be read to each company in his regiments. See Chapter IV.

66. Fitzhugh Lee, *Report,* pp. 23, 24.

67. Peachy Gilmer Breckinridge was *a former major of Virginia State Troops.* He enlisted as a private in his brother James's Co. C, was promoted to Color Sergeant, then to Lieutenant the day before, and finally Acting Captain of Co. B, 2nd VA Cavalry, in which role he was killed on 5/24/64. His brother James, who was wounded in the arm, wrote to their sister Lucy: "...We dismounted and made the [initial] assault [on the front of the fort] and were repulsed. Gilmer was grazed by a ball on the wrist. We then changed our position [to the eastern side of the fort] and charged again through some obstructions of fallen trees and sharpened limbs (abatis). Gilmer pushed on ... under heavy fire. *He got within 50 yards of the parapet, when he was seen to fall, struck somewhere in the body ... every man near him being killed or wounded...he did not speak after he fell.*" (A postwar account embellished: "A few 2nd VA Cavalrymen succeeded in crossing the moat (ditch) and led by Captain Gilmer Breckinridge mounted the parapet. Here they were met by a deadly musketry fire and driven back, Captain Breckinridge losing his life." (No early account substantiates any Confederate "mounting the parapet.") The family name "Peachy" commemorated "Colonel Samuel Peachy, who came to Richmond County around 1659 and later settled in Williamsburg." (Letter from Jane W. Breckinridge to Mr. Harrison R. Tyler from Fincastle, VA dated 8 May 1997.)

68. Copy, *Autobiography of H.* (Henry) *St. George Tucker Brooke* (born July 1844, died 1911), *2nd Virginia Cavalry, Company B, Fitzhugh Lee's Brigade, written for his children;*

68–71; sent by his Grand-daughter Mrs. Sara Wilson H. Saunders of Lynchburg, VA to Harrison R. Tyler on 18 May 1997; Mr. Tyler shared it with the Author. (Comment: It may seem that a combat veteran's memory would fade after forty years, when Brooke wrote his *Autobiography*, but the Author's own violent combat experiences in Vietnam on 23–24 August 1966, 47 years ago as this is written, seem as though they happened to him yesterday.)

69. Roster, Driver, *2nd Virginia Cavalry*, p. 199.

70. Lyman A. Smith, *Memorial of Adjt. M.W. Smith: A Tribute to a Beloved Son and Brother* (Newark, NJ: 1864), pp. 41–42; cited in: Edward G. Longacre, *Army of Amateurs, General Benjamin F. Butler and the Army of the James, 1863–1865* (Harrisburg, PA: Stackpole Books, 1997), p. 110.

71. Charles T. Price, *An Account and Brief History of Company C, 2nd Virginia Cavalry*, cited in Driver, *2nd Virginia Cavalry*, p. 121.

72. Whitehead, *The Campaigns of Thomas T. Munford*, p. 2.

73. Stiles, *4th Virginia Cavalry*, p. 50.

74. Paul B. Means: "We captured that day [12 May at Brook Church] an entire wagon load of Spencer rifles and their special ammunition. It was a splendid, long range breechloader and shot seven times without reloading [using a tubular magazine in the buttstock]. I carried one of them during the remainder of my service in the ranks, and was very much attached to it." The 5th North Carolina Cavalry was recruited as a Partisan regiment, which allowed the officers and men to retain captured enemy property for their own use. Paul B. Means, "Additional Sketch Sixty-Third Regiment (Fifth Cavalry)," *North Carolina Regiments 1861–1865*, Vol. 3: pp. 600–601.

75. *Ibid.*, pp. 604–607. Also: Paul B. Means, "Brook Church Fight, James B. Gordon Killed"; R.A. Brock, ed., "and Something about the Fifth North Carolina Cavalry," *Southern Historical Papers*, Vol. 24, Richmond, VA, 1901, pp. 139–144.

76. Means, "Additional Sketch," p. 601. Major James H. McNeill was a 37-year old Minister; he was promoted to Colonel on 1/5/1865 and was killed at Chamberlain Run, VA on 3/31/1865. (Source: "North Carolina Troops 1861–65, A Roster.")

77. Wild's Report of 25 May 1864, in *O.R.*, Ser. I, Vol. 36, Pt. II, pp. 270–271.

78. Captain William Davis Parlin, from a speech he gave at Natick, MA during the early 1890s, manuscript, pp. 20–22, Courtesy The Eaton Family of Watchung, NJ; Simonton, *Campaign Up the James River*, pp. 485, 486.

79. Simonton, *ibid.*, pp. 485–486; cited in Trudeau, *Like Men of War*, p. 219.

80. "M.W.S." Letter in the Washington *Daily Morning Chronicle*, cited by Trudeau in *Like Men of War*, p. 217.

81. Zimmerman Davis, "Capt. Mulligan's Company—In May 1864-Dates of Some Battles 37 Years Ago," *Charleston News and Courier*, ____, 1903; quoted in Hutchinson, *"My Dear Mother & Sisters,"* p. 179; also quoted in Besch, et al., p. 3.

82. "Newspaper Casualty Reports" from the undated *Charleston Daily Courier*, sent to Edwin W. Besch by Randolph W. Kirkland of Charleston, SC on 31 May 1997. Mr. Kirkland commented: "I think in the casualty reports that the casualties up to May 24th had been lumped into Drury's Bluff."

83. Lt. Julius M. Swain, Report of 25 May 1864, in *O.R.*, Ser. I, Vol. 36, Pt. II, p. 272.

84. Simonton, *Campaign Up the James River*, p. 486.

85. Lt. Swain, Report of 31 May 1864, in *O.R.*, Ser. I, Vol. 6, Pt. II, p. 31.

86. Fitzhugh Lee, *Report*, pp. 24, 25.

87. Ferguson, *Memoranda*, p. 4.

88. Fitzhugh Lee, *Report*, 24–25.

89. Ferguson, *Memoranda*, 25 and 26 May 1864.

90. Letter of Lt. Col. H. Biggs at Chief Quartermaster's Office, Fort Monroe to Chief Quartermaster dated 25 May 1864, Collection from the Manuscript Division, Library of Congress.

91. "The Attack on Wilson's Wharf ... Steamers Fired Into," *New York Times*, Vol. XIII, No. 2955(?), p. 1, column 2, bottom.

92. "H.J.W.," "The Rebel Attack on Wilson's Wharf ... In Camp, May 25, 1864," *New York Times*, May 27, 1864, p. 1, column 2, top.

93. "H.J.W.," "Gen. Butler's Army," *New York Times*, Sunday, May 29, 1864, p. 1, column 4.

94. Report of Brig. Gen. Edward W. Hinks to Maj. Gen. Butler from City Point—8 p.m., in *O.R.*, Ser. I, Vol. 36, Pt. III, pp. 181–182.

95. *Ibid.*, p. 205.

96. From Butler's "Headquarters in the Field," May 25, 1864—7:30 a.m.; in *O.R.*, Ser. I, Vol. 36, Pt. II, p. 269.

97. Apparently an estimate of "200" enemy killed and wounded was shared throughout Wild's two regiments. Ruphus Wright to dear wife, 25 May 1864, filed with affidavit of Elizabeth Wright, 21 August 1865, Letters & Orders Received, ser. 4180, Norfolk, VA, Asst. Subasst. Comr., RG 105 (A-7945), Quoted in *Freedom*; "Documents," C.R. Gibbs, *Black, Copper, and Bright*, p. 202. Ruphus Wright enlisted on 25 July 1863; he and Elizabeth Wright were married by Chaplain Henry M.

Turner on 3 December 1863. Private Wright was one of 156 casualties (17 killed, 114 wounded, 25 missing) suffered by the 1st Regiment, USCT at Baylor's Farm near Petersburg on 15 June 1864; he received a gunshot wound to the abdomen and died on 21 June 1864 at Hampton General Hospital. (C.R. Gibbs, *ibid.*, pp. 81, 203, Elizabeth & Ruphus Wright "Marriage Certificate" illustrated on p. 121.)

98. Copies in a Box of "Wild Correspondence" at USAMHI.

99. Brig. Gen. Edward W. Hinks to Maj. Gen. B.F. Butler, from City Point, Va., May 28 (1864), in *O.R.*, Ser. I, Vol. 36, Pt. III, pp. 287–288.

100. Typescript copy of George R. Minor's Letter to his Mother dated "May 30th, 1864" from "Atley's [*sic*, Atlee's] Station, Va."; enclosed with a letter from Lt. Col. Robert J. Driver, Jr., USMC (Ret.) dated 4 November 1996. May 1864 casualties for 1st and 2nd Virginia Cavalry Regiments, are from Robert J. Drivers' two regimental histories, respectively. George R. Minor survived the war and lived until 1910. Information about the Minor Family from Ancestry.com was provided by Henry H. McCawley, Jr. of Mobile County, AL on 26 August 2013.

Chapter VI

1. From Butler's "Headquarters in the Field," May 25, 1864—7.30 a.m.; in *O.R.*, Ser. I, Vol. 36, Pt. II, pp. 269–270.

2. *Ibid.*, p. 270.

3. B.F. Butler telegraph message to Hon. E.M. Stanton, Secretary of War dated May 26, 1864—10:45 AM, received 2:10 PM; in *O.R.*, Ser. I, Vol. 36, Pt. III, p. 234.

4. *The Sentinel*, Richmond, Thursday Morning, May 26, 1864, p. 1, column 1.

5. Report of Brig. Gen. Edward A. Wild, May 25, 1864, in *O.R.*, Ser. I, Vol. 36, Pt. II, p. 171.

6. *Christian Recorder*, 28 June 1864, cited in C.R. Gibbs, p. 126.

7. "Return of Casualties....," in *O.R.*, Ser. I, Vol. 36, Pt. II, pp. 16–17.

8. _____. "Civil War Surgery: Desperate Measures for Desperate Wounds Part 1," *Resident & Staff Physician*, Vol. 44, No. 10, October 1998, p. 90.

9. Turner's Letter in the *Christian Recorder* of 25 June 1864; cited in C.R. Gibbs, p. 126.

10. *Ibid.*

11. "...The enemy, after desperate fighting, were repulsed and driven back in disorder, leaving between 200 and 300 in killed and wounded on the field. One rebel major [*sic*]

was killed, a rebel Colonel was made prisoner [Not true!], and 10 privates were also captured"; "Movements on the Peninsula," *Harper's Weekly*, 11 June 1864.

12. Combined from: Irving P.W. Whitehead, "Meadow Bridge and Fort Kennon," *The Campaigns of Thomas T. Munford and the 2nd Virginia Cavalry*, p. 96; Irving Whitehead, "Meadow Bridge and Fort Kennon," in: "History of the Second Virginia Cavalry," × 90, p. 96.

13. "Ft. Kennon," Driver, *2nd Virginia Cavalry*, p. 179.

14. Horatio Nelson, *Diary*. Private Nelson was mortally wounded at "Symaria" (Samaria or St. Mary's Church) north of Charles City Court House on 24 June 1864 and died during the night of 26 June.

15. _____, "Civil War Surgery: Desperate Measures for Desperate Wounds Part 1," *Residents & Staff Physicians*, Vol. 44, No. 10, October 1998, p. 90.

16. _____, "The Attack on Fort Powhatan" [*sic*, which describes the attack on Wilson's Wharf], "Headquarters of General Butler, May 25, 1864"; Frank Moore, editor; Document 77, "Operations in Virginia," *Rebellion Record 1862–65*, Vol. XI, (New York: Van Nostrand, 1868), p. 504.

17. *Ibid.*

18. *O.R.*, Ser. I, Vol. 36, Pt. III, p. 234.

19. Wild's Report, 25 May 1864.

20. "Roll of the Second Virginia Cavalry," H.B. McClellan, *The Life and Campaigns of Major-General J.E.B. Stuart* (Secaucus, NJ: The Blue & Grey Press, 1885/1993), pp. 423, 426, 428, 429.

21. *Ibid.*, "1st Virginia Cavalry," p. 467.

22. Stiles, *4th Virginia Cavalry*, p. 120.

23. Driver, *2nd Virginia Cavalry*, p. 121.

24. Gill, *Reminiscences*, p. 99.

25. Fitzhugh Lee, *Report*, p. 25; J.D. Ferguson, *Memoranda*, p. 4; Grant to Halleck, 29 May 1865, in *O.R.*, Ser. I, Vol. 36, Pt. III, p. 289; Sheridan, 1 June 1864, in *ibid.*, pp. 262, 469; Lt. Col. William Stokes Halliburton Letter date 29 May 1864, in *Saddle Soldiers*, pp. 140, 141; Edwin W. Besch & Kenneth A. Bako, "Haw's Shop-Enon Church," Civil War Sites Advisory Commission Survey, for the National Park Service, 1993, p. 4.

26. Phoebe Pember, who served during the entire war at Chimborazo Hospital in Richmond, thought the *high mortality from secondary amputations* was mostly due to nutrition of the soldiers. She wrote: "*Poor food and great exposure had thinned the blood and broken down the system so entirely that secondary amputations performed in the hospital almost invariably resulted in death, after the second year of war. Only cases*

under my observation that survived were two Irishmen, and it was really so difficult to kill an Irishman that there was little cause for boasting on the part of the officiating surgeon;" in Pember P: *A Southern Woman's Story, Life in Confederate Richmond* (Reprint, St. Simon's Island, GA: Mockingbird Books, 1987), p. 77, New York: G.W. Carleton, 1879); cited in Dr. Julian Chrisholm, "Civil War Surgery: All Those Amputations—Part 1," *Resident & Staff Physician*, Vol. 45, No. 2, February 1999, p. 84.

27. *The Civil War Letters of James Michael Barr*, pp. 242–244, 247, 250–251, 253–254, 258–260.

Chapter VII

1. "The War News," Richmond *Examiner*, Thursday, May 26, 1864, p. 1.

2. "The Affair in Charles City County," Richmond *Examiner*, Saturday, May 28, 1864, p. 1.

3. Handwritten copy, "Report of the Military Services of Edward A. Wild, Brig. Gen. U.S. Vols. (concluded)," pp. 125–126, Folder 2149, "First Use of Black Troops in the Union, Mass. MOLUS Paper—General Wild," Archives, USAMHI.

4. Grant had about 50,000 Federal effectives after detachments; Robert E. Lee had 43,000 troops, total 93,000 men; North Anna casualties: official Federal losses were 1,973 killed, wounded, and captured; Confederate casualties are estimated at 304 killed, 1,573 wounded, and 200 captured, a total of 2,017 men. Total reported and estimated casualties are thus 3,990 (or "some 4,000"), to which must be added 650 Federal sick for the North Anna Campaign. J. Michael Miller, *The North Anna Campaign "Even To Hell Itself" May 21–26 1864* (Lynchburg, VA: H.E. Howard, Inc., 1989), pp. 6, 7, 138.

5. Simonton, *Campaign Up the James River*, pp. 486, 487.

6. Captain William Davis Parlin, speech at Natick, MA in early 1890s, manuscript, p. 22, Courtesy The Eaton Family of Watchung, NJ.

7. William A. Gladstone Letter to Ed Besch dated 26 August 2006, p. 9.

8. Richard J. Sommers, *Richmond Redeemed*, pp. 193–194.

9. Eric J. Whittenberg, "Confederate Cavalry Command Dilemma....," *America's Civil War*, Vol. 14, No. 6, January 2002, p. 28.

10. "Lee, Fitzhugh ("Fitz"). CSA gen. 1835–1905. Va."; in Boatner, *Dictionary*, p. 475; "Lee, Fitzhugh, CSA," in Faust, *Encyclopedia*, p. 429.

11. "Attack on Fort Powhatan" [*sic*, Wilson's Wharf], *Rebellion Record*, p. 504.

12. Boatner, *Dictionary*, p. 402; Faust, *Encyclopedia*, pp. 362–363.

13. Boatner, *ibid.*, pp. 775, 776; Grant cited in Trudeau, *The Last Citadel*, p. 32.

14. Trudeau, *ibid.*

15. Gerard Peterson, "The Beast of New Orleans," *Civil War Illustrated*, May-June 1993, pp. 29–33, 62–64, 66.

16. Gladstone, *Men of Color* pp. 12, 13.

Chapter VIII

1. Gladstone, *Men of Color*, pp. 4, 61.

2. "War Graph" of "USCT Recruitment" and "USCT Strength Levels," in *Civil War Times*, Vol. 53, No. 1, February 2014, p. 16.

3. Glatthar, 5. "Black Glory: The African-American Role in Union Victory," in Borritt, *Why the Confederacy Lost*, p. 152.

4. *Ibid.*, pp. 152, 153.

5. An Advertisement illustrated in Gladstone, *Men of Color*, p. 61.

6. General Cobb cited in Bell Irvin Wiley & Hirst D. Mulhollen, *Embattle Confederates, An Illustrated History of Southerners at War* (New York: Harpers & Row, 1964), p. 241.

7. (Forrest erroneously believed that 500 of 700 Federal troops had been killed, many drowning in the Mississippi River.) Forrest's report to Lt. Gen. Leonidas Polk, his immediate superior, of 15 April 1864, in *O.R.*, Ser. I, Vol. 32, Pt. I, p. 612. Most of the report is cited in Wyeth, p. 333; Forrest also described the Action at Fort Pillow in a letter to President Davis, and quoted in Wyeth, p. 185. Forrest's conclusion is cited by Wills, *A Battle from the Start*, p. 185.

8. Gladstone, *Men of Color*, Appendix VIII, Index of Battles, pp. 208–212.

9. Brig. Gen. E.W. Hinks, "HDQRS. Third Division, Eighteenth Army Corps, In the field, Va., June 26, 1864," in *O.R.*, Ser. I, Vol. 40, Pt. II, p. 460.

10. Gladstone, *Men of Color*, pp. 4–5.

11. Stephen D. Lutz, "The 1st Kansas Colored Infantry was the first black regiment to strike a blow for ending slavery," *America's Civil War*, Vol. 16, No. 1, March 2003, p. 62; "79th Regiment," in: Dyer, *Compendium*, p. 1735; Fox, *Regimental Losses*, p. 9; Gladstone, *Men of Color*, pp. 15, 16.

12. Lawrence Lee Hewitt, "Port Hudson, 22 May–9 July 1863," Frances H. Kennedy, ed., *The Civil War Battlefield Guide* (Boston: Houghton Mifflin, 1990), pp. 148, 149.

13. Glatthaar, "Black Glory," in *Why the*

Confederacy Lost, pp. 153, 154. Quote is from the *New York Times* of 11 June 1863.

14. Glatthaar, *ibid.*, pp. 41, 42.

15. Fox, *Regimental Losses...*, pp. 450, 451.

16. Lieutenant-General Ulysses S. Grant, cited in Trudeau, *The Last Citadel*, pp. 126–127.

17. *Ibid.*, p. 123.

18. "Battle of Rhode Island," Boatner, *Encyclopedia of The Revolutionary War*, p. 792.

19. "The Black Troops," *Harper's Weekly*, 20 August 1864, p. 531.

20. "The Civil War: Joseph P. Reidy, 'Black Men in Navy Blue During the Civil War,' reprinted from *Prologue*: Quarterly of the NARA," Fall, 2001, Vol. 33, No. 3, pp. 1–2, Note 3 on p. 10. www.navyandmarine.org/ondeck/1862blackinblue.htm.

21. *Ibid.*, p. 2.

22. *Ibid.*

23. *Ibid.*, pp. 2–3.

24. "Muster Rolls of Vessels," RG 24, NARA, cited in *ibid.*, pp. 3–4.

25. Ivan Musicant, *Divided Waters, The Naval History of the Civil War* (Edison, NJ: Castle Books, 1995/2000), p. 74.

26. Michael Foster, *Ledger-Enquirer*, cited in "African-Americans served in both Civil War Navies," a paper published by The National Civil War Naval Museum, Columbus, Georgia, undated, p. 1.

27. Edwin W. Besch, Michael Hammerson, and Dave W. Morgan, "Raphael Semmes, the English 'Confederate Parson,' and his Maiden Sister Louisa: A Cased Presentation Revolver, a Magnificent Silver-Mounted Sword, and a 'Mammoth' Silk Confederate National Flag," *Military Collector & Historian*, Vol. 53, No. 4, Winter, 2001–2002, p. 150.

28. Glatthaar, "Black Glory," *Why the Confederacy Lost*, p. 138.

29. Quoted in: Isaac W. Heysinger, *Antietam and the Maryland and Virginia Campaigns of 1862* (New York: Neale Publishing, 1912), pp. 122–123.

30. Quoted from: *The Fremantle Diary, Being the Journal of Lieutenant Colonel James Arthur Fremantle, Coldstream Guards, on His Three Months in the Southern States*, in: Jacob Hoke, *The Great Invasion of 1863, Or, General Lee in Pennsylvania* (Dayton, OH: W.J. Shuey, 1887), pp. 489–490; and Richard Rollins, "Black Confederates at Gettysburg," in Richard Rollins, ed., *Black Southerners in Gray, Essays on Afro-Americans in Confederate Armies*, Vol. XI, *Journal of Confederate History* Series (Murfreesboro, TN: Southern Heritage Press, 1994), p. 137.

31. Richard Rollins, *Black Southerners in Gray*, *ibid.*, p. 9; Bell Irvin Wiley, *Embattled*

Confederates, An Illustrated History of Confederates at War (New York: Bonanza Books, 1964), p. 234.

32. *O.R.*, Ser. IV, Vol. II, p. 941.

33. Arthur W. Bergeron, Jr., Chapter 8, "Role of Blacks in Mobile Defense," in *Confederate Mobile* (Jackson: University Press of Mississippi, 1991), pp. 105, 175.

34. *O.R.*, Ser. I, Vol. 52, Pt. II, p. 586; Daniel Malloch, "Cleburne's Proposal," *North & South, Vol. 11, No. 2, Dec. 2008, pp. 68, 70–76.

35. Edward Younger, ed., *Inside the Confederate Government: The Diary of Robert Garlich Hill Kean, Head of the Bureau of War* (New York: Oxford University Press, 1957), p. 192.

36. *O.R.*, Ser. 3, p. 1315.

37. Noah Andre Trudeau, *The Last Citadel: Petersburg, Virginia June 1864–April 1865* (Boston: Little, Brown, 1991), p. 325.

38. General Orders No. 14, of 23 March 1865 published in the Act of Congress; *O.R.* Ser. IV, Vol. 3, p. 1161.

39. *O.R.*, Ser. IV, Vol. 3, p. 1144.

40. General Orders No. 14, in *ibid.*, pp. 1161, 1162.

41. Quoted by Rollins in *Black Southerners in Gray, Essays*, p. 27.

42. *O.R.*, Ser. I, Vol. 46, Pt. III, p. 1370.

43. Trudeau, *The Last Citadel*, p. 356.

44. *O.R.*, Ser. I, Vol. 3, Appendix, p. 194; Trudeau, *ibid.*

45. R.M. Doswell, "Union Attack on Confederate Negroes," *Confederate Veteran* 23, Sept. 1915, p. 404; quoted by Rollins in *Black Southerners in Gray, Essays*, pp. 27–28.

46. Earl Schenk Miers, ed., *John Beauchamp Jones, A Rebel War Clerk's Diary* (New York: Sangamon Press, In. 1866/1958), p. 530.

47. Major Darrel L. Choat, USMC, "Enough is Enough," *Marine Corps Gazette*, June 2012, p. 42.

Chapter IX

1. Drawer 150, Sheet 46, No. 3, National Archives and Record Administration (NARA) facility in Maryland. Major General Godfrey Weitzel was born in Cincinnati, Ohio in 1835 and graduated 2nd in the Class of 1855 at West Point. He served with distinction at Fort Pickens, Florida in 1861, and with General Butler in Louisiana. As chief engineer of the Army of the James, he was engaged in actions at Swift Creek and near Drewry's Bluff, and he constructed the defenses at Bermuda Hundred, sites on the James River, and at Deep Bottom. (*The Union Army*, Vol. 8.)

2. "Sat Aug 6th" Diary entry in: *George L. Brooks Papers* (edited by John M. Pierson,

Dover, OH in 1996), p. 11; (Brooks was) "Company [sic, Regimental Commissary] Sergeant, Field & Staff, 143rd Regiment Ohio National Guard," Archives, USAMHI, Carlisle, PA; copy sent by Courtesy of Mr. Timothy R. Brookes, J.D. of East Liverpool, OH with "Letter to Fort Pocahontas Historian, Charles City, VA" dated 2 Dec. 2003, and forwarded to the Author by Mr. Harrison R. Tyler of Sherwood Forest Plantation, Charles City, VA on 27 January 2004. (Hereafter: "Brooks Diary.")

3. O.R., Ser. I, Vol. 36, Pt. III, pp. 287–288.

4. Box, "Wild Correspondence," USAMHI.

5. "10th Regiment Infantry," and "37th Regiment Infantry, Regiments, U.S. Colored Troops," Frederick H. Dyer, A Compendium of the War of the Rebellion, pp. 1725, 1730, respectively. (Hereafter: Dyer, Compendium.)

6. O.R., Ser. I, Vol. 40, Pt. I, "Reports," p. 24; Pt. II, p. 555; "Statistics of Ammunition-June 11, 1864, at Wilson's Wharf," copy in "Wild Papers," USAMHI, Carlisle, PA.

7. Reports of Colonels Holman and Duncan dated, respectively, 20 and 25 June 1864; in O.R., Series I, Vol. 36, Pt. III, pp. 263–269.

8. U.S. Military Telegraph message dated 24 July 1864, in Box "Wild Correspondence," USAMHI.

9. Wild's Notes in Box "Correspondence," USAMHI; "Wild, Edward Augustus, Union gen. 1825–1891," Boatner, Civil Dictionary, p. 919.

10. Frances H. Casstevens, Edward Augustus Wild, pp. 189, 192–194.

11. "143rd Infantry Regiment," and "163rd Infantry Regiment, Ohio," in Dyer, Compendium, pp. 1550, 1552, respectively; O.R., Series I, Vol. 36, Pt. III, pp. 739, 774.

12. The regiments had replaced their old state-issue (.69 caliber?) muskets with Enfield P1853 .577 caliber rifle-muskets, issued at the Columbus, Ohio arsenal on 15 May 1864, the day they left for Washington, DC. (Brooks Diary, p. 1.)

13. "Marston, Gilman," 1811–1890," Boatner, Dictionary, p. 514.

14. Letter of Captain Albert R. Arter, provided by Harrison R. Tyler. It was found in a cigar box in Hanoverton(?), Columbiana County, eastern Ohio in 1980. An unsigned "New Arter Letter 3" from "Headquarters June 19th 18—Wilson's Landing on James River" and addressed to "M Arter Dear Father" was posted 5/5/2007 on http://www.fortpocahontas.org/Arter3.html. Since the letter was posted at "Headquarters," it probably was written by Lieutenant Theodore Arter, Adjutant of the 143rd Ohio Infantry Regiment. Much information duplicates that written by Captain Albert R. Arter four days later.

15. "143rd Regiment," Official Roster of the Soldiers of the State of Ohio.

16. Linn Diary.

17. Ibid.

18. Ibid.

19. Brooks Diary, p. 5.

20. Linn Diary.

21. 163rd Ohio Order Book.

22. Linn Diary.

23. Ibid.

24. O.R., Ser. I, Vol. 40, Pt. I, "Reports," p. 264, and Pt. III, "Correspondence, etc.," pp. 498–499, 739; "33rd New York Independent Battery, Light Artillery," Dyer, Compendium, p. 1403. The 33rd NY Battery had supported assaults on Petersburg during 15–18 June 1864 and was then assigned to Fort Pocahontas where it remained until January 1865. (Dyer, ibid.)

25. Brooks Diary; Todd, American Military Equipage, Vol. III, pp. 1044, 1046. In February 1864, the colonel of the 1st U.S. Colored Cavalry Regiment had rejected "577 Merrill carbines & appendages, cartridge boxes, & cap boxes, & 34 Burnside .54 cal. carbines, and 16,000 cartridges which I do not require," possibly because the entire regiment had not been mounted, and was still not mounted by late June 1864. (Notes the author made from reviewing the regimental file at USAMHI, Carlisle, PA.)

26. Brooks Diary, various entries; 143rd Regiment Ohio Volunteer Infantry, 163rd Ohio Volunteer Infantry, in "Roll of Honor of [deceased] Ohio Soldiers," in Official Roster of the Soldiers of the State of Ohio in the War of the Rebellion 1861–1866, Vol. IX, 141st–184th Regiments—Infantry (Cincinnati: Ohio Valley Press, 1889), pp. 750–751, 761–762, respectively.

27. Linn Diary.

28. Brooks Diary, p. 13.

29. Linn Diary.

30. Brooks Diary, p. 14.

31. Quoted in Martin A. Haynes, Company I, A History of the Second Regiment, New Hampshire Volunteer Infantry, in the War of the Rebellion (Lakeport, NH: 1896), p. 250.

32. Dyer, Compendium, p. 1730. On 27 September 1864, Pvt. Gray Barnes "deserted at Wilson's Wharf when in arrest and guarded by men of the 2nd New Hampshire Provost Guard"; however, Company H recruited 14 men at Wilson's Wharf during 2–16 June. (Microfilm Muster Rolls at NARA.)

33. Dyer, ibid., p. 1387; ordnance reports in Archives at USAMHI.

34. Dyer, ibid., p. 1403.

35. Dyer, ibid., p. 1347; Todd, Military Equipage, p. 985; "Sharps Rifles," John D. McAulay, Civil War Breech Loading Rifles (Lincoln, RI: Andrew Mobray, Inc., 1987), p. 88.

36. Dyer, *ibid.*, p. 1366; Todd, *ibid.*, p. 1003; *The Union Army*, Vol. 3.

37. Dyer, *ibid.*, p. 1440; Todd, *ibid.*, p. 1051; "Ordnance Returns, 2nd Qtr, 1864," at NARA.

38. Dyer, *ibid.*, p. 1470; Todd, *ibid.*, p. 1055.

39. Dyer, *ibid.*, p. 1720.

40. Dyer, *ibid.*, p. 1381; Todd, p. 1045. New York artillery, cavalry, and infantry units that served in the 1st brigade, 3rd division, Xth Corps and/or the Separate Brigade, Army of the James, were also researched in Frederick Phisterer, *New York in the War of the Rebellion 1861–1865*, Part III, "Sketches of Organizations," (Albany: Weed, Parsons & Co., 1890), pp. 29, 62, 226, 237, 317–318, 338, 348–349, 369, 371, 445–446, and 511–512 without finding more information.

41. "Carr, Joseph Bradford. 1828–95"; Boatner, *Dictionary*, p. 128.

42. Casstevens, *Edward A. Wild*, pp. 197–201.

43. *Ibid.*, p. 204; "Ord, Edward Otho Cresap, b. Cumberland, Md., USMA 1839," Faust, *Encyclopedia*, pp. 547–548.

44. Casstevens, *Edward A. Wild*, p. 205.

45. *Ibid.*

46. *Ibid.*, p. 209.

47. *Ibid.*, pp. 210, 259, 260.

Chapter X

1. Statement on inside cover, *Civil War Sites Advisory Commission Report on the Nation's Civil War Battlefields* (Washington, DC: Civil War Sites Advisory Commission, July 1993).

2. *Ibid.*, pp. 39, 60.

3. Paul M. Nasca, Dennis B. Blanton, Charles M. Downing, & Veronica L. Deitrick; *Archaeology at Fort Pocahontas: Results from the 1997 Field Season*; Prepared for Harrison Tyler, Sherwood Forest; Prepared by: William and Mary Center for Historical Research, Dep't. of Anthropology, The College of William & Mary, Williamsburg, VA, 1998; p. 1. (Afterwards: *Archaeology … 1997.*)

4. *Ibid.*, pp. 7, 9.

5. *Ibid.*, pp. 9–10.

6. "Arnold's Raid," Mark Mayo Boatner III, *Encyclopedia of the American Revolution* (New York: David McKay, 1966), p. 1149; Edwin W. Besch, "Virginians Arm for Conquest, Defense, and Revolution, 1607–1783," MS, p. 1564. (Hereafter: Besch, "Virginians Arm….")

7. Captain Johann Ewald, *Diary of the American War, A Hessian Journal* (New Haven & London: Yale University Press, 1979), pp. 258–259; quoted in: Besch, *ibid.*

8. *The George Washington Papers*, XXI, p. 255; Van Doren, *Secret History of the American Revolution*, p. 420; Freeman, *George Washing-*

ton, V, p. 257; referenced by Editor Tustin in Ewald, *ibid.*, Note 12, p. 421; all in Besch, *ibid.*, p. 1564, Notes 44 and 45 on p. 1857.

9. Quote by D. Gardiner Tyler, in his *A History & Pictorial Review of Charles City County* (Expert Graphics, 1990). p. 84.

10. Robert Armistead Stewart, *History of Virginia's Navy of the Revolution* (Richmond: Mitchell & Hotchkiss, Printers, 1933), p. 93; Thomas Jefferson's "Notes of 1781, Thursday, 4 January 1781," *Thomas Jefferson Papers*, vol. 5, p. 262; Lyon Gardiner Tyler, *Letters and Times of the Tylers*, vol. I, p. 77, quoted in: D. Gardiner Tyler, *Charles City County Virginia During the Period of the Revolutionary War 1775–1783* (Charles City County Bicentennial Committee, 1976), p. 11; referenced in: Besch, *ibid.*, p. 1566, Note 48 on p. 1858. A wine bottle seal embossed "1771" and a 1783 New Jersey coin, and ceramics, including Chinese porcelain, found at the site of the main house indicate Kennons was occupied at the time of Arnold's raid.

11. "Thomas Nelson, Jr., B.G." letter to Governor Jefferson from Holt's (Providence Forge, north of Charles City) dated 7 p.m., 8 January 1781, *Thomas Jefferson Papers*, vol. 5, p. 362.

12. *Archaeology … 1997*, pp. 10–13.

13. "Fort Pocahontas"; www.fortpocahontas.org.

14. William Tyler in conversation with Ed Besch in May 2013.

15. Eric Pfeiffer, "Former President John Tyler's (1790–1862) grandchildren still alive," *Yahoo News*, 26 January 2012.

16. Eric Pfeiffer, "Former President John Tyler's grandchildren…."

17. Harrison Ruffin Tyler, quoted in: Don Amira, "President John Tyler's Grandson on Still Being Alive," nymagwww/daily/intel/2012/01/president-tyler-granson-alive.html.

18. "Julia Gardner Tyler—Later life and death," en.wikipedia.org/wiki/Julia_Gardiner_Tyler.

19. Lion Gardiner published his critical *Relation of the Pequot War* in East Hampton in 1660. (Robert Seager II, *and Tyler too….*, p. 19.)

20. Information provided by Payne Tyler in 2013.

21. Christopher J. Leahy, "Tech degree, not ancestry, key to success," *Virginia Tech magazine*, Winter, 2007, pp. 1–3, www.vtmagazine.vt.edu/winter07/feature5.html.

22. *Ibid.*, p. 2.

23. Information provided by Harrison and Payne Tyler.

24. "Fort Pocahontas," www.fortpocahontas.org/Preservation.html.#TOP.

25. *Archaeology … 1997*, pp. 1, 7.

26. Jameson M. Harwood (Author) & Dennis B. Blanton (Project Director), *"NO*

DANGER OF SURRENDER" An Historical Archeological Perspective of the Civil War Battle of Wilson's Wharf, Charles City County, Virginia; WMCAR Project No. 00–23 Prepared For: American Battlefield Protection Program, By: William and Mary Center for Archeological Research, 8 June 2001; pp. 1, 35.

27. Author's interviews with Joe Funk and Patty Finegan at Fort Pocahontas on 18 May 2013. Joe and Patty traveled from their home in Shrewsbury, Pennsylvania to coordinate and participate in the reenactments since 1997.

Bibliography

Manuscript Sources

Arter, Captain A. (Albert) R., Co. C, 143rd Regiment, Ohio National Guard. Letter to "Dear Friend" from Wilson's Landing, Virginia June 23[,] 1864. Typescript copy found in a cigar box at Hanoverton, Columbiana County, Ohio, in 1980. Copy given the author by Harrison R. Tyler.

Assistant Adjutant General's Office, Record Group (RG) 94, National Archives and Records Administration (NARA), Washington, D.C.

Atkins, James E. "Preliminary" draft of a "previously hidden history of Adam Boykin," who enlisted in Co. H, 37th Infantry Regiment, U.S. Colored Troops at Fort Pocahontas. Copy courtesy of James E. Atkins.

Besch, Edwin W. "Virginians Arm for Conquest, Defense, and Revolution, 1607–1783."

Besch, Edwin W., and Kenneth A. Bako, independent consultants. *Civil War Sites Advisory Commission Survey Form (Revised Draft)*, July 25, 1993, Subject: "Wilson's Wharf ... Kennon's Landing"; submitted to the National Park Service (NPS). Copies provided by the NPS to the Congressional Civil War Sites Advisory Commission and the Virginia State Historic Preservation Officer.

Besch, Edwin W., John M. Bingham, and Robert L. Brown. "The Confederate Fifth South Carolina Cavalry and its Battle Flag and Enfield Arms." 1997.

Biggs, Lt. Col. H. Letter from Chief Quartermaster's Office, Fort Monroe, to Chief Quartermaster dated 25 May 1864. Collection of the Manuscript Division, Library of Congress.

Breckinridge, Jane W. Letter to Harrison R. Tyler from Fincastle, VA, dated 8 May 1997.

Brief Summary: "10th United States Colored Infantry." Microfilm Publication M-1821, Compiled Military Service Records of Volunteer Soldiers Who Served with the United States Colored Troops: Infantry Organizations, 8th through 13th, including the 11th (new), 2000. 3, RG 94. www.fold3.com/pdf/M1821.pdf.

Brooke, H. St. George Tucker. Typescript copy, undated: "Autobiography of H. St. George Tucker Brooke, written for his children, 2nd Virginia Cavalry, Company B, Fitzhugh Lee's Brigade." Charlottesville: University of Virginia Library, and copy provided by Mrs. Sara W. Saunders in 1997.

Brown, Sergeant John D., Company D, 5th South Carolina Cavalry Regiment. *Orderly Book* of Company D, 5th SC Cavalry (1863–64). South Carolina Dept. of Archives & History, Columbia, SC.

Clark, Henry: "Edward Crafts Hobson, A Biographical Sketch Read Before the Vermont Historical Society, January 25, 1865."

Civil War diaries covering 3 May–15 Sept. 1864 of two brothers, John Brownhill Linn and Thomas Buchanan Linn, 143rd Ohio Infantry Regiment, Civil War Miscellaneous Collection, Archives, U.S. Army Military History Institute, Carlisle, Pennsylvania.

Complete Descriptive Roll of the U.S. Steamer *Dawn* on 30 June 1864. NARA.

Complete Descriptive Roll of the Steamer *Young America* on 30 June 1864. NARA.

Descriptive Books, 1st and 10th Infantry Regiments, U.S. Colored Troops, NARA, Washington, D.C.

Endsley, Private Thomas L., Co. H, 143rd Ohio Infantry Regiment. Certificate given him for his "100 Days" Service in the Ohio National Guard. Copy sent the author by the recipient's great-great-grandson, Donald W. ("Dack") Dalrymple, Washington, D.C., on 24 May 2010.

Ferguson, Major, Assistant Adjutant General J.D. (James Du Gue). *Memoranda of the Itinerary and Operations of Major General Fitzhugh Lee's Cavalry Division of the A.N.V.—from May 4th to October 19th, 1864, inclusive.* Copy provided by J. Michael Miller.

_____. "5th South Carolina Cavalry," microfilm, RG 94, NARA, Washington, D.C.

_____. "1st Virginia Cavalry" File, Eleanor S. Brockenbrough Library, Museum of the Confederacy, Richmond, VA.

Forrest, Nathan Bedford. Forrest's "Testimony: Ku Klux Klan Conspiracy." *Report of the Joint Select Committee to Inquire into the Conditions of Affairs in the Late Insurrectionary States,* made to two houses of Congress, 19 February 1872, 42nd Congress, 2nd Session, *Senate Report*, Vol. 13, pp. 20, 32–35.

Hall, Henry, and James Hall. *Cayuga in the Field, A Record of the 19th New York Volunteers, All of The Batteries of the 3rd New York Artillery, and the 75th New York Volunteers....* Auburn, NY:1873.

Gill, John. *Reminiscences of Four Years as a Private in the Confederate Army.* Baltimore: Sun Printing, 1904, copy at Preston Library, Virginia Military Institute, Lexington, VA.

Hackley, Woodford B. *The Little Fork Rangers, a sketch of Company D, Fourth Virginia Cavalry.* Richmond: Dietz, 1927.

Halliburton, Lloyd. *Saddle Soldiers. The Civil War Correspondence of General William Stokes of The 4th South Carolina Cavalry.* Orangeburg, SC: Sandlapper, 1993.

Hay, Thomas Hobson, ed., *Cleburne and His Command by Capt. Irving A. Buck, Assistant Adjutant General, Cleburne's Division, C.S.A., and Pat Cleburne, Stonewall Jackson of the West.* Monographs, Sources, and Reprints in Southern History. Jackson, TN: McCowat-Mercer Press, Inc., 1959.

Haynes, Martin A., Company I. *A History of the Second Regiment, New Hampshire Volunteer Infantry in the War of the Rebellion.* Lakeport, NH: 1896.

_____. "History of the 5th S.C.C.," Copy of Report sent to Professor W.J. Rivers, Recording Agent, December 1868. Courtesy Robert L. Brown, Columbia, SC.

Hutchinson, Calvin Gibbs, Acting Assistant Paymaster on USS *Commodore Morris* ordered to USS *Pequot* 24 Oct. 1863. *Nos. 1 and 2, Diary. No. 2 Diary* (begun) Charlestown, MA December 27, 1858. Ronald E. Fischer Collection, Charlottesville, VA.

Hutchinson, Olin Fulmer. *"My Dear Mother & Sisters," Civil War Letters of Capt. A.B. Mulligan, Co. B, 5th South Carolina Cavalry—Butler's Division, Hampton's Corps 1861–1865.* Spartanburg, SC: The Reprint Company, 1992.

Lee, Fitzhugh. *Report of Major General Fitzhugh Lee of the Operations of His Cavalry Division, A.N.V. (Army of Northern Virginia) from May 4, 1864 to September 19, 1864.* Collection of the Eleanor S. Brockenbrough Library, Museum of the Confederacy, Richmond, VA.

Loewen, James W. Letter to Edwin W. Besch dated May 24, 1999, from Department of Sociology at The Catholic University of America, Washington, D.C., w/10-page attachment re: Fort Pillow, Fort Pocahontas, and Nathan Bedford Forrest, etc.

_____. Logbook of USS *Dawn.* Microfilm copy, RG 24 Stack 18w-1, Row 2, NARA, Washington, D.C.

_____. Logbook of the U.S. Tug *Young America.* Microfilm copy, RG 24, 18W4, Row 13, Comp 19, NARA.

Mays, Thomas D., ed. *Let Us Meet in Heaven: The Civil War Letters of James Michael Barr, 5th South Carolina Cavalry.* Abilene, TX: McWhiney Foundation Press, McMurray University, 2001.

McIntosh, Alexander S., Co. B, 143rd Ohio Infantry Regiment. Letter to "Dear Daughter" from "Fort Pocahontas," Aug. 18, 1864. Courtesy Mr. Timothy R. Brookes, J.D., of East Liverpool, OH.

McIntosh, Private William T. Letter to "Dear Brother" (A.F. McIntosh), from "Wilson's Landing, Va." dated June 20, 1864, 3 pp. Courtesy Mr. Timothy R. Brookes, J.D., of East Liverpool, OH.

McKinstry, The Honorable Alexander. *The Code of Ordinances of the City of Mobile* (parts prescribing treatment of slaves, license requirements, slave tags, fines and number of lashes for owners' and slaves' offenses, etc.). Mobile: S.H. Goetzel of 37 Dauphin Street, 1859. Courtesy George Ewert, Director, Museum of Mobile.

Means, Paul B. "Additional Sketch Sixty-Third Regiment (Fifth Cavalry), *North Carolina Regiments 1861–1865,* Vol. III, pp. 600–601.

Medical Record Cards Files, 1st and 10th Regiments, U.S. Colored Troops, NARA.

Miers, Earl Schenk, ed. *John Beauchamp Jones: A Rebel War Clerk's Diary.* New York: Sangamon, 1866/1958.

Military Service and pension records of Union Soldiers in the Civil War, Record Group 94, NARA, Washington, D.C.

Minor, George A. Letter to his Mother dated 30 May 1864 from "Atley's [*sic*; Atlee's] Station, Va." Copy sent the author by Lt. Col. Robert J. Driver, Jr., U.S. Marine Corps (Ret.) on 4 Nov. 1996.

_____. *Morning Reports; Regimental Letter, Order, and Detail Book,* 10th Regiment, USCT, NARA.

Nelson, Horatio. *Diary.* Excerpts in Harold "John" Howard, ed. *"If I am killed on this trip, I want my horse kept for my brother": The Diary of the Last Weeks in the Life of a Young Confederate Cavalryman. Horatio Nelson, Co. A, 4th Virginia Cavalry, 1844–1864.* The Manassas Chapter of the United Daughters of the Confederacy, 1980. Copy in author's collection.

_____. *Official Roster of the Soldiers of the State of Ohio in the War of the Rebellion 1861–1866,* Vol. IX: "141st-148th Regiments-Infantry." Cincinnati: Ohio Valley Press, 1889.

_____. *Order Books* for Companies A and E, *Morning Reports* for Company I, 1st U.S. Colored Cavalry Regiment. Archives, U.S. Army Military History Institute, Carlisle, Pennsylvania.

_____. *Order Book, 163rd Ohio National Guard Regiment: Companies B, D, F, H, K.* Archives, U.S. Army Military History Institute, Carlisle, Pennsylvania.

Parlin, Captain William Davis, Company E, 1st Regiment, U.S. Colored Troops. A speech he gave during the early 1890s at Natick, Massachusetts, manuscript copy. Courtesy the Eaton Family of Watchung, New Jersey.

Pierson, John M., ed. *The George L. Brooks Papers, Company* [*sic*; Commissary] *Sergeant, 143rd Regiment, Ohio National Guard.* Dover, Ohio 1996. Archives, U.S. Army Military History Institute, Carlisle, PA. Brooks "borrowed a 'diary' of one of my fellow soldiers— Granville S. Watson of Salem [, Ohio], for procuring therefrom the ... necessary dates, and [he] proceed[ed] to fill up, with a brief narration of such facts as can be called into life by memory." Copy sent by Mr. Timothy R. Brookes, J.D., of East Liverpool, OH with "Letter to Fort Pocahontas Historian, Charles City, VA," dated 2 Dec. 2003, and forwarded to the author by Harrison R. Tyler.

Powell, Lt. Col. E. Henry, 10th USCT. "The Colored Soldier in the War of the Rebellion," War Paper no. 3, read 10 January 1893 before the Vermont Commandery of the Loyal Legion.

Price, Charles T. *An Account and Brief History of Company C, 2nd Virginia Cavalry.* Fincastle, VA: George Honts III, 1907, in Irving Powell Whitehead Papers, Alderman Library, University of Virginia, Charlottesville, Virginia.

Rigby, Private Timothy, Co. I, 143rd Infantry Regiment, Ohio National Guard. "Civil War Letters," typed copy, provided by Mr. Timothy R. Brookes, J.D., of East Liverpool, OH.

Rich, Lt. Lewis Bennet. Letter to "Dear Friends at Home" dated 16 May 1864 from Chesapeake Hospital. JPEG Files, copy sent the author via e-mail from William Kerry and Stephen Kerry on 24 May 2006.

Salley, A.S., Jr., compl. *South Carolina Troops in Confederate Service*, vol. 1. Columbia, SC: R.L. Bryan, 1913.

Saunders, Mrs. Sara Wilson H., of Lynchburg, VA. Letter to Harrison R. Tyler dated 18 May 1997.

Simonton, Edward. "The Campaign Up the James River to Petersburg: Experiences and Observations of a Company Officer, By Captain Edward Simonton, First U.S. Colored Infantry, Brevet Lieut. Col. U.S. Volunteers," in *Glimpses of the Mortal Struggle*, Series 5, Minnesota Commandery, Military Order of the Loyal Legion of the United States, pp. 490–495.

Sketch Map: On 1 June 1864, Brig. Gen. Godfrey Weitzel, Chief Engineer Officer (Butler's) Department of Virginia and North Carolina, signed *"Sketch(es)"* of the fortifications at *"Wilson's Wharf or Landing"* and *"Fort Powhattan"* [sic] that were prepared *"By* [i.e., at Weitzel's] *Order"* by Capt. John W. Donn, Coast Survey. NARA, Maryland facility.

Smith, Lyman Arnold. "Tribute (A), To a Beloved Son and Brother" (Adjutant Myron W. Smith, 1st Infantry Regiment, U.S. Colored Troops), a funeral sermon in 1864.

Stillwell, Lewis D. "History of the 1st and 2nd Regiments, New Hampshire Volunteers." In *New Hampshire and The Civil War*, Vol. 1, No. 1, New Hampshire Civil War Centennial Commission, 1962.

Swank, Walbrook D., Colonel USAF (Ret.). *Courier for Lee and Jackson 1861–1865 Memoirs*. Shippensburg, PA: Burd Street Press, 1993.

Tustin, Joseph P., ed. *Captain Johann Ewald, Field Jaeger Corps, Diary of the American War, A Hessian Journal*. New Haven: Yale University Press, 1979.

Tyler Family Papers, Margaret Cook Special Collection, Earl Gregg Swem Library, the College of William & Mary, Williamsburg, Virginia.

Tyler, Lyon Gardiner, ed., *Narratives of Early Virginia 1606–1625*. New York, 1907.

_____. *U.S., Statutes at Large, Treaties, and Proclamations of the United States of America*, vol. 12. Boston, 1863.

Virginia Military Institute Archives Manuscript "015, W.J. Black Diary." (Major John J. Shoemaker's) *Operations Report for Shoemaker's Battery, Horse Artillery Battalion, Sept. 1, 1864*.

Vodray, Colonel William H., 143rd Ohio Infantry Regiment. Letter to: "Dear Brother" from "Fort Pocahontas, Va. August 27th, 1864." Courtesy Mr. Timothy R. Brookes, J.D. of East Liverpool, OH.

Weist, Jacob R. *Medical Department in the War: A Paper Delivered Before the Commandery of the Loyal Legion of the United States, October 6, 1886*. Cincinnati: H.C. Sherric, 1886.

Wells, Edward L. *Hampton and His Cavalry in '64*. 1899.

_____. *A Sketch of the Charleston Light Dragoons From the Earliest of the Corps*. Charleston, 1888.

Whitehead, Irving Powell. *The Campaigns of Thomas T. Munford in the 2nd Virginia Cavalry*. Typed manuscript on microfilm no. 910, Deposit 1940, Irving P. Whitehead Papers, Alderman Library, University of Virginia, Charlottesville, Virginia.

Wild, Edward A. Boxes "Wild Correspondence" & "Wild Papers," Massachusetts Commandery, Military Order of Loyal Legion of the United States Collection (MOLLUS), Archives, U.S. Army Military History Institute, Carlisle Barracks, Pennsylvania.

_____. Handwritten "1864. Report of the Military Services of Edward A. Wild, Brig. Gen. U.S. Volunteers (concluded): "1864, March–May 24–August 4; My Military Biography from March 13, 1864.-till mustered out Jan. 15, 1866"; written in 1873; pp. 125–126, Folder 2149, "First Use of Black Troops in the Union," Mass. MOLLUS Paper-General Wild, Archives, U.S. Army Military History Institute, Carlisle Barracks, Pennsylvania. (The paper states that "one and a half regiments" fought at Wilson's Wharf," but above is written in small letters [by Wild later?] "10th Regt" over "one" and "1st Regt" over "and a half." The reverse is true.)

_____, papers. Southern Historical Collection, Manuscript Department, University of North Carolina, Chapel Hill, North Carolina.

Willis, Byrd C. *Byrd Charles Willis Papers 1861–1865.* Accession 23975, *Papers, 1861–1900 of Byrd C. Willis (1847–1911)* ... Library of Virginia, Richmond.

Wright, Captain Benjamin S., Company F, 143rd Ohio Regiment. Letter from "Wilson's Wharf, Va." to: "Mr. J. Easterly, Mr. B.F. Wright, & 'Friend Easterly'"; dated June 20, July 8, and July 23, 1864. Copies provided by Mr. Timothy R. Brookes, J.D., East Liverpool, OH.

Young, William H. *Journal of an Excursion, From Troy, N.Y. To Gen. Carr's Head Quarters, at Wilson's Landing (Fort Pocahontas) on the James River, Va. During the month of May 1864. By one of the party.* Troy, NY: Privately printed, 1871.

Younger, Edward, Jr., ed. *Inside the Confederate Government: The Diary of Robert Garlich Hill Kean, Head of the Bureau of War.* New York: Oxford University Press, 1957.

Newspapers

Buckeye State, a Republican newspaper printed in New Lisbon, the county seat of Columbiana County, Ohio: Undated Letter by I.P. Farmer, 143rd Ohio Infantry Regiment. Copy provided by Mr. Timothy R. Brookes, J.D., of East Liverpool, OH.

Charlotte (NC) Observer, November 1901: "A Confederate Plan for Arming the Slaves," in R.A. Brock, ed., *Southern Historical Society Papers* 24 (1901): p. 174.

Christian Recorder. African Methodist Episcopal Church. Philadelphia, 25 June 1864: Chaplain Henry M. Turner's Letter re: Action at Wilson's Wharf on 24 May 1864.

Columbiana County, Ohio, Newspaper Abstracts: *Reveille Echo*, "Home News Notes," Courtesy Carol Willsey Bell, State Library of Ohio, pp. 1, 32.

Daily Richmond Enquirer and Public Advertiser, May–June 1864, Newspaper & Current Periodical Room, Serial and Government Publications Division, Library of Congress.

Harper's Weekly, 20 August 1864: editorial "The Black Troops."

Harper's Weekly, May 7, 1864, p. 302: Daniel Tyler, "Buried Alive." (The Account of Private Daniel Tyler, Battery F, 2nd U.S. Colored Light Artillery Regiment, of his life, and the Confederate attack on Fort Pillow, Tennessee on 12 April 1864.)

Memphis Daily Appeal, 3 December 1863.

Milledgeville (GA) Southern Recorder, 19 January 1864.

Montgomery Daily Advertiser, microfilm files, Alabama Department of Archives & History, Montgomery, Alabama.

New York Times, 9 January 1864, p. 1, col. 6: "Tewksbury, "General Butler's Department, Invasion of North Carolina by Gen. Wild's Colored Battalions."

New York Times, May 27, 1864: "H.J.W., The Rebel Attack on Wilson's Wharf ... In Camp," p. 1, col. 2, top.

New York Times. Robert C. Kennedy, "On This Day: November 5, 1864," http://www.nytimes.com/learning/general/onthisday/harp/1105.html.

New York Times, Thursday, December 22, 1864, 4 pages.

Richmond (VA) Examiner, 9 January 1862 and various dates in May 1864.

(Richmond, VA) Sentinel: Tuesday morning, 21 March; Thursday morning, 19 March, and 25, 26, 27 May 1864, microfilm archive, Library of Virginia, Richmond.

Wellsville (OH) Union. Letters to the Editor by Pvt. Geo. J. Luckey dated on Thursdays in 1864: 16 and June 23 June, 14 July. Copies Courtesy of Mr. Timothy R. Brookes, J.D. of East Liverpool, Ohio, February 2004.

Primary Printed Sources

Berlin, Ira. *Many Thousands Gone: The First Two Centuries of Slavery in North America.* Cambridge, MA: Harvard University Press, 1998.

Birkett, Courtney J., Douglas E. Ross, Kristie R. Martin, Susanne D. Sell, Jack A. Gary, and Stephanie A. Santillo. *Fort Pocahontas: Results from the 2000 Field Season.* WMCAR Report No. 00–07 (Draft), Prepared for Harrison Tyler by William & Mary Center for Archeological Research, 10 November 2000.

Blanco, Richard, ed. *The American Revolution 1775–1783: An Encyclopedia.* 2 vols. New York: Garland, 1993.

Boatner, Mark M., III. *The Civil War Dictionary,* rev. ed. New York: Vintage Books, 1991; New York: Oxford University Press, 1992.

_____. *Encyclopedia of the American Revolution.* New York: David McKay, 1996.

Butler, Benjamin F. *Butler's Book: Autobiography and Personal Reminiscences of Benj. Butler.* Boston: A.M. Thayer, 1892.

Casstevens, Frances H. *Edward A. Wild and the African Brigade in the Civil War.* Jefferson, NC: McFarland, 2003.

Calvin D. Coles, compl. *Atlas to Accompany the Official Records of the Union and Confederate Armies.* Washington, D.C.: Government Printing Office, 1891–1895, rpt. New York: Fairfax Press, 1983.

_____. *Civil War Sites Advisory Commission Report on the Nation's Civil War Battlefields.* Washington, D.C.: Civil War Sites Advisory Commission, July 1993.

Dyer, Frederick H. *A Compendium of the War of the Rebellion, Compiled and Arranged from Official Records of the Federal and Confederate Armies.* Des Moines, Iowa: Dyer Publishing, 1908; reprint Dayton, OH: Morningside Bookshop, 1978.

Faust, Patricia L. *Historical Times Illustrated Encyclopedia of the Civil War.* New York: Harpers & Row, 1986.

"Fort Pocahontas." www.fortpocahontas.org. See also: www.fortpocahontas.org/Preservation. html.#TOP.

Fox, William F., Lt. Col., U.S.V. *Regimental Losses in the American Civil War 1861–1865.* Dayton, OH: 1898; The Press of Morningside Bookshop, 1985.

Gibbs, C.R. *Black, Copper & Bright.* Silver Spring, MD: Three Dimensional Publishing, 2002. A history of the First Regiment, U.S. Colored Troops, featuring a biography of the Rev. (later Bishop) Henry McNeil Turner, African Methodist Episcopal Church, and Chaplain, 1st Regt, USCT.

Harwood, Jameson M. (author), and Dennis B. Blanton (project director). *"No Danger of Surrender": An Historical Archaeological Perspective of the Civil War Battle of Wilson's Wharf, Charles City County, Virginia.* WMCAR Project No. 00–23, Prepared for American Battlefield Protection Program by William & Mary Center for Archeological Research, 8 June 2001.

Nasca, Paul M., Dennis B. Blanton, Charles M. Downing, and Veronica L. Detrick. *Archaeology at Fort Pocahontas: Results from the 1997 Field Season.* Prepared for Harrison Tyler, Sherwood Forest by the William & Mary Center for Historical Research, Dep't. of Anthropology, the College of William & Mary, Williamsburg, VA, 1998.

Nichols, James L. *General Fitzhugh Lee: A Biography.* Lynchburg, VA: H.E. Howard, 1989.

Tyler, D. Gardiner. *A History & Pictorial Review of Charles City County.* Expert Graphics, 1990.

_____. "United States Colored Troops." http://en.wikipedia.org/wiki/United_States_ Colored_Troops.

_____. "United States Colored Troops," *Union Regimental Index, The Civil War Archive,* 1998–2009, http://civilwararchive.com/unioncol.htm.

United States. Naval War Records Office. *Official Records of the Union and Confederate Navies,* Series I, 27 vols. Washington, D.C.: Government Printing Office, 1894–1922.

United States. War Department. *The War of the Rebellion: A Compilation of the Official Records of the Union and Confederate Armies.* 130 vols. Washington, D.C.: Government Printing Office, 1880–1901.

Virginia Census for Years 1860 and 1870.

Secondary Sources

Alexander, E. Curtis. *Wilson's Wharf: Afro-Virginia Infantry Regiments Defeat Lee's Cavalry at Fort Pocahontas.* Chesapeake, NY: ECA Associates Press, 2006.

Ambrose, Stephen E., ed. *A Wisconsin Boy in Dixie: The Selected Letters of James K. Newton.* Madison: University of Wisconsin Press, 1961.

Ancestry.com.

Axelrod, Alan. "Battle of Gettysburg, Third Day cavalry battles." en.wikipedia.org/wiki/Battle of_ Gettysburg,_Third_Day_cavalry_battles.

_____. *Generals South, Generals North: The Commanders of the Civil War Reconsidered.* Guilford, CT: Lyons Press, 2011.

Bergeron, Arthur W. *Confederate Mobile.* Jackson: University Press of Mississippi, 1991.

Bergeron, Arthur W., and Lawrence W. Hewitt, eds. *Louisianan Free Men of Color in Gray.* University of Missouri Press, 2002.

Berlin, Ira, et al., eds. *Freedom: A Documentary History of Emancipation, 1861–1867.* Series II. London: Cambridge University Press, 1982.

Besch, Edwin W., and Kenneth A. Bako, independent consultants. "Engagement at St. Mary's Church-Nance's Shop, 24 June 1864." (Summary) on Civil War Sites Advisory Commission Survey Form prepared during mid–1993 under contract to the National Conference of Historic State Preservation Officers for the Congressional Civil War Sites Advisory Commission and the National Park Service.

_____. "Trevilian Raid, Battle of Trevilian Station," Civil War Sites Advisory Form, prepared in 1993 under contract to the National Conference of Historic State Preservation Officers for the Congressional Civil War Sites Advisory Commission and the National Park Service.

Blake, Michael. *American Civil War Cavalry.* London: Almark, 1973.

Boritt, Gabor, ed. *Why the Confederates Lost.* New York, Oxford: Oxford University Press, 1992.

Brooks, Ulysses Robert. *Butler and His Cavalry, 1861–1865.* Columbia, SC: The State Co., 1909.

Cappon, Lester J., PhD. *Virginia's Newspapers, 1821–1835.* New York: Appleton-Century or University of Virginia, 1936.

Catton, Bruce. *The Army of the Potomac: A Stillness at Appomattox.* New York: Doubleday, 1953.

_____. "Civil War Surgery: All Those Amputations," Part 1, *Resident & Staff Physician* 45, no. 2 (February 1999): 79–85.

_____. "Civil War Surgery: Desperate Measures for Desperate Wounds," Part 1, *Resident & Staff Physician* 44, no. 10 (October 1998): 88–92.

Coates, Earl J., and John D. McAulay. *Civil War Sharps Carbines & Rifles.* Gettysburg, PA: Thomas Publications, 1996.

Connery, William. "Outline of the Lives of General Edward A. Wild and General Fitzhugh Lee." Presentation at the Fort Pocahontas Reenactment on 21 May 2005.

Cornish, Dudley Taylor. *The Sable Arm: Black Troops in the Union Army, 1861–1865.* Lawrence: University Press of Kansas, 1956/1987.

Copland, Mary Ruffin. *Confederate History of Charles City County, Virginia.* Harrison Harwood Chapter, UDC, 1959.

Davis, David Brion. *Directory of Naval Fighting Ships*, vol. 8, U.S. Naval Historical Center, Washington, D.C.

_____. *The District of Columbia Emancipation Act*, U.S. National Archives & Records Administration (NARA), Washington, D.C. www.archives.gov/exhibits/featured_documents_emancipation_act/.

_____. *Slavery in the Colonial Chesapeake.* Williamsburg: Colonial Williamsburg Foundation, 1986/ 1987.

Driver, Robert J., Jr. *The 1st Virginia Cavalry.* Lynchburg, VA: H.E. Howard, 1991.

_____. *The 2nd Virginia Cavalry.* Lynchburg, VA: H.E. Howard, 1995.

_____. *The 5th Virginia Cavalry.* Lynchburg, VA: H.E. Howard, 1997.

Fortier, John. *15th Virginia Cavalry.* Lynchburg, VA: H.E. Howard, 1993.

Freeman, Douglas Southall. *Lee's Lieutenants: A Study in Command,* vol. 3.

_____. *R.E. Lee: A Biography,* vol. 4. (Freeman books are editions published in Taiwan; acquired by the author while on R&R from Vietnam in 1966.)

Freemantle, Lt. Col. James Arthur, Coldstream Guards. "The Freemantle Diary, Being the Journal of Lieutenant Colonel James Arthur Freemantle, Coldstream Guards, on His Three Months in the Southern States" In Jacob Hoke, *The Great Invasion of 1863, Or, General Lee in Pennsylvania.* Dayton, OH: W.J. Shuey, 1887.

Gladstone, William A. *Men of Color.* Gettysburg, PA: Thomas Publications, 1993.

Glatthaar, Joseph T. *Forged in Battle: The Civil War Alliance of Black Soldiers and White Officers.* New York: Free Press, 1990.

Graves, Robert Ewell. *Black Defenders of America.* Chicago: Johnson, 1974.

Hargrove, Hondon B. *Black Union Soldiers in the Civil War.* Jefferson, NC: McFarland, 1988.

Hartley, Chris J. *Stuart's Tarheels: James B. Gordon and His North Carolina Cavalry in the Civil War.* Jefferson, NC: McFarland, 2011.

Hearn, Chester G. *Mobile Bay and the Mobile Campaign: The Last Great Battles of the Civil War.* Jefferson, NC: McFarland, 1993.

Heysinger, Isaac W. *Antietam and the Maryland and Virginia Campaigns of 1862.* New York: Neale, 1912.

Hollandsworth, James G., Jr. *The Louisiana Native Guards: The Black Military Experience During The Civil War.* Baton Rouge & London: Louisiana State University Press, 1995.

Horn, Stanley F. *The Army of Tennessee.* Wilmington, NC: Broadfoot, 1987.

Jordan, Ervin L, Jr. *Black Confederates and Afro-Yankees in Civil War Virginia.* Charlottesville: University of Virginia Press, 1995.

Katcher, Philip. *Confederate Cavalryman 1861–1865.* Oxford, UK: Osprey, 2002.

Katcher, Philip, and Rick Scollins. *Flags of the American Civil War 1: Confederate.* London: Osprey, 1992.

Kennedy, Frances H. *The Civil War Battlefield Guide.* Boston: Houghton Mifflin, 1990.

Korn, Jerry, and the editors of Time-Life Books. *Pursuit to Appomattox: The Last Battles.* Alexandria, VA: Time-Life Books, 1987.

Longacre, Edward G. *Army of Amateurs: General Benjamin F. Butler and the Army of the James, 1863–1865.* Mechanicsburg, PA: Stackpole, 1997.

Mast, Greg. *State Troops and Volunteers: A Photographic Record of North Carolina's Civil War Soldiers,* vol. 1. Raleigh: North Carolina Department of Cultural Resources, 1995.

McAulay, John D. *Civil War Breechloading Rifles.* Lincoln, RI: Andrew Mobray, 1987.

McClellan, H.B. *The Life and Campaigns of Major-General J.E.B. Stuart.* Secaucus, NY: The Blue & Grey Press, 1885/1993.

McMillan, Malcom C., ed. *The Alabama Confederate Reader.* Tuscaloosa: University of Alabama Press, 1963/1992.

McPherson, James M. *Battle Cry of Freedom: The Civil War Era.* New York, Oxford: Oxford University Press, 1988.

_____. *The Negro's Civil War: How American Blacks Felt and Acted During the War for the Union.* New York: Ballantine, 1991.

Miller, J. Michael. *The North Anna Campaign: "Even to Hell Itself," May 21–26, 1864.* Lynchburg, VA: H.E. Howard, 1989.

Moebs, Thomas Truxtun. *Black Soldiers-Black Sailors-Black Ink: Research Guide on African-Americans in U.S. Military History, 1526–1900.* Chesapeake Bay and Paris: Moebs, 1994.

Murphy, John M., M.D. *Confederate Carbines & Musketoons.* Dallas, TX: Taylor, 1986.

Musicant, Ivan. *Divided Waters: The Naval History of the Civil War.* Edison, NJ: Castle Books, 1995/ 2001 edition.

Musick, Michael P. *6th Virginia Cavalry.* Lynchburg: H.E. Howard, 1990.

Nanzig, Thomas P. *3rd Virginia Cavalry.* Lynchburg, VA: H.E. Howard, 1989.

Phisterer, Frederick P. (Late Captain, U.S. Army). *New York in the War of the Rebellion 1861–1865.* Albany: Weed, Parsons, 1890.

Quarles, Benjamin. *The Negro in the Civil War.* Boston: Little, Brown, 1955.

Redkey, Edwin S. *A Grand Army of Black Men: Letters from African-American Soldiers in the Union Army.* New York: Cambridge University Press, 1992.

Reid, Whitelaw. *Ohio in the War: Her Statesmen, Her Generals, and Soldiers,* Vol. II, *The History of Her Regiments and Other Military Organizations.* Cincinnati & New York: Moore, Wilstock & Baldwin, 1868.

Schiller, Herbert M., M.D. *The Bermuda Hundred Campaign, "Operations on the South Side of the James River, Virginia—May 1864."* Dayton, OH: Morningside, 1988.

Seager, Robert, II. *And Tyler, Too: A Biography of John & Julia Gardner Tyler.* New York: McGraw-Hill, 1963.

Sifakis, Stewart. "South Carolina 5th Cavalry Regiment." In *Compendium of Confederate Armies: South Carolina and Georgia.* Facts on File, 1995.

Sommers, Richard, J. "John Dunovant." In William C. Davis, ed. *The Confederate Generals,* vol. 2. National Historical Society, 1991.

Starr, Stephen A. *The Union Cavalry in the Civil War,* vol. 2. Baton Rouge: Louisiana State University Press, 1981.

Stewart, James, Jr., ed. *The Union Army: A history of military affairs in the loyal states 1861–1865—Records of the Regiments in the Union Army—Cyclopedia of battles—memoirs of soldiers.* Vol. 8. Madison, WI: Federal Publishing, 1908. Excerpts sent to the author 2004.

Stiles, Kenneth. *4th Virginia Cavalry.* Lynchburg, VA: H.E. Howard, 1995.

Thomas, Emory M. *The Confederate Nation 1861–1865.* Hagerstown, NY: Harper & Row, 1979.

Todd, Frederick P., ed. *American Military Equipage, 1851–1872,* vols. 2 and 3, *State Forces.* Square Press, 1983, 1993.

Trudeau, Noah Andre. *The Last Citadel: Petersburg, Virginia June 1864-April 1865.* Boston: Little, Brown, 1991.

_____. *Like Men of War: Black Troops in the Civil War 1862–1865.* Boston: Little, Brown, 1998.

Tyler, D. Gardiner. *Charles City County Virginia During the Period of the Revolutionary War 1775–1783.* Charles City County Bicentennial Committee, 1976.

Tyler, Lyon Gardiner, ed. *Narratives of Early Virginia 1606–1625.* New York, 1907.

_____. "U.S. Colored Troops—The Regiments," http://www.idea-classroom.org/IDEAS/ civilwar/ 189~ colregts.html.

_____. *U.S. Statutes at Large, Treaties, and Proclamations of the United States of America,* vol. 12. Boston, 1863.

Wallace, Lee A. *A Guide to Virginia Military Organizations 1861–1865.* Lynchburg, VA: H.E. Howard, 1986.

Whittenberg, James P. & Coski, John M. *Charles City County, An Official History.* Salem, West Virginia: Don Mills, Inc., 1989.

Wiley, Bell Irwin. *The Life of Johnny Reb: The Common Soldier of the Confederacy.* Baton Rouge: Louisiana University Press, 1978.

Wiley, Bell Irwin, and Hirst D. Mulhollen. *Embattled Confederates: An Illustrated History of Confederates at War.* New York: Harper & Row, 1964.

Williams, George W. *A History of the Negro Troops in The War of the Rebellion 1861–1865.* New York: Harper & Brothers, 1888. Ch. XI, "The Army of the Potomac (1864)," erroneously calls the Action at Wilson's Wharf the "Battle of Fort Powhatan" and contains other errors.

Wills, Brian Steel. *A Battle from the Start: The Life of Nathan Bedford Forrest.* New York: HarperPerennial, 1992.

Winters, John D. *The Civil War in Louisiana.* Baton Rouge & London: Louisiana University Press, 1963.

Wyeth, John Allan. *That Devil Forrest: Life of General Nathan Bedford Forrest.* Baton Rouge: Louisiana State University Press, 1959.

Articles and Pamphlets

Amira, Don. Harrison Ruffin Tyler, quoted in "President John Tyler's Grandson on Still Being Alive," nymagwww/daily/intel/2012/01/president-tyler-grandson-alive.html.

Anderson, Bryce A. "War Along the James," *North & South* 6, no. 3 (April 2003): pp. 12–13.

Barrow, Charles Kelly, J.H. Segars, and R.B. Rosenberg. "Forgotten Confederates, An Anthology About Black Southerners." *Journal of Confederate History* Series 14. Atlanta, GA: Southern Heritage Press, 1994, pp. 172.

Beard, Rick. "$10 a month: The men of the USCT would not tolerate second rate status." *Civil War Times* 53, no. 1 (February 2014): pp. 48–55.

Beckman, James A. "A visit to a notorious Tavern, nearly ended the West Point career of a young cadet named Jefferson Davis." *America's Civil War* 13, no. 5 (November 2000).

Besch, Edwin W. "Large Quantities of English and Austrian Infantry Weapons were used by Both Sides during the American Civil War." *Military Collector & Historian, The Journal of the Company of Military Historians* 65, no. 3 (Fall 2013): pp. 204–218.

Besch, Edwin W., Michael Hammerson, and Dave W. Morgan. "Raphael Semmes, the English 'Confederate Parson,' and his Maiden Sister Louisa: A Cased Presentation Revolver, a Magnificent Silver-Mounted Sword, and a 'Mammoth' Silk Confederate 2nd National Flag." *Military Collector & Historian* 53, no. 4 (Winter 2001–2002): pp. 146–160.

_____. "Black Confederates in Gray." Pamphlet, unknown source.

_____. "Black Confederate Soldiers, American Civil War (1861–1865)." 8 photos of body servants, www.blackconfederatesoldiers.com/confederate_uniforms_58.html.

Broadwater, Robert P. "The black and mixed race troops of the Louisiana Native Guards offered to serve both South and North." *America's Civil War* (March 2004): pp. 18, 20, 70, 72.

Choate, Maj. David L., USMC. "Enough Is Enough." *Marine Corps Gazette* (June 2012): pp. 42–44.

Cimprest, John. "Congress erupts over arming freed slaves." *America's Civil War* 25, no. 3 (July 2012).

_____. "Fort Pillow During the Civil War." *North & South* 9, no. 6 (December 2006): pp. 60–70.

Doswell, R.M. "Fitzhugh Lee." en.wikipedia.org/wiki/Fitzhugh_Lee.

_____. "Union Attack on Confederate Negroes." *Confederate Veteran* 23 (September 1915): p. 404.

Faust, Patricia L. *Historical Times Illustrated Encyclopedia of the Civil War.* New York: Harpers & Row, 1986.

Foster, Michael. "African-Americans served in both Civil War Navies." *Columbus (GA) Ledger-Enquirer,* and a paper published by the National Naval Museum, Columbus, GA.

Garrison, Webb. "Genealogy of John Tyler (28 March 1790–18 January 1862)." www.sherwood_forest.org/genealogy.html.

_____. "Scores of hostages were pawns in the power struggle of the American Civil War." *America's Civil War* 12, no. 2 (June 1995).

Gladstone, William A. Letter and 12-page attachment to the author dated 26 August 2008, reviewing *Black, Copper & Bright,* by C.R. Gibbs, and making other comments about black Union soldiers.

_____. "150th Anniversary of Black Soldiers," speech script, c. 2011.

Green, Michael S. "The Political Genius of Candidate Lincoln." *North & South* 13, No. 6 (November–December 2012), pp. 40–48.

Hatch, Thorn. "Custer." *America's Civil War* 26, no. 5 (November 2013): pp. 50–57.

_____. "History of the Colored troops in the American Civil War," http://americancivilwar.com/ histofcolored_troops.html.

Howland, Chris. "Foiled at Fort Wagner." *America's Civil War* 26, no. 5 (November 2013): pp. 58–61.

Hudson, Leonne. "Valor at Wilson's Wharf." *Civil War Times Illustrated* 37, no. 1 (March 1998): pp. 46–52.

Hull, Mark M. "Concerning the Emancipation of the Slaves: A Proposal by Major-General Patrick Cleburne, CSA." *The Journal of Mississippi History* 58, no. 4 (Winter 1996): pp. 377–379.

Jones, Hari. "The Color of Bravery: United States Colored Troops in the Civil War." *Hallowed Ground* 14, no. 2 (Summer 2013): pp. 26–31.

_____. "Julia Gardiner Tyler—Later Life and Death." en.wikipedia.org/wiki/Julia_ Gardiner_Tyler.

Leahy, Christopher J. "Tech degree, not ancestry, key to success." *Virginia Tech* (Winter 2007): pp. 1–3. www.vtmagazine.vt.edu/winter07/feature5.html.

Levine, Bruce. "The myth of the black Confederates." washingtonpost.com.editors ... washingtonpost.com/...the_myth_of_the_black_confederates.

Longacre, Edward G. "Brave Radical Wild." *Civil War Times Illustrated* 19, no. 3 (June 1980): pp. 8–19.

Lutz, Stephen D. "The 1st Kansas Colored Cavalry was the first black regiment to strike a blow for ending slavery." *America's Civil War* 16, no. 1 (March 2003): pp. 62, 64, 66.

Mallock, Daniel. "Cleburne's Proposal, After the Confederate rout at Missionary Ridge in 1863, Cleburne came to the conclusion that unless a new source of manpower was tapped, the Confederacy was doomed." *North & South* 11, no. 2 (December 2008): pp. 64–72.

Maynard, W. Barksdale. "Civil War Jamestown, Defending the Confederacy at Fort Poca-hontas." *Colonial Williamsburg* 35, no. 4 (Autumn 2013): pp. 74–81.

McPherson, James M. "Central to the War." *North & South* 10, no. 4 (June 2008): pp. 56–59.

McElfresh, Earl B. "Fighting in *Strange* Ground; Can poor planning and bad maps explain the Confederate defeat at Gettysburg?" *Civil War Times* 52, no. 4 (August 2013): pp. 30–37.

_____. "Missouri Opens Park Honoring the 1st Kansas." *Civil War Times* 52, no. 1 (February 2013): p. 15.

Neeley, Mark E., Jr., "ONE COUNTRY, ONE DESTINY—Abraham Lincoln's First Inau-gural Address." *North & South* 13, no. 5 (January 2012).

_____. "Order of Battle, Battle of Plymouth (1864)" [in North Carolina], en.wikipedia.org/ wiki/Battle_ of_Plymouth(1864)#Order_of_Battle.

Padgett, Vernon R., Ph.D. "Did Black Confederates Serve in Combat?" www.dixiescv.org/ fact_did-blacks-serve.html.

Pfeiffer, Eric. "Former President John Tyler's (1790–1862) grandchildren still alive." Yahoo News, 26 January 2012.

Reid, Bill G. "Confederate Opponents of Arming the Slaves, 1861–1865." *The Journal of Mis-sissippi History* 22 (1960).

Reidy, Joseph P. "Black Men in Navy Blue During the Civil War." www.navyandmarine.org/ ondeck/ 1862blackinblue.htm.

Rhea, Gordon, "Fellow Southerners!" *North & South* 13, no. 5, January 2012.

Rice, Charles. "The black soldiers who served in the Confederate Army are the real forgotten Heroes of the Civil War." *America's Civil War* (November 1995).

Rollins, Richard, ed. *Black Southerners in Gray: Essays on Afro-Americans in Confederate Armies.* Murfreesboro. TN: Southern Heritage Press, 1963.

Sampson, Myra Chandler, and Kevin M. Levin. "The Loyalty of Silas Chandler: Was he a 'heroic black Confederate' fighting for the cause?" *Civil War Times* 51, no. 1 (February 2012): pp. 30–35.

Shoaf, Dana B. "Sea Change, Thoughts & Comments." *Civil War Times* 52, no. 1 (February 2013).

Silverman, Jason H., and Susan R. Silverman. "Blacks in Gray: Myth or Reality?" *North & South* 5, no. 3 (April 2002): pp. 35–41.

Soodalter, Ron. "The day New York tried to Secede." *America's Civil War* 24, no. 6 (January 2012): pp. 44–51.

Sturcke, Roger, and Anthony Gero. "3 March 1865." www./history.com/this-day-in-history/freemen's-bureau-created.

_____. "Zouave Dress for the 10th United States Colored Troops, 1863–1864, A Probability." *Military Collector & Historian* 49, no. 3 (Fall 1997).

Towns, W. Stuart. "Haunting the South for a Century and More Lost Cause Rhetoric and Ritual." *North & South* 14, no. 1 (May 2012): pp. 40–48.

_____. "Trevilian Station, Battle of." www.trevilianstation.org.

Turner, Arlin, ed. "George W. Caleb's Recollections of General Forrest," *Journal of Southern History* 21 (May 1955): pp. 315, 316.

Urwin, Gregory J.W. "We Cannot Treat Negroes ... As Prisoners of War: Racial Atrocities and Reprisals in Civil War Arkansas." *Civil War History* 42, no. 3 (September 1966).

_____. "USCT Recruitment War Graph" and "USCT Strength Levels." *Civil War Times* 53, no. 1 (February 2014): p. 16.

Westphal, Tim. "Black Confederate Participation" in "The Stonewall Brigade." www.stonewallbrigade. com/articles_black_confeds.html.

Whittenberg, Eric J. "Confederate Cavalry Command Dilemma." *America's Civil War* 14, no. 6 (January 2002): pp. 26–32, 56.

Williams, Edward F., III. "Confederate Victories at Fort Pillow, 'with help from Nathan Bedford Forrest, Alfred T. Mahan, Thomas Jordan, J.P. Pryor, and H. Kenneth Humphreys.'" (Pamphlet) Memphis, TN: Historical Holiday Trails Inc., 1973; 2nd printing, 1984.

Williams, Scott K. "Black Confederates in the Civil War," www.usgennet.org/usa/mo/county/stlouis/ blacks.htm.

Wills, Brian Steel. "A Devil of a Mess in Tennessee: What Possessed Nathan Bedford Forrest's Troops to Massacre Their Foes at Fort Pillow?" *America's Civil War* 27, no. 1 (March 2014): pp. 34–41.

Index

275